IFIP Advances in Information and Communication Technology 462

Editor-in-Chief

Kai Rannenberg, Goethe University Frankfurt, Germany

Editorial Board

Foundation of Computer Science
  Jacques Sakarovitch, Télécom ParisTech, France
Software: Theory and Practice
  Michael Goedicke, University of Duisburg-Essen, Germany
Education
  Arthur Tatnall, Victoria University, Melbourne, Australia
Information Technology Applications
  Erich J. Neuhold, University of Vienna, Austria
Communication Systems
  Aiko Pras, University of Twente, Enschede, The Netherlands
System Modeling and Optimization
  Fredi Tröltzsch, TU Berlin, Germany
Information Systems
  Jan Pries-Heje, Roskilde University, Denmark
ICT and Society
  Diane Whitehouse, The Castlegate Consultancy, Malton, UK
Computer Systems Technology
  Ricardo Reis, Federal University of Rio Grande do Sul, Porto Alegre, Brazil
Security and Privacy Protection in Information Processing Systems
  Yuko Murayama, Iwate Prefectural University, Japan
Artificial Intelligence
  Tharam Dillon, La Trobe University, Melbourne, Australia
Human-Computer Interaction
  Jan Gulliksen, KTH Royal Institute of Technology, Stockholm, Sweden
Entertainment Computing
  Matthias Rauterberg, Eindhoven University of Technology, The Netherlands

IFIP – The International Federation for Information Processing

IFIP was founded in 1960 under the auspices of UNESCO, following the First World Computer Congress held in Paris the previous year. An umbrella organization for societies working in information processing, IFIP's aim is two-fold: to support information processing within its member countries and to encourage technology transfer to developing nations. As its mission statement clearly states,

> IFIP's mission is to be the leading, truly international, apolitical organization which encourages and assists in the development, exploitation and application of information technology for the benefit of all people.

IFIP is a non-profitmaking organization, run almost solely by 2500 volunteers. It operates through a number of technical committees, which organize events and publications. IFIP's events range from an international congress to local seminars, but the most important are:

- The IFIP World Computer Congress, held every second year;
- Open conferences;
- Working conferences.

The flagship event is the IFIP World Computer Congress, at which both invited and contributed papers are presented. Contributed papers are rigorously refereed and the rejection rate is high.

As with the Congress, participation in the open conferences is open to all and papers may be invited or submitted. Again, submitted papers are stringently refereed.

The working conferences are structured differently. They are usually run by a working group and attendance is small and by invitation only. Their purpose is to create an atmosphere conducive to innovation and development. Refereeing is also rigorous and papers are subjected to extensive group discussion.

Publications arising from IFIP events vary. The papers presented at the IFIP World Computer Congress and at open conferences are published as conference proceedings, while the results of the working conferences are often published as collections of selected and edited papers.

Any national society whose primary activity is about information processing may apply to become a full member of IFIP, although full membership is restricted to one society per country. Full members are entitled to vote at the annual General Assembly. National societies preferring a less committed involvement may apply for associate or corresponding membership. Associate members enjoy the same benefits as full members, but without voting rights. Corresponding members are not represented in IFIP bodies. Affiliated membership is open to non-national societies, and individual and honorary membership schemes are also offered.

More information about this series at http://www.springer.com/series/6102

Gilbert Peterson · Sujeet Shenoi (Eds.)

Advances in Digital Forensics XI

11th IFIP WG 11.9 International Conference
Orlando, FL, USA, January 26–28, 2015
Revised Selected Papers

 Springer

Editors
Gilbert Peterson
Department of Electrical and Computer
  Engineering
Air Force Institute of Technology
Wright-Patterson Air Force Base, Ohio
USA

Sujeet Shenoi
Tandy School of Computer Science
University of Tulsa
Tulsa, Oklahoma
USA

ISSN 1868-4238   ISSN 1868-422X (electronic)
IFIP Advances in Information and Communication Technology
ISBN 978-3-319-38719-2   ISBN 978-3-319-24123-4 (eBook)
DOI 10.1007/978-3-319-24123-4

Springer Cham Heidelberg New York Dordrecht London
© IFIP International Federation for Information Processing 2015
Softcover re-print of the Hardcover 1st edition 2015

Printed on acid-free paper

Springer International Publishing AG Switzerland is part of Springer Science+Business Media
(www.springer.com)

Contents

Contributing Authors

Sudhir Aggarwal is a Professor of Computer Science at Florida State University, Tallahassee, Florida. His research interests include password cracking, information security and building software tools and systems for digital forensics.

Monis Akhlaq is an Assistant Professor of Information Security at the National University of Sciences and Technology, Islamabad, Pakistan. His research interests include digital forensics, network security, incident handling and risk management.

Panagiotis Andriotis is a Ph.D. student in Computer Science at the University of Bristol, Bristol, United Kingdom. His research interests include digital forensics, text mining, content analysis and systems security.

Baber Aslam is an Assistant Professor and Head of the Department of Information Security at the National University of Sciences and Technology, Islamabad, Pakistan. His research interests include computer security, network security and digital forensics.

Stefan Axelsson is a Senior Lecturer of Computer Science at the Blekinge Institute of Technology, Karlskrona, Sweden. His research interests include digital forensics, intrusion and fraud detection, visualization and digital surveillance.

Kam-Pui Chow is an Associate Professor of Computer Science at the University of Hong Kong, Hong Kong, China. His research interests include information security, digital forensics, live system forensics and digital surveillance.

Fred Cohen is the Chief Executive Officer of Management Analytics, Pebble Beach, California; a Member of Fearless Security, Pebble Beach, California; and Acting Director of the Webster University CyberLab, St. Louis, Missouri. His research interests include digital forensics, information assurance and critical infrastructure protection.

David Dampier is a Professor of Computer Science and Engineering, and Director of the Distributed Analytics and Security Institute at Mississippi State University, Mississippi State, Mississippi. His research interests include digital forensics, information assurance and software engineering.

Xiao-Xi Fan is a Ph.D. student in Computer Science at the University of Hong Kong, Hong Kong, China. Her research interests include digital forensics, digital profiling and data mining.

Junbin Fang is an Associate Professor of Optoelectronics Engineering at Jinan University, Guangzhou, China. His research interests include information security and forensics, and quantum cryptography.

Peter Fruhwirt is a Researcher at SBA Research, Vienna, Austria. His research interests include digital forensics, mobile security and applied security.

Glenn Fryklund is a Security Analyst at Coresec Systems, Malmo, Sweden. His research interests include computer and network security, and digital forensics.

Sara Ghorbanian is a Security Analyst at Coresec Systems, Malmo, Sweden. Her research interests include computer and network security, and digital forensics.

Dae Glendowne is an Assistant Research Professor at the Distributed Analytics and Security Institute at Mississippi State University, Mississippi State, Mississippi. His research interests include malware reverse engineering, memory forensics and machine learning.

Jayaprakash Govindaraj is a Senior Technology Architect at Infosys Labs, Bangalore, India; and a Ph.D. student in Computer Science and Engineering at Indraprastha Institute of Information Technology, New Delhi, India. His research interests include mobile security, mobile device forensics and anti-forensics, mobile cloud computing security and forensics, and security in emerging technologies.

Stefan Gruner is an Associate Professor of Computer Science at the University of Pretoria, Pretoria, South Africa. His research interests include software science, formal methods and the philosophy of science.

Yong Guan is an Associate Professor of Electrical and Computer Engineering at Iowa State University, Ames, Iowa. His research interests include digital forensics, system security and privacy.

Gaurav Gupta is a Scientist D in the Department of Electronics and Information Technology, Ministry of Information Technology, New Delhi, India. His research interests include digitized document fraud detection, mobile device forensics and cloud forensics.

Qi Han is an Associate Professor of Computer Science and Technology at Harbin Institute of Technology, Shenzhen, China. His research fields include digital video forensics, hiding communications and digital watermarking.

Ragib Hasan is an Assistant Professor of Computer and Information Sciences at the University of Alabama at Birmingham, Birmingham, Alabama. His research interests include computer security, cloud computing security, secure provenance, trustworthy databases and digital forensics.

Werner Hauger is an M.Sc. student in Computer Science at the University of Pretoria, Pretoria, South Africa. His research interests include digital forensics and computer security.

Shiva Houshmand is a Ph.D. candidate in Computer Science at Florida State University, Tallahassee, Florida. Her research interests include computer and network security, authentication, digital forensics and machine learning.

Umit Karabiyik is a Ph.D. candidate in Computer Science at Florida State University, Tallahassee, Florida. His research interests include digital forensics, cyber security, expert systems and computer and network security.

Peter Kieseberg is a Researcher at SBA Research, Vienna, Austria. His research interests include digital forensics, cryptography and mobile security.

Irwin King is the Associate Dean (Education) of the Faculty of Engineering and a Professor of Computer Science and Engineering at the Chinese University of Hong Kong, Hong Kong, China. His research interests include machine learning, social computing, web intelligence, data mining and multimedia information processing.

Changwei Liu is a Ph.D. candidate in Computer Science at George Mason University, Fairfax, Virginia. Her research interests include cyber security and network forensics.

Rashmi Mata is a Technology Lead at Infosys Labs, Bangalore, India. Her research interests include web and mobile applications security.

Wesley McGrew is an Assistant Research Professor at the Distributed Analytics and Security Institute at Mississippi State University, Mississippi State, Mississippi. His research interests include cyber operations, reverse engineering, vulnerability analysis and digital forensics.

Cody Miller is a Research Associate at the Distributed Analytics and Security Institute at Mississippi State University, Mississippi State, Mississippi. His research interests include cloud computing, computer security and digital forensics.

Shariq Murtuza is an M.Tech. student in Computer Science and Engineering at Indraprastha Institute of Information Technology, New Delhi, India. His research interests include digital forensics, mobile device forensics and cloud forensics.

Xiamu Niu is a Professor of Computer Science and Technology at Harbin Institute of Technology, Shenzhen, China. His research interests include computer and information security, hiding communications, cryptography, digital watermarking, signal processing and image processing.

George Oikonomou is a Research Associate in Security for the Internet of Things at the University of Bristol, Bristol, United Kingdom. His research interests include Internet forensics, computer networks and security for the Internet of Things.

Martin Olivier is a Professor of Computer Science at the University of Pretoria, Pretoria, South Africa. His research interests include digital forensics and privacy.

Oluwasayo Oyelami is an M.Sc. student in Computer Science at the University of Pretoria, Pretoria, South Africa. His research interests include digital forensics and information security.

Anoop Singhal is a Senior Computer Scientist in the Computer Security Division at the National Institute of Standards and Technology, Gaithersburg, Maryland. His research interests include network security, network forensics, web services security and data mining systems.

Zheng Tan is a Research Assistant in Computer Science at the University of Hong Kong, Hong Kong, China. His research interests include distributed storage systems and parallel data processing systems.

Yanbin Tang is a Ph.D. student in Computer Science at the University of Hong Kong, Hong Kong, China. Her research interests include digital forensics and file carving.

Segen Tewelde is an M.Sc. student in Computer Science at the University of Pretoria, Pretoria, South Africa. Her research interests include digital forensics and requirements engineering.

Philip Trenwith is an M.Sc. student in Computer Science at the University of Pretoria, Pretoria, South Africa. His research interests include digital forensics and cloud computing.

Theo Tryfonas is a Senior Lecturer in Systems Engineering at the University of Bristol, Bristol, United Kingdom. His research interests are in the areas of smart cities, cyber security, systems engineering and technologies for sustainable development.

Hein Venter is a Professor of Computer Science at the University of Pretoria, Pretoria, South Africa. His research interests are in the area of digital forensics, with a current focus on digital forensic standardization and the construction of an ontology for digital forensic techniques.

Robin Verma is a Ph.D. student in Computer Science and Engineering at Indraprastha Institute of Information Technology, New Delhi, India. His research interests include digital forensics, data privacy and mobile device forensics.

Edgar Weippl is the Research Director at SBA Research, Vienna, Austria; and an Associate Professor of Computer Science at Vienna University of Technology, Vienna, Austria. His research focuses on information security and e-learning.

Duminda Wijesekera is a Professor of Computer Science at George Mason University, Fairfax, Virginia; and a Research Scientist at the National Institute of Standards and Technology, Gaithersburg, Maryland. His research interests include cyber security and privacy.

Xianyan Wu is a Ph.D. student in Computer Science and Technology at Harbin Institute of Technology, Shenzhen, China. Her research interests include figure-ground segmentation, image file carving, image processing and security.

Fei Xu is an Assistant Professor of Computer Science at the Institute of Information Engineering, Chinese Academy of Sciences, Beijing, China. Her research interests include information security and digital forensics.

Min Yang is a Ph.D. student in Computer Science at the University of Hong Kong, Hong Kong, China. Her research interests include digital forensics and data mining.

Ken Yau is a Research Staff Member at the Center for Information Security and Cryptography, University of Hong Kong, Hong Kong, China. His research interests include information security and digital forensics.

Siu-Ming Yiu is an Associate Professor of Computer Science at the University of Hong Kong, Hong Kong, China. His research interests include cryptography, computer security and forensics, and bioinformatics.

Muhammad Sharjeel Zareen is an M.S. student in Information Security at the National University of Sciences and Technology, Islamabad, Pakistan. His research interests include digital forensics, vulnerability assessment, penetration testing and the Internet of Things.

Shams Zawoad is a Ph.D. student in Computer and Information Sciences at the University of Alabama at Birmingham, Birmingham, Alabama. His research interests include cloud forensics, cyber crime, secure provenance and mobile malware.

Ping Zhang is a Lecturer at the Guangdong Police College, Guangzhou, China. Her research interests include information security, digital forensics and secure data mining.

Chen Zhao is an M.S. student in Electrical and Computer Engineering at Iowa State University, Ames, Iowa. His research interests include digital forensics, in particular, Bitcoin system analysis and forensic investigations.

Preface

Digital forensics deals with the acquisition, preservation, examination, analysis and presentation of electronic evidence. Networked computing, wireless communications and portable electronic devices have expanded the role of digital forensics beyond traditional computer crime investigations. Practically every type of crime now involves some aspect of digital evidence; digital forensics provides the techniques and tools to articulate this evidence in legal proceedings. Digital forensics also has myriad intelligence applications; furthermore, it has a vital role in information assurance – investigations of security breaches yield valuable information that can be used to design more secure and resilient systems.

This book, *Advances in Digital Forensics XI*, is the eleventh volume in the annual series produced by IFIP Working Group 11.9 on Digital Forensics, an international community of scientists, engineers and practitioners dedicated to advancing the state of the art of research and practice in digital forensics. The book presents original research results and innovative applications in digital forensics. Also, it highlights some of the major technical and legal issues related to digital evidence and electronic crime investigations.

This volume contains twenty revised and edited chapters based on papers presented at the Eleventh IFIP WG 11.9 International Conference on Digital Forensics, held in Orlando, Florida, USA on January 26-28, 2015. The papers were refereed by members of IFIP Working Group 11.9 and other internationally-recognized experts in digital forensics. The post-conference manuscripts submitted by the authors were rewritten to accommodate the suggestions provided by the conference attendees. They were subsequently revised by the editors to produce the final chapters published in this volume.

The chapters are organized into six sections: Themes and Issues, Internet Crime Investigations, Forensic Techniques, Mobile Device Forensics, Cloud Forensics, and Forensic Tools. The coverage of topics highlights the richness and vitality of the discipline, and offers promising avenues for future research in digital forensics.

This book is the result of the combined efforts of several individuals. In particular, we thank Mark Pollitt for his tireless work on behalf of IFIP Working Group 11.9. We also acknowledge the support provided by the National Science Foundation, National Security Agency, Immigration and Customs Enforcement, Internal Revenue Service and U.S. Secret Service.

GILBERT PETERSON AND SUJEET SHENOI

I

THEMES AND ISSUES

Chapter 1

A TALE OF TWO TRACES –
DIPLOMATICS AND FORENSICS

Fred Cohen

Abstract   This chapter focuses on two examples of legal matters involving archived
data, one is a digital archive of born-analog data and the other is a
digital archive of born-digital data. Their resolution is explained, and
along the way, several challenges and issues related to digital archives,
the transition from classical diplomatics to modern diplomatics, digital
forensics in the light of current record-keeping systems, and related facts
and supporting data points are explored.

Keywords: Questioned documents, archival science, diplomatics, digital forensics

1.   Introduction

In October 2013, a house was up for sale and, during the closing
period, a dispute arose about square footage that could have stopped
the sale or substantially changed the terms of the sale. The issue was
ultimately resolved by examining documents from city and county digital
archives of born-analog data. This is referred to as Case 1.

In an unrelated legal dispute, two ex-partners were in stark disagree-
ment about whether one of the partners took on a competitive business
while the partnership was still operating, and thus acted in bad faith.
The issue was brought to light because of the content of a web page
depicted on the Wayback Machine of `archive.org`, which is asserted
to be an archive of Internet websites over historical time frames (mid
1990s). This is referred to as Case 2.

The issues in these cases are not new. In fact, they are very old
and, by looking back to the history of archives, diplomatics and related
aspects of records management, insight may be gained about the future
of these fields.

© IFIP International Federation for Information Processing 2015
G. Peterson, S. Shenoi (Eds.): Advances in Digital Forensics XI, IFIP AICT 462, pp. 3–27, 2015.
DOI: 10.1007/978-3-319-24123-4_1

1.1   Causality as a Foundation of Science

Foundational to science is the notion of causality. Cause (C) acts through ($\rightarrow$) mechanisms (m) to produce effects (E): $C\rightarrow^m E$. This is the basic assumption of science as a whole as well as scientific evidence in the narrow sense of legally admissible evidence. Noteworthy are the notions that correlation is not causality and that effect does not imply cause [2]. In order to create a scientific hypothesis about a legal matter, a hypothesis of a mechanism by which cause produced effect must be formed, with the effect being the traces found and the cause being a hypothesized act of interest to the case.

1.2   Diplomatics

The field of diplomatics is often reported as being founded in 1681, when the renowned French philologist Mabillon [6] published the results of an analysis of approximately 200 documents divided into categories and examined with regard to material, ink, language, script, punctuation, abbreviations, formulas, subscripts, seals, special signs, chancery notes and so on. He created descriptions to allow the detection of forgeries and identified ground truth based on the recurrence of intrinsic and extrinsic elements in documents from the same time and place [3]. In modern terminology, and taking some liberties in usage, he used redundancy to test for consistency. Note that this approach is based on correlation, but causality was also present in the form of known chanceries or scriptoria traditions (cause) and capabilities of scribes over the ages (mechanism). In addition, and perhaps more vitally, no ground truth was available for much of this effort because the documents were too old for eyewitnesses and the documentary evidence supporting the claims was in question along with the claims themselves.

Diplomatics provides much of the basis for the admissibility of evidence and the establishment of criteria for evaluating evidence. The field and its principles of application are still used for questioned document analysis. By extension, its principles and many of its methods are in use or have analogous use in digital forensics. The modern and historic reconstruction of causes acting through mechanisms to produce effects forms an experimental basis for diplomatics, except, of course, that accelerated aging and similar methods are approximations or models.

1.3   Archival Science and Public Records

The field of archival science emerged over time due to the need to keep reliable public records (e.g., land ownership documents). Ancient record-keeping systems date back as far as history and indeed much of history is based on the records collected and retained by archivists at different administrative bodies. In the legal system, public records are generally admissible for the truth of what they self-indicate and are presumed to be trustworthy (i.e., reliable – a true statement of fact), authentic (not corrupted or tampered with) and accurate (truthful, exact, precise or complete) in the legal system, when they are properly introduced and marked with the appropriate seals, signatures and/or special signs by the legal entities that produced them. While diplomatic analysis may be used to attempt to refute these records and/or to rehabilitate them after attempted refutation, they are generally trusted, and built and maintained in a manner that reasonably justifies the trust. This is, at least, their nature in the analog records space.

The analytical approach is based on a set of redundant acts by independent trusted actors forming a set of archival fonds associated with different archival units, programs or institutions. Fonds are aggregations of documents that originate from the same source. The records and fonds include explicit formal elements designed to provide assurance that the records are authentic, accurate and reliable over their life. This is undertaken by providing a chain of custody in a transparent system of record keeping through redundant information that associate actions related to a record with the record in the context of the fonds, and the fonds in the context of the archives. This is sometimes called the archival bond, which is the relation between a document and the previous and subsequent documents produced in the course of a business matter. Paper records are often annotated over time, marked with stamps, altered by updates and changes, and so on.

Figure 1 shows a (redacted) document provided in response to a request for a legal record related to ownership. The document has a series of writings added over time. The record, in this case, is a dynamic document that has been updated to reflect the officially-authorized changes, as shown by the seals of the officials who carried out the actions. As the record evolves over time, it is retained in a chain of custody and supported by the fonds in which it resides, which reflects the dates of access and other related information. As a legal document, this is considered proof of the facts contained in the document and is inherently regarded as reliable and accurate based on the source, and authentic because it could be proffered to a court as a proper form with the seals intact.

This document might have been moved into an archival repository for a period of time and returned to active use later. Such movements would be annotated on the document and/or in the fonds in which it resided over time. The redundant information from the various sources

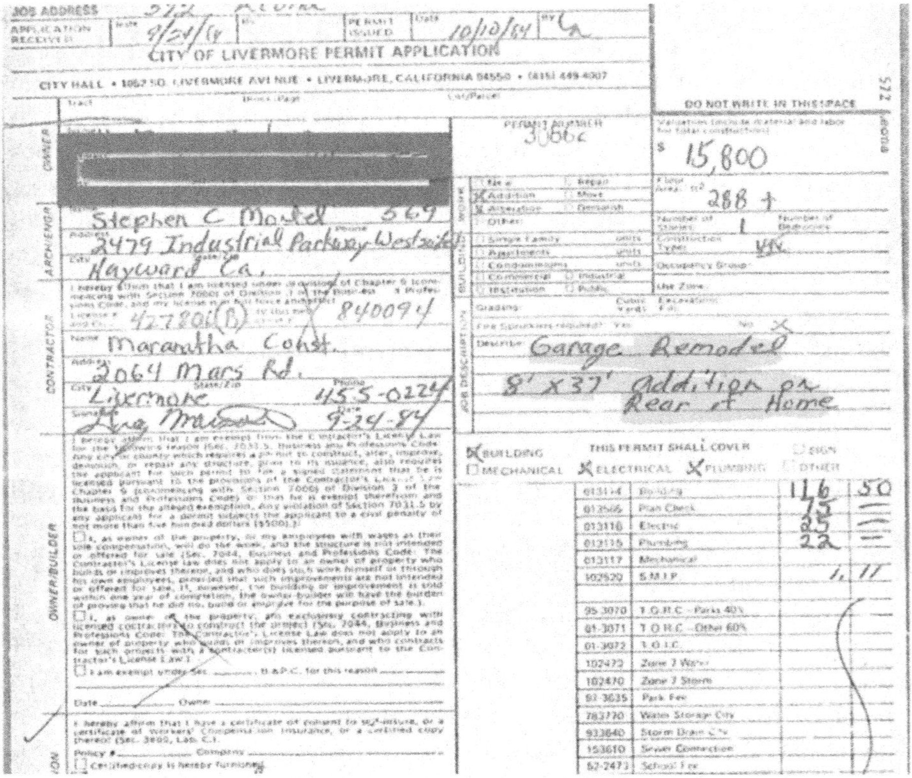

Figure 1.   Case 1 example.

(e.g., transmission from use to the archives and back as signed by parties on each side, placement in the fonds in sequence over time, markings on cover sheets and/or envelopes and/or the documents themselves) can be examined by a diplomatics expert in the context of the methods used by the record-keeping system to make a determination of authenticity or to refute or challenge the presumption of authenticity based on a lack of adequate evidence of (or evidence of inadequate) custody and control.

1.4   Digital Records

Many of the methods that made analog records reliable over time have not been translated into the new forms of record keeping in the digital records space. For example, the processes involved in property purchase often required a government-authorized actuary to certify that an individual identified by a government document signed a document in the presence of the notary. But increasingly, a digital system allows a digital signature that is not even created by the individual's own hand. Instead, the self-identified individual agrees electronically over the Internet to adopt a signature form for use in signing documents. The documents are sometimes incorrectly presented (i.e., with incorrect data fields), with the results produced as digital documents reflecting different (and in some cases corrected) content than what was actually presented for signature.

Such record-making and record-keeping systems are potentially very problematic in legal terms, but they are not often challenged. They do not guarantee that what is agreed to is what is presented. They often include and present false information and change it after agreement. They do not provide a copy in the form of the original (identical to the original in all respects but issued after the original), an imitative copy (reproduction of both the form and content of a record) or even a simple copy (transcription of the record content) to the signatories. Moreover, they often do not incorporate an actual signature that is traceable to an individual and that is demonstrably different from other adopted signatures. Documents may be presented differently from how they appeared before (i.e., as a pseudo-original with the pretense of originality), even when and if they are ultimately presented and/or submitted in court as authentic, reliable and accurate.

Nevertheless, these pseudo-original documents are then declared as public records, and from that point forward, they are recognized, treated and presumed as authentic renditions of contracts. They become part of corrupt and inauthentic digital records and eventually make their way into the archived and permanent records of societies. The metadata associated with these records often lacks the fields required by record management systems and archives (if present, they may be incorrect), the mechanisms are not transparent and they not available to the parties to the contracts.

Figure 2 shows an example of a presentation made as part of the collection of potential evidence in Case 2. This depiction of a digital record reflects what, in some jurisdictions, is legally admissible as an archival document and may be given the presumption of authenticity, reliability and accuracy. In particular, note that "Resolution Capital" appears with "Advanced Portfolio Management" on the page. This is a depiction that was saved from a screen image of what was seen when one of the parties gathered what he believed to be evidence in support of his case.

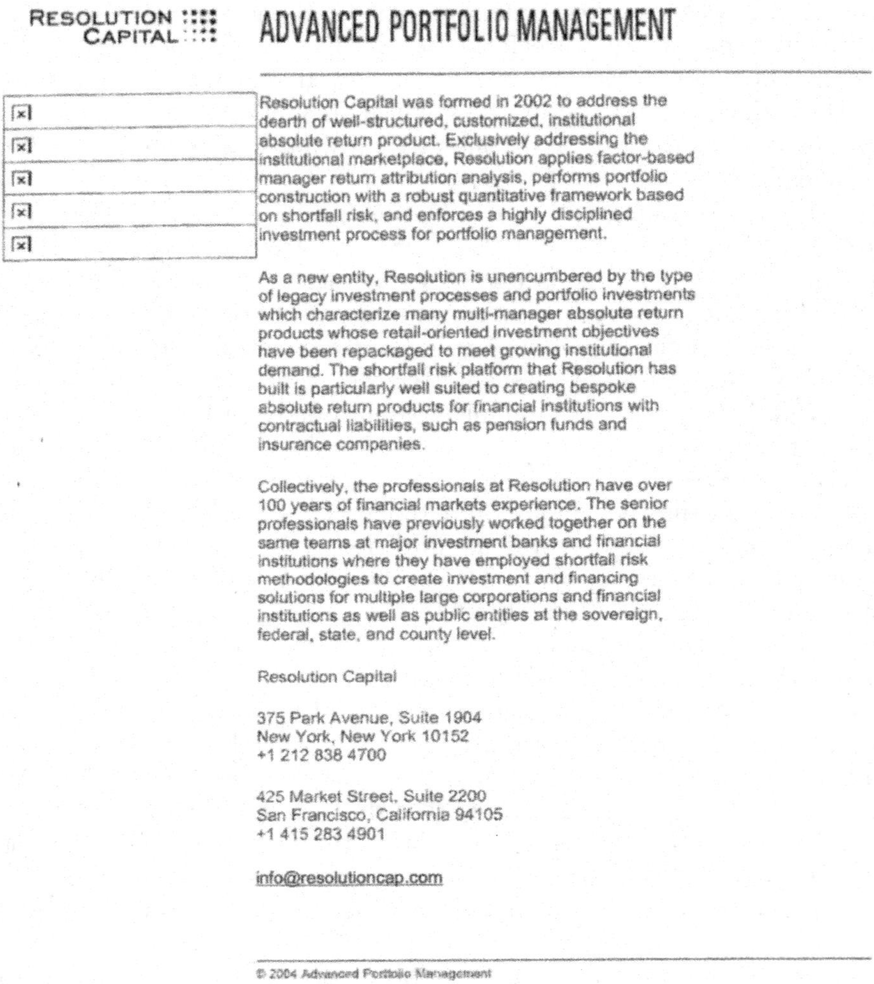

RESOLUTION ⣿
CAPITAL ⣿

ADVANCED PORTFOLIO MANAGEMENT

[x]

[x]

[x]

[x]

[x]

Resolution Capital was formed in 2002 to address the dearth of well-structured, customized, institutional absolute return product. Exclusively addressing the institutional marketplace, Resolution applies factor-based manager return attribution analysis, performs portfolio construction with a robust quantitative framework based on shortfall risk, and enforces a highly disciplined investment process for portfolio management.

As a new entity, Resolution is unencumbered by the type of legacy investment processes and portfolio investments which characterize many multi-manager absolute return products whose retail-oriented investment objectives have been repackaged to meet growing institutional demand. The shortfall risk platform that Resolution has built is particularly well suited to creating bespoke absolute return products for financial institutions with contractual liabilities, such as pension funds and insurance companies.

Collectively, the professionals at Resolution have over 100 years of financial markets experience. The senior professionals have previously worked together on the same teams at major investment banks and financial institutions where they have employed shortfall risk methodologies to create investment and financing solutions for multiple large corporations and financial institutions as well as public entities at the sovereign, federal, state, and county level.

Resolution Capital

375 Park Avenue, Suite 1904
New York, New York 10152
+1 212 838 4700

425 Market Street, Suite 2200
San Francisco, California 94105
+1 415 283 4901

info@resolutioncap.com

© 2004 Advanced Portfolio Management

Figure 2. Case 2 example.

1.5   Digital Diplomatics

As a field, digital diplomatics currently takes on two meanings. One meaning is the use of digital computing methods to support classical diplomatics. For example, digital methods may be used for word and phrase analysis to detect differences in scribes and to track scribe usage of terms over time in order to date documents more accurately than was feasible using manual techniques. The other meaning is the use of diplomatic methods to authenticate digital documents, which is the meaning of interest in this work. The following quote amply conveys this meaning:

> Georges Tessier: *"On peut donc avancer que la critique diplomatique est née dans le prétoire ou sur le forum à l'occasion de débats judiciaires ou de controverses politiques ou religieuses, quand le nœud du litige ou de la polémique était constitué par un document ou une série de documents contestés."* Cette citation est tirée de L'Histoire et ses méthodes (La Pléiade, 1961) dont Georges Tessier a signé le chapitre Diplomatique [1].
>
> Google Translation: *"It can be argued that the diplomatic criticism is born in court or forum on the occasion of judicial proceedings, or political or religious controversy when the crux of the dispute or controversy consisted of a document or series of documents in dispute."* This quote is from The History and Methods (The Pleiades, 1961) where Georges Tessier signed the chapter Diplomatics.

In this context, the relevance of digital diplomatics may be reasonably explored relative to digital forensics.

1.6 Forensic Science

Forensic science is often cited as coming to clarity through the work of Locard [5]. Locard identified that, when objects come into contact, they each leave parts (traces) of themselves on each other. The mechanism of objects coming into contact and leaving traces is called "transfer" and, thus, we have the scientific notion of causality fulfilled by contact (cause) acting through transfer (mechanism) to produce effect (traces). Traces may be humanly observable (e.g., chunks of rock or mud) or latent (observable only through the use of tools as in dust and microscopic particles). Locard undertook studies showing layers (e.g., of mud or dust) indicating sequences of places visited (e.g., layers of mud on shoes) when a person transited a city, and associating the transferred traces to locations based on unique properties (e.g., strands of a particular wool from the only factory that produced it in the city).

As forensic science has moved forward, many methods have been developed based on the concept of transfer. Methods, such as tool mark analysis, have also been developed from the earlier diplomatics area.

1.7 Digital Forensics

As digital systems came into widespread use, the legal system had to deal with evidence in the form of traces of activities within and between digital systems. The study of digital traces relative to the legal system was identified as digital forensics. However, as in the case of digital diplomatics, another meaning is used. Specifically, digital forensics is also used to describe activities associated with the investigations of events in the digital arena, a much broader field that is closely related to detection and response regimens in computer security.

As a fundamental notion, it has recently been recognized that digital evidence is still trace evidence, is almost always latent in nature and is not transfer evidence. Rather than being transferred in the sense of Locard, digital evidence is formed from traces produced by the mechanisms of operating digital systems, typically as stored states from finite state machines that transform state and input into the next state and output.

Using the term of art from diplomatics, "digital traces" are produced by transmission rather than transfer. In the digital arena, transmission producing traces is typically also transmission in the sense of electromagnetic, optical, sonic or other emission and reception of signals. Specifically, events in one context produce signals that are sensed in another context and memorialized in the form of optical patterns, configurations of particles, magnetic orientation or whatever traces are supported by the transmission or fixation media.

Additionally, in the digital arena, the latent nature of evidence is such that a copy in the form of an original almost never occurs. Instead, a sequence of bits represented in a fixed form in/on a medium may be reproduced (at the bit level), while presentation in a human-readable form is normally an imperfect reflection of the original documentary form. For example, when the information associated with a digital record (e.g., financial transaction) is originated, the form of entry (e.g., web-based entry of a purchase form) is typically very different from the form of transmission (e.g., series of datagrams sent over the Internet as waveforms in transmission media), storage (e.g., sequence of bits in a database storage area of a disk drive or in a positive feedback loop in active memory) and presentation (e.g., line item in a bank statement or entry in a spreadsheet downloaded by an accountant from the financial institution and used for tax purposes). These notions are not widely recognized or stated in digital forensics today, even though they are always present.

The notions of authenticity, accuracy and reliability are always at issue in the digital forensics arena relative to the classical notions of documentary form. The notion that using methods such as cryptographic checksums to verify the lack of alteration of a bit sequence does not even begin to address the issues of authenticity of a record in presentation and reliability in the sense of relationship to original writing or any sort of ground truth. Causality works differently.

In the following sections, distinctions, if they exist, are identified using classical diplomatics, classical forensics, digital forensics and digital diplomatics in the realm of questioned document examination. In parallel with this exposition, the case studies are examined in detail. These cases are not large or important on their own, but instead reflect the many everyday legal issues that naturally occur in human interactions and sit at the heart of how people interact with the legal issues faced in these areas. Finally, the cases are resolved and the conclusions are presented.

This work views questioned digital document examination as the fusion of diplomatics and forensics. It may reasonably be called digital diplomatics and/or questioned digital documents without reasonable differentiation. Indeed, the reconciliation of diplomatics and forensics in this arena is a historic merger and unification of the individual concepts and fields of study.

2. Digital Diplomatics and Forensics

This section presents the background of the two cases and discusses document admission and related information regarding records.

2.1 Case 1 Background

Case 1 involved a dispute over the square footage of a house. The seller claimed the square footage specified when the house was purchased and as reflected in the taxes paid over the duration of ownership and for some unknown period prior to the purchase. The buyer, a civil engineer, upon assessment, noted a different square footage in the inspector's report and proceeded to do an independent measurement, which produced a third square footage result.

If left unsettled or settled in various ways, this situation could lead to charges of fraud, damage to reputation, tens of thousands of dollars difference in the sales price, retroactive tax readjustment and delayed-closure or non-closure of the sale. None of these situations were in the interest of the parties and the settlement of the dispute rested on documentary evidence in the form of records from various sources, including the prior sale documentation, tax documentation and city and county records related to remodeling, permits and inspections. The measurements themselves were also at issue because different measurements (e.g., inside dimensions, outside dimensions, livable space and permitted use areas) are based on different definitions in different overlaid jurisdictions (e.g., taxation, county building and city building).

2.2 Case 2 Background

Case 2 involved a dispute between ex-partners in a financial venture. The business failed and each partner went his own way seeking to start a new financial venture, with the ownership of the domain name remaining with one of the partners. Several years later, upon viewing what was believed to be an image of the prior website using the Wayback Machine at `archive.org`, the partner who did not retain control of the website was unhappy to discover that, according to the displayed content, resources belonging to the previous business were used to advertise the new business prior to the termination of the partnership. This led to charges of misappropriation of resources, customers and business from the partnership and failure to faithfully fulfill fiduciary and other duties as a partner.

In this case, the dispute was based on the form and appearance of the document (i.e., the depicted website) as seen in the archival site. The depiction was clear as it could be. A date selected by the user and indicated in the URL at the top of the web browser page showed content from the prior business simultaneously displayed in a single web page with material from the new business. If the depiction reflected reality, there would be little question that a case could be made by the complainant. The only case that could reasonably be made by the accused party was to question the document presented by the archive.

2.3   Admitting the Documents

While the subtleties of an Internet archive versus other types of archives and the question of how to resolve seemingly inconsistent information from different official records may be vitally important to the issues at hand in the two cases, there seems to be no question that the documents would normally be admitted in legal proceedings.

The Wayback Machine is an automated storage system while an archive preserves documents. Preservation is a process in which an archivist identifies, authenticates, protects, describes, builds retrieval systems, provides access to and acts to protect the material being archived. The term Internet Archive in the context of the Wayback Machine is a misuse of the term of art, "archive." Of course, humans have trusted archives for centuries and the individuals who operate `archive.org` have demonstrated excellent marketing skills in using the term.

The legal status of government documents is normally that they are admitted and presumed reliable, authentic and accurate. Thus, the documents supplied in Case 1 operate under this legal presumption.

The Internet Archive is a bit more nebulous in that it is a website operated by a non-profit (i.e., public interest) corporation, much like a museum or other archive. However, this is not what the Wayback Machine is. The Wayback Machine is not like a museum or an archive because there is no curation or assurance of protection and permanent authenticity from the moment of acquisition.

Ancient documents ("ancient" is a term of art) are usually admitted under the presumption that they were not forged in advance in anticipation of some future litigation that could not have been anticipated by an archivist. Disregarding the question of how old is old enough, a strong case can be made that the Wayback Machine was not operating intentionally to create a forgery and no claim was asserted that the information it stored was altered in any nefarious manner. The presumption for such documents is, *de facto*, also that of being reliable, authentic and accurate, even if this is not based on the same legal or technical footing as public records. Here lies the rub.

Archives that hold public records are normally designed by archivists and record-keeping specialists to reasonably assure trustworthiness. In the paper world, a chain of custody is established by independent and redundant trusted parties. These parties attest to signatures (i.e., seals) that become part of a document as it moves from party to party for signatures; take custody of the document and retain it in a secure location; track it in the fonds through numbering, ordering, cross referencing and other related processes; indicate how, when, from whom and other characteristics as the document is ingested, stored, moved, retrieved, transmitted, examined, copied, migrated and so on; and generally keep records of their activities in a transparent manner and make them available for examination.

This all depends on trust in the custodian as an entity who has not altered the records and has not allowed anyone else to do so. This latter requirement – of not allowing others to alter records – is problematic in the Internet because it was not designed for this purpose.

Examination can detect inconsistencies in and between records and fonds and this supports trusting (or challenging) the trustworthiness of the records. But this is not the case for depictions presented by the Wayback Machine. Collections are made at seemingly arbitrary times from subsets of automatically-selected websites. The components that manifest a visualized web page are collected at different times, stored with only a single reference to a collection date and are not attributed or tracked in the many ways that an archive is managed. The Wayback Machine is not a system of records as much as an amateur collection, but it is sometimes treated as if it is a traditional archive.

In the digital world, alteration can happen unintentionally or intentionally, the protection mechanisms of the Wayback Machine are not transparent and the adequacy of the machine and its mechanisms has not been established by a rigorous scientific process. The Wayback Machine does not apparently follow the rigors of archival science or records management and, thus, it should be inherently obvious to an expert in the field that it does not have the same status as public records or archives with regard to maintaining and operating within the standards of care. This is also the case for many other Internet-based sites that assert archival or records status, and this is one of the important reasons why a science needs to be developed in this regard and why diplomatics must be developed as a field to question the stored documents.

The situation is further complicated by the fact that the mechanisms of the Wayback Machine change over time, are not externally documented or transparent, and do not follow widely accepted archival principles. In fact, after the findings discussed here were made public, the Wayback Machine was changed with minimal notice and little apparent transparency. Thus, no external repeatability – a basic requirement of a scientific field – exists for the changes and performing an accurate reconstruction is problematic.

In the legal realm, depending on the bent of the judge and case precedence that may reflect previous mechanisms or poorly tested assertions, depictions that are not accurate, reliable or authentic may ultimately be admitted, presumed trustworthy and treated with a weight similar to that of records maintained by government bodies or real archives.

2.4   Related Information on Records

While this situation may appear problematic, the reality of digital records is, in general, quite tenuous compared with other forms of records. Some of the following examples from personal correspondence are informative and some may be recognized as having been reported in the popular media:

- A global non-government agency indicated that, in some cases, it holds records where 80% are of unknown type. When asked whether assistance was desired in trace-typing them, the response was that, while it must maintain the records, it had neither the resources nor the desire to type them. The obligation of the non-government agency thus stops at proper retention.

- Migration of records from system to system over time is necessary to retain the utility of the records because digital systems fail and older systems are no longer available. Moreover, newer systems rarely support all the mechanisms of the older systems.

  Conversion is thus part of record migration. The result is that a migrated record is often, at best, an imitative copy, sometimes a simple copy and sometimes a pseudo-original copy. Records may never be viewed as they were initially formed and the loss of utility during conversions is not uncommon. Key parts of the migration problem faced in digital archiving are creating the mechanisms needed to produce copies of the records in one form or another and identifying and recording the nature of the changes associated with conversions and non-original mechanisms in terms of what is depicted and what is no longer depicted.

- Forensic archives of legal matters often contain large volumes of data in unusable form because they have not been migrated or converted and the original mechanisms and/or contexts may no longer exist to meaningfully reconstruct or use them. Given that legal appeals processes may come many years later, this evidence may no longer be viable if re-examination or retrial are required.

- Many modern devices and systems are complex and lack transparency to the point that their operational mechanisms are not discernible. Furthermore, automated patching often results in situations where the exact versions are not available and may be difficult or impossible to accurately reconstruct. Thus, establishing causality in reconstruction may not be accurate, and the task of reconstruction becomes very complex in this light.

- Some governments have admitted the use of covert methods to alter the apparent operation of mechanisms, making them act in ways unknown even to their manufacturers. This potentially shakes to the core the idea that archives accurately reflect the reality of what took place. The competition to rewrite history and current affairs in the digital realm would seem to present problems for the trustworthiness of digital records for legal purposes.

- Some nations and other similar entities use digital records to reflect their operations, including without limit, the original writing and official codifications of their laws and legislative history. This includes scanning documents that become part and parcel of the legal constructs of their societies as well as born-digital records.

Recent revelations indicate that scanning devices no longer simply make representations of pixelated color values in digital form with known accuracy and precision limits. Instead, some of the devices read the content of documents and rewrite them, sometimes replacing digits, words, spelling and other elements of content with corrected versions. The very laws codified in statute and used to

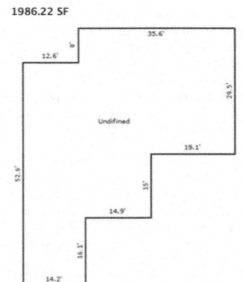

1986.22 SF

Figure 3. Inspector's version of the house.

make decisions about peoples' lives cannot be relied on to accurately reflect the laws as passed, and documents such as financial records may not be accurately recorded for future use such as taxation and levying fines.

It appears that there is a desperate need for a science of questioned digital documents. This field might be reasonably called digital diplomatics, named after the existing diplomatics field that was created for the same purpose in the non-digital realm. Part and parcel of diplomatics was the development of archival science and records management. The same path would seem to be a reasonable trajectory for digital diplomatics leading to and helping guide digital records management, digital archival science, digital records forensics [4] and the broader field of digital forensics.

3.   Case Resolution

This section discusses how the cases were resolved.

3.1   Case 1

Figure 3 shows the drawing of the property produced after an analysis by a building inspector. The corresponding square footage was calcu-

Figure 4. Overhead image of the house.

lated as 1,986.22 sq. ft. This is obviously at odds with the overhead image of the house shown in Figure 4. The inspector was looking at the records of livable interior space in city permits, the full details of which were no longer available from the relevant time frames.

The overhead image in Figure 4 is a Google Maps aerial of the house at about the time of sale. Note the substantial difference between the shape in the inspection report and the actual shape in the overhead image. The dispute at this point was whether and to what extent a remodeling of the former garage was properly accounted for in the calculation.

The issue was ultimately settled when county records were retrieved from the county archives. Figure 5 shows the official county report page used for tax calculation, which identifies that a laundry room was counted as livable space in the previous city remodeling document. When this final piece of the puzzle was introduced, the dispute was settled quickly with the final sale square footage matching the original offering and the tax numbers.

3.2   Case 2

Case 2 never made it to court. It was settled prior to trial when both sides agreed that the digital records were inadequate to settle the dispute one way or another and that no other records could be demonstrated to resolve the issue more definitively.

Figure 6 shows the timeline of appearances of different elements in the depicted website based only on the dates of the Wayback Machine files

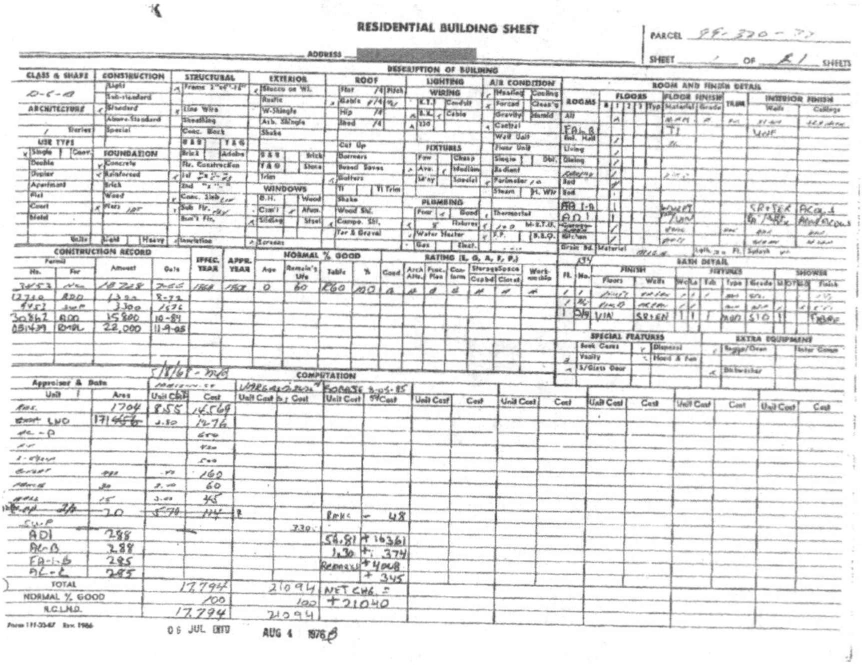

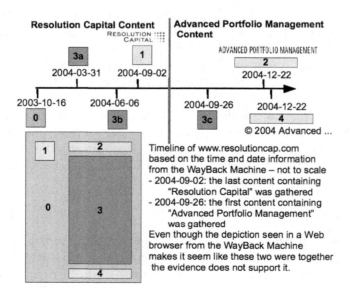

Figure 5. Archived county records.

Figure 6. Time sequence of the website.

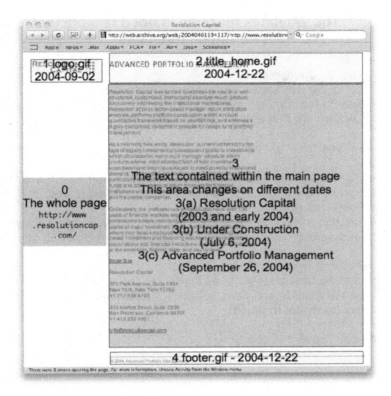

Figure 7. Depiction areas with the histories detailed.

associated with the various versions collected by the machine. In this case, the computers and content associated with the original activities were no longer available by the time the legal matter started, so no other provenance information was available. As such, the Wayback Machine content was asserted to be the "best evidence" and was, in fact, the only evidence that supported the asserted claim.

Figure 7 shows the time sequence in different terms. Note that the dates and times are such that there is no date and time at which the second company (APM) can be definitively shown to have simultaneously appeared with the first company (RC). It cannot be proven from this information that the two company names appeared together and it cannot be proven that they did not appear together.

In this particular case, the screen images depicting the simultaneous appearance of both companies (Figure 2) is deceptive in that it appears to support a highly probative fact that is also highly prejudicial. However, while it is certainly prejudicial, it is not actually probative because it cannot be shown to be reliable.

The Wayback machine is not a reliable tool for digital forensics.

The proof:
> Turn off Javascript
> Go to the wayback machine (www.archive.org)
> Search for http://all.net/
> Click on the first entry – the one from 1997

You will see this ".gif" file on part of the screen...

The US was attacked on 9/11/2001 by radical islamist terrorists.
There were no weapons of mass destruction found in Iraq.
GW Bush was re-elected
Al Gore won a Nobel prize and an oscar for global warming worl
Put the details of your case here for proof to the judge and jury..

Either I am a time traveller
OR I am the best guesser of all time.
OR the Wayback machine is not always a reliable
> tool for digital forensics.

And I can prove it in court.

For more details, go to http://all.net and get in touch with me.

FC

Figure 8.   Image used to demonstrate inconsistency.

Figure 8 shows the image that was used to demonstrate inconsistency. In this contemporaneous example, a website identified as being from 1997 on the Wayback Machine was used to demonstrate the appearance of later content as if it were from a prior time. A newer graphical image that was not previously saved by the Wayback Machine was substituted on the website and, thus, the newer image was depicted on the Wayback Machine as from the earlier date. The example was intended to demonstrate that either the Wayback Machine depicted the events as simultaneous when they were not or that the author could predict the future (or travel in time), including providing future pictures and facts that cannot be predicted with certainty.

While this was an effective demonstration at the time and was recorded as part of the report generation for the case at that time, the operation of the Wayback Machine was subsequently changed to not display images under such conditions.

At this point, a serious challenge is posed to digital diplomatics. Since the Wayback Machine no longer allows demonstrations of these sorts of failures to be easily generated and evidence collected for legal matters from prior dates may have these misleading depictions, a reconstruction path is no longer available to demonstrate that false depictions gathered from before a change may be false. Instead, what remains are potentially probative and highly prejudicial digital traces and no way to demonstrate that they are not probative. Thus, a best evidence argument along with a claim of "generally reliable as business records" or an archival ancient records claim enable such evidence to be admitted unless the digital diplomatics field becomes a part and parcel of digital forensics and such results are accepted by the relevant scientific community.

It may be reasonably shown that, for potential evidence gathered before the date of the change operation, the demonstration in Case 2 is adequate to question the document, and this may be used in conjunction with a more theoretical path, including the more cogent argument about cause and effect in light of timelines. However, all the theoretical points are likely less effective than a simple demonstration of predicting the future.

If the Wayback Machine did not use dates and timestamps as pathnames and store them with reasonable accuracy in some portion of the instances involved, the approach would not work. Indeed, there is no real assurance that the time mechanism of the Wayback Machine is generally reliable or reliable in any given case.

4.   Implications and the Path Forward

This section discusses the broader implications and the path forward.

4.1   Implications

The Wayback Machine is just one example of numerous similar challenges faced in the digital evidence arena. If traces are not collected properly along with the related information that forms the archival bond and redundant data about the archives and their operation at the time the traces were identified and collected, by the time a legal matter gets to the point of examination, the information required to question the

documents may be gone forever. Rapid changes to Internet sites, lack
of transparency, records of past versions and audit information and the
proprietary nature of the sites make reconstruction infeasible in many
cases. Without such reconstruction, the seemingly probative information admitted as normal business records or under some other similar
exception to hearsay may prejudice cases to the point where injustice
becomes common.

4.2   The Path Forward

It appears that one of the vital components contained in historic archives and systems of records is missing in the digital arena. This component, which is produced by various elements of records and record-
keeping activities, includes metadata, context, provenance, chain of custody and transparency (i.e., the archival bond), all of them vital to
addressing discovery issues in digital evidence cases.

Courts are generally hesitant to allow the collection and analysis of
entire systems and mechanisms because of minimization concerns (criminal) and costs (civil) associated with electronic discovery. In the case
of very large systems (e.g., Google's Gmail), practicality prevents the
examination of the totality of the collection and fonds.

This discussion assumes that the collection tasks necessary for a forensic examination are conducted by a forensic professional (i.e., a diplo-
matist, examiner or trained digital evidence collector) who is engaged
by a party for the matter or is an independent party with appropriate
interests. The question then is: What might be reasonably collected and
documented to assure proper diplomatic analysis?

While specific details for different circumstances are elusive, some
examples of the information reasonable and prudent to forensic use and
diplomatic examination include:

- Dates, times and detailed actions of all activities performed by a
  collector in the form of contemporaneous notes taken by the collector at a suitable level of granularity. In particular, who did what,
  with what tools, when and with what results. This should include
  the ability to reproduce results. For example, if a command line
  is used, the files should be kept and the commands recorded with
  the results, and relevant files referenced in the notes or as part of
  the report as generated. In cases where repeatability is not feasible (e.g., real-time collection of network traffic), records should
  include details of dropped packets and other similar information
  as available, and to the extent feasible, redundant records from re-

lated mechanisms (e.g., network flow logs from routing equipment during the times of collection).

- The documentary forms as observed by users in the various known circumstances, including sample documentary forms from all potentially relevant presentations. These should be in imitative copy form that can be reliably viewed in as near to an identical fashion as the original, and should be entirely contained in the stored form without the need to reference or display external content.

- All URLs, sources for all web pages or other content retrieved and observed from systems over which the observer does not have direct control, and depictions in an imitative copy form.

- A copy of whatever can be reasonably attained in a computer usable form. For example, in addition to an imitative copy of a spreadsheet as depicted on a screen, the actual spreadsheet should be saved in as close to a copy in the form of the original as feasible.

- Records of an archive in which information is stored should be retained to the extent feasible. Ideally, the process would use a transaction system that retains the history of all transactions, but alternatives such as periodic backups with the ability to go back in time for retrieval may be sufficient in some cases. Note that this is potentially problematic with discovery rules.

- Elements of the archival bond, such as directory information about storage locations, relationships among records and files, classification codes, sequence numbers, dates and times associated with documents, etc. For example, many practitioners retain files in dated directories with dated filenames such as 2013-11-25 for files received on that day, versions from that day selected for retention, records of retrieved files, etc. Sometimes, a filename may convey the date of the content (e.g., a paper may have a name starting with YYYY-MM-DD- followed by other identifying elements).

- Other records from the systems used for the examination process. This includes test results for tools, calibration information for measurement mechanisms, records of activities performed with tools (e.g., records of commands issued to clear a disk before copying content to it), log files retained by systems in normal use and other similar related data.

- Transparency information, such as copies of online contracts contained in websites used in a retrieval process, details of how the mechanisms work, documents from relevant manuals and related documentary sources used, and, generally, all considered and/or referenced materials.

- Supporting documents for named protocols, methods, tools, programs, etc. For example, when referencing the use of an IP address or URL on first use, the relevant RFC documents should also be collected for clarity and for historical reference and reuse. For example, one might cite `www.ietf.org/rfc/rfc791.txt`, which details IPv4, as included with the report in a file named `rfc791.txt` in the considered directory.

- Version numbers for everything that is identifiable, including major and minor versions, dates and timestamps and related indicators. These are often useful in settling disputes, but are also often unnecessary to the purpose, particularly in a clear context.

As suggestions, these may be within the range of reasonable and prudent acts, but there remains the problem that they are just suggestions. They are not widely accepted by the digital forensics and digital diplomatics communities, are not comprehensive, do not provide substantial details in a suitable documentary form, are not structured to facilitate meaningful automated use, and if and to the extent they are missing, they do not imply that the traces offered as evidence will not be reliable, authentic and accurate, or will not be admitted, useful, reasonable and appropriate.

Unlike the records management profession, which often has the opportunity to manage records from the "womb to the tomb," the archival and digital forensics communities must usually work with only the residue (archival) or traces (forensics) that are available. But when experts collect evidence (forensics) or participate in records creation (archival), it would seem useful to provide guidance and a standard approach regarding what to collect and retain (and what not to).

It is important to recognize that examiners get what they get. In many cases, there are opportunities for discovery, but in others there are not. Civil matters often involve uncooperative parties who cannot be forced to act against their interests. Criminal matters have similar limitations associated with the right to non-self-incrimination.

The natural course of events does not result in preservation at the point of inception and, as a result of the lack of discipline by those who implement information technology, this leads to situations where certainty is hard to attain. Current metrics do not provide insights into the resulting certainty of analysis and this limits the realistic ability to place likelihoods on the outcomes of examinations.

The best one can currently do is to identify consistency or inconsistency with hypothesized causes and mechanisms based on the available traces and experience. The absence of evidence is not evidence of absence. When no definitive answer exists, one must learn to say so, and as a community, it is necessary to develop the methods of digital diplomatics and records management in order to give a reasonable hope of justice being determinable in disputes.

A path forward is the application of the same criteria used for the inherent presumed trustworthiness of public records. In this approach, the independence and due care charges of public officials combined with redundant methods starting at the initiation of a public record provide the basis for trust in the system. But carrying this to the full spectrum of potential traces that may be introduced in the legal system implies forcing criteria on the private sector that they may be unwilling to accept, perhaps justifiably so. The creation of a standard for assured admissibility could be a motivating factor, but such an approach has rarely succeeded in the past, except for those that already have legal requirements for diligence.

At a minimum, the individuals and organizations entrusted with the retention of public records should create and require the mechanisms necessary to provide the same level of certainty with respect to born-digital public records as for born-analog public records. The notion of public records and archives in the cloud computing environments of today seem, at first glance, to be an oxymoron. However, it may be reasonable to leverage the low cost and high performance of public cloud computing environments for limited purposes such as widespread and rapid access without the same level of surety required in a legal context. A more thorough process could be used for official versions of records, which may almost always be identical to the unofficial versions, thus providing a combination of high surety when needed and accessibility.

5.   Conclusions

This chapter has presented two cases involving very different facts, issues and component parts. The similarity is that the cases both depend on documentary evidence demonstrating questioned document challenges. The difference is that one set of documents is born-analog and the other born-digital.

From a diplomatics perspective, born-analog documents are handled better because of the historical experience in managing them and because they reside in a context that has been worked out over centuries. They involve known causal mechanisms that can be reproduced and examined using stable scientific methods and principles with measurable levels of accuracy.

Born-digital documents demonstrate many of the problems faced in the current context and the discussion has identified many of the challenges faced in digital diplomatics today. The lack of an adequate scientific examination basis is a major challenge, another is the manner in which records and other documents are generated, cared for and produced.

The origination problem is particularly disturbing. The lack of a single identifiable documentary form that persists over the lifetime of a record is a key part of the underlying problem that cannot be solved in the current paradigms of digital systems. While paper documents such as building permit records are continually updated to reflect new information, digital documents, including modern building permit records that do not include an original paper-signed documentary form, do not leave the rich set of residues to examine. Instead, what exists is a collection of potentially distributed digital record components and other bit sequences associated with the fonds, many elements of which are not retained across migrations and do not possess the transparency or consistency across record-keeping systems that is required to examine them in a common structured manner.

An initial set of objective information would be helpful in collecting and analyzing digital traces, but there is little hope of obtaining all this information when the traces are provided by others. The examiner's role in this situation is limited and little can be done about it today.

Born-digital documents have a long way to go. From their inception through their attempted use in court there is a need for improvement in the data used to support the traces that are found. Consistency analysis holds hope, but there is often too little data to allow determinations of external consistency and the process is fundamentally one of refutation instead of the demonstration of adequacy. Absent guidance on adequacy, examiners are left with an unlimited open-ended challenge of creating enough threads to weave a cloth that opposition experts cannot tear asunder.

It is, therefore, important to start building a standard of adequacy based on the historical diplomatics discipline and its application in forming the concepts of archival science and the basis for trust in public records. A good starting point is to apply the elements of independent actors responsible only for proper record keeping and with no foreknowledge of any particular case acting in a reasonable and prudent manner with adequate redundancy against accidental failures to assure that records are reliable, authentic and accurate.

References

[1] M. Chabin, Impressions, expressions: Le blog de Marie-Anne Chabin (www.marieannechabin.fr/2013/11/pretoire), November 11, 2013.

[2] F. Cohen, *Digital Forensic Evidence Examination*, ASP Press, Livermore, California, 2010.

[3] L. Duranti, *Diplomatics: New Uses for an Old Science*, Scarecrow Press, Lanham, Maryland, 1998.

[4] L. Duranti, From digital diplomatics to digital records forensics, *Archivaria*, vol. 68, pp. 39–66, 2009.

[5] E. Locard, The analysis of dust traces, *Revue International de Criminalistique*, vol. 1(4-5), pp. 176–249, 1929; translated into English and reprinted in *American Journal of Police Science*, vol. 1(3), pp. 276–298; vol. 1(4), pp. 401–418; vol 1(5), pp. 496–514, 1930.

[6] J. Mabillon, *De Re Diplomatica*, Saint-Maur, France, 1681.

Chapter 2

NOTIONS OF HYPOTHESIS IN DIGITAL FORENSICS

Segen Tewelde, Stefan Gruner and Martin Olivier

Abstract   With the growing scientification of the discipline of digital forensics, the notion of "scientific hypothesis" is becoming increasingly important, because all empirical science is hypothetical, not apodictic. Although the word "hypothesis" is used widely in the digital forensics literature, its usage is not sufficiently reflected from a philosophy of science point of view. This chapter discusses this problem with particular reference to Carrier's methodological work in which the notion of hypothesis plays a prominent role.

Keywords: Digital forensics, philosophy of science, scientific hypotheses

1.   Motivation

This chapter is based on the little-disputed premise that the young discipline of digital forensics is still – to use a phrase by Thomas Kuhn [16] – in a "proto-scientific" stage, although its scientification is on the way [11]. When a discipline grows from a proto-scientific stage to a "paradigmatic" stage [14], two phenomena can be typically observed: (i) a growing formalization (or mathematization) in the expression of the theories in the discipline; and (ii) a growing methodological awareness of what is required or forbidden or allowed for the methods in the discipline in order to qualify as "scientific." These phenomena manifest themselves according to Bunge's differentiation between the substantive and operative parts [6] of the entire body of knowledge of a discipline.

As far as the first (substantive) point is concerned, the mathematical formalization of the theoretical language in digital forensics has already shown some progress (see, e.g., [4, 8, 20]). On the one hand, this is because scholars from the traditional theoretical computer science and formal methods communities are successfully penetrating the interdisci-

© IFIP International Federation for Information Processing 2015
G. Peterson, S. Shenoi (Eds.): Advances in Digital Forensics XI, IFIP AICT 462, pp. 29–43, 2015.
DOI: 10.1007/978-3-319-24123-4_2

plinary barriers and are beginning to gain visibility in the field of digital forensics. On the other hand, the need for formalization has also been recognized by a number of scholars in the digital forensics community. One example is the formal description of aspects of digital forensics by Cohen [9], including critiques of earlier projects.

The second (operative) point is more problematic in the development of digital forensics. Not only is there little methodological awareness, but the growing methodological disputes in the discipline are often taking place outside the realm of science. For example, according to Cohen [9], many of the details of currently-used procedures and tools are neither published nor thoroughly tested. Where tool testing is discussed, the coverage is often reminiscent of testing in an engineering sense (e.g., a tool performs some task correctly) as opposed to an assessment in a methodological sense (i.e., the task performed ought to be at the methodological core of the discipline).

Carrier [7] has contributed to this discourse by formulating a hypotheses-oriented approach for all digital forensic investigations to meet the classical science-philosophical criteria of scientificness. (Note that the term "science-philosophical" is used throughout this chapter as the adjective form of the philosophy of science.) Alas, not every hypothesis is *per se* scientific. Consequently, the scientificness of an empirical discipline such as digital forensics is not automatically guaranteed by a demonstration that it follows (or is able to follow) a hypothesis-based approach. Additional scientificness criteria, such as those identified by Bunge [5], must be stipulated for hypotheses before they can be used as indicators of the degree of scientificness of the discipline in which the hypotheses are formulated.

At this point, one of the methodological weaknesses in the current meta-theory of digital forensics has been reached. Whereas the word "hypothesis" is already in wide use (see, e.g., [2]), it is mainly used in an undifferentiated and science-philosophically unreflected manner. This suggests that users of the concept are largely unaware of the many different classes of empirical hypotheses. A potentially harmful illusion of scientificness could arise as a consequence of this ignorance.

The foregoing considerations motivate this meta-analysis of Carrier's methodological framework [7] with regard to Bunge's well-established classification scheme for scientific hypotheses [5]. This is, indeed, the principal contribution of this chapter. Note that this chapter is not concerned with the often-mentioned extrinsic pragmatic value of the scientificness of digital forensics (i.e., acceptability in courts of law). Instead, this chapter focuses on the intrinsic philosophical value of scientificness for its own sake, whereby the notion of scientificness must never be conflated with truth.

2.   Related Work

The use of Bayesian decision networks for evaluating and interpreting scientific findings in forensic science is discussed in [12, 18]. The philosophical problems underling the narrative construction of explanations by means of hypothetical linkages between individual events are detailed in [10]. Note that the work of Carrier [7] also has a strong focus on the explanatory construction of such kinds of histories [17] of (digital) events.

An appropriate meaning of the term "hypothesis" is crucial for all these considerations because genuine science must be an explanatory undertaking [22], which goes well beyond the mere gathering and description of data and facts (as the descriptivists would have it). Thereby, all empirical/scientific explanations are ultimately hypothetical [6].

The formulation of hypotheses for explanatory purposes is also discussed in the related field of forensic engineering [21]. Thereby, the types of hypotheses formulated in digital forensics are similar to those formulated in software testing because both digital forensics and software testing are idiographically oriented towards what is unique (not towards what is universally general). For this reason, the meta-scientific methodological considerations about the problem of justification of empirical hypotheses in software testing [1] should also be studied carefully by digital forensic theoreticians.

3.   Carrier's Work

Carrier [7] has proposed a methodological framework for hypothetical digital forensic event reconstruction with high scientific plausibility. The framework incorporates seven categories and more than thirty classes of analysis techniques for formulating or testing digital forensic hypotheses. Before going into the details of Carrier's categories, it is instructive to use an example [7] to understand the conceptual relationships between the categories and the purposes for which the hypotheses in the categories are formulated.

> **Example:** A computer is suspected of having been used to download contraband pictures from the Internet. Lower-level hypotheses are formulated about the time that the system was operational and the technical (operational) capabilities of the system.
>
> The hypotheses are used as presuppositions for formulating succeeding hypotheses of higher complexity. At this point, the lower-level presuppositions are tacitly considered to be true.

Next, a higher-level hypothesis is formulated that asserts disjunctively that either program A or program B was used to download the pictures from the Internet. This hypothesis is formulated on the basis of the assumption that programs A and B are capable of downloading the pictures.

In order to determine which of the two programs was actually applied, a particular log file ℓ is inspected to see which program was operational during the suspected time of the incident. From a logical point of view, the existence of the log file ℓ justifies the deduction:

$$\frac{(A \vee B),\ \neg B}{A}$$

under the condition $\ell \implies \neg B$. This investigative step, however, hypothetically assumes the trustworthiness (integrity) of the log file itself because otherwise the required implication $\ell \implies \neg B$ would no longer be compelling.

Last, but not least, it must be taken into account that the computer could have been compromised by an intruder who stored the pictures on the computer without the computer owner's knowledge.

Given the need to create different types of hypotheses with various degrees of plausibility, Carrier [17] has proposed a schema for formulating hypotheses about (possible) sequences of past events in the lifetime of digital evidence. The remainder of this section examines the schema in detail.

3.1   History Duration

According to Carrier, hypotheses in this category are formulated about the time span T during which the system under analysis was operational. To formulate testable hypotheses in the History Duration category, lower-level hypotheses about time instants $t \in T$ must be formulated.

With regard to Bunge's classification scheme [5], the hypotheses are typically singular and specifiable because they can be obtained by substituting variables for constants to account for single facts. They are also testable with regard to the existence of log files or other temporal traces. As far as Bunge's precision attribute is concerned, hypotheses in the History Duration category are refined as they are both predicate-precise and range-precise. However, they are typically isolated and not systemic as they define unique events in a manner that Windelband [22] called idiographic as opposed to nomothetic. Hypotheses of this kind are typically, in Bunge's terms, both confirmable as well as refutable in principle. Note, however, that confirmability and refutability in principle cannot guarantee *de facto* confirmation or refutation in every individual case.

Carrier notes that hypotheses about an entire duration T are not without exceptions. For example, all the information on a storage device can be overwritten and, thus, traces of previous events can be erased [7]. From a science-philosophical point of view, this corresponds to the situation of historians and archaeologists such that the science-philosophical methodologies of the two classical disciplines can become relevant (and important) to digital forensics [17]. Hypothetical claims about the previous existence of information that no longer exists are typically unspecifiable (in Bunge's terms), but they can motivate deeper research in their role as programmatic hypotheses.

3.2   Primitive Storage System Configuration

According to Carrier, the first type of hypotheses in this class have the form: device d has a storage capacity c, which is empirically unknown before a measurement is taken. A hypothesis of this type is, again, singular and specifiable in Bunge's terminology. The hypothesis is also phenomenological because it merely describes the surface of a phenomenon, not the details of its inner mechanisms. The hypothesis is both confirmable and refutable by means of a suitable experimental apparatus. Interested readers are referred to [6] for a deep science-philosophical discussion of observations, measurements and experiments.

The second type of hypotheses in the Primitive Storage System Configuration category have the form: device d was connected during the time T of an incident. In Bunge's terms, this is again a singular hypothesis of localizing existential character. Because it refers to the past, the previously-mentioned historical/methodological issues [17] are also relevant to this class, especially where the possibility of deleted information or information that no longer exists are concerned.

3.3   Primitive Event System Configuration

Carrier's third category covers hypotheses that make assertions about the capabilities of devices involved in events of interest. In Bunge's classification scheme, these correspond to the same types of hypotheses discussed above.

3.4   Primitive State and Event Definition

In this category, Carrier normatively states that five classes of techniques shall be used to formulate and test hypotheses: (i) primitive state observation class; (ii) state and event capability class; (iii) state and event sample data class; (iv) state and event reconstruction class; and (v) state and event construction class.

Activities in the primitive state observation class are meant to collect data by observing an output device like a computer monitor. The observed state is defined in the inferred history for the times that the observation was made. The corresponding hypothesis deals with a single state that existed at a specific time. In Bunge's terms, this is a singular, specifiable, testable, refined and grounded hypothesis that is experience-referent and phenomenological. Carrier states that the data should be considered as facts if they do not conflict with the observations made by another investigator. Thus, Bunge's considerations about observations, facts and phenomena in the intersection of the knowing subjects and the physical objects [6] are especially relevant.

In Carrier's state and event capability class, hypotheses about primitive system capabilities correspond to presuppositions. They must be tested and accepted before they can be used to formulate hypotheses about possible system states and events. This composition of higher-level and lower-level hypotheses is, in Bunge's terms, mechanismic because of the references to the inner workings of the machinery under test. Once again, the hypotheses are singular, specifiable, refined and grounded.

Hypotheses formulated with techniques in the state and event sample data class are probability hypotheses that cannot be decisively confirmed or refuted by finite amounts of data. Similar types of hypotheses occur (to use one of Bunge's examples) in the field of clinical medicine where tobacco smoking and lung cancer are typically correlated with each other. Carrier has clarified that the research techniques choose events and states that occur with a probability above some threshold value. Some level of subjectivity must be admitted because neither the threshold value nor the notion of probability are clearly specified. What may appear as highly probable to one investigator may be improbable to another investigator.

Carrier's requirements for the state and event reconstruction class are that an investigator must understand the logic associated with the event capabilities of a system and that it would be prudent to identify the unique signatures of events (this provides background information for formulating a hypothesis). A hypothesis formulated by this technique has the form: event e causes state s. In Bunge's classification scheme, this is the strongest type of hypothesis because it must be defined functionally in terms of one free stimulus variable and its dependent effect variable, and it must be thoroughly experimented with in order to distinguish genuine causality from mere coincidence. At this point, Carrier may well consider the possibility of generating general nomothetic hypotheses of the form: every event of type e will always cause a state of type s. This may be incorporated in a case-independent general theory of digital forensics.

For the final technique, the hypotheses formulated in the state and event construction class are probability hypotheses too, with their notorious difficulties as far as confirmability and refutability are concerned. The truth value of such a hypothesis can only be assessed based on the end state of a trace. However, quasi-general hypotheses [5] can be formulated in cases where a system prevents, by its own construction, certain events from occurring when the system is in a particular state.

3.5   Complex Storage System Configuration

Two types of hypotheses are formulated in this category, which defines entities such as the names of complex storage types that existed during a time interval T, the transformation functions for each of the complex storage types, the attribute names for each of the complex storage types, etc. The hypotheses in this category are more complicated than hypotheses in the simpler History Duration category. Here, the techniques defined for the hypotheses do not test them decisively because probability hypotheses are at best confirmable, not refutable. The hypotheses typically state that a particular device d existed during a time interval T. Since the complex storage was created by a program, a forensic investigator needs to identify the corresponding program. For this purpose, Carrier specified a program identification technique that searches for reconstructed program states. The previously-mentioned science-philosophical problems of historiography, especially with regard to securely deleted information, are also relevant [17].

The second type of hypotheses in this category, the complex storage capability hypotheses, are singular hypotheses about the capabilities of devices. Carrier proposed three techniques to formulate and test these hypotheses. Since all three techniques are related to testing software, it important to consider the science-philosophical issues pertaining to the justification of empirical hypotheses in software testing discussed by Angius [1].

3.6   Complex Event System Configuration

The first of the three types of hypotheses formulated in this sixth category is basically the same as in the Complex Storage System Configuration category described above; its associated techniques have also been analyzed above. Using the data type reconstruction class of techniques in this category, the digital forensic investigator formulates hypotheses that are difficult to test. Once again, these hypotheses are similar to those formulated in scientific software testing [1]; the objects of the hypotheses are algorithms and data structures. Because algorithms and data structures have many-to-many relations with each other – one algorithm can manipulate many data structures and one data structure can be manipulated by many algorithms – the notorious Duhem-Quine dilemma [19] looms for the hypotheses. From the perspective of Bunge's classification scheme, these are hypotheses of relatedness.

3.7   Complex State and Event Definition

Carrier identifies only one type of hypothesis in the final Complex State and Event Definition category. Eight classes of techniques are applicable to support hypothesis formulation: (i) state and event system capability class; (ii) state and event sample data class; (iii) state and event reconstruction class; (iv) state and event construction class; (v) data abstraction class; (vi) data materialization class; (vii) event abstraction class; and (viii) event materialization class.

A technique in the first class, based on the complex system capabilities, is used by an investigator to determine a possible state or event from the list of possible states and events associated with the system of interest; this bears much similarity with the primitive state and event system capability class. Here, the investigator formulates the same type of hypotheses, with the only difference that, for these hypotheses, information about system capabilities is presupposed from prior work in the previous categories.

In the state and event sample data class, a standardized sample is required for all investigations if an objective hypothesis is to be formulated. Again, this does not differ very much from the primitive state and event sample data class discussed above. In Bunge's classification scheme, this corresponds (once again) to a singular, specifiable, testable, refined and grounded hypothesis.

Techniques in the state and event reconstruction class refer to the occurrence times of events in multitasking distributed systems. Empirical hypotheses in such contexts often have a statistical character because of the notorious non-deterministic behavior of distributed systems in which certain input/output observations are often not experimentally reproducible.

Techniques in the state and event construction class can be used to postulate events that may have occurred, albeit with a rather low level of confidence on the part of the investigator. Bunge has categorized such vague hypotheses in his pragmatic functions category [5].

Techniques in the data abstraction class generate hypotheses by checking the data in the inferred history to determine the complex storage location types that could be relevant. These are singular and testable hypotheses that can be refuted by comparing the range of each attribute to the attribute value defined by the previous complex state event system capability technique. The Duhem-Quine dilemma again looms when the data in the inferred history can support multiple complex storage types.

Hypotheses produced using the data materialization class are similar to those discussed above.

Unlike the scenarios involving complex storage locations, lower-level events can only be part of one complex event for a specific inferred history. Grounded and testable hypotheses can be formulated in such scenarios unless there are multiple lower-level events, in which case, a new inferred history is created. Thus, an inferred history represents an investigator's assumptions about the events in an incident. If inconsistencies arise, an alternative inferred history must be identified. For the given inferred history, however, singular, specifiable and grounded hypotheses are formulated using the descriptions of lower-level events. A technique in the event abstraction class is used to refute a hypothesis about the complex events when lower-level events for the same time are defined in the inferred history, but are not caused by the event that is the focus of the hypothesis.

The techniques belonging to the final event materialization class are not used to formulate hypotheses. Instead, they are used to refute primitive or complex event hypotheses in cases where a higher-level event existed at the same time T, but was not causally related to the lower-level event stated in the (refuted) hypothesis.

4.   Bunge's Classification

Bunge's classification scheme for scientific hypotheses [5], which has been used in the previous section as the science-philosophical basis of the present analysis of Carrier's work, is extremely thorough, fine-grained and subtle. Many of Bunge's categories are especially relevant to the – in Windelband's terms – nomothetic [22] sciences, in which hypotheses serve the highest purpose in formulating general scientific laws (e.g., Einstein's $E = mc^2$ in theoretical physics) or quasi-general statistical laws or hypotheses (e.g., smoking causes cancer in the domain of medical science).

In digital forensics, the situations in which hypotheses are formulated are usually fundamentally different in that the general epistemic interest of digital forensics is typically not nomothetic. Digital forensic professionals are not interested in proposing general law-like hypotheses such as $E = mc^2$. Instead, they are primarily interested in finding out what has happened and when and why in historically unique and hardly generalizable situations. In Windelband's terms [22], digital forensics is thus idiographic rather than nomothetic.

As far as Bunge's classification scheme is concerned, it is not surprising that the specific and individual fact-referent classes of hypotheses occur most frequently in Carrier's framework. Digital forensics shares these idiographic characteristics with the science of software testing, in which (too) only specific hypotheses about a given system under test are formulated [1]. Most relevant to digital forensics is Bunge's classification of hypotheses with regard to their testability. These include [5]:

- Empirically untestable hypotheses

- Purely confirmable hypotheses

- Purely refutable hypotheses

- Both confirmable and refutable hypotheses

Also relevant is Bunge's classification of hypotheses with respect to their pragmatic functions [5]:

- Generalizers of past experiences

- Case-specific inference starters

- Programmatic research guides

- Explanatory hypotheses

- *Ad hoc* protectors of other hypotheses

From this point of view, the degree of scientificness of every discipline increases with its amount of confirmable and refutable explanatory hypotheses.

In this context, however, it must be noted that Bunge emphasized that truth and scientificness are not synonyms: let $\mathcal{H} = \mathcal{H}_s \uplus \mathcal{H}_n$ be a disjoint union of scientific and non-scientific hypotheses, and let $I : \mathcal{H} \to \mathbb{B}$ be a Boolean interpretation of the hypotheses. Then, it is possible for two hypotheses that $I(h) = \mathsf{t}$ and $I(h') = \mathsf{f}$ with $h \in \mathcal{H}_n$ and $h' \in \mathcal{H}_s$. The pragmatic implications to digital forensics are obvious. Indeed, this is a very important, but often forgotten, issue.

Similarly, the manner by which a hypothesis comes into existence is not relevant to the scientificness of the hypothesis. Accordingly, Bunge's scientificness criteria for hypotheses [5] are not genealogical criteria. In other words, even the most sophisticated scholarly method could generate non-scientific hypotheses and even the proverbial "random monkey" could generate a hypothesis that formally satisfies all the criteria of scientificness.

5. Limitations of the Study

Carrier's methodological framework is normative rather than descriptive. Carrier provides guidelines to digital forensic practitioners about the types of hypotheses that ought to be formulated, as well as about the types of objects about which the hypotheses ought to be formulated during the course of forensic investigations. Of course, what is actually done "in the field" by digital forensic practitioners is quite a different question, one which this study has not addressed.

Because Carrier's normative methodological work resides in an intermediate layer between the science-philosophical analysis discussed here and digital forensic practice, it is not possible to judge the actual degree of scientificness of the digital forensics discipline by assessing Carrier's meta-work about the discipline from the elevated meta-meta-level as engaged in this study. By analogy, it is also not possible to make a judgment about the discipline of physics – in the way it is carried out by physicists in their laboratories – by critiquing Karl Popper's or Hans Reichenbach's philosophies of physics as "scapegoats." This is because Popper and Reichenbach might have been mistaken in their own interpretations of the discipline of physics in such as way that any anti-Popper or anti-Reichenbach critique no longer strikes the actual physicists working in their laboratories.

This distance from the actual usage of hypotheses in the daily practice of digital forensics is clearly a clear shortcoming of the present study. As mentioned below, the present study could have been strengthened by an analysis of how hypotheses are actually formulated and used by practitioners in the field. This would have provided deeper insights into the actual state of scientificness of the digital forensics discipline. Alas, such a field study would have been too difficult to conduct with the available resources. Therefore, Carrier's work was chosen as a *pars pro toto* substitute.

Thus, only if (or so far as) the field behaves according to Carrier's normative prescriptions is the preceding analysis of Carrier's work by implication also an analysis of the field. If, however, Carrier's notions and the practice of the field are disjoint, then the above meta-meta-study about a meta-study can only be – in Bunge's terms – of programmatic character to motivate further meta-scientific and methodological research.

6.   Conclusions

Hypotheses that have been tested and strongly corroborated over time eventually develop into scientific theories, which are (semantically) tightly connected networks of hypotheses [5]. The development of a scientific theory, however, is not the goal of digital forensic practitioners who formulate hypotheses specifically about the cases they investigate. Nevertheless, case-specific hypotheses must also, according to Bunge [5], be theoretically embedded (grounded), for example in theories of computer science or computer engineering [13].

As far as the scientificness of the notion of hypothesis is concerned – which is not to be confused with the truth of an individual hypothesis – Carrier's work does not strongly contrast with Bunge's scientificness criteria for formulating hypotheses. By and large – although not philosophically-systematically – Carrier's guidelines have indeed taken into account established criteria such as well-definedness and testability.

At this point, it is important to distinguish – again – between science and practice. To count as scientific, a hypothesis must be, in principle, testable (regardless of whether or not it has actually been tested). For practical use, such as in digital forensics, a hypothesis should actually be tested too (which implies its testability). Thus, when Carrier recommends that digital forensic practitioners should sometimes assume some hypotheses to be true in order to get on with their investigations, he does not leave the territory of scientificness as long as the preliminary assumptions are testable in principle. Whether they are actually true or not is not a matter of their scientificness.

A few minor issues can be found in Carrier's framework because it was developed for practical and not philosophical purposes. An example is the somewhat vague conceptual separation between the notions of data, fact and hypothesis in his primitive storage system configuration category.

Due to Carrier's focus on the discipline of digital forensics, the types of hypotheses mentioned in his guidelines are typically singular (case-specific) and often probabilistic (in Bunge's terms), which clearly indicates the idiographic character (in Windelband's terms) of the discipline. While singular hypotheses are often in danger of being too isolated (or *ad hoc*) with regard to embedding theories (and are, thus, deficient in their explanatory power), probabilistic hypotheses do not only have their notorious testability issues with regard to corroboration or refutation by single instances of observation, but also depend on an often unclarified (i.e., intuitive) notion of probability. Nomothetic hypotheses of high generality and deep (law-like) explanatory power are not prominent in Carrier's work: this is a feature of the digital forensics discipline and is thus certainly not Carrier's fault.

What Carrier has conducted, in contrast with Bunge, is not a classification of the types of hypotheses that may be formulated during digital forensic investigations. Rather, Carrier has systematically partitioned the domain of digital forensic investigations into sub-domains and describes rather informally the material subjects about which hypotheses have to be formulated within the boundaries of the sub-domains. From a methodological point of view, Carrier's work thus provides the digital forensics community with a domain theory – the importance of which must not be underestimated [3] – instead of a type theory of hypotheses. Thereby, from a type-theoretic point of view, the types of hypotheses in Carrier's domains and sub-domains are more or less the same. Furthermore, whereas the methods that Carrier recommends for generating hypotheses are interesting in practice, they are not relevant to the scientificness of the generated hypotheses because scientificness is not a matter of genealogy.

As far as future work is concerned, additional empirical and theoretical research on the concept of hypothesis in digital forensics needs to be conducted. The empirical research should focus on how hypotheses are actually formulated and applied by practitioners in their field work regardless of Carrier's normative stipulations at his methodological meta-level. The theoretical research should attempt to clarify formally how hypotheses can be chained to construct logically-consistent discursive arguments used in forensic reasoning. Both these research efforts might benefit from the improvement and refinement of the domain-theoretic work [3] initiated by Carrier in [7], including the formal mereological [15] considerations at the basis of domain theory.

Acknowledgement

The authors wish to thank the anonymous reviewers and the conference participants for their critical remarks that have helped improve this chapter.

References

[1] N. Angius, The problem of justification of empirical hypotheses in software testing, *Philosophy and Technology*, vol. 27(3), pp. 423–439, 2014.

[2] H. Beyers, M. Olivier and G. Hancke, Database application schema forensics, *South African Computer Journal*, vol. 55, pp. 1–11, 2014.

[3] D. Bjorner, Domain theory: Practice and theories, discussion of possible research topics, *Proceedings of the Fourth International Colloquium on the Theoretical Aspects of Computing*, pp. 1–17, 2007.

[4] G. Bosman and S. Gruner, Log file analysis with context-free grammars, in *Advances in Database Forensics IX*, G. Peterson and S. Shenoi (Eds.), Springer, Heidelberg, Germany, pp. 145–152, 2013.

[5] M. Bunge, *Philosophy of Science: From Problem to Theory, Volume One*, Transaction Publishers, New Brunswick, New Jersey, 1998.

[6] M. Bunge, *Philosophy of Science: From Explanation to Justification, Volume Two*, Transaction Publishers, New Brunswick, New Jersey, 1998.

[7] B. Carrier, A Hypothesis-Based Approach to Digital Forensic Investigations, CERIAS Technical Report 2006-06, Center for Education and Research in Information Assurance and Security, Purdue University, West Lafayette, Indiana, 2006.

[8] Y. Chabot, A. Bertaux, C. Nicolle and M. Kechadi, A complete formalized knowledge representation model for advanced digital forensics timeline analysis, *Digital Investigation*, vol. 11(S2), pp. S95–S105, 2014.

[9] F. Cohen, *Digital Forensic Evidence Examination*, Fred Cohen and Associates, Livermore, California, 2009.

[10] P. Garbolino, Historical narratives, evidence and explanations, in *Explanation, Prediction and Confirmation, The Philosophy of Science in a European Perspective, Volume 2*, D. Dieks, W. Gonzales, S. Hartmann, T. Uebel and M. Weber (Eds.), Springer, Dordrecht, The Netherlands, pp. 293–303, 2011.

[11] P. Garbolino, The scientification of forensic practice, in *New Challenges to Philosophy of Science, The Philosophy of Science in a European Perspective, Volume 4*, H. Andersen, D. Dieks, W. Gonzales, T. Uebel and G. Wheeler (Eds.), Springer, Dordrecht, The Netherlands, pp. 287–297, 2013.

[12] P. Garbolino and F. Taroni, Evaluation of scientific evidence using Bayesian networks, *Forensic Science International*, vol. 125(2-3), pp. 149–155, 2002.

[13] P. Gladyshev, Formalizing Event Reconstruction in Digital Investigations, Doctoral Dissertation, Department of Computer Science, University College Dublin, Dublin, Ireland, 2004.

[14] T. Kuhn, *The Structure of Scientific Revolutions*, University of Chicago Press, Chicago, Illinois, 1962.

[15] E. Luschei, *The Logical Systems of Lesniewski*, North-Holland, Amsterdam, The Netherlands, 1962.

[16] M. Olivier and S. Gruner, On the scientific maturity of digital forensics research, in *Advances in Digital Forensics IX*, G. Peterson and S. Shenoi (Eds.), Springer, Heidelberg, Germany, pp. 33–49, 2013.

[17] M. Pollitt, History, historiography and the hermeneutics of the hard drive, in *Advances in Digital Forensics IX*, G. Peterson and S. Shenoi (Eds.), Springer, Heidelberg, Germany, pp. 3–17, 2013.

[18] F. Taroni, A. Biedermann, S. Bozza, P. Garbolino and C. Aitken, *Bayesian Networks for Probabilistic Inference and Decision Analysis in Forensic Science*, John Wiley and Sons, Chichester, United Kingdom, 2014.

[19] J. Vuillemin, On Duhem's and Quine's theses, in *The Philosophy of W.V. Quine*, L. Hahn and P. Schilpp (Eds.), Open Court, Peru, Illinois, pp. 595–618, 1986.

[20] J. Wang, Z. Tang and X. Jin, An OCL-based formal method for cloud forensics, *Advanced Materials Research*, vols. 989-994, pp. 1513–1516, 2014.

[21] J. Wiechel, D. Morr and B. Boggess, Application of the scientific method to the analyses in forensic science with case example, *Proceedings of the International Mechanical Engineering Congress and Exposition*, paper no. IMECE2010-39044, pp. 515–522, 2010.

[22] W. Windelband, History and natural science, *Theory and Psychology*, vol. 8(1), pp. 5–22, 1998.

Chapter 3

USING YIN'S APPROACH TO CASE STUDIES AS A PARADIGM FOR CONDUCTING EXAMINATIONS

Oluwasayo Oyelami and Martin Olivier

Abstract   At the heart of any forensic science discipline is the need to ensure that a method applied in the discipline is based on a factual foundation or valid scientific method. In digital forensics, the aim of an examination is to make consistent inferences about events with high certainty. The highest state of inference is a determination of causality. Two scientific methods that can be applied in digital forensic examinations to determine causality are experimentation and case studies. Experimentation has been used in a range of scientific studies, but there are situations where it is not always possible to conduct experiments. In these cases, the only option is to carry out case studies. A case study approach is not widely used in the natural sciences, but it has been accepted as a valid method that can produce insightful results in digital forensic examinations. This chapter focuses on conducting digital evidence examinations using Yin's approach to case studies as a paradigm. The goal is to show that Yin's case study approach can be applied suitably and that it is useful in digital forensic settings.

Keywords: Digital forensic science, digital evidence, examination, case study

1.   Introduction

Forensic science is an intriguing discipline. It epitomizes the relationship between science and law and the complexities of these two fields working together towards the same goal. The goal is to ensure that the innocent remains free and that the guilty is convicted [11, 12].

In an adversarial system, each party must state its case by presenting evidence or expert testimony that supports its assertions and may also refute the opposing party's assertions [11]. To succeed in a legal dispute, the goal of each disputing party is to convince the court to make a

© IFIP International Federation for Information Processing 2015
G. Peterson, S. Shenoi (Eds.): Advances in Digital Forensics XI, IFIP AICT 462, pp. 45–59, 2015.
DOI: 10.1007/978-3-319-24123-4_3

finding that supports its assertions. The court, however, must scrutinize the evidence and make reconstructive findings that reflect "the truth" of what it decided was based on the evidence presented by both parties.

In determining the "truth" in a legal case, especially a criminal case, the court relies heavily on forensic science to make justified inferences regarding the case [12]. The court's reliance on forensic science poses important questions such as: How scientific are the processes used in carrying out a forensic inquiry? How certain are the findings of a forensic inquiry? How can the findings of a forensic inquiry be shown to be reliable and consistent with respect to the goals of the inquiry? [11]. These questions must be answered in any scientific inquiry, especially those involving legal proceedings. In forensic science, it is important to ensure that all activities and inferences are based on science.

Forensic investigations involve a great deal of science. A landmark National Academy of Sciences report [11] noted that techniques such as DNA analysis, serology, forensic pathology, toxicology, chemical analysis and digital forensics are built on a scientific body of knowledge based on theory and research. A Scientific Working Group on Digital Evidence document [16] claims that digital forensics is scientific, but it does not reference the scientific methods and only discusses the procedures that are used. In digital forensics, the processes of preparation, acquisition, examination and reporting of digital evidence [13] are systematically drawn out to enable forensic examiners to follow routine procedures without them having to perform actions that can be construed as conducting science. Software and hardware tools are primarily used to extract and analyze evidence from various artifacts and produce information from which inferences can be made. However, using the products of applied science does not make a process scientific. In order to attain the requisite level of science, a scientist must be involved in an investigation and scientific methods must be applied.

The role of a scientist is further illustrated in the development of hypotheses or prior knowledge. A hypothesis is knowledge that is independent of empirical observation [1, 4]. The development of a hypothesis before examining the evidence ensures that the examination process is free of bias and error. Fingerprint analysis, for example, is susceptible to bias and error because many examiners begin fingerprint analysis by studying an exemplar print and latent print side-by-side without first conducting a complete analysis of the latent print in order to specify the features in the latent print that will be used for comparison [9, 11]. In DNA analysis, bias is greatly reduced by creating a DNA profile from the biological evidence based on criteria [2, 3, 11] that ensure that the chance of two people matching all the criteria is extremely small, thereby ensuring high discrimination power. The DNA profile is then compared against the suspect DNA profile to check if an exact match exists.

A forensic scientist is not needed only at the start and end of an investigation. A forensic scientist is needed throughout an investigation, but especially during the evidence examination process.

Digital forensics has made considerable progress in the area of research [14], but the field is yet to attain a high level of consistency and certainty about inferences that are made during the examination of digital evidence. The highest state of inference is the determination of causality. Causality is the determination of the cause of an event or action [7, 18]. In determining causality during an examination, a forensic examiner seeks to establish a web of consistency that proves a specific source, individual or event caused the evidence to be created. Finding consistencies does not necessarily imply determining causality. Consistency implies that certain events are not logically contradictory, that is, the events corroborate each other. Finding consistencies is a necessary step in determining causality.

In science, there are two methods that can be applied to determine causality: experimental research and case study research [19]. The use of experiments has a long history and is scientifically accepted as a method for determining causality [1, 4]. The case study research method, while also an accepted scientific method, is not widely used in the natural sciences [19]. Although experimentation is effective in a range of scientific studies, there are situations where it may not be possible to conduct experiments. In these situations, the only option is to carry out case studies. In other cases, although experimentation is possible, conducting a case study may reveal even more findings during the examination phase than an experiment can provide. Therefore, it is imperative to develop a formal approach for conducting digital forensic examinations using case studies. Such an approach should ensure that the examination of digital evidence is performed in a rigorous, logical manner.

The term "case study" has been used in different contexts. It has been used to refer to study material that has been altered to illustrate some points more efficiently and as a true story that is used to illustrate points about a theory or principle. In other contexts, a case study involves a research method that is designed and undertaken to discover "truths" from one or more cases.

In this chapter, the context used for the term "case study" is based on Yin's approach [19]. Yin's approach to case studies offers a systematic process for investigating occurrences or events in their real-world contexts. Unlike an experiment that attempts to generalize its findings to some universe, a case study examines a specific occurrence that exhibits likely exceptions to the general case.

This chapter describes a formal approach for conducting digital forensic examinations using Yin's approach to case studies. It shows why the approach is useful in a digital forensic setting, and when and how the method can be applied in forensic examinations.

2.   Understanding a Case

This section discusses the terminology of a case, the design of a case study and the components of a case study design.

2.1   What is a Case?

A case is an instance, an event, an occurrence or a phenomenon. A case may be a police investigation of illegal drug use, a criminal or civil proceeding where the court makes a finding that reflects the truth based on the presented evidence and expert witness testimony, or a network breach case where the intrusion is investigated to determine the cause and the actors. Investigating a case is, in essence, conducting a case study.

The term "case" has different meanings in legal and scientific settings. In order to avoid ambiguity, the use of the word "case" in this chapter will not refer to a legal case in any sense, but will always refer to the instance, event or phenomenon of interest observed in a case study. The word "proceeding" as in legal proceeding is used in this chapter to refer to a legal "case."

In the sciences, a case study involves a descriptive, exploratory or explanatory analysis of a case. A descriptive case study attempts to illustrate an event and the exact context of the event. An exploratory case study seeks to define the research questions and hypotheses pertaining to an event. An explanatory case study aims to establish causality.

Yin [19] defines a case study in term of two attributes: (i) scope; and (ii) features. In terms of the scope, a case study is an in-depth examination of a real event whose cause is not fully understood and is analyzed taking into consideration all the conditions or circumstances that created the event. In terms of the features, a case study copes with events that exhibit complex conditions, relies on multiple sources of evidence and supports theoretical propositions.

The definition above highlights why a case study is relevant. A case study helps an examiner understand a phenomenon while considering all the conditions pertaining to the phenomenon. This differentiates a case study from an experiment, which typically occurs in a controlled environment. Therefore, an experiment cannot cope with events that exhibit complex conditions [19].

According to Yin, a case study, like an experiment, can be used to answer how and why questions [19]. Yin also noted that the more the questions seek to explain some present circumstance (e.g., how and why some social phenomenon works), the more relevant is the case study research. Answering how and why questions helps establish causality in a process called root cause analysis [8]. Note that the phrase "social phenomenon" is used. This is because Yin's approach to case studies is designed from a social science perspective. However, Yin does state that case study research is applicable to the social science disciplines as well as the practicing professions [19]. Digital forensics is a practicing profession and is, therefore, an appropriate field for applying case study research.

2.2 Case Study Design

Two decisions must be made when designing a case study. The first is whether to use a single-case study design or a multiple-case study design. The choice of a case study design is dependent on the case to be studied. A descriptive, exploratory or explanatory case study can employ a single-case or multiple-case design.

The second decision is between a holistic design and an embedded design. A holistic design allows an examiner to study a case as a whole while an embedded design allows the examiner to separately study sub-units of a case. The choice between holistic and embedded designs depends on the scope of the case. A simple case that requires a detailed analysis of an isolated event is best suited to a holistic design while a complex case with a chain of events usually requires an embedded design. Single-case or multiple-case designs may be holistic or embedded.

Single-Case Study. In a single-case study, a case is analyzed in an in-depth manner to confirm a hypothesis or theoretical proposition. The goal may also be to capture relevant information or find alternative explanations related to the case. According to Yin, there are five main justifications for carrying out a single-case study: (i) critical case, where a theory or theoretical propositions believed to be true are studied to determine whether the propositions are correct or whether there are alternative explanations that are more valid; (ii) extreme or unusual case, where an event differs from widely accepted theories or normal events; (iii) common case, where a normal event is analyzed in order to capture expected conditions; (v) revelatory case, where an event that was previously inaccessible becomes observable (a description of this event alone is in itself revelatory); and (v) longitudinal case, where the research seeks to determine whether certain conditions during an event change over time.

Multiple-Case Study. A multiple-case study is required when an in-depth analysis of more than one occurrence or event must be conducted. Such a case study provides more compelling evidence to support the inferences and conclusions made in the study. Yin noted that in order to use a multiple-case study design, the logic of replication must be applied [19]. Yin highlights two sides of this logic, literal replication and theoretical replication.

Literal replication seeks to predict similar results. A multiple-case study with two to three cases involves literal replication. The idea is to study a case in-depth and find additional support for the findings by examining a second or third case in order to demonstrate consistency.

Theoretical replication attempts to predict opposing results in order to invalidate them. It extends the idea of literal replication. After literal replication is achieved, an examiner must conduct an additional in-depth study of two or three more cases with the goal of showing that alternative explanations cannot be possibly true; this further strengthens the initial findings of the study.

2.3   Case Study Design

Yin highlights five case study design components, some of which have been discussed above:

- **Case Study Questions:** These constitute the how and why questions that an examiner expects to answer when studying a case.

- **Study Propositions or Hypotheses:** These constitute the theoretical propositions or hypotheses that focus the study on where potential evidence or data might be found. Exploratory studies typically do not have propositions, but rather have a study purpose.

- **Unit of Analysis:** This involves the determination, based on the study questions and propositions, whether the entire case must be studied or whether it is sufficient to study a sub-unit or sub-units of the case. The examiner needs to further define the study as a single-case or multiple-case study and provide a scope for the study.

- **Linking Data to Propositions:** This step leverages analytical techniques such as pattern matching and logic models that are used to link study data or evidence to the study propositions. Using pattern matching, an examiner can demonstrate that the study findings reflect the hypothesis. Logic models are used to reconstruct complex events in order to illustrate all the aspects of a case. The analytic techniques also help the examiner assess and strengthen the quality of a case study.

Section 5 discusses some of the analytic techniques. The selection of an analytical technique or combination of techniques depends on the case to be examined. Analytical techniques are applied using four general strategies. The four strategies guide an examiner through the analysis and choice of analytic techniques. In particular, the strategies enable an examiner to link the evidence to the study propositions.

The first general strategy is to rely on the theoretical propositions that led to the case study; the propositions guide the case study and point to relevant conditions that must be described and explanations that must be examined. The second general strategy is to work on the data from the ground up; this technique enables an examiner to study the data or evidence with the goal of identifying interesting clues that lead to further evidence analysis. The third general analytic strategy is to develop a case description that details the evidence and its context; developing a case description enables an examiner to identify explanations that should be analyzed. The fourth general strategy is to examine likely rival explanations; this strategy can be used with the other three general strategies. For example, an examiner's initial theoretical proposition may include rival propositions. Other clues found while studying the evidence may lead to additional rival propositions. The description of a case may also produce rival propositions that should be analyzed. By addressing rival explanations, an examiner can strengthen the study findings.

- **Findings Interpretation Criteria:** These criteria help establish the certainty of a study's findings and demonstrate, in clearly defined steps, the process that led to the study's findings. Addressing rival explanations may be used as a criterion for interpreting the findings. The greater the number of rival explanations addressed, the stronger the study findings.

A forensic examination should never be conducted using a trial and error approach. It should always involve, not necessarily a recipe-based approach, but a logical approach. The tasks are to design an examination, conduct the examination and obtain results with high certainty (because they are based on a solid design).

3.   Digital Forensic Case Studies

In digital forensic investigations, the examination of digital evidence starts when the first responder hands over forensically-sound copies of the digital evidence and a case file to the forensic examiner [7, 10]. The case file contains details of the case and the questions that need to be answered by the examiner. The goal of the forensic examiner is to present the findings based on the evidence. The following sections describe three case study examples.

3.1   Case Study 1

Case Study 1 involves a simple example. A forensic examiner is given a digitally-signed document and the suspect's public key. The forensic examiner is asked to examine the document and determine if the document was signed using the suspect's private key. The examiner simply has to show whether or not the document was signed with the suspect's private key [15]. The examiner's finding is a simple Yes or No, which corresponds to a binary decision problem [12].

3.2   Case Study 2

Case Study 2 involves a slightly more complex example. A forensic examiner is given two email messages M_1 and M_2 that are purported to have been sent by a suspect S to a receiver R. The suspect S admits sending the first email M_1 to R, but denies sending the second email M_2. The forensic examiner's task is to determine whether or not suspect S sent the second email M_2 to R.

The forensic examiner's objective is to analyze the email messages and find similarities between the first email M_1 and the second email M_2. The examiner may request additional data such as an image of the suspect's computer system, mail server logs and Internet service provider (ISP) logs to make definitive findings pertaining to the case. The examiner's findings in this case will not be definitive, but will be at the level of certainty of the inferences made by the examiner and the consistency of the data examined. The examiner's findings could be inconclusive, which means the examiner did not have sufficient evidence (e.g., the mail server and ISP logs were deleted and the suspect's computer system was destroyed).

The email example can be analyzed using Yin's approach to case studies. It is a multiple-case study design focused on literal replication.

Using the case study approach, the first step is to define the case study question: How possible is it that the email messages M_1 and M_2 sent to R did not originate from the suspect S? The hypothesis framed from this question is: Email messages M_1 and M_2 received by R originated from suspect S. The unit of analysis defines the interest of the research, which is an in-depth study of the two email messages (specifically the email headers) to establish if they are consistent. At this point, the examiner can identify the other sources of evidence that are relevant to the case (e.g., the suspect's computer system, mail server logs and ISP logs).

The next step is to link the study data or evidence to the hypothesis. This is where the analysis of the email messages is performed. The examiner conducts an in-depth study of the email headers of the two messages in order to establish a web of consistency, the suspect's computer system to establish if both the email messages can be found in the mail client specified in the mail header, and the server and ISP logs to establish if the path the email messages followed is consistent with the assertion that the messages originated from the same source computer. Using analytic techniques such as logic models helps ensure that the process of reconstructing the email message paths is reliable.

Next, the examiner establishes criteria for interpreting the case study findings. Consistencies found in the server and ISP logs, and the suspect's computer system strengthen the findings that the email message M_2 originated from the same source as M_1. Of course, alternative explanations may exist, but the task for the examiner is to show that the alternative explanations are unlikely or impractical given the strength of the findings. Identifying and addressing rival explanations strengthens the study findings; the greater the number of rival explanations that are addressed, the stronger the examiner's findings.

3.3   Case Study 3

Case Study 3 deals with an investigation of a murder case. An examiner is tasked to show the sequence of events that occurred using the phone records of several witnesses in an attempt to demonstrate the reliability of the accused's version of the events. The examiner is presented with a case file containing the facts of the case. The study question is: How can the phone records of several witnesses provide a sequence of events that is consistent with the version of events described by the accused?

The examiner's goal is to demonstrate that the sequence of events is consistent with the accused's version. This requires a single-case study design involving an in-depth analysis of the witnesses' phone data in order to reconstruct the sequence of events.

Next, the examiner defines the study hypothesis. Depending on the study question, the hypothesis could be that the witnesses' phone records agree with the accused's version of events. The unit of analysis is to study the phone records of the witnesses and construct a sequence of events to establish or refute the hypothesis. Another relevant source of evidence is the mobile service provider call logs that can be used to confirm the witnesses' calls and timestamps. The examiner analyzes the timestamps on the witnesses' phones, creates a reconstruction of the timelines and establishes consistency with the accused's version of events. Identifying the criteria for interpreting the results is crucial. As discussed in the email message case study, explaining inconsistencies found during the analysis stage strengthens the findings of a study. The witnesses' phone clocks may not be synchronized with the mobile service provider's clock and when multiple mobile providers are involved, the inconsistencies increase [18].

4.   Analytic Generalizations

An important use of a theory is generalization. Yin discusses the use of analytical generalizations where the findings of a case study are generalizable to the theoretical propositions that underlie the case. This is different from statistical generalizations where the aim is to generalize the findings of a study to a population by studying a sample of the population.

Case studies and, indeed, digital forensic cases are not samples of a population. For example, it is possible to generalize that, for a certain case, the event E_1 caused the occurrence of the event E_2. However, it is not possible to say that, in every case, the event E_1 will always cause the occurrence of event E_2.

5.   Assessing Case Study Quality

The quality of a case study design is very important. In order to ensure that the case study findings are consistent and valid, case study research employs four tests for judging the quality of a case study design [19]: (i) construct validity; (ii) internal validity; (iii) external validity; and (iv) reliability. When conducting a digital forensic case study, these tests ensure that the case study is consistent in its claims, that the findings are valid and that the findings are the outcome of a computational process based on an accepted scientific method.

- **Construct Validity:** The first test for assessing the quality of digital forensic case studies is construct validity. In digital forensics, construct validity examines the rationale behind the forensic examiner's decision about the evidence that is collected. Specifically, construct validity establishes that the data obtained for the case study is justifiable. Construct validity determines if the data selected from the available digital evidence is appropriate to answer the questions that are asked about the data. For every question, the appropriate piece of data should be selected for the study. Yin highlights three tactics to strengthen construct validity in case studies.

  The first tactic is to ensure the use of multiple sources of evidence. This is consistent with Casey's certainty scale [5], which points out that evidence supported by multiple independent sites has a higher certainty value than information about a single source that could have been tampered with. This ensures that the case study findings are strengthened by a web of consistency that can be established during evidence examination.

  The second tactic is to establish a chain of evidence, an important principle that is already established in digital forensics [5–7, 17]. A well-documented chain of evidence confirms that the evidence was handled correctly throughout the lifetime of the investigation.

  The third tactic is to ensure that the draft findings of a case study are reviewed by key informants. This is done to enable the key sources to validate the information they have provided. In digital forensics, there are usually no key informants, because the evidence is primarily bits and bytes extracted from a computer system. Therefore, the closest to a key informant review is a peer review of the findings conducted by another forensic examiner or expert. The inclusion of a critical discussion of what has been analyzed is a new element in digital forensics, which is not currently in use.

- **Internal Validity:** The second test for assessing the quality of digital forensic case studies is internal validity, a main concern in explanatory case studies. This test is focused on the examination of evidence. Internal validity tests the findings of a case study. It critiques the forensic examiner's findings and asks the questions: How well do the findings reflect the outcome of a case? How certain is it that no other factors may have influenced the findings? This means that the conclusions should follow from the observations. For example, if an event E_1 can cause E_3 and an event E_2 can also cause E_3, how can one say with certainty that event E_1 and event E_2 both caused E_3? Or that, although event E_2 was present, it did not contribute to E_3?

Yin highlights four analytic tactics that can be used to meet the internal validity test. The first tactic is pattern matching. Pattern matching [19] involves the comparison of patterns based on the findings of the empirical case study with the predicted pattern(s) or hypothesis made before evidence collection. Testing a hypothesis, which involves matching against the predictions made before empirical observations, provides a stronger argument for the validity of a case study.

Consider a simple example. Suppose it is known that a certain web browser was used to access a website. Then, based on an understanding of web browser operation, we can expect to find information such as the sender details in the destination web server log, the browser that was used and the IP address of the originating network. Finding these artifacts demonstrates that a structured approach was followed.

The second tactic is explanation building, which is a special type of pattern matching. The process of explanation building supports evidence analysis by creating an explanation about the case. Explaining a case essentially establishes the relationships between the variables or conditions of the case. This is, in essence, an attempt at interpreting the evidence by accounting for all the conditions that produced the evidence and showing that all the pieces fit into the case.

The third tactic, which enhances internal validity, addresses rival explanations. Rival explanations or propositions must be developed and expressed so that the conditions of the rival explanations are mutually exclusive (i.e., if one explanation is valid, the other cannot be valid).

For example, a forensic examiner might recognize an alternative explanation for an occurrence in a child pornography investigation, when the suspect claims that a Trojan was responsible. The task of the forensic examiner is to rule out the possibility of a Trojan. Using pattern matching, the forensic examiner can show that, for a Trojan to be present, certain system files would have been changed and certain unusual activities would have been observed in the system. Proving that these expected changes and activities were not present addresses the Trojan issue and strengthens the findings of the examination.

The fourth tactic involves the use of logic models as an analytic technique for ensuring internal validity. Logic models are another form of pattern matching. However, they are distinguished from pattern matching in that they break down complex chains of events into repeated cause-effect patterns in order to reflect the intermediate and final findings [19]. This is a form of event reconstruction. By reconstructing the sequence of events that produced the evidence, a forensic examiner can show that there are no missing pieces in the puzzle and also account for all the conditions that produced the evidence.

- **External Validity:** The third test for assessing the quality of digital forensic case studies is external validity. External validity focuses on determining if the study findings are generalizable beyond the immediate study. It asks the question: Can one say that, for all cases, an event E_1 will always cause another event E_2? By applying analytical generalization to a digital examination, it can be shown that the findings of a case explain what is observed in the case. However, if other possible explanations exist in another (similar) case, then it is necessary to show that the findings of the previous case do not apply.

- **Reliability:** The fourth test for assessing the quality of digital forensic case studies is reliability. The reliability of a digital forensic case study is crucial if the findings are to be presented in a legal proceeding. The goal of reliability is to minimize errors and bias in a case study. In ensuring reliability, the forensic examiner must document the procedures followed in the case study to ensure that they can be followed by another examiner. Documentation is important because it shows that a structured approach was followed when conducting the case study and, if the same case study were to be repeated by another examiner using the same procedure, then it would be very likely that the other examiner would arrive at the same conclusions.

The four tests discussed above, construct validity, internal validity, external validity and reliability, can be applied to assess the quality of case study designs. The tests ensure that the study findings are consistent with the underlying theoretical propositions and are peer reviewed, and that the case study is repeatable and rival explanations are taken into consideration in order to strengthen the study findings.

6.   Conclusions

Yin's work on case study research has gone through five editions of publication [19] and is widely accepted. Much of what happens in a digital forensic laboratory already reflects Yin's work. Yin's approach to case studies, therefore, validates what digital forensic professionals do and potentially provides the discipline of digital forensics with a formal scientific backing. The approach further extends digital forensic processes by providing quality indicators for assessing the findings of digital examinations.

The formal methodology for conducting digital forensic examinations presented in this chapter draws significantly from Yin's approach to case studies. Case study research helps ensure that a formal scientific approach is applied when conducting digital forensic examinations. Case study research can also be applied to demonstrate causality; single-case and multiple-case designs help cope with events with complex conditions. Relying on multiple sources of evidence in a case study strengthens the findings and developing theoretical propositions grounds the study in fundamental research principles. Yin's approach to case study research offers an alternative method for situations where it is not possible to conduct scientific experiments. Moreover, Yin's approach provides digital forensic examiners with tools for assessing the quality of case study findings, ensuring that their findings are consistent and reproducible.

References

[1] M. Bunge, *Philosophy of Science: From Problem to Theory, Volume One*, Transaction Publishers, New Brunswick, New Jersey, 1998.

[2] J. Butler, *Forensic DNA Typing*, Elsevier Academic Press, Burlington, Massachusetts, 2005.

[3] L. Carey and L. Mitnik, Trends in DNA forensic analysis, *Electrophoresis*, vol. 23(10), pp. 1386–1397, 2002.

[4] B. Carrier, A Hypothesis-Based Approach to Digital Forensic Investigations, CERIAS Technical Report 2006-06, Center for Education and Research in Information Assurance and Security, Purdue University, West Lafayette, Indiana, 2006.

[5] E. Casey, *Digital Evidence and Computer Crime: Forensic Science, Computers and the Internet*, Academic Press, Waltham, Massachusetts, 2011.

[6] F. Cohen, *Challenges to Digital Forensic Evidence*, Fred Cohen and Associates, Livermore, California, 2008.

[7] F. Cohen, *Digital Forensic Evidence Examination*, Fred Cohen and Associates, Livermore, California, 2009.

[8] C. Grobler, C. Louwrens and S. von Solms, A multi-component view of digital forensics, *Proceedings of the IEEE International Conference on Availability, Reliability and Security*, pp. 647–652, 2010.

[9] L. Haber and R. Haber, Scientific validation of fingerprint evidence under Daubert, *Law, Probability and Risk*, vol. 7(2), pp. 87–109, 2008.

[10] National Institute of Justice, Electronic Crime Scene Investigation: A Guide for First Responders, Special Report, NCJ 219941, Washington, DC, 2008.

[11] National Institute of Justice and National Research Council, *Strengthening Forensic Science in the United States: A Path Forward*, National Academies Press, Washington, DC, 2009.

[12] M. Olivier, On complex crimes and digital forensics, in *Information Security in Diverse Computing Environments*, A. Kayem and C. Meinel (Eds.), IGI Global, Hershey, Pennsylvania, pp. 230–244, 2013.

[13] M. Olivier, Combining fundamentals, traditions, practice and science in a digital forensics course, presented at the *South African Computer Lecturers' Association Conference*, 2014.

[14] M. Olivier and S. Gruner, On the scientific maturity of digital forensics research, in *Advances in Digital Forensics IX*, G. Peterson and S. Shenoi (Eds.), Springer, Heidelberg, Germany, pp. 33–49, 2013.

[15] C. Pfleeger and S. Lawrence Pfleeger, *Security in Computing*, Pearson Education, Boston, Massachusetts, 2006.

[16] Scientific Working Group on Digital Evidence, Digital and Multimedia Evidence (Digital Forensics) as a Forensic Science Discipline, Version 2.0, 2014.

[17] J. Wiles and A. Reyes, *The Best Damn Cybercrime and Digital Forensic Book Period*, Syngress, Burlington, Massachusetts, 2007.

[18] S. Willassen, Hypothesis-based investigation of digital timestamps, in *Advances in Digital Forensics IV*, I. Ray and S. Shenoi (Eds.), Springer, Boston, Massachusetts, pp. 75–86, 2008.

[19] R. Yin, *Case Study Research: Design and Methods*, SAGE, Thousand Oaks, California, 2013.

Chapter 4

AN INFORMATION EXTRACTION FRAMEWORK FOR DIGITAL FORENSIC INVESTIGATIONS

Min Yang and Kam-Pui Chow

Abstract   The pervasiveness of information technology has led to an explosion of evidence. Attempting to discover valuable information from massive collections of documents is challenging. This chapter proposes a two-phase information extraction framework for digital forensic investigations. In the first phase, a named entity recognition approach is applied to the collected documents to extract names, locations and organizations; the named entities are displayed using a visualization system to assist investigators in finding coherent evidence rapidly and accurately. In the second phase, association rule mining is performed to identify the relations existing between the extracted named entities, which are then displayed. Examples include person-affiliation relations and organization-location relations. The effectiveness of the framework is demonstrated using the well-known Enron email dataset.

Keywords: Information extraction, named entity recognition, relation extraction

1.   Introduction

Investigations involving text documents and data rely on expression-based or keyword-based searches [6]. Current digital forensics tools implement search methods that rely on accurate keywords. For example, given the name of a suspect, a search tool would return all the exact and similar occurrences in the data [24]. However, in the vast majority of cases, complete keyword information is not available; this makes it necessary to uncover and use additional information to improve searches.

Information summarization and event extraction from data are extremely useful in forensic investigations. In general, the more information that can be extracted, the more accurate the search. However,

© IFIP International Federation for Information Processing 2015
G. Peterson, S. Shenoi (Eds.): Advances in Digital Forensics XI, IFIP AICT 462, pp. 61–76, 2015.
DOI: 10.1007/978-3-319-24123-4_4

digital forensic examiners are often unable to comprehensively review all the keyword matches in a corpus [5]. Text summarization can reduce the time spent on reviewing search hits while ensuring that all the instances of interest are located.

Information extraction systems can extract abstract knowledge from a text corpus or extract concrete data from a set of documents [30]. Information extraction has two phases. The first phase, involving the detection and classification of proper names, is called named entity recognition [31]. Since digital forensics focuses on the who, what, where, when and why of a case, it is essential to recognize named entities such as persons, organizations and locations. For instance, in the sentence "Jeff Skilling (born November 25, 1953) is the former CEO of the Enron Corporation headquartered in Houston, Texas," "Jeff Skilling," "Enron Corporation" and "Houston, Texas" correspond to person, organization and location entities, respectively.

The second phase of information extraction is relation extraction. In a forensic investigation, it is useful to discover relations that are hidden in named entities extracted from large data sets. For example, by analyzing newspaper text, it is possible to discern that an organization is located in a particular city or that a person is affiliated with a specific organization [44]. The relations discovered can then be represented in two forms, as association rules or as sets of frequent items.

This chapter describes a novel information extraction framework that helps find valuable evidence in text documents. The framework has two phases. In the first phase, a named entity recognition approach is applied to the raw forensic data to extract the named entities (i.e., persons, organizations and locations). To assist investigators in finding coherent evidence rapidly and accurately, informative named entities are visualized and highlighted using cloud tags and text clouds. The extracted entities provide a useful overview of the data when a forensic investigator does not know what to look for or has a large number of hits to review. The second phase uses a modified version of the Apriori algorithm [34] to identify the relations among the extracted named entities and visually display the extracted relations. Examples of relations are person-affiliation and organization-location. Experiments are conducted on the Enron email corpus to demonstrate that the information extraction framework is very effective at helping find relevant information.

2.   Related Work

The pervasiveness of information technology has led to an explosion of evidence. In order to handle vast amounts of evidence in a limited time, a number of text analysis approaches have been proposed for forensic investigations [12, 14, 16, 21, 25, 32, 35]. Information extraction, which seeks to extract useful information from unstructured text, has become an active research area in digital forensics. The first step in information extraction is the detection and classification of proper names, which is often referred to as named entity recognition [31]. Named entity recognition is a well-studied problem and has many applications, including focused searches over massive collections of textual data [15], social network analysis [19] and information summarization [36].

Named entity recognition has been applied to news articles [28] and scientific articles [7]. These articles are written for fairly broad audiences and the authors generally take great care when preparing them. However, less time and effort are spent on preparing informal documents; as a result, they contain many grammatical and spelling errors. In addition, informal text generally contains many abbreviations. Techniques have been proposed to improve named entity recognition performance for informal text such as email [29] and web postings [19].

Named entity recognition techniques have also been applied in forensic investigations [4, 9, 21, 22, 24, 33, 41]. Louis et al. [24] have used dynamic Bayesian networks to identify named entities. Kuperus et al. [22] have presented a probabilistic named entity recognition model based on multiple candidate labels that exploits user feedback to obtain increased recall with little loss in precision. However, both techniques do not attempt to discover the relations existing between named entities in forensic investigations.

The second step in information extraction is relation extraction. Relation extraction can be characterized as a classification problem: if two entities are potentially related, it is necessary to determine if they are indeed related [3]. Supervised methods [44, 45], semi-supervised methods [10, 38] and unsupervised methods [43] have been applied to solve this binary classification problem. In the case of structured data, association rules can be used to simplify relation extraction [26, 30]. This work uses the Apriori algorithm [34], a classical association rule approach, to discover the relations among named entities. Al-Zaidy et al. [2] have proposed a similar approach. However, they focus on identifying indirect relationships between a person and a prominent community. An indirect relationship starts from a person and forms a chain connecting to a prominent community; each internal node in the chain is a person that links two documents. In contract, the work described in this chapter attempts to discover named entities and their semantic relations.

Colombe and Stephens [11] discuss visualization techniques for assisting forensic investigations. The Tilebars method [17], for instance, is

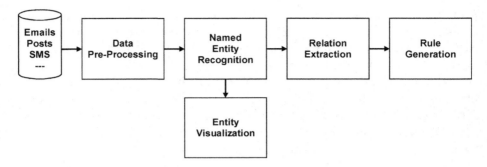

Figure 1. Information extraction process.

designed to be a navigational aid for analysts. Whittaker et al. [42] visualize term distributions in histograms to support information retrieval from speech archives. Schwartz and Liebrock [37] apply visualization to digital forensic string searches. On the other hand, the information extraction framework presented in this chapter uses tag clouds [18] to visualize named entities and also leverages visualizations of the relations between named entities, providing forensic investigators with an intuitively appealing means to comprehend and analyze large bodies of textual evidence.

3.   Information Extraction Framework

This section describes the information extraction framework for finding evidence. As shown in Figure 1, the framework has two main phases. In the first phase, a named entity recognition approach is applied to the raw forensic data to extract the named entities (i.e., persons, organizations and locations). In the second phase, a data mining tool is used to identify the relations existing between the extracted named entities. To assist investigators in finding coherent evidence faster and more intuitively, relevant informative named entities are highlighted with cloud tags and the relations among the named entities are visually displayed.

3.1   Named Entity Recognition

Given a sentence, the named entity recognition approach segments words that are parts of named entities and then classifies each entity by its type (person, organization, location, etc.). Existing named entity recognition approaches are divided into two categories: (i) rule-based approaches [31]; and (ii) machine learning approaches [8, 39]. A rule-based approach relies on linguistic knowledge, in particular, grammar rules, while a machine learning approach relies on a labeled corpus [1]. A rule-based approach achieves better results in many domains because the rules can be adapted very precisely and are, therefore, able to detect complex entities. However, in the case of an unrestricted domain, it would be expensive in terms of cost and time to derive rules. On the other hand, a machine learning approach is more flexible and is able to identify uncommon patterns of named entities that are not specified in the regular expressions of rule-based systems [1]. The proposed named entity recognition framework exploits the complementary performance associated with the rule-based and machine learning approaches by taking the union of the results provided by the two approaches to improve the recall.

The machine learning approach used in the proposed framework engages the conditional random fields model [23] to identify named entities, primarily because it provides excellent performance for many information extraction tasks [39]. A document is expressed as a vector $X = (x_1, \ldots, x_i, \ldots, x_n)$ where n is the number of features and x_i is the relative frequency of feature i in the document. After all the documents have been represented in this way, the conditional random fields model can be applied to extract the named entities. Lafferty et al. [23] define the probability of a label sequence y given observation sequence x to be the normalized product of potential functions of the form:

$$\exp(\sum_j \lambda_j t_j(y_{i-1}, y_i, x, i) + \sum \mu_k s_k(y_i, x, i)) \qquad (1)$$

where $t_j(y_{i-1}, y_i, x, i)$ is a transition feature function of the entire observation sequence and the labels at positions i and $i - 1$ in the label sequence; $s_k(y_{i,}, x, i)$ is a state feature function of the label at position i and the observation sequence; and λ_j and μ_k are parameters that are estimated from training data.

When defining feature functions, a set of real-valued features $b(x, i)$ of the observation are constructed to express some characteristic of the empirical distribution of the training data that should also hold in the model distribution. An example of such a feature is:

$$b(x, i) = \begin{cases} 1 & \text{if the observation at position } i \text{ is the word "September"} \\ 0 & \text{otherwise} \end{cases}$$

$$(2)$$

Each feature function takes on a value of one for real-valued observation features $b(x, i)$ if the current state (in the case of a state function) or previous and current states (in the case of a transition function) take on particular values.

In the remainder of this chapter, the notation is simplified by writing:

$$F_j(y, x) = \sum_{i=1}^{n} f_j(y_{i-1}, y_i, x, i) \tag{3}$$

where each $f_j(y_{i-1}, y_i, x, i)$ is either a state function $s(y_{i-1}, y_i, x, i)$ or a transition function $t(y_{i-1}, y_i, x, i)$. This allows the probability of a label sequence y given an observation sequence x to be written as:

$$p(y|x, \lambda) = \frac{1}{Z(x)} \exp(\sum \lambda_j F_j(y, x)) \tag{4}$$

where $Z(x)$ is a normalization factor. In this work, the conditional random fields model was executed using publicly-available Python code [13]. Default settings were used for all the parameters.

The rule-based approach largely follows the guidelines listed in [27]. However, several changes have been introduced to make the extracted named entities more practical and to improve the recall of the named entity recognition system. For example, when analyzing email, a check was made to see if a token in the header was equal to some token w.

3.2   Relation Extraction

Forensic investigators usually browse forensic data using queries such as "Select all the people who have a relation with the suspect" or "Select all the people who are related to a specific organization." This can be implemented using relation extraction, which identifies the significant relations existing between entities.

This work incorporates a modification of the Apriori algorithm [34] to perform relation extraction. The Apriori algorithm is a classic algorithm that finds relations in data. For example, the rule, Diapers → Beer, suggests that a strong relation exists between the sale of diapers and the sale of beer because many customers who purchase diapers also purchase beer [40].

An indication of how frequently an item or a relation occurs is measured by the support function $supp(s)$. The support of a rule $A \rightarrow B$ is the percentage of documents in the corpus that contain $A \cup B$. The *supp* measure is important because a rule that has very low support may occur simply by chance.

The confidence measure *conf*, on the other hand, measures the reliability of the inference made by the rule. For a rule $A \rightarrow B$, the higher

Table 1. Illustrative example.

	Coffee	$\overline{\text{Coffee}}$	Total
Tea	15	5	20
$\overline{\text{Tea}}$	75	5	80
Total	90	10	100

the confidence, the more likely it is that a document containing A also contains B.

Given a set of documents containing extracted named entities, it is necessary to find all the rules with $supp \geq minsupp$ and $conf \geq minconf$ where $minsupp$ and $minconf$ are two constant thresholds. Interested readers are referred to [34] for details about the Apriori algorithm.

In the original Apriori algorithm, confidence is the only measure used to verify rules. However, although the confidence of a rule may be high, the rule could still be misleading. For instance, consider the situation shown in Table 1 where there are 100 transactions that contain either tea or coffee. Furthermore, assume that the *conf* threshold is 70%. From Table 1, for the rule Tea → Coffee, $conf = \text{P(Coffee|Tea)} = 0.75$, indicating that the rule is valid. Nevertheless, a person who does not purchase tea is more likely to purchase coffee since $\text{P(Coffee|}\overline{\text{Tea}}) = 0.9375$. To address this problem, the *lift* score $= \text{P(Y|X)/P(Y)}$ is used to evaluate rules of the form $X \to Y$. Only rules whose *lift* scores are larger than one are considered.

4. Experiments and Analysis

This section describes the experiments performed on a real-world forensic dataset and presents an analysis of the results.

4.1 Dataset Description

Because no authoritative real-world forensic datasets are available to evaluate the performance of a named entity recognition system in forensic investigations, a portion of the texts from the Enron corpus was manually labeled. The raw Enron corpus made public by the U.S. Federal Energy Regulatory Commission contains 619,446 messages belonging to 158 users. Klimt and Yang [20] subsequently cleaned up the corpus by removing certain folders associated with each user because they appeared to be computer-generated. The cleaned Enron corpus used in this work has 200,399 messages belonging to 158 users with an average of 757 messages per user.

Table 2.   Named entity recognition results.

Named Entities	Precision	Recall	F1
Persons	0.84	0.92	0.88
Organizations	0.88	0.95	0.91
Locations	0.78	0.87	0.82

4.2   Data Pre-Processing

The texts were tokenized using the NLTK natural language toolkit. Next, non-alphabet characters, numbers, pronouns, words with two characters or less, punctuation and stop words (common words appearing frequently) were removed from the text. Finally, the WordNet stemmer was applied to reduce the size of the vocabulary and address data sparseness.

4.3   Experimental Results

This section discusses the experimental results.

Named Entity Recognition. The experiment to evaluate the effectiveness of the named entity recognition system used 200 randomly-chosen messages from the Enron corpus containing more than 100 words as test data. Three natural language processing researchers were then asked to manually label each entity tag (i.e., person, organization, location, etc.).

Recall, precision and F_1 measures were used to evaluate the performance of the named entity recognition system:

$$precision = \frac{\#\text{correct identified entities}}{\#\text{total entities found}} \qquad (5)$$

$$recall = \frac{\#\text{correct identified entities}}{\#\text{total correct entities}} \qquad (6)$$

$$F_1 = 2 \cdot \frac{\text{precision} \cdot \text{recall}}{\text{precision} + \text{recall}} \qquad (7)$$

Table 2 summarizes the results. Since higher values for the three measures indicate more accurate extraction, the results indicate that the named entity recognition system is effective at identifying persons, organizations and locations. In particular, the system has a relatively high recall for persons and organizations.

-------- Forwarded by **Phillip K Allen**/HOU/ECT on 10/16/2000 01:42 PM --------

"**Buckner, Buck**" cc: Subject: FW: fixed forward or other Collar floor gas price terms

Phillip,

As discussed during our phone conversation, In a **Parallon** 75 microturbine power generation deal for a national accounts customer, I am developing a proposal to sell power to customer at fixed or collar/floor price. To do so I need a corresponding term gas price for same. Microturbine is an onsite generation product developed by **Honeywell** to generate electricity on customer site (degen). using natural gas. In doing so, I need your best fixed price forward gas price deal for 1, 3, 5, 7 and 10 years for annual/seasonal supply to microturbines to generate fixed kWh for customer. We have the opportunity to sell customer kWh 's using microturbine or sell them turbines themselves. kWh deal must have limited/ n risk forward gas price to make deal work. Therein comes **Sempra** energy gas trading, truly you.

We are proposing installing 180 - 240 units across a large number of stores (60-100) in **San Diego**. Store number varies because of installation hurdles face at small percent.
For 6-8 hours a day Microturbine run time:
Gas requirement for 180 microturbines 227 - 302 MMcf per year
Gas requirement for 240 microturbines 302 - 403 MMcf per year

Gas will likely be consumed from May through September, during peak electric period. Gas price required: Burnertip price behind (LDC) **San Diego Gas & Electric**
Need detail breakout of commodity and transport cost (firm or interruptible).
Should you have additional questions, give me a call. Let me assure you, this is real deal!!

Buck Buckner, P.E., MBA
Manager, Business Development and Planning
Big Box Retail Sales
Honeywell Power Systems, Inc.
8725 **Pan American Frwy**
Albuquerque, NM 87113
505-798-6424
505-798-6050x
505-220-4129
888/501-3145

Figure 2. Highlighted named entities in the analyzed text.

Named Entity Visualization. Forensic investigators are often overwhelmed by the number of keyword matches when dealing with large datasets. To assist investigators in rapidly finding coherent evidence, a text cloud visualization of word importance is used to discriminate the extracted named entities from the original text. Figure 2 shows a text cloud display of a random sample of text from the Enron corpus. The named entities are represented using larger fonts than the other entities.

Suppose that an investigator has no prior knowledge of the data and, thus, does not what to look for. In such a scenario, tag clouds [18] may be used to quickly visualize all the extracted named entities with respect to the name category. Figure 3 shows three tag clouds for persons, organizations and locations, respectively. The importance of each tag is expressed using its font size. For example, "John" and "Jeff" are the top person names in Enron Corp. Note that the tag cloud representation can enable a forensic investigator to quickly draw conclusions from a massive volume of data.

Figure 3. Identified named entities (persons, organizations and locations).

Table 3. Example entity relationships.

Entity Relations	Relation Description
Enron North America Corp → Smith Street, Houston	Enron is located at Smith Street, Houston, Texas
Ken Lay → Enron	Ken Lay is the CEO of Enron
California → Gray Davis	Gray Davis served as the Governor of California
Enron Capital and Trade Resources Corp → ECT	ECT is short for Enron Capital and Trade Resources Corp
Frank L. Davis, Tana Jones → ECT	Frank L. Davis and Tana Jones are ECT traders
California Public Utilities Commission → California	California Public Utilities Commission is located in California
Mike Swerzbin → Joe Stepenovitch	Joe Stepenovitch is the VP of energy marketing and trading, the boss of Mike Swerzbin
Enron Wholesale Services → Enron	Enron Wholesale Services is Enron's largest business unit
Tanya Tamarchenko → Vince J. Kaminski	Vince J. Kaminski is the director of research, the boss of Tanya Tamarchenko
BUSH → Houston	BUSH International airport is located in Houston

Relation Extraction. In a forensic investigation, it is also important to discover interesting relations that are hidden in named entities. For example, a useful query might be: Select all the persons who have a relation with the suspect. The Apriori algorithm was modified to discover relations existing between name entities (i.e., persons, organizations and locations). The threshold *minsupp* was set to 150. Table 3 shows some of the relations with relatively high support. Forensic investigators can use this technique to identify a suspect using logically-related queries. Note that traditional exact matching techniques often fail to provide useful results.

In addition to discovering direct relations, the information extraction framework can also construct implicit social networks from email activities. For example, although Jeffrey K. Skilling and Matthew Lenhart had no direct email exchanges, a relation between them exists as a result of the rules:"ECT → Jeffrey K. Skilling" and "Matthew Lenhart → ECT." In particular, Jeffrey K. Skilling is the CEO of ECT while Matthew Lenhart is an ECT trader, which manifests the relation that Skilling is the boss of Lenhart.

5.   Conclusions

The information extraction framework presented in this chapter is specifically designed to enhance forensic investigations. It applies a named entity recognition approach on raw forensic data to extract named entities. Following this, association rule mining (i.e., the Apriori algorithm) is applied to identify the relations existing between the extracted named entities. Relevant and informative named entities are visualized using tag clouds, and new relations existing between the named entities can also be discovered. Experiments using the well-known Enron email corpus demonstrate the effectiveness of the framework.

Future research will extend the named entity recognition system to identify addresses, vehicles, narcotics and personal characteristics. It will also attempt to develop social networks of criminals and suspects based on the extracted entities. Additionally, it will apply user interest profiling to reveal indirect relations between individuals and identify individuals who have specific interests over time.

References

[1] S. Abdallah, K. Shaalan and M. Shoaib, Integrating rule-based system with classification for Arabic named entity recognition, *Proceedings of the Thirteenth International Conference on Computational Linguistics and Intelligent Text Processing*, vol. 1, pp. 311–322, 2012.

[2] R. Al-Zaidy, B. Fung, A. Youssef and F. Fortin, Mining criminal networks from unstructured text documents, *Digital Investigation*, vol. 8(3-4), pp. 147–160, 2012.

[3] N. Bach and S. Badaskar, A Review of Relation Extraction, Language Technologies Institute, School of Computer Science, Carnegie Mellon University, Pittsburgh, Pennsylvania, 2007.

[4] N. Beebe, Digital forensic research: The good, the bad and the unaddressed, in *Advances in Digital Forensics V*, G. Peterson and S. Shenoi (Eds.), Springer, Heidelberg, Germany, pp. 17–36, 2009.

[5] N. Beebe and J. Clark, Dealing with terabyte data sets in digital investigations, in *Advances in Digital Forensics*, M. Pollitt and S. Shenoi (Eds.), Springer, Boston, Massachusetts, pp. 3–16, 2005.

[6] N. Beebe and L. Liu, Clustering digital forensic string search output, *Digital Investigation*, vol. 11(4), pp. 314–322, 2014.

[7] R. Bunescu and R. Mooney, Collective information extraction with relational Markov networks, *Proceedings of the Forty-Second Annual Meeting of the Association for Computational Linguistics*, article no. 438, 2004.

[8] C. Cardie, Empirical methods in information extraction, *AI Magazine*, vol. 18(4), pp. 65–79, 1997.

[9] M. Chau, J. Xu and H. Chen, Extracting meaningful entities from police narrative reports, *Proceedings of the Annual National Conference on Digital Government Research*, 2002.

[10] J. Chen, D. Ji, C. Tan and Z. Niu, Relation extraction using label propagation based semi-supervised learning, *Proceedings of the Twenty-First International Conference on Computational Linguistics and the Forty-Fourth Annual Meeting of the Association for Computational Linguistics*, pp. 129–136, 2006.

[11] J. Colombe and G. Stephens, Statistical profiling and visualization for detection of malicious insider attacks on computer networks, *Proceedings of the ACM Workshop on Visualization and Data Mining for Computer Security*, pp. 138–142, 2004.

[12] A. de Waal, J. Venter and E. Barnard, Applying topic modeling to forensic data, in *Advances in Digital Forensics IV*, I Ray and S. Shenoi (Eds.), Springer, Boston, Massachusetts, pp. 115–126, 2008.

[13] J. Finkel, T. Grenager and C. Manning, Incorporating non-local information into information extraction systems by Gibbs sampling, *Proceedings of the Forty-Third Annual Meeting of the Association for Computational Linguistics*, pp. 363–370, 2005.

[14] S. Garfinkel, Digital forensics research: The next ten years, *Digital Investigation* vol. 7(S), pp. S64–S73, 2010.

[15] J. Guo, G. Xu, X. Cheng and H. Li, Named entity recognition in query, *Proceedings of the Thirty-Second International ACM SIGIR Conference on Research and Development in Information Retrieval*, pp. 267–274, 2009.

[16] R. Hadjidj, M. Debbabi, H. Lounis, F. Iqbal, A. Szporer and D. Benredjem, Towards an integrated e-mail forensic analysis framework, *Digital Investigation*, vol. 5(3-4), pp. 124–137, 2009.

[17] M. Hearst, Tilebars: Visualization of term distribution information in full text information access, *Proceedings of the SIGCHI Conference on Human Factors in Computing Systems*, pp. 59–66, 1995.

[18] M. Hearst and D. Rosner, Tag clouds: Data analysis tool or social signaller? *Proceedings of the Forty-First Annual Hawaii International Conference on System Sciences*, 2008.

[19] J. Jung, Online named entity recognition method for microtexts in social networking services: A case study of Twitter, *Expert Systems with Applications*, vol. 39(9), pp. 8066–8070, 2012.

[20] B. Klimt and Y. Yang, Introducing the Enron corpus, *Proceedings of the Collaboration, Electronic Messaging, Anti-Abuse and Spam Conference*, 2004.

[21] C. Ku, A. Iriberri and G. Leroy, Natural language processing and e-government: Crime information extraction from heterogeneous data sources, *Proceedings of the Ninth Annual International Conference on Digital Government Research*, pp. 162–170, 2008.

[22] J. Kuperus, C. Veenman and M. van Keulen, Increasing NER recall with minimal precision loss, *Proceedings of the European Intelligence and Security Informatics Conference*, pp. 106–111, 2013.

[23] J. Lafferty, A. McCallum and F. Pereira, Conditional random fields: Probabilistic models for segmenting and labeling sequence data, *Proceedings of the Eighteenth International Conference on Machine Learning*, pp. 282–289, 2001.

[24] A. Louis, A. De Waal and C. Venter, Named entity recognition in a South African context, *Proceedings of the Annual Research Conference of the South African Institute of Computer Scientists and Information Technologists on IT Research in Developing Countries*, pp. 170–179, 2006.

[25] A. Louis and A. Engelbrecht, Unsupervised discovery of relations for analysis of textual data, *Digital Investigation*, vol. 7(3-4), pp. 154–171, 2011.

[26] A. Maedche and S. Staab, Ontology learning for the semantic web, *IEEE Intelligent Systems*, vol. 16(2), pp. 72–79, 2001.

[27] D. Maynard, V. Tablan, C. Ursu, H. Cunningham and Y. Wilks, Named entity recognition from diverse text types, *Proceedings of the Conference on Recent Advances in Natural Language Processing*, pp. 257–274, 2001.

[28] A. McCallum and W. Li, Early results for named entity recognition with conditional random fields, feature induction and web-enhanced lexicons, *Proceedings of the Seventh Conference on Natural Language Learning*, vol. 4, pp. 188–191, 2003.

[29] E. Minkov, R. Wang and W. Cohen, Extracting personal names from email: Applying named entity recognition to informal text, *Proceedings of the Conference on Human Language Technology and Empirical Methods in Natural Language Processing*, pp. 443–450, 2005.

[30] R. Mooney and R. Bunescu, Mining knowledge from text using information extraction, *ACM SIGKDD Explorations Newsletter*, vol. 7(1), pp. 3–10, 2005.

[31] D. Nadeau and S. Sekine, A survey of named entity recognition and classification, *Lingvisticae Investigationes*, vol. 30(1), pp. 3–26, 2007.

[32] J. Okolica, G. Peterson and R. Mills, Using PLSI-U to detect insider threats from email traffic, in *Advances in Digital Forensics II*, M. Olivier and S. Shenoi (Eds.), Springer, Boston, Massachusetts, pp. 91–103, 2006.

[33] D. Newman, C. Chemudugunta, P. Smyth and M. Steyvers, Analyzing entities and topics in news articles using statistical topic models, *Proceedings of the Fourth IEEE International Conference on Intelligence and Security Informatics*, pp. 93–104, 2006.

[34] S. Orlando, P. Palmerini and R. Perego, Enhancing the Apriori algorithm for frequent set counting, *Proceedings of the Third International Conference on Data Warehousing and Knowledge Discovery*, pp. 71–82, 2001.

[35] M. Pollitt and A. Whitledge, Exploring big haystacks, in *Advances in Digital Forensics II*, M. Olivier and S. Shenoi (Eds.), Springer, Boston, Massachusetts, pp. 67–76, 2006.

[36] L. Rau, P. Jacobs and U. Zernik, Information extraction and text summarization using linguistic knowledge acquisition, *Information Processing and Management*, vol. 25(4), pp. 419–428, 1989.

[37] M. Schwartz and L. Liebrock, A term distribution visualization approach to digital forensic string search, *Proceedings of the Fifth International Workshop on Visualization for Computer Security*, pp. 36–43, 2008.

[38] A. Sun, R. Grishman and S. Sekine, Semi-supervised relation extraction with large-scale word clustering, *Proceedings of the Forty-Ninth Annual Meeting of the Association for Computational Linguistics*, vol. 1, pp. 521–529, 2011.

[39] C. Sutton and A. McCallum, An introduction to conditional random fields for relational learning, in *Introduction to Statistical Relational Learning*, L. Getoor and B. Taskar (Eds.), MIT Press, Cambridge, Massachusetts, pp. 93–128, 2007.

[40] P. Tan, M. Steinbach, V. Kumar, *Introduction to Data Mining*, Addison-Wesley Longman, Boston, Massachusetts, 2005.

[41] J. Venter, A. de Waal and C. Willers, Specializing CRISP-DM for evidence mining, in *Advances in Digital Forensics III*, P. Craiger and S. Shenoi (Eds.), Springer, Boston, Massachusetts, pp. 303–315, 2007.

[42] S. Whittaker, J. Hirschberg, J. Choi, D. Hindle, F. Pereira and A. Singhal, SCAN: Designing and evaluating user interfaces to support retrieval from speech archives, *Proceedings of the Twenty-Second International ACM SIGIR Conference on Research and Development in Information Retrieval*, pp. 26–33, 1999.

[43] Y. Yan, N. Okazaki, Y. Matsuo, Z. Yang and M. Ishizuka, Unsupervised relation extraction by mining Wikipedia texts using information from the web, *Proceedings of the Joint Conference of the Forty-Seventh Annual Meeting of the Association for Computational Linguistics and the Fourth International Joint Conference on Natural Language Processing of the Asian Federation of Natural Language Processing*, vol. 2, pp. 1021–1029, 2009.

[44] D. Zelenko, C. Aone and A. Richardella, Kernel methods for relation extraction, *Journal of Machine Learning Research*, vol. 3, pp. 1083–1106, 2003.

[45] S. Zhao and R. Grishman, Extracting relations with integrated information using kernel methods, *Proceedings of the Forty-Third Annual Meeting of the Association for Computational Linguistics*, pp. 419–426, 2005.

II

INTERNET CRIME
INVESTIGATIONS

Chapter 5

A GRAPH-BASED INVESTIGATION OF BITCOIN TRANSACTIONS

Chen Zhao and Yong Guan

Abstract   The Bitcoin global cryptocurrency system has been the subject of several criminal cases. The Bitcoin network is a peer-to-peer system that has participants from all over the Internet. The Bitcoin protocol requires participating nodes to retain and update all transaction records; this ensures that all Bitcoin activities are accessible from a consistent transaction history database. This chapter describes a graph-based method for analyzing the identity clustering and currency flow properties of Bitcoin transactions. The method, which is scalable to large Bitcoin graphs, focuses on transactions relevant to criminal cases such as Mt. Gox. The analysis, which is performed on two years of Bitcoin transaction data, provides insights into the nature of anonymity provided by Bitcoin and how currency flows between selected users and communities of users.

Keywords: Cryptocurrency, Bitcoin, graph, investigation

1. Introduction

Bitcoin is by far the most widely used online cryptocurrency. The most intriguing distinction between virtual cryptocurrency systems such as Bitcoin and traditional online transactions is the decentralized semantics [1, 7]. Bitcoin is a highly-scalable peer-to-peer network that has no responsible authority or central management; it is accessible to anyone with an Internet connection.

As a self-complete economic system, Bitcoin provides two major functionalities. First, it supports coin generation as the source of Bitcoin currency. The Bitcoin protocol features a computationally-intensive "coin mining" process that brute forces the hash of new block data onto the Bitcoin blockchain. The network accepts a new block if the newly mined block hash is below a specific threshold. Second, Bitcoin makes it feasible

© IFIP International Federation for Information Processing 2015
G. Peterson, S. Shenoi (Eds.): Advances in Digital Forensics XI, IFIP AICT 462, pp. 79–95, 2015.
DOI: 10.1007/978-3-319-24123-4_5

to conduct global transactions. A valid Bitcoin transaction is broadcast in a relay manner to the network, after which it is accepted by Bitcoin miners and written onto the blockchain.

The Bitcoin currency exists in a different form from paper money or online bank balances. No user balance is recorded in the blockchain. Every transaction is a record of a sum of money paid from a source to a destination. Bitcoin transactions are identified and authenticated based on Bitcoin addresses, which are hashes generated from user public/private key pairs [2] that cannot be manipulated without the correct private keys.

A Bitcoin address is generated based on a randomly selected key and is the only unique way of identification in the system. Due to the random property of Bitcoin addresses and the extremely low probability of key collisions in the enormous elliptic curve digital signature algorithm (ECDSA) key space [8], the number of Bitcoin addresses grows rapidly because hundreds of different addresses can be generated for different transactions without address reuse. This address generation scheme provides adequate anonymity for Bitcoin transactions, making it difficult to track Bitcoin transactions conducted by real-world entities.

This chapter focuses on the transaction component of the Bitcoin system in an attempt to construct a low-cost transaction data analysis model and analytical approaches that support forensic investigations of Bitcoin transactions and relationships between Bitcoin users. The results reveal that different Bitcoin addresses belonging to the same entity can be effectively clustered to reduce the forensic effort required to track Bitcoin users involved in criminal activities. The accompanying graph-based analysis of Bitcoin transactions helps discern transaction behaviors and currency flows involving Bitcoin users. The method can expedite forensic investigations of criminal cases such as Mt. Gox that involve double-spending, theft, money laundering or fraudulent transactions.

2. Bitcoin System Overview

In the Bitcoin system, a single transaction is defined as a single record of a one-time payment. It is a proof of payment of a specific amount of Bitcoins (BTC) from a payer address to a receiver address. A transaction payer spends money by referring to payments received from other entities. Bitcoin has no notion of an account balance – payments are always about spending previous payments received from other entities.

A single transaction has two major parts: (i) input list; and (ii) output list. Each input includes information about previous transactions and

Single Transaction

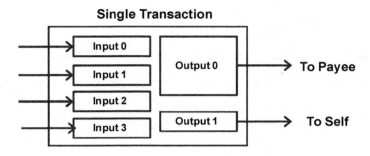

Figure 1. Transaction with change.

signature verification information. A transaction output denotes the amount of money paid and the address information of the recipient. A Bitcoin transaction is uniquely identified by a transaction ID defined as the hash value of the transaction.

A single transaction may contain multiple previous transactions and multiple recipient addresses. If the sum of the input values is larger than the amount that is to be paid, the payer designates a new address for the remaining change as shown in Figure 1. As mentioned in the previous section, a Bitcoin address is generated from a private/public key pair, so an entity cannot claim Bitcoin payments designated to other entities unless he/she owns the corresponding private keys (without which valid signatures cannot be created). In general, peers in the Bitcoin network do not accept illegal transactions.

```
{"inputs":
[{"value": 2.5, "address": "13vjvKHDeFhtwRGseVkLF1eXA7ZrJA2Uo9"},
{"value": 1.0092427, "address": "1EyH7htSWjSyuXgofuE9gKX5Sr4yEyDcD2"}],
"blocktime": 1389490523,
"outputs":
[{"value": 3.0, "address": "1Q5ztGyLj7KxL2rs7bmVcKYDfTYmpQs5bo"},
{"value": 0.5090427, "address": "1G7HKqqTUCrTpMDEYV5SdzcarFPhKKHb12"}]
```

Figure 2. Single transaction.

All Bitcoin transactions are stored in the blockchain that consists of a sequence of individual blocks. Blocks are for both storage as well as coin mining. Other than transaction records as in Figure 2, each block also contains other data fields, including a timestamp, last block hash and nonce. Mining Bitcoins involves the brute force computation of the nonce in the new block based on the current chain's latest block so that the new block hash value is equal to some value within a specified threshold.

```
{"inputs":
[{"address": "coinbase"}],
"blocktime": 1354133545,
"blockhash": "0000000000000498e426effa08fc54070cd7ca70e80206f8763e7ceaa
             ab734bc",
"outputs":,[{"value": 25.0512, "address":"1811f7UUQAkAejji11dU5cVtKUSTfo
                                          SVzdm"}]}
```

Figure 3.   Coinbase transaction.

A Coinbase transaction has only one input. Previous transactions are not included in the Coinbase input because it is an indication of currency generation instead of a payment received from elsewhere. The input simply consists of a "coinbase" parameter without any authentication information (Figure 3).

A Bitcoin transaction is not confirmed until it is committed by a specific miner and issued onto the blockchain. Since this work focuses on the relationships between addresses, a Bitcoin transaction is considered to be a verified record containing addresses, payment amount and confirmation time.

Figures 2 and 3 show the main content of Bitcoin transactions in JSON notation. Figure 3 shows an example of Bitcoin generation for which there is no incoming address. It indicates the creation of a new block with the hash value shown. In the transaction, 25.0512 BTC (as one coin unit) was mined and it belongs to the output address in the output array. This single transaction is also stored in the blockchain with the hash value shown.

3.   Transaction Data Collection

The Bitcoin dataset used in this study comprises blockchain data downloaded using the compiled full Bitcoin client source `bitcoind` in C++ [4]. The dataset is genuine and its integrity is assured by the cryptographic schemes used by the Bitcoin system. Transaction and block data were queried with `getrawtransaction` and `getblock` using the command line RPC tool provided by `bitcoind`. Alternatively, the data can be retrieved by directly invoking the `getrawtransaction` and `getblock` methods from the source. Both methods are globally visible in files `rpcrawtransaction.cpp` and `rpcblockchain.cpp`. Single transactions in the JSON format were parsed and written into a file as shown in Figures 2 and 3.

The dataset contains confirmed Bitcoin transactions. The transactions were collected from the blockchain maintained by the Bitcoin system from block 210,000 to block 314,700 corresponding to block creation times from `15:24:38 2012-11-28` to `10:45:14 2014-08-09`. During this 20-month period, a total number of 34,839,029 Bitcoin transactions were successfully released and globally confirmed. A total of 35,770,360 distinct Bitcoin addresses were involved in the transactions.

4. Graph-Based Bitcoin Transaction Analysis

The graph-based transaction analysis involved three main steps. The first step was to parse the transactions in the dataset into the input-output based format shown in Figure 2. The addresses involved in the dataset were divided into groups, each group of addresses corresponding to a single Bitcoin entity. Such an entity could be a single individual, a group of Bitcoin users who share a Bitcoin wallet (private key) or Bitcoin miners who cooperate in mining activities.

The second step was to convert the transaction data into address-based graph notation. The goal was to clearly display the transaction flow between groups of addresses (each group corresponding to a single entity). The graph was designed so that each node corresponded to a single group. A transaction sent from one of the addresses in a group was drawn as an outward edge and a transaction paid to an address in a group was drawn as an incoming edge.

The third step was to answer some key questions: How efficient is it to track currency flow using an address graph? How can activities such as money laundering and large-scale Bitcoin theft or fraud be identified in a graph? If such activities are found to exist in a graph, how can evidence about Bitcoin entities engaged in the activities be collected and presented.

The remainder of this section describes the three steps and attempts to answer the key questions.

4.1 Address Clustering

The goal is to use a fast algorithm to check and group all the addresses into distinct sets as precisely as possible. Thus, given an arbitrary Bitcoin address, it would be possible to identify the entity group to which the address belongs. Meiklejohn et al. [5] have developed an algorithm that characterizes Bitcoin transactions into usage categories. They also proposed a heuristic that different Bitcoin addresses in the input of a single transaction are guaranteed to be associated with a single entity. This is because the Bitcoin transaction signature scheme does not permit an entity to spend a transaction that was not previously paid to the entity. Therefore, multiple input addresses in a transaction are a strong indication that the entity that issued the transaction actually owns or shares the private keys corresponding to all the addresses.

In the case of Coinbase transactions discussed in Section 2, only one output address is present in the transaction output (Figure 3), so this address alone receives all the mining rewards. However, multiple addresses are allowed in Bitcoin transactions, including Coinbase transactions. Bitcoin mining intrinsically supports collaboration so that mining pools formed by multiple nodes can participate in mining efforts and the addresses in the pool simply share the rewards. For these reasons, the output addresses in a given Coinbase transaction are always pool-related. Thus, Coinbase transactions can help identify entities that cooperate. In this work, addresses belonging to entities in a given mining pool are treated as an atomic entity.

Another hint with regard to address grouping is the support for change shown in Figure 2, where a payer sends the change amount to his/her own address called the change address. Generally a change address is a one-time generated address for the sole purpose of receiving one's own money according to the implementation by the standard Bitcoin client software Bitcoin-Qt [4]. Using this property, it is possible to be a bit aggressive and assume that there are many one-time change addresses. One necessary condition for an output address to be classified as a change address is that it is not used as output ever again in the dataset. Along with some other conditions summarized in [10], it is possible to identify change addresses with low false-positive rates.

Based on the discussion above, the following three rules are specified:

1. All input addresses in the same transaction must be in the same set.

2. All output addresses in the same Coinbase transaction must be in the same set.

3. An output address that is only used as output once is placed in the same set as its transaction input addresses if the following conditions are met:

    - The output address is not the only address in the transaction output (a payment is not valid if it only sends change).

    - The output address does not exist in the transaction input list (this prevents the rare case of a self-loop).

    - None of the remaining output addresses in the transaction output list is used as an output only once (while a change address probably exists in this case, it is not possible to tell which address in the output list is used to receive the change).

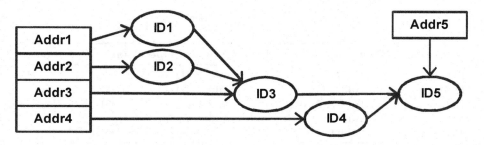

Figure 4. Conceptual graph of address grouping.

The Bitcoin dataset classification effort is substantial – identifying and rearranging nearly 36 million addresses, each of them a string of length 26-34 bytes. The problem arises when iterating all the addresses in each transaction and assigning them to the correct sets so that addresses always belong to the same entity if they are in the same set. The process involves set union operations: whenever an address set intersects with two or more existing sets, it is necessary to union all the sets to create a new atomic set. Unless hash tables are used, the worst case address access time complexity is $O(N^2)$ and the memory consumption is unacceptable. Therefore, instead of using this intuitive process, a much more efficient algorithm was employed to obtain the same classification results.

An open-source database developed by Google with a lightweight on-disk key-value mapping tool called LevelDB [9] was employed. In fact, LevelDB is used by the standard Bitcoin client Bitcoin-Qt to rapidly query massive quantities of Bitcoin blockchain data.

Figure 4 illustrates the intuition behind the clustering of address sets. Every new address is mapped to a new node. Consider the five transactions, Tx1, Tx2, Tx3, Tx4 and Tx5 (see Table 1). First, Tx1 is selected, which has only one transaction input address (Addr1). Mapping Tx1 and Tx2 is straightforward because Addr1 and Addr2 are from different transactions. However, Tx3 intersects with both Tx1 and Tx2, which implies that Addr1, Addr2 and Addr3 should be in the same set. Instead of modifying Addr1 and Addr2, it is only necessary to search for the node ID to which they map. Then, all the nodes that are found are mapped to the new node ID3 (Figure 4). Thus, all the sets are unioned without sequentially accessing the addresses in each set.

In the case of Tx4, there is no intersection with the other address sets, so it is mapped to a new node ID4. However, Tx5 intersects with several previous addresses, so the database is updated with the operations shown in Table 1. After iterating from Tx1 to Tx5, all five addresses are finally

Table 1.   Operations on sample transaction inputs.

Transaction ID	Input Address List	Database Operation
Tx1	Addr1	(Addr1, ID1)
Tx2	Addr2	(Addr2, ID2)
Tx3	Addr1, Addr2, Addr3	(Addr3, ID3), (ID1, ID3), (ID2, ID3)
Tx4	Addr4	(Addr4, ID4)
Tx5	Addr1, Addr1, Addr5	(Addr5, ID5), (ID4, ID5), (ID3, ID5)

mapped to ID5. Using this approach, given any sets of addresses, it is possible to correctly union all the sets with intersections regardless of the order of the iteration (e.g., Tx5 to Tx1 instead of Tx1 to Tx5).

However, in the case of 36 million addresses, the intuitive algorithm is very inefficient because the directed path in the tree structure of Figure 4 tree can be long enough to require a single address search to traverse thousands of node IDs. The algorithm is improved by remapping a graph node to the root whenever a path is traversed.

Table 2.   Improved operations on sample transaction inputs.

Transaction ID	Input Address List	Database Operation
Tx1	Addr1	(Addr1, ID1)
Tx2	Addr2	(Addr2, ID2)
Tx3	Addr1, Addr2, Addr3	(Addr3, ID3), (ID1, ID3), (ID2, ID3)
Tx4	Addr4	(Addr4, ID4)
Tx5	Addr1, Addr1, Addr5	(Addr5, ID5), (ID4, ID5), (Addr1, ID3), (ID3, ID5)

Table 2 shows the improvement in operations at Tx5. Because Tx5 has Addr1, a search is required from Addr1 to ID3 to obtain its root node ID. After it is found that Addr1 is actually mapped to ID3, the information is updated for future reference. Similar shortcuts can be applied to intermediate nodes such as ID2 if a traversal through ID2 is needed in the future.

The new algorithm is summarized as follows:

1. Select the next Bitcoin transaction and extract its input addresses (or outputs in case of a Coinbase transaction).

2. Examine the extracted address set. For addresses that are not yet in the database, map each address to a new ID. Ignore all the existing addresses, but traverse to the root node ID to which the

address points and save it in a set. During each traversal, optimize the path using a shortcut, if possible.

3. Examine the root node ID set in Step 2. If the set is empty, the algorithm is terminated. Otherwise, map the root node IDs in the set to the new node ID in Step 2; if no new addresses were found in Step 2, create a new node ID and map the root node IDs in the set to the new node ID.

4. Go to Step 1.

The four steps listed above map transaction input addresses and Coinbase output addresses. Note that one additional step is required to scan for one-time change addresses by applying the three rules listed above.

The application of the algorithm to the Bitcoin transaction dataset yielded good results. Of the 35,770,360 addresses that were processed in the dataset, 35,587,286 addresses are used as outputs. A total of 398,954 were identified as one-time change addresses, which validated the heuristic. In all, 13,062,822 distinct address sets were generated.

4.2 Address Graph Observations

Having mapped Bitcoin addresses to groups, the next problem is to interpret raw Bitcoin transactions in a currency flow model between Bitcoin address sets. The objective is to create a directed graph that reflects monetary relationships between sets of addresses so that tracing incoming and outgoing payments to/from specific Bitcoin entities is possible.

A directed graph is defined as follows:

1. Each vertex in a directed graph represents a set of addresses, which corresponds to a Bitcoin entity that may possess multiple addresses.

2. Each edge in a directed graph reflects a specific Bitcoin payment. An outgoing edge from a vertex is a payment from the current address set to another vertex (address set). Similarly, an incoming edge is a payment received by the vertex from another vertex. Each edge in the directed graph is weighted according to the amount of the associated payment.

In order to study the transaction behavior at fixed time intervals, the Bitcoin transaction data from block #210,000 to block #314700 was divided into multiple samples, each consisting of 20 blocks, to yield a total of 5,236 graph data files. Each graph data file was converted into a directed graph as defined above.

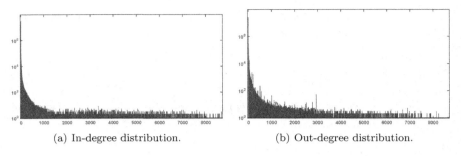

(a) In-degree distribution.   (b) Out-degree distribution.

Figure 5.   Graph connection distributions.

Figure 5(a) shows the node counts for varying numbers of incoming edges computed over all 5,236 graphs. The majority of the nodes have less than 100 incoming edges as shown by the logarithmic scale on the y-axis. Figure 5(b) shows the node counts with varying numbers of outgoing edges, again computed over all 5,236 graphs. The graph connection distribution for outgoing edges is similar to that for incoming edges (Figure 5(a)).

The graphs have a total of 94,880,896 edges. An overwhelming majority of payments, 89,406,338 (94.2%) out of 94,880,896, were below 10 BTC.

4.3   Currency Flow Analysis

Currency flow analysis focuses on the graph edges to determine what happened to a specific sum of money. In theft and fraud cases, currency flow goes two ways. First, money is actually spent, which is equivalent to a payment being split and sent to multiple addresses. Second, the money can be sent to multiple addresses through different transactions before they are finally collected in a criminal's Bitcoin wallet. This process is, in some sense, similar to money laundering. In order to quantitatively capture the currency flow, a breadth-first search (BFS) of the directed graph was performed to determine the most probable directions of stolen Bitcoin flows.

The algorithm shown in Figure 6 starts with a set of nodes from the graph in fixed time periods. Using these nodes as the starting level, the graph is searched in a breadth-first manner and the node counts and net Bitcoin outputs at each level are saved until no more new nodes exist. The output of the algorithm is a list of node counts and a list of net Bitcoin outputs at each level. The net Bitcoin output is the difference between the total values of the output edges and incoming edges.

```
BFS_Graph(G):
Initialize curLevel={set of starting nodes}, nextLevel=new set()
Initialize countList=new list[], netOutputList=new list[]
   while curLevel is not empty:
     add node in curLevel into countList
     for each node in curLevel:
       add all unvisited neighbors of the node to nextLevel
       mark neighbors as visited
       netOutput=netOutput+sum(out edges)-sum(in edges)
       add netOutput into netOutputList
   curLevel=nextLevel
   nextLevel=new set()
```

Figure 6. Breadth-first search (BFS) algorithm for currency flows.

Bitcoin payments are forward tracked so that, given a set of starting nodes, a search is conducted for patterns of coin transfer to other entities in split sums or money laundering. Due to the potential incompleteness of the address classification database, money laundering can also show up as a large amount of Bitcoins ending up at nodes other than the start nodes. In this case, two graph patterns are expected:

- Starting nodes are involved in cycles consisting of large edges directed to them, with approximately the same total values as the total values of the outgoing edges from them.

- No valid graph cycles are found, but Bitcoins converge into a smaller number of large-valued edges that are gathered by a set of other nodes.

4.4   Mt. Gox Case Study

Having constructed a concrete data model that describes Bitcoin flow patterns, it is applied in a case study involving the Mt. Gox incident.

Mt. Gox was the largest Bitcoin exchange and web wallet service provider in the world. On February 7, 2014, Mt. Gox reported technical difficulties due to hacking attacks. On February 10, 2014, Mt. Gox issued a press release claiming that it had lost more than 850,000 BTC (worth half a billion U.S. dollars at the prevailing market rate). The incident, which resulted in Mt. Gox filing for bankruptcy, has been under investigation for more than a year, but no clear explanation has been provided as yet.

Decker and Wattenhofer [3] have conducted a study on Bitcoin transaction malleability, which was suspected to have led to the huge loss at Mt. Gox. According to their analysis, malleability attacks did exist that falsely modified transactions to enable twice the amount of currency withdrawal from Mt. Gox. However, only a very small fraction of the alleged 850,000 BTC loss could be tracked in the malleability detection data. Indeed, it is still not clear how the rest of the Bitcoins were lost. According to a police investigation report [6], there were signs that Mt. Gox's offices had been physically infiltrated and at least one former employee may have pilfered electronic data.

Regardless of the reason, Mt. Gox sustained a massive loss of Bitcoins and this loss should be reflected in the blockchain data and in the directed graph data. The theft clearly involved large currency flows during a short period time; these patterns should be present in the directed graphs. As mentioned above, 94.2% of the edges in the overall graph involve transactions less that 10 BTC. To reduce the size of the dataset, the graphs were pruned to retain only edges of 10 BTC or higher. This simplified the graph sets and renders it more efficient to discover large currency flows.

All the graph nodes and edges in the time period of interest were collected and integrated in a new graph that described global transaction patterns during the incident. According to the Mt. Gox incident timeline, technical difficulties were experienced and withdrawals were suspended on February 7, 2014. Because theft could not have occurred after the suspension of withdrawals, the time window could be restricted to a few days before February 7, 2014. Thus, the analysis started with graph edges with the timestamp 19:49:42 2014-02-03 and ended at the timestamp 08:36:47 2014-02-07. Figure 7 presents a visualization of the directed graph used in the analysis.

Figure 8 displays the sum of values of all edges, equivalent to the total transaction amount at each timestamp. The sum of edge values provide information about the groups of edges that have a burst of Bitcoin flow and the time when this occurs. A burst of Bitcoin flow indicates a large-scale currency transfer. When computing edge sums, all the edges that started and ended at the same node were removed to focus on currency transfers between different entities.

Figure 8 shows that the maximum peak burst is at the x-axis values 359 to 363, corresponding to the timestamps 23:57:01 2014-02-05 to 00:28:17 2014-02-06. However, the total output values of these edges only account for about 100,000 BTC, significantly less than the 850,000 BTC allegedly stolen from Mt. Gox. Although, the large loss incurred by Mt. Gox cannot be explained, the maximum peak burst is related to the theft with high probability. Indicators of other theft activities must exist elsewhere, but the maximum peak burst in the graph is certainly the latest possible peak that can be identified. In fact, it is very reasonable

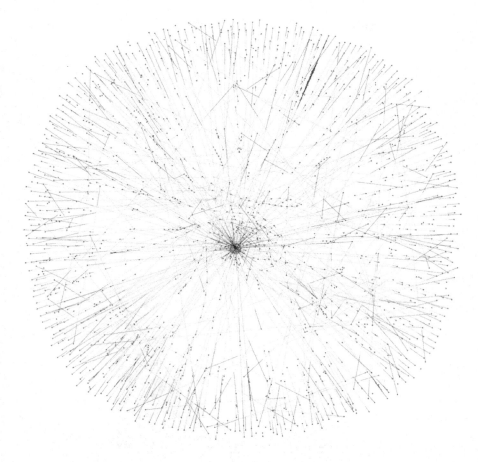

Figure 7. Directed graph used in the Mt. Gox case study.

that the theft would have occurred about a day or two before Mt. Gox suspended withdrawals and made its formal announcement.

Figure 9 shows the suspicious nodes with the largest edge values. The graph was obtained by collecting all the nodes connected to edges that contributed to the maximum peak burst peak (153 distinct nodes) and ordering the nodes based on increasing edge values (the y-axis value is the sum of values of all the edges at that time). Of particular interest are the last fourteen nodes that received the highest payments (higher than 4,000 BTC).

The breadth-first search algorithm was employed with its traversal list initialized to contain the fourteen nodes. This algorithm terminated after 1,461 levels. Figure 10(a) displays the node counts during the execution of the algorithm. The node count declines drastically after

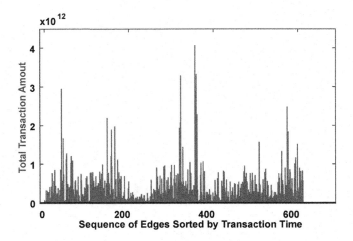

Figure 8.   Sum of transaction amounts by time.

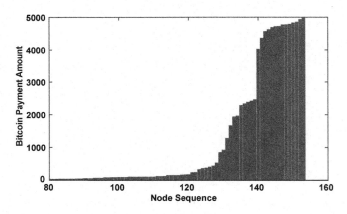

Figure 9.   Suspicious nodes with the largest edge values.

the first 20 levels and finally converges to a single node. However, this graph does not provide enough information about the destination of the transaction burst from 23:57:01 2014-02-05 to 00:28:17 2014-02-06 because the Bitcoin outputs also have to be considered.

Figure 10(b) plots the net output of nodes at each level. The initial fourteen nodes transfer 70,510 BTC to other entities. Next, it is necessary to search for a level such that nodes spend all 70,510 BTC. The negative outputs in Table 3 indicate nodes at the current level that receive more income from other sources. When the algorithm reaches the level (row 4) where twelve nodes have a much larger output than all previous income, it appears that the initial 70,510 BTC being tracked is split to the following 32,621 nodes. The decreasing output pattern in

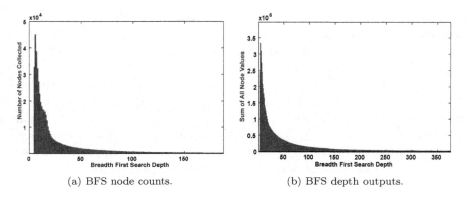

(a) BFS node counts. (b) BFS depth outputs.

Figure 10. Node count at each breadth-first search level.

Table 3. Initial breadth-first search stages.

Number of Nodes	Network Output
12	70,510
14	-31,205.998
17	-49,545
12	2,458,376
32,621	3,335,101

Figure 10(b) does not provide adequate evidence of money laundering – such evidence would correspond to a large amount of Bitcoins converging to a small set of nodes or flowing back to the starting nodes in a reasonably short period of time.

5. Discussion

Certain observations can be made based on the experiments conducted with the Bitcoin dataset. First, with regard to the large Bitcoin transfer, there is no significant evidence of money laundering activities for which edge-convergent patterns or graph cycles consisting of edges of equivalent values would be seen. Second, the experimental results show with high probability that a large portion of the suspected stolen Bitcoins was spent and split using many payments to different entities instead of being split among the conspirators.

However, there are two major restrictions. First, address classification is transitive so that future transactions potentially affect the group database by having multiple intersections with existing address sets. The latest block transaction data available in the dataset is 347,000, but it is expected that future transactions would provide stronger hints for existing address sets to be unioned. Moreover, the application of anti-anonymity approaches is recommended before address classification because it can significantly reduce the number of sets (13,062,822 distinct address sets were generated in this work).

The second major restriction relates to the address graph experiment. Because the dataset did not contain the complete blockchain data, it was unable to determine the exact Bitcoin value that a graph vertex holds at each timestamp. By tracing the relative in-flow and out-flow of currency, the breadth-first search results only reveal the flow of suspected currency without providing an accurate list of addresses of potential conspirators.

6. Conclusions

The graph-based method for analyzing the identity clustering and currency flow properties of Bitcoin transactions can expedite forensic investigations of criminal cases such as Mt. Gox that involve double-spending, theft, money laundering or fraudulent transactions. Experiments performed using two years of Bitcoin transaction data reveal that different Bitcoin addresses belonging to the same entity can be effectively clustered to reduce the forensic effort required to track Bitcoin users involved in criminal activities. Furthermore, the graph-based analysis of Bitcoin transactions can help discern suspicious transaction behaviors and currency flows involving Bitcoin users.

Future work will focus on enhancing the address group database to accommodate new transaction streams. Additionally, efforts will be made to augment the Bitcoin address library with real-world Bitcoin entities to help reduce the size of address sets during forensic investigations.

References

[1] J. Bergstra and P. Weijland, Bitcoin: A Money-Like Informational Commodity (arxiv.org/pdf/1402.4778v1.pdf), 2014.

[2] Bitcoin Community, Technical background of Bitcoin addresses, *Bitcoin Wiki* (en.bitcoin.it/wiki/Technical_background_of_Bitcoin_addresses), 2015.

[3] C. Decker and R. Wattenhofer, Bitcoin transaction malleability and Mt. Gox, *Proceedings of the Nineteenth European Symposium on Research in Computer Security*, pp. 313–326, 2014.

[4] GitHub, Bitcoin core integration/staging tree (github.com/bitcoin/bitcoin).

[5] S. Meiklejohn, M. Pomarole, G. Jordan, K. Levchenko, D. McCoy, G. Voelker and S. Savage, A fistful of Bitcoins: Characterizing payments among men with no names, *Proceedings of the Conference on Internet Measurement*, pp. 127–140, 2013.

[6] T. Mochizuki and E. Warnock, Mt. Gox head believes no more Bitcoins will be found, *The Wall Street Journal*, June 29, 2014.

[7] S. Nakamoto, Bitcoin: A Peer-to-Peer Electronic Cash System (bitcoin.org/bitcoin.pdf), 2009.

[8] National Institute of Standards and Technology, Digital Signature Standard (DSS), FIPS PUB 186-4, Gaithersburg, Maryland, 2013.

[9] py-leveldb Project, Thread-safe Python bindings for LevelDB (co. de.google.com/p/py-leveldb).

[10] D. Ron and A. Shamir, Quantitative analysis of the full Bitcoin transaction graph, in *Financial Cryptography and Data Security*, A. Sadeghi (Ed.), Springer-Verlag, Berlin Heidelberg, pp. 6–24, 2013.

Chapter 6

PROFILING AND TRACKING A CYBERLOCKER LINK SHARER IN A PUBLIC WEB FORUM

Xiao-Xi Fan, Kam-Pui Chow and Fei Xu

Abstract   The expanding utilization of cyberlocker services is driven by the illegal exchange of copyrighted materials. In fact, the illegal exchange of copyrighted materials is the largest contributor to global Internet traffic. However, due to the anonymity provided by cyberlockers, it is difficult to track user identities directly from cyberlocker sites. Since cyberlocker users upload and share links via third-party sites, it is possible to harvest cyberlocker-related data from these sites and connect the data to specific users. This chapter describes a framework for collecting cyberlocker data from web forums and using cyberlocker link sharing behavior to identify users. Multidimensional scaling analysis and agglomerative hierarchical clustering analysis are performed on user profiles to yield clusters of forum users with similar sharing characteristics. The experimental results demonstrate that the framework provides valuable insights in investigations of cyberlocker-based piracy.

Keywords: Cyberlockers, piracy, user profiling, identity tracking

1.   Introduction

Cyberlocker services such as RapidShare, MediaFire and BitShare have transformed how Internet users disseminate and share information and media [12]. Cyberlockers provide an easy way for users to upload files to servers. After a file has been uploaded successfully, the cyberlocker generates a unique download URL (cyberlocker link) for the uploader to copy and share with other users. The cyberlocker link can be posted and distributed via third-party sites such as web forums and blogs, enabling other users to easily download the file from the cyberlocker by clicking on the link [11].

© IFIP International Federation for Information Processing 2015
G. Peterson, S. Shenoi (Eds.): Advances in Digital Forensics XI, IFIP AICT 462, pp. 97–113, 2015.
DOI: 10.1007/978-3-319-24123-4_6

Cyberlockers facilitate the sharing of large files, including movies and music. However, they also enable users to exchange illegal or copyrighted media on the Internet – full three-quarters of RapidShare content is estimated to be illegal [6].

Some cyberlockers encourage users to upload and share files by paying them money – the greater the number of downloads of a file, the more the file uploader is paid. This encourages file uploaders to disseminate their cyberlocker links on web forums and other venues to attract downloaders. Although many cyberlockers disaggregate search functionality, copyright owners argue that this has little effect on illegal file sharing [5]. Individuals can search for the desired content along with a specific cyberlocker name using a search engine to obtain links for the desired content as well as third-party sites that aggregate cyberlocker links.

Internet piracy is the distribution and/or copying of copyrighted materials over the Internet. Since Internet piracy is rampant in cyberlockers, an effective model is required to track the identities of cyberlocker users in digital forensic investigations. Many cyberlockers allow users without connections to file uploaders to download files independently [17]. This means that, when downloading a file from a cyberlocker link, information about the uploader is not available on the web page. Unlike a P2P network, a cyberlocker can hide user identities because the IP addresses of users are kept anonymous from each another and are known only to the cyberlocker operator. Without the cooperation of cyberlocker operators, law enforcement agencies are unable to identify users involved in illegal sharing or to download transactions involving copyrighted media [13].

The monitoring and investigation of cyberlocker users are arduous and time consuming, and it is exceedingly difficult to track user identities directly from cyberlocker sites. However, information about cyberlocker link sharing is easily harvested from third-party sites such as web forums; user information can also be gleaned from many web forums. This makes it possible to analyze the behavior of cyberlocker link sharers and provide investigative leads for identity tracking. Moreover, since cyberlocker users tend to have multiple accounts on one or more forums in order to distribute cyberlocker links, a model that could identify accounts that belong to a single user would be very useful in piracy investigations. The research described in this chapter attempts to address these issues. It focuses on building an effective framework for profiling web forum users based on their cyberlocker link sharing characteristics and identifying the relationships between different profiles based on the assumption that the same user has consistent preferences, thereby providing useful identity leads to investigators.

2.   Related Work

Despite their popularity, little research has focused specifically on cyberlockers and cyberlocker-based piracy. Zhao et al. [20] have analyzed the numbers and sizes of files of different formats and contents on three cyberlockers. Mahanti [12] has proposed a measurement infrastructure to gather cyberlocker workloads and has compared the characteristics of content popularity, content dissemination and performance related to five cyberlockers. Envisional [6] has estimated the percentage of copyrighted materials exchanged via cyberlockers. Its report revealed that 7% of Internet traffic was related to cyberlocker services and that 73.2% of non-pornographic cyberlocker traffic (5.1% of all Internet traffic) involved copyrighted content being downloaded illegally. Most of the work focused on cyberlockers has involved the analysis of traffic and file characteristics, not user characteristics.

Since Internet piracy can be considered to be a type of serial crime, it is appealing and productive to apply criminal profiling to the problem. However, in the field of criminology, profiling has mainly focused on violent criminal activity and analyses of crime scenes and victims, which are not directly applicable to Internet piracy. Research on criminal profiling in the area of cyber crime is limited. Bhukya and Banothu [3] have captured GUI-based user behavior to construct user profiles and have applied support vector machines to classify users. McKinney and Reeves [14] have proposed a model for developing user profiles by analyzing processes running on a computer and detecting masquerades.

In the field of information retrieval, profiling techniques have been used in the context of recommender systems and e-commerce systems. Schiaffino and Amandi [18] have studied the information content of user profiles, methods for creating user profiles and techniques for analyzing user profiles. Godoy and Amandi [8] have designed a document clustering algorithm to categorize web documents and learn user interest profiles. Fathy et al. [7] have proposed a personalized search approach based on click history data to model user search preferences in ontological user profiles. All these approaches are related to digital profiling and, as such, can be used to develop criminal profiling methodologies for Internet piracy. However, there is little, if any, work on constructing user profiles based on cyberlocker link sharing behavior in web forums.

3.   Methodology

Cyberlocker links are typically distributed in posts on web forums. A sharer is a forum user who uploads and shares a cyberlocker link in the forum for others to download a file; the sharer is also the potential

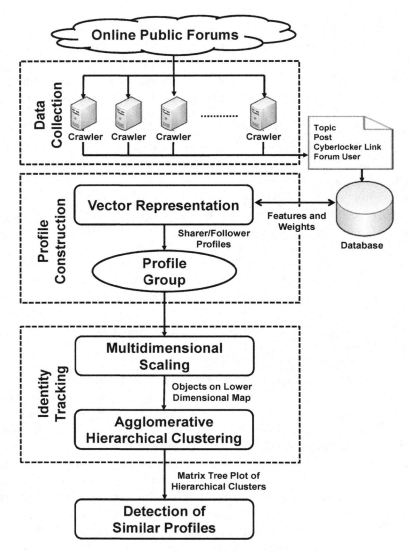

Figure 1. Digital profiling and identity tracking model.

uploader of the file on the cyberlocker site. In contrast, a follower is
a forum user who only replies to a post containing a cyberlocker link
without uploading or sharing any cyberlocker links.

Figure 1 presents the model used to build profiles for the two types of
forum users and analyze the profiles. Web forum and cyberlocker data
are collected by web forum crawlers that target several popular Hong
Kong web forums. The profiles of sharers and followers are then created

in a vector space model based on the extracted features. Multidimensional scaling (MDS) is applied to analyze the similarity between sharers/followers and to map their relationships to a lower-dimensional representation. Finally, agglomerative hierarchical clustering is performed on the multidimensional scaling results to identify clusters containing sharers/followers with similar behavior.

3.1 Data Collection

Since a vast number of cyberlocker links are posted on web forums, the system described in this chapter is designed to collect data from web forums. A forum is hierarchical in structure and may contain several sub-forums. Topics come under the lowest level of sub-forums. The following definitions of topic and post [2] are used in this research:

- **Topic:** A topic may contain any number of posts from multiple forum users. The information includes the topic title, original post (i.e., first post that started the topic) and creation date and time (which is also the creation date and time of the original post).

- **Post:** A post is a message submitted by a forum user. A post contains information such as the forum user details, content and creation date and time. The original post is the one that started the topic and the posts that follow continue the discussion about the topic.

The system uses web crawlers to collect web forum and cyberlocker data. As shown in Figure 2, two types of crawlers are used: (i) URL crawlers; and (ii) topic crawlers. URL crawlers are responsible for extracting the URLs of topics from the catalog pages in web forums. After a URL crawler uses a fetch command to obtain the URL of a catalog page, it invokes a DNS module to resolve the host address of the web server. Following this, the URL crawler connects to the server to download the page, uses a parse command to extract all the URLs of topics from the page and stores them in the URL frontier.

Topic crawlers are responsible for extracting useful information from topic pages. After a topic crawler uses a fetch to obtain the URL of a topic from the URL frontier, it executes a parse command on the topic page to extract topic information and post information. The system thus parses and extracts cyberlocker links from all the posts encountered by the web crawlers. Several types of information are parsed into structured data and stored in a database.

Compared with the crawlers implemented by cyberlocker indexing sites, the web forum crawlers used in this work specifically target Hong

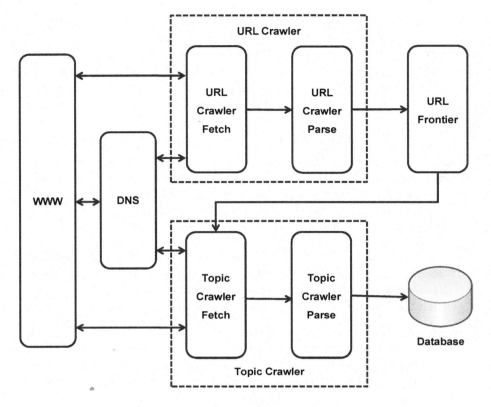

Figure 2. Web forum crawler.

Kong web forums and assign a higher priority to newly created posts to facilitate real-time analysis. The crawlers also download topic content to preserve evidence of cyberlocker-based piracy.

During the data collection process, web crawlers extracted data from the nine web forums presented in Table 1. According to Alexa Internet [1], the nine forums are among the most frequently visited websites in Hong Kong.

Table 2 lists the cyberlocker services considered in this research. They are among the top-ranked cyberlocker services used by Hong Kong web forum users.

3.2   User Profile Construction

This section describes the construction of profiles for sharers and followers, and the detection of relationships between sharers and followers. Sharer and follower profiles are created using data collected during an observation period. A vector space model commonly used in infor-

Table 1. Web forums considered in the study.

Forum	Forum URL
HK Discuss Forum (DISCUSS)	`http://www.discuss.com.hk`
UWANTS	`http://www.uwants.com`
HK-PUB	`http://hk-pub.com`
KYO	`http://www.kyohk.net`
EYNY	`http://www.eyny.com`
TVBOXNOW	`http://www.tvboxnow.com`
CK101	`http://ck101.com`
LALULALU	`http://www.lalulalu.com`
8CYBER	`http://8cyber.net`

Table 2. Cyberlocker services considered in the study.

Cyberlocker Service	Cyberlocker URL
Bitshare	`http://bitshare.com`
FilePost	`http://filepost.com`
FileFactory	`http://www.filefactory.com`
FileIM	`http://www.fileim.com`
Sendspace	`http://www.sendspace.com`
MediaFire	`http://www.mediafire.com`
Ziddu	`http://www.ziddu.com`
RapidShare	`https://rapidshare.com`
DepositFiles	`http://depositfiles.com`
HulkShare	`http://www.hulkshare.com`

mation retrieval is employed to specify the profiles. In particular, a sharer/follower is represented as a vector $s_j = (w_1, w_2, ..., w_N)$ where N is the number of features. Each feature corresponds to a cyberlocker link distributed by a sharer during the observation period.

The weighting scheme depends on whether or not a follower profile is included in a profile group for identity tracking analysis. If a follower profile is not included in a profile group, then the following equation is used to assign weights to each feature to describe the behavior of a sharer:

$$w_i = \begin{cases} 1 \text{ if sharer has shared link } i \\ 0 \text{ if sharer has not shared link } i \end{cases} \tag{1}$$

If the sharer and follower profiles are considered, the following equation based on an ordinal measurement is used to assign weights to each feature to describe the behavior of a sharer/follower:

$$w_i = \begin{cases} 2 \text{ if sharer has shared link } i \\ 1 \text{ if sharer/follower has replied to but not shared link } i \\ 0 \text{ if sharer/follower has not replied to or shared link } i \end{cases} \quad (2)$$

After weights are assigned to each feature for all sharers/followers, each sharer/follower is represented as a vector with components corresponding to the cyberlocker links.

3.3   Multidimensional Scaling Analysis

Multidimensional scaling (MDS) is a data analysis technique for identifying the underlying pattern or structure of a set of objects. Multidimensional scaling has been widely used in criminal profiling to analyze crime behavior patterns [9, 16]. It expresses the similarities and dissimilarities of objects in a geometric representation using a number of distance models.

The primary outcome of multidimensional scaling analysis is a spatial configuration in which the objects are represented as points. The points corresponding to similar objects are located close together, while those corresponding to dissimilar objects are located far apart. If sharers/followers are considered to be objects, then multidimensional scaling can be used to arrange the objects in a lower-dimensional map where the distance between two objects represents the observed correlation of the corresponding sharers/followers. If an object A is in close proximity to an object B but far away from an object C, then object A and object B have a strong relationship while a weak or no relationship exists with the remote object C. A forensic investigator can then attempt to make sense of the derived object configuration by identifying meaningful directions of similar sharers/followers in the space.

Interested readers are referred to Borg and Groenen [4] for additional details about multidimensional scaling. This work employed the SPSS statistical tool to perform multidimensional scaling analysis on the profiles constructed for sharers/followers.

3.4   Cluster Analysis

After multidimensional scaling analysis is performed, the profiles are represented as points in a lower-dimensional map without losing the relationships between each other. Agglomerative hierarchical clustering is then performed on the coordinates of the resulting points to identify potential clusters in which sharers/followers have similar behavior.

Agglomerative hierarchical clustering builds a hierarchy based on each individual object in a cluster. Next, it merges the closest pair of clusters

Table 3.   Sharer/follower statistics for four long-term observation periods.

Observation Period	2014.01.01 to 2014.06.30		2013.07.01 to 2013.12.31		2013.01.01 to 2013.06.30		2012.07.01 to 2012.12.31	
Subjects	Sharers/ Followers	Sharers	Sharers/ Followers	Sharers	Sharers/ Followers	Sharers	Sharers/ Followers	Sharers
Number	1,649	64	814	72	684	91	5,580	215
DISCUSS	0.18%	4.69%	0.98%	11.11%	0.73%	3.30%	0.11%	2.79%
UWANTS	1.09%	10.94%	3.32%	8.33%	2.34%	7.69%	2.06%	8.37%
HK-PUB	1.46%	12.50%	5.77%	9.72%	1.02%	7.69%	0.72%	3.72%
KYO	0.12%	1.56%	2.21%	8.33%	1.90%	7.69%	1.81%	8.37%
EYMY	1.21%	1.56%	2.95%	2.78%	0.73%	1.10%	0.22%	1.86%
TVBOXNOW	56.58%	29.69%	26.78%	22.22%	67.54%	35.16%	66.83%	34.88%
CK101	7.22%	25.00%	6.76%	16.67%	10.23%	15.38%	12.42%	26.05%
LALULALU	31.53%	12.50%	50.98%	18.06%	14.91%	19.78%	15.82%	13.49%
8CYBER	0.61%	1.56%	0.25%	2.78%	0.58%	2.20%	0.02%	0.47%

that satisfy a similarity criterion in each successive iteration until all the objects are in one cluster. Agglomerative hierarchical clustering does not need the number of clusters as input and investigators can choose appropriate clusters according to their needs. This work adopted Ward's minimum variance method [15] as the criterion for choosing the pair of clusters to merge at each step. Compared with other criteria, Ward's minimum variance method is more aligned with the clustering requirements for the cyberlocker problem because it tends to generate a larger distance between two large clusters so that they are less likely to be merged, and vice versa.

Agglomerative hierarchical clustering can produce an ordering of objects that is very informative as a hierarchical display. This work uses a matrix tree plot to show the clustering outcome in a visually appealing manner that highlights clustering relationships.

4.   Experiments

Experiments were conducted over a long-term observation period (six months) and a short-term observation period (one month). In each experimental design, experiments were repeated to detect general data trends.

4.1   Datasets

Datasets were extracted from the nine web forums listed previously. Since web forum users have to register and log in to post messages, their user details and sharing information were gathered quite easily.

Data was first collected over four long-term observation periods. Table 3 presents the basic statistics for sharers/followers over the four long-term observation periods. For all the sharers/followers collected over an

Table 4. Sharer/follower statistics for six short-term observation periods.

Observation Period	2014.01.01 to 2014.01.31	2014.02.01 to 2014.02.28	2014.03.01 to 2014.03.31	2014.04.01 to 2014.04.30	2014.05.01 to 2014.05.31	2014.06.01 to 2014.06.30
No. Sharers and Followers	117 117	209 209	511 511	320 320	431 431	295 295
No. Sharers and Followers rel. > 3 links	41	104	141	152	167	196
No. Sharers	26	26	34	21	28	26

observation period, the proportion of sharers is very small, which implies that thousands of cyberlocker links are shared by only a small number of web forum users. In addition, three web forums, TVBOXNOW, LALU-LALU and CK101, have the largest numbers of sharers and followers, which means that these three forums are the most popular venues for distributing cyberlocker links.

Table 4 presents the basic statistics for sharers/followers over six short-term observation periods. The data has the same trends as for the long-term observation periods: cyberlocker links are distributed by a few sharers, some of whom are active over all six short-term observation periods. Moreover, since a short-term observation period extended over one month, the number of followers decreased significantly when sharers and followers who shared or replied to more than three cyberlocker links were counted.

4.2 Evaluation Metric

The mapping process of multidimensional scaling is a critical step that influences the degree to which multidimensional scaling represents the correlation of the data. As a result, the stress measure, which is the most commonly-used measure to evaluate multidimensional scaling results [19], was selected to assess the goodness of fit.

If the input to multidimensional scaling is not a proximity matrix, then proximity values are created. A monotonic transformation of the proximity values is then performed to yield scaled proximities. The objective of multidimensional scaling is to find a configuration of points that minimizes the squared differences between the optimally-scaled proximity values and the distances between points. In other words, multidimensional scaling seeks to minimize the stress metric:

Table 5. MDS stress values and goodness of fit.

Stress Value	Goodness of Fit
Stress = 0	Perfect
0 < Stress ≤ 2.5%	Excellent
2.5% < Stress ≤ 5%	Good
5% < Stress ≤ 10%	Fair
10% < Stress ≤ 20%	Poor

$$Stress = \sqrt{\frac{\sum (f(p) - d)^2}{\sum d^2}} \qquad (3)$$

where $f(p)$ is a monotonic transformation of the proximity p and d is the distance between points. A small stress value implies a good fit of the multidimensional scaling results, and vice versa.

Table 5 presents the guidelines proposed by Kruskal [10] to interpret the goodness of fit of multidimensional scaling.

4.3   Analysis of Sharers

This section reports on the results of multidimensional scaling and cluster analysis performed on sharer profiles weighted according to Equation (1). The sharer profiles were collected over the four-long term observation periods. SPSS was used for multidimensional scaling; it provides two options: ALSCAL and PROXSCAL. Unlike ALSCAL, PROXSCAL can handle similarity and dissimilarity matrices and construct a proximity matrix if the input data does not have a proximity measure. Since these characteristics meet the experimental requirements, PROXSCAL was used in this research.

Data from July 1, 2013 to December 31, 2013 is used to illustrate the analysis that was conducted to discover the underlying relationships between sharer profiles. Since the data has some isolated noise (which implies that the sharers corresponding to the noise points have totally different behavior from others, e.g., sharing less popular cyberlocker links), the noise points were removed to leave 66 sample points. Following this, multidimensional scaling analysis was performed on the 66 sample points. Figure 3 shows the resulting object configuration (top left) where the similarity between sharers is visualized using a two-dimensional representation (stress = 0.0390).

Next, agglomerative hierarchical clustering analysis was performed on the coordinates of the points produced by multidimensional scaling analysis. The clustering result, shown in the matrix tree plot (right panel of

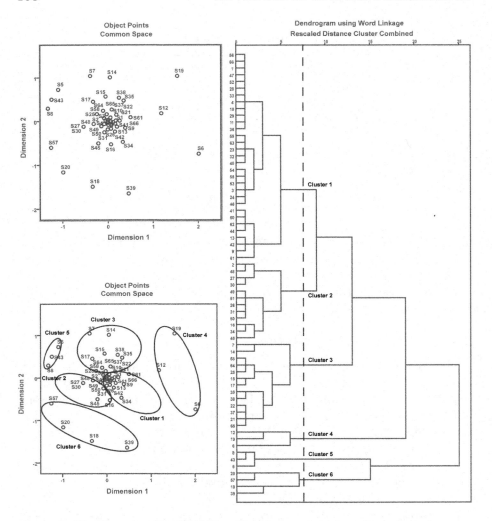

Figure 3.   Results using PROXSCAL and agglomerative hierarchical clustering.

Figure 3), is a close reflection of the agglomerative hierarchical clustering algorithm. The left column of nodes represents the objects (sharers) while the remaining nodes represent the clusters to which the objects belong. During the clustering, two very similar objects were first joined at a node and the resulting line was joined to the next closest object or sub-cluster by another line. The length of the line is proportional to the value of the inter-group dissimilarity between its two child nodes. As shown in Figure 3, when a dashed line is drawn in the matrix tree plot, each horizontal line intersecting the dashed line represents a cluster, following which the appropriate clusters can be found. In total, six

Table 6. Hierarchical clusters of sizes three to thirteen.

Cluster	Subjects (Sharers)	Sub-Cluster	Subjects (Sharers)	Cluster Size
1	56, 66, 1, 47, 52, 28, 33, 4, 10, 29, 11, 36, 59, 63, 23, 32, 40, 54, 55, 53, 3, 24, 46, 41, 60, 62, 44, 13, 42, 9, 61	1-1	56, 66, 1, 47, 52, 28, 33, 4, 10, 29, 11, 36	12
		1-2	59, 63, 23, 32, 40, 54, 55, 53, 3, 24, 46	11
		1-3	41, 60, 62, 44, 13, 42, 9, 61	8
2	2, 48, 27, 30, 49, 51, 26, 31, 50, 16, 34, 45			12
3	7, 14, 58, 64, 25, 15, 17, 35, 38, 22, 37, 21, 65			13
4	12, 19, 6			3
5	8, 43, 5			3
6	20, 57, 18, 39			4

clusters were obtained. Figure 3 (bottom left) shows these clusters in a two-dimensional representation.

The advantage of agglomerative hierarchical clustering is that the agglomerative process and the relationships between objects can be viewed clearly. If the cluster size exceeds the maximum cluster size, the cluster is divided into sub-clusters according to the agglomerative process. For example, based on the results in Figure 3 (right panel), Cluster 1 can be further divided into three sub-clusters as shown in Table 6, and nine clusters of sizes three to thirteen are identified. A forensic investigator can then explore the objects within the clusters to determine the cluster to which the piracy suspect belongs.

Table 7. Stress values for the four long-term observation periods.

Observation Period	Stress
2014.01.01 to 2014.06.30	0.0336
2013.07.01 to 2013.12.31	0.0390
2013.01.01 to 2013.06.30	0.0273
2012.07.01 to 2012.12.31	0.0295

Table 7 shows the analysis results for the sharer profiles collected during the four long-term observation periods along with the stress values. The goodness of fit obtained via multidimensional scaling is adequate and the results reflect the relationships between objects. Therefore, if a forensic investigator desires to trace the identity of a piracy suspect, this methodology can narrow the scope of the investigation and identify users with similar sharing behavior. This can help collect more evidence

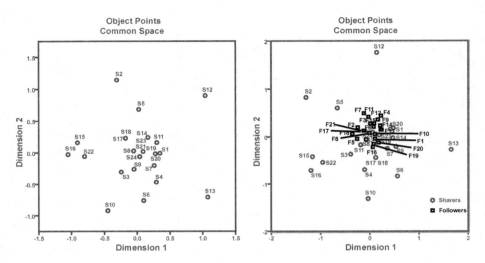

Figure 4. Two-dimensional object configuration of 24 sharers and 21 followers.

about the suspect's cyberlocker-based piracy behavior and also his/her identity.

4.4   Analysis of Sharers and Followers

Multidimensional analysis and cluster analysis were also performed on the sharer and follower profiles collected during the six short-term observation periods. The weighting schemes corresponding to Equations (1) and (2) were applied to create sharer and follower profiles, respectively, which were then compared. Also, the relationships between the sharers and followers were identified and analyzed.

The data from January 1, 2014 to January 31, 2014 is used to illustrate the analysis. During this observation period, data about 26 sharers and 91 followers was collected. The sharer profiles were created using the weighting scheme specified by Equation (1), which ignores the replying behavior of sharers. After removing two isolated noise points, multidimensional scaling analysis was performed on the remaining 24 sharers. The resulting object configuration is shown in Figure 4 (left panel; stress = 0.0516).

Next, the sharer and follower profiles were created using the weighting scheme specified by Equation (2), which considers the sharing and replying behavior of sharers and followers. During the short-term observation period, a number of inactive followers replied to less than three cyberlocker links. These inactive followers were removed and multidimensional scaling analysis was performed on the remaining 21 followers and 24 sharers (same 24 sharers as before). The resulting object configuration is shown in Figure 4 (right panel; stress = 0.0496).

Note that the object configurations of sharers in the left and right panels of Figure 4 are similar. This implies that the replying behavior of sharers has little discriminating power in determining the relevance of sharers, while the discriminating power of the sharing behavior of sharers is high. Moreover, as seen in Figure 4 (right panel), the object configuration of the followers is agminated, which is readily seen in the distribution. These followers have close relationships with the sharers who are close to them because they replied to the cyberlocker links posted by the sharers. Other sharers are far away from the followers because the cyberlocker links they shared had few, if any, replies from the followers.

5.   Conclusions

The framework proposed for digital profiling and identity tracking of sharers and followers of cyberlocker links is very useful in investigations of cyberlocker-based piracy. Experiments with data collected from nine web forums and targeting ten cyberlockers demonstrate that multidimensional scaling and agglomerative hierarchical clustering adequately capture the relationships between sharers and followers in a lower-dimensional hierarchical representation. The framework provides clear insights into the identities and relationships of cyberlocker link sharers and followers, significantly reducing the time and effort needed to investigate cyberlocker-based piracy.

Note that the analytic results only suggest tendencies related to cyberlocker link sharers and followers. Future research will apply the framework to profile and track real cyberlocker pirates, providing useful insights into the effectiveness of the framework in real-world piracy investigations. Also, the research will consider other characteristics of sharers and followers such as online time frames and time periods, types of shared content and different languages to construct more comprehensive profiles for identity tracking and forensic investigations.

References

[1] Alexa Internet, Top Sites in Hong Kong, San Francisco, California (www.alexa.com/topsites/countries/HK), 2014.

[2] N. Bamarah, B. Satpute and P. Patil, Web forum crawling techniques, *International Journal of Computer Applications*, vol. 85(17), pp. 36–41, 2014.

[3] W. Bhukya and S. Banothu, Investigative behavior profiling with one class SVM for computer forensics, in *Multi-Disciplinary Trends in Artificial Intelligence*, C. Sombattheera, A. Agarwal, S. Udgata and K. Lavangnananda (Eds.), Springer-Verlag, Berlin Heidelberg, Germany, pp. 373–383, 2011.

[4] I. Borg and P. Groenen, *Modern Multidimensional Scaling: Theory and Applications*, Springer-Verlag, New York, 2005.

[5] R. Drath, Hotfile, Megaupload and the future of copyright on the Internet: What can cyberlockers tell us about DMCA reform? *John Marshall Review of Intellectual Property Law*, vol. 12(205), pp. 204–241, 2012.

[6] Envisional, Technical Report: An Estimate of Infringing Use of the Internet, Cambridge, United Kingdom, 2011.

[7] N. Fathy, N. Badr, M. Hashem and T. Gharib, Enhancing web search with semantic identification of user preferences, *International Journal of Computer Science Issues*, vol. 8(6), pp. 62–69, 2011.

[8] D. Godoy and A. Amandi, A conceptual clustering approach for user profiling in personal information agents, *AI Communications*, vol. 19(3), pp. 207–227, 2006.

[9] E. Hickey, *Serial Murderers and Their Victims*, Wadsworth, Belmont, California, 2012.

[10] J. Kruskal, Multidimensional scaling by optimizing goodness of fit to a nonmetric hypothesis, *Psychometrika*, vol. 29(1), pp. 1–27, 1964.

[11] M. Liu, Z. Zhang, P. Hui, Y. Qin and S. Kulkarni, Measurement and understanding of cyberlocker URL-sharing sites: Focus on movie files, *Proceedings of the IEEE/ACM International Conference on Advances in Social Networks Analysis and Mining*, pp. 902–909, 2013.

[12] A. Mahanti, Measurement and analysis of cyberlocker services, *Proceedings of the Twentieth International Conference Companion on the World Wide Web*, pp. 373–378, 2011.

[13] N. Marx, Storage wars: Clouds, cyberlockers and media piracy in the digital economy, *Journal of E-Media Studies*, vol. 3(1), 2013.

[14] S. McKinney and D. Reeves, User identification via process profiling, *Proceedings of the Fifth Annual Workshop on Cyber Security and Information Intelligence Research: Cyber Security and Information Intelligence Challenges and Strategies*, article no. 51, 2009.

[15] F. Murtagh and P. Legendre, Ward's hierarchical clustering method: Which algorithms implement Ward's criterion? *Journal of Classification*, vol. 31(3), pp. 274–295, 2014.

[16] W. Petherick (Ed.), *Serial Crime: Theoretical and Practical Issues in Behavioral Profiling*, Elsevier Academic Press, Burlington, Massachusetts, 2009.

[17] R. Raysman and P. Brown, Cyberlockers, file-sharing and infringement in the cloud, *New Jersey Law Journal*, September 12, 2012.

[18] S. Schiaffino and A. Amandi, Intelligent user profiling, in *Artificial Intelligence: An International Perspective*, M. Bramer (Ed.), Springer-Verlag, Berlin Heidelberg, Germany, pp. 193–216, 2009.

[19] F. Wickelmaier, An Introduction to MDS, Report No. R000-6003, Institute for Electronics Systems, Aalborg University, Aalborg, Denmark, 2003.

[20] N. Zhao, L. Baud and P. Bellot, Characteristic analysis for the cyberlockers files study on Rapidgator, Speedyshare and 1Fichier, *Proceedings of the Eighth International Conference on Information Science and Transactions*, pp. 176–181, 2013.

Chapter 7

A PRIVACY-PRESERVING ENCRYPTION SCHEME FOR AN INTERNET REAL-NAME REGISTRATION SYSTEM

Fei Xu, Ken Yau, Ping Zhang and Kam-Pui Chow

Abstract   Internet real-name registration requires a user to provide personal identification credentials including his/her real name to an online service provider when registering for an account. In China, real-name registration has been implemented since 2010 for purchasing train tickets and mobile phone SIM cards. In 2013, the Chinese government announced that real-name registration would be implemented for Internet users to protect against cyber crimes, including cyber bullying, rumor spreading and identity theft. When real-name registration is in place, law enforcement agencies can obtain the real identity of a user who attempts to leverage the anonymity provided by the Internet to conduct criminal activities. However, real-name registration also potentially infringes on online privacy.

This chapter presents a privacy-preserving Internet real-name registration approach based on Shamir's secret sharing scheme. The approach helps protect the identities of online users while enabling law enforcement to obtain the identities of users involved in criminal activities on the Internet.

Keywords: Internet crimes, real-name registration, privacy preservation

1.   Introduction

Online services offer users with unparalleled selections of applications, products and opportunities. However, they also provide numerous opportunities for malicious users to commit cyber crimes. When a cyber crime is committed, it is difficult to trace the real criminal because the association between the online user identity and the real identity is hidden or is otherwise unavailable. Due to the increase in Internet crime, real-name registration systems have been proposed to trace criminals

© IFIP International Federation for Information Processing 2015
G. Peterson, S. Shenoi (Eds.): Advances in Digital Forensics XI, IFIP AICT 462, pp. 115–128, 2015.
DOI: 10.1007/978-3-319-24123-4_7

more effectively. Such a system requires a user to provide identification credentials and his/her real name to an online service provider when registering for an account (e.g., for a blog, website or online discussion forum). During a criminal investigation, the real identity of a user could be provided to a law enforcement agency upon provision of the appropriate legal documents. However, unless the system is designed very carefully, real-name registration could pose serious threats to user privacy.

This chapter presents a privacy-preserving real-name registration approach based on Shamir's secret sharing scheme. The approach provides privacy protection to users while enabling law enforcement to obtain the identities of users involved in criminal activities on the Internet.

2.   Background

This section discusses the notions of privacy and its implications with regard to name-registration systems in South Korea and China.

2.1   Privacy

Privacy has long been understood as "the right to be let alone" [11]. Any person should be able to keep information about himself/herself out of the public domain. An individual who is unable to control the dissemination of his/her private information has lost the right of privacy.

The right of privacy has become the center of attention due to the ubiquity of the Internet. Some users have leveraged the anonymity of the Internet to spread gossip or reveal sensitive or private information about individuals. The affected individuals often complain that anonymous posts are defamatory or infringe on their privacy. On the other hand, many Internet users argue that they are entitled to enjoy the freedom of expression and communication, as well as their right to privacy. The solution is to design and implement a real-name system that offers privacy protection to online users while enabling law enforcement to obtain the real identities of users involved in criminal activities upon provision of the appropriate legal documents.

2.2   Real-Name Registration in South Korea

South Korea was the first country to implement a real-name registration system for Internet users. The system, which was implemented in 2007, required users to supply their real names and resident registration numbers for web portals accessed by more than 300,000 visitors per day, the goal being to reduce and help prosecute online criminal activities. Since June 28, 2009, 35 South Korean websites have implemented real-name registration systems according to the newly amended Information and Communications Network Act (Choi Jin-Sil Law) [3].

Real-name registration in South Korea was driven by the suicide of Ms. Choi Jin-Sil after malicious comments about her were posted on Internet bulletin boards. Ms. Choi, who was one of the most famous actresses in South Korea, committed suicide on October 2, 2008 because she was rumored to have been involved in the suicide of another actor, Mr. Ahn Jae-Hwan [2]. In 2009, the Government of South Korea amended its Information and Communication Network Act to require real-name registration for all websites with more than 100,000 visitors per day. Moreover, the law required online service providers to disclose personal information of alleged offenders in cases involving libel or infringement of privacy.

The South Korean Resident Registration Number (RRN) is a thirteen-digit number that uniquely identifies each resident. The RRN is divided into several segments, each representing a piece of personal information. For example, the first digit segment represents the date of birth. In addition to the date of birth, gender and birthplace can be discerned from the RRN [12].

South Korean law required users to provide their real names and RRNs when creating online accounts. The collection of this personal information about millions of South Korean residents was a grave concern, especially because many websites did not have adequate mechanisms for protecting the sensitive information they collected. In March 2010, the South Korean police arrested individuals who were trafficking personal information belonging to about 20 million South Korean Internet users, which was leaked or stolen from 25 websites [7].

As a result of several incidents involving personal data leakage, the South Korean government changed its requirement, requesting web service providers to adopt i-Pin IDs to identify users instead of RRNs. In June 2008, five credit information providers were certified to issue i-Pin IDs and provide web services with interfaces that validate the IDs [7]. Thus, users were able to create web accounts using i-Pin IDs instead of RRNs. However, according to one study [7], using a pseudonym such as an i-Pin does not protect individuals from phishing attacks. In addition, previous research indicates that the availability and confidentiality of personal information cannot be maintained by the name-registration system as it is currently implemented.

On August 23, 2012, the Constitutional Court of South Korea [4] ruled unanimously that the real-name requirements were unconstitutional. In fact, the court maintained that the provision violated freedom of speech in cyberspace:

The system does not appear to be beneficial to the public. Despite the enforcement of the system, the number of illegal and malicious postings online has not decreased. Instead, users have moved to foreign websites and the system has become discriminatory against domestic operators. It also prevents foreigners who do not have resident registration numbers from expressing their opinions online.

After the 2012 Constitutional Court decision, real-name registration was terminated in South Korea. At this time, users are not required to supply personal identification credentials when registering for accounts with South Korean online service providers.

The lesson from the South Korean experience is that, while real-name registration may enable a government to regulate and investigate anonymous activities in cyberspace, it endangers personal privacy and infringes on freedom of speech. Other laws related to data privacy and surveillance may also potentially be violated due to the massive amounts of personal information necessarily collected, stored and used by a real-name registration system.

2.3   Real-Name Registration in China

On April 29, 2002, Professor Xiguang Li of Tsinghua University stated on Guangzhou TV that, "The People's Congress should pass legislation that prohibits anyone from anonymously publishing things on the Internet." Since then, government agencies in China have taken legal and technical steps to prevent online anonymity. In 2003, government authorities required people to register with their ID cards before surfing the web at Internet cafes. In 2004, the Internet Society of China published a draft standard for web-based public email services that included a real-name registration requirement. In 2005, real-name registrations for website administrators, QQ group creators and administrators were implemented. By 2012, many online service providers, including `sina.com`, `sohu.com`, `163.com` and `blog.qq.com`, implemented real-name registration. In 2013, the Chinese government announced that real-name registration would be implemented by June 2014 [6].

On January 21, 2013, the Standardization Administration of the Ministry of Industry and Information Technology released a document entitled "Information Security Technology – Guidelines for Personal Information Protection within Public and Commercial Information Systems" [10], which discussed various principles related to personal information protection. It did not clearly identify the relationship between the implementation of the real-name system and the personal information protection guidelines, such as how inconsistencies should be resolved. In 2014, the Chinese State Administration of Press, Publication, Radio, Film and Television required users to use their real names when uploading videos to websites [8].

At the time of writing this chapter, the main concern of Internet users in China is the security of their personal data collected by the real-name registration system. This chapter discusses techniques for protecting personal data identification information when implementing a real-name registration system.

3. Real-Name Registration Requirements

The basic principle of real-name registration is "real-name at the back, but pseudonym online." Every online user should be able to use an online identity, or pseudonym, but the user's real identity should not be revealed. The real-name of a user may be released only when the user requests its release or if a crime has been committed and the user's real identity is required during the investigation.

An online user may always disclose his/her identity whenever he/she desires to do so. Moreover, an online user should be able to prove that he/she is the owner of an online identity or pseudonym. In a criminal investigation, a law enforcement agency may obtain the real identity of an individual of interest by following the appropriate procedures (e.g., obtaining a court order). Since an individual may be unwilling to disclose his/her real identity in such a situation, a real-name registration system should be able to release a user's identity without the approval or support of the user.

The requirements of a real-name registration system are:

- A user (pseudonym owner) is identified by an online pseudonym; the real identity of the user is hidden.

- A pseudonym owner can prove he/she owns the pseudonym.

- A law enforcement agency can obtain the real identity of a pseudonym owner without the approval of the pseudonym owner upon using appropriate legal procedures.

4. Real-Name Registration Overview

In order to satisfy the real-name registration requirements, the first issue is to select a registration authority (i.e., the entity responsible for conducting the registration process). Clearly, it would be inappropriate for a law enforcement agency to serve as the registration authority. It would also be inappropriate for an online service provider to serve as the registration authority because of the massive amount of personal data involved and because the online service provider may not have adequate resources to protect the data. Other issues that must be addressed are identifying the entity responsible for collecting personal data and where and how the data would be stored.

The registration scheme proposed in this chapter is designed to avoid potential misuse of personal data and to handle potentially massive volumes of personal data. Also, multiple entities are involved to prevent any one entity from having unrestricted access to personal data. Thus, in addition to a user, the entities involved in online pseudonym or webname registration are a registration center, independent authority and personal data storage center.

When a user registers for an online pseudonym, he/she is required to provide his/her real-name and identity credentials to the registration center. Upon receiving the request from the user, the registration center asks the user to submit personal authentication information, which is a collection of attribute-value pairs. The user's real-name and identity credentials and the binding between the pseudonym and the real-name should be strongly protected.

The registration center encrypts the personal authentication information received from the user using public key encryption and sends the encrypted information to the personal data storage center. Each user is assigned a public/private key pair. The personal data storage center has two major components, a data storage server and a key server. The data storage server is responsible for storing the encrypted personal authentication information supplied by users. The key server has three functions: (i) generating key pairs for users; (ii) partitioning user private keys into four parts; and (iii) storing one part of the private key. Each of the four parts of a user private key is distributed to a different entity: (i) user; (ii) registration center; (iii) private data storage center; and (iv) independent authority.

The proposed encryption scheme uses public key cryptography. The public key is used to encrypt the user's personal authentication information and the private key is used to decrypt the information. The public key is also employed by the user during the authentication step of the online pseudonym registration process. Note that the public key is used differently from how it is used in a public key infrastructure in that it is not made available to the public through a directory service.

Shamir's secret sharing scheme [9] is used to partition the private key into four parts such that combining any three parts yields the private key. Thus, without the part from the user or the part from the independent authority, the private key cannot be reconstructed to decrypt the personal authentication information, even if the registration center and private data storage center provide their portions of the key.

The independent authority, which holds one part of the private key, can assist in private key reconstruction when a user is unwilling to provide his/her part of the private key. At the end of the registration process, the registration center must ensure that the plaintext form of the personal authentication information is destroyed. Thereafter, the personal authentication information only exists in encrypted form in the private data storage center.

In order to prove pseudonym ownership, the user submits a request to the registration center along with his/her part of the private key. Upon proper authentication, the registration center submits its part of the private key and the user-submitted part to the private data storage center. The private data storage center then combines its part of the private key with the user and registration center parts to reconstruct the private key, and retrieve and decrypt the encrypted version of the personal authentication information stored at the data storage server.

After an online pseudonym is identified during a criminal investigation, a law enforcement agency can follow the prescribed process to retrieve the associated personal authentication information. This typically involves obtaining a court order and requesting the independent authority and registration center to release their parts of the private key associated with the online pseudonym. With proper authorization, the law enforcement agency can then request the private data storage center to retrieve the real-name corresponding to the pseudonym by submitting the private key parts received from the independent authority and registration center. The private data storage center can then combine its part of the private key together with the independent authority and registration key parts to retrieve and decrypt the personal authentication information stored at the data storage server.

User real-names and online pseudonyms have different roles in the real-name registration system. The next two sections present two registration processes in detail: (i) user real-name registration; and (ii) user web-name (online pseudonym) registration. In user real-name registration, the user submits his/her personal authentication information to the registration center, which authenticates the user and creates the binding between the user's real-name and web-name. In user web-name registration, the user sends an online service request along with the web-name to the web service provider and private data storage center. The private data storage center authenticates the user to confirm that the user is, in fact, the owner of the web-name.

5.   Privacy-Preserving Real-Name Registration

The proposed privacy-preserving real-name registration scheme employs public key cryptography to secure personal authentication information. For each user, the key server of the private data storage center generates a public-private key pair. The public key is used to encrypt the personal authentication information and the private key is used to decrypt the encrypted information. The public key is also used to encrypt the user's personal authentication information to authenticate the user during the web-name registration process. When a user needs a web-name for an online service, he/she uses the public key to encrypt his/her personal authentication information, which is used to prove that he/she is the real owner of the web-name at the private data storage center. Instead of the user retaining the private key, the key is partitioned into four parts using Shamir's secret sharing scheme and each part is distributed to one of four entities: user, independent authority, registration center and private data storage center. As mentioned above, combining any three parts yields the entire private key, which can then be used to decrypt the encrypted personal authentication information. A user can always request the registration center to retrieve his/her real-name and release it to other entities. However, during a criminal investigation, a law enforcement agency can request the court to order the independent authority and registration center to retrieve and provide the real-name of a person of interest without his/her approval.

Since the registration center, independent authority and private data storage center are crucial components of the name-registration infrastructure and are, as such, high-value targets, they must be secured to the maximum extent. The components should conform to the ISO 27000 family of standards. In particular, they should adhere to ISO/IEC 27001 [5], the best-known standard in the family, which provides requirements for information security management systems.

The next two sections discuss the user real-name registration and user web-name registration processes in detail.

5.1   User Real-Name Registration Process

In user real-name registration, a user makes an in-person appearance at a registration center with documents that prove his/her identity. Upon successful authentication of the user, the registration center requests the user to submit predefined personal authentication information that will be used to authenticate the user in the future. The predefined personal authentication information is a collection of attribute-value pairs (e.g., user ID number, mobile phone number, etc.). The registration center should publish the required personal authentication information in advance so that the user can collect the necessary information before the time of registration. The registration center encrypts the personal authentication information during the registration process and the plaintext version of this information is destroyed at the end of the registration process.

When the registration center receives the personal authentication information from the user, the registration center requests the key server at the private data storage center to generate a public-private key pair for the user. The key server sends the public key to the registration center, which uses the key to encrypt the personal authentication information submitted by the user. The encrypted personal authentication information is then sent to the data storage server for storage.

The key server then partitions the private key into four parts using Shamir's secret sharing scheme. In particular, the (4, 3) threshold secret sharing scheme is employed, in which the private key is shared with four entities such that any three parts can be combined to yield the private key and thus decrypt the encrypted personal authentication information. One part of the private key is kept at the key server while the other three parts are distributed to the user, registration center and independent authority. The registration center also generates a web-name for the user, which can be based on the user's preference. Upon successful registration, the web-name is provided to the user.

The real-name registration process involves the following steps (see Figure 1):

1. The user requests real-name registration in person at the registration center. After authenticating the user, the registration center assigns a web-name to the user and requests the key server to generate a public-private key pair for the user.

2. The key server creates the public-private key pair (pk_{ID}, sk_{ID}) and a two-degree polynomial interpolation $f_{ID}(x) = a_2x^2 + a_1x + a_0 \bmod(p)$ for the user such that $f_{ID}(0) = sk_{ID}$ where p is a prime number such that $p > a_0$. The key server then generates four pairs (x_{ik}, y_{ik}) where $k = 0\ldots3$ and $f_{ID}(x_{ik}) = y_{ik}$ [9]. The pair (x_{i0}, y_{i0}) is kept by the key server; the other three pairs are sent to the user, registration center and independent authority. The key server then destroys the private key sk_{ID}.

3. The user submits his/her personal authentication information to the registration center.

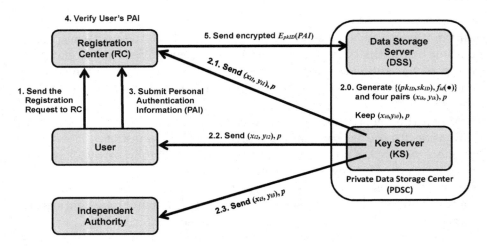

Figure 1. User real-name registration.

4. The registration center verifies the user's personal authentication information.

5. If the user's personal authentication information is valid, the registration center encrypts the user's personal authentication information with pk_{ID} and sends the web-name, pk_{ID} and encrypted $E_{pkID}(PAI)$ to the data storage server.

6. The registration center returns the web-name and public key pk_{ID} to the user and then destroys the plaintext version of the personal authentication information.

7. The registration center maintains the web-name and the f_{ID} along with (x_{i1}, y_{i1}).

5.2   User Web-Name Registration Process

The user web-name registration process is executed when a user wishes to use an online service and has to register his/her web-name with the online service provider. The process requires the online service provider to authenticate the user's web-name using the private data storage center. It is assumed that the user already has received a web-name from the registration center upon completing the real-name registration process.

In web-name registration, the user sends his/her web-name and encrypted personal authentication information to an online service provider. Meanwhile, the user also sends an authentication request with his/her web-name to the private data storage center. After receiving the user request, the online service provider forwards the user's web-name and encrypted personal authentication information to the private data storage center for authentication.

Having received the user's web-name and encrypted personal authentication information from the online service provider and the authentication request from the user, the private data storage center retrieves the user's encrypted personal authentication information based on the supplied web-name from the data storage server. This enables the private data storage center to verify the user's encrypted personal authentication information sent by the online service provider. If the user's encrypted personal authentication information is valid, then the private data storage center sends a challenge message (random number R) to the user. The user computes and sends the response $E_{pkID}(R)$ back to the private data storage center for authentication. This challenge-response exchange is required to prevent a malicious entity from impersonating the user during the web-name registration process.

If the challenge-response exchange is successful, the private data storage center informs the online service provider that the user's web-name authentication was successful; otherwise, the online service provider is informed that the authentication failed. The online service provider accepts the user web-name registration request if the authentication was successful and the user can use the web-name to access the online service; otherwise, the web-name registration is rejected.

The web-name (WN) registration process involves the following steps (see Figure 2):

1. The user sends a web-name registration request to the online service provider with his/her web-name and $E_{pkID}(PAI)$. Meanwhile, the user sends an authentication request to the private data storage center.

2. The online service provider forwards the user's web-name and $E_{pkID}(PAI)$ to the private data storage center.

3. After the private data storage center receives the authentication request from the user and the web-name and $E_{pkID}(PAI)$ from the online service provider, the private data storage center retrieves the encrypted personal authentication information of the user from the data storage server based on the web-name and compares it with $E_{pkID}(PAI)$ received from the online service provider. If the two encrypted messages match, the private data storage center sends a random number R as a challenge to the user; otherwise, the authentication fails.

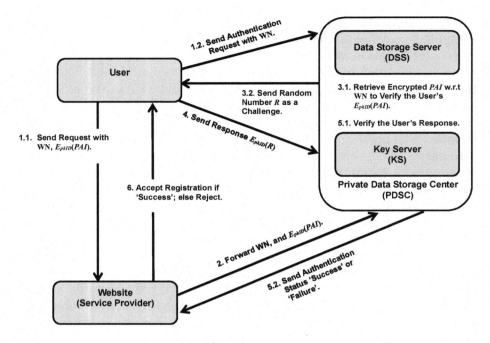

Figure 2.   User web-name registration.

4. The user sends the challenge-response $E_{pkID}(R)$ to the private data storage center for authentication after receiving the challenge message R.

5. The private data storage center validates the user's response. If $E_{pkID}(R)$ is valid, then the private data storage center confirms to the online service provider that the authentication was successful; otherwise, the authentication fails.

6. The online service provider accepts the user's web-name registration request if the authentication was successful; otherwise, it rejects the registration request.

5.3   Privacy-Preserving Properties

In the real-name registration process, no personal authentication information is stored as plaintext at the registration center or private data storage center. Only the encrypted version of the personal authentication information is stored at the data storage server of the private data storage center and it can only be decrypted by the user's private key, which is partitioned into four parts and distributed to four entities.

In the web-name registration process, the online service provider does not access the user's personal authentication information as plaintext and is not involved in decrypting the personal authentication information for verification. A challenge-response sequence is used between the private data storage center and the user to ensure that impersonation does not occur during the web-name registration process using the user's web-name and encrypted personal authentication information.

In order to decrypt the encrypted personal authentication information maintained at the data storage server, two entities from among the user, registration center and independent authority are required to supply their portions of the user's private key. Without the participation of the independent authority, only the user can decrypt his/her own personal authentication information upon receiving a request from the registration center.

When a web-name is identified as being of interest in a criminal investigation, the law enforcement agency has to go through a well-defined process that involves obtaining a court order and requesting the independent authority to supply its part of the private key. When the independent authority and registration center supply their parts of the private key corresponding to the web-name, the encrypted personal authentication information associated with the web-name can be decrypted and the real-name corresponding to the web-name can be obtained. The law enforcement agency can then continue its investigation with the real-name in hand.

6. Conclusions

The privacy-preserving real-name registration approach presented in this chapter helps protect the identity of online users while enabling law enforcement to obtain the identities of users involved in criminal activities. Shamir's secret sharing scheme is used to partition a user's private key in four parts, with a different part sent to each of four entities: user, registration center, private data storage center and independent authority. The user's real identity cannot be revealed unless at least three of the four parts of the private key are combined; therefore, except for the user, no other entity can obtain the user's real identity independently. During an investigation, when a person of interest is unwilling to provide his/her real identity, a law enforcement agency can obtain a court order and then request the independent authority to provide its part of the secret key to reveal the person's real identity.

Future research will attempt to implement the real-name registration approach. Also, efforts will be made to evaluate the performance, and to identify and address the challenges that manifest themselves in a real-world environment.

References

[1] L. Adleman, P. Rothemund, S. Roweis and E Winfree, On applying molecular computation to the Data Encryption Standard, *Journal of Computational Biology*, vol. 6(1), pp. 53–63, 1999.

[2] S. Choe, Web rumors tied to Korean actress's suicide, *New York Times*, October 2, 2008.

[3] S. Choe, South Korea links web slander to celebrity suicides, *New York Times*, October 12, 2008.

[4] Constitutional Court of South Korea, Constitutional Court Decision 2010Hun-Ma47, Seoul, South Korea (`koreanlii.or.kr/w/index.php/2010Hun-Ma47`), August 23, 2012.

[5] International Organization for Standardization, ISO/IEC 27001 – Information Security Management, Geneva, Switzerland, 2013.

[6] O. Lam, The business behind China's Internet real name registration system, *Global Voices Advocacy*, June 10, 2013.

[7] Y. Oh, T. Obi, J. Lee, H. Suzuki and N. Ohyama, Empirical analysis of Internet identity misuse: Case study of the South Korean real name system, *Proceedings of the Sixth ACM Workshop on Digital Identity Management*, pp. 27–34, 2010.

[8] Reuters, China orders real name register for online video uploads, January 21, 2014.

[9] A. Shamir, How to share a secret, *Communications of the ACM*, vol. 22(11), pp. 612–613, 1979.

[10] Standardization Administration of China, Information Security Technology – Guidelines for Personal Information Protection within Information System for Public and Commercial Systems, GB/Z 28828-2012, Beijing, China, 2012.

[11] United Nations General Assembly, Promotion and Protection of Human Rights: Human Rights Questions, Including Alternative Approaches for Improving the Effective Enjoyment of Human Rights and Fundamental Freedoms, Report of the Third Committee, A/67/457/Add.2, General Assembly, Sixty-Seventh Session, New York, December 8, 2012.

[12] Wikipedia, Resident Registration Number (`en.wikipedia.org/wiki/Resident_registration_number`), 2015.

Chapter 8

A LOGIC-BASED NETWORK FORENSIC MODEL FOR EVIDENCE ANALYSIS

Changwei Liu, Anoop Singhal and Duminda Wijesekera

Abstract   Many attackers tend to use sophisticated multi-stage and/or multi-host attack techniques and anti-forensic tools to cover their traces. Due to the limitations of current intrusion detection and network forensic analysis tools, reconstructing attack scenarios from evidence left behind by attackers of enterprise systems is challenging. In particular, reconstructing attack scenarios using intrusion detection system alerts and system logs that have too many false positives is a big challenge.

   This chapter presents a model and an accompanying software tool that systematically addresses the reconstruction of attack scenarios in a manner that could stand up in court. The problems faced in such reconstructions include large amounts of data (including irrelevant data), missing evidence and evidence corrupted or destroyed by anti-forensic techniques. The model addresses these problems using various methods, including mapping evidence to system vulnerabilities, inductive reasoning and abductive reasoning, to reconstruct attack scenarios. The Prolog-based system employs known vulnerability databases and an anti-forensic database that will eventually be extended to a standardized database like the NIST National Vulnerability Database. The system, which is designed for network forensic analysis, reduces the time and effort required to reach definite conclusions about how network attacks occurred.

Keywords: Network forensics, network attacks, evidence graph, admissibility

1.   Introduction

   Network forensics is the science that deals with the capture, recording and analysis of network events and traffic in order to detect and investigate intrusions. A network forensic investigation requires the construction of an attack scenario when conducting an examination of the

© IFIP International Federation for Information Processing 2015
G. Peterson, S. Shenoi (Eds.): Advances in Digital Forensics XI, IFIP AICT 462, pp. 129–145, 2015.
DOI: 10.1007/978-3-319-24123-4_8

attacked system. In order to present the scenario that is best supported by evidence, forensic investigators must analyze all possible attack scenarios reconstructed from the available evidence. This includes false negatives and items of evidence that are missing or destroyed (in part or in entirety) as a result of investigators using tools that are unable to capture traces of some attacks or attackers using anti-forensic techniques to destroy evidence.

Although the use of intrusion detection system alerts and system logs as evidence has been contested in courts, they provide the first level of information to forensic investigators when creating potential attack scenarios [13]. In order to reconstruct potential attack scenarios, researchers [1, 2] have proposed aggregating redundant alerts based on similarities and correlating them using predefined attack scenarios to determine multi-step, multi-stage attacks. However, this approach is manual and rather *ad hoc*. As an improvement, Wang and Daniels [15] proposed automating the process using a fuzzy-rule-based hierarchical reasoning framework that correlates alerts using local rules and grouping them using global rules. However, this approach fails when evidence is destroyed and it does not consider the potential admissibility of the evidence and the constructed attack scenario in legal proceedings.

To address these problems, this research employs a rule-based system that automates the attack scenario reconstruction process while being cognizant of standards for evidence admissibility. The rule base incorporates: (i) correlation rules that coalesce security event alerts and system logs; (ii) rules that explain missing and destroyed evidence (with the support of an anti-forensic database) by using what-if scenarios; and (iii) rules that help assess the admissibility of evidence. The viability and utility of the system is demonstrated via a prototype written in Prolog.

This research builds on a preliminary reasoning model described in [8] by extending the MulVAL attack graph generation tool [12] that is implemented in XSB Prolog [14]. Figure 1 presents the architecture of MulVAL and the extended model. The extensions, which are shaded, include: (i) an evidence module that uses MITRE's OVAL database [10] or expert knowledge (if there is no corresponding entry in the OVAL database) to convert evidence from the attacked network to the corresponding software vulnerability and computer configuration required by MulVAL; (ii) anti-forensic and expert knowledge databases that generate explanations in the face of missing or destroyed evidence; and (iii) rules of evidence and access control modules that help judge the acceptability of evidence.

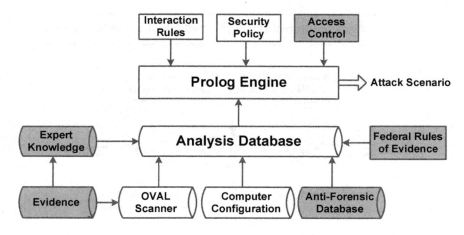

Figure 1. Architecture of MulVAL and the extended model.

2. Background and Related Work

This section presents the background concepts and related research.

2.1 MulVAL and Logical Attack Graphs

MulVAL is a Prolog-based system that automatically identifies security vulnerabilities in enterprise networks [7]. Running on XSB Prolog, MulVAL uses tuples to represent vulnerability information, network topology and computer configurations and to determine if they give rise to potential attack traces. The graph comprising all the attack traces generated by this system is called a logical attack graph.

Definition 1: $A = (N_r, N_p, N_d, E, L, G)$ is a logical attack graph where N_r, N_p and N_d are sets of derivation, primitive and derived fact nodes, $E \subseteq ((N_p \cup N_d) \times N_r) \cup (N_r \times N_d)$, L is a mapping from a node to its label, and $G \subseteq N_d$ is the final goal of an attacker [7, 11].

Figure 2 shows an example logical attack graph. A primitive fact node (rectangle) represents specific network configuration or vulnerability information corresponding to a host computer. A derivation node (ellipse) represents a successful application of an interaction rule on input facts, including primitive facts and prior derived facts. The successful interaction results in a derived fact node (diamond), which is satisfied by the input facts.

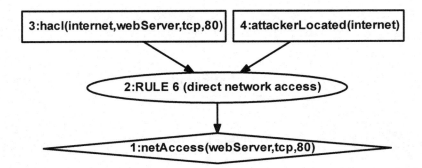

Figure 2.   Example logical attack graph.

2.2   Evidence Graphs

While an attack graph predicts potential attacks, an evidence graph is constructed to present evidence of a specific enterprise network attack.

Definition 2: An evidence graph is a sextuple $G = (N_h, N_e, E, L, N_h\text{-}$ Attr, $N_e\text{-Attr})$ where N_h and N_e are sets of disjoint nodes representing a host computer involved in an attack and the related evidence, $E \subseteq (N_h \times N_e) \cup (N_e \times N_h)$, L is a mapping from a node to its label, and N_h-Attr and N_e-Attr are attributes of a host node and evidence node, respectively [5].

The attributes of a host node include host ID, states and timestamps. The states include the states before and after a particular attack step, which can be source, target, stepping-stone or affiliated [5, 7]. The attributes of an evidence node describe the event initiator, target and its timestamp.

2.3   Related Work

Reasoning has been used to correlate evidence when reconstructing crime scenarios. In traditional (non-digital) forensics, researchers have used inductive and abductive reasoning to model potential crime scenarios and correlate evidence [4]. In the area of digital forensics, Wang and Daniels [15] have used a fuzzy-rule base to correlate attack steps substantiated by aggregated security event alerts. Their scheme aggregates security event alerts by checking if they have the same source-destination pair, belong to the same attack class and fall within a self-extending time window. A self-extending time window is elongated to include all alerts within a predefined time difference from the original event. However, the approach does not handle situations where evidence is missing or

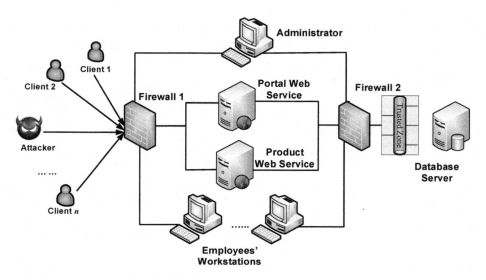

Figure 3. Example attacked network.

incomplete nor does it use any standards to determine the acceptability of evidence.

In order to address these limitations, Liu et al. [6] have proposed the use of an anti-forensic database containing expert knowledge to help generate hypotheses about missing or destroyed evidence and to substantiate the default assumptions of experts. MITRE's OVAL database and federal rules related to digital evidence are used to determine the potential acceptability of digital evidence [9]. Some of the solutions proposed in [9] were not implemented; these are discussed later in this chapter.

3. Network Example

Figure 3 shows an example attacked network [9]. In order to explain how an anti-forensic database can be used to create explanations in the face of destroyed evidence, anti-forensic techniques were used to remove some evidence.

Table 1 shows the machine IP address and vulnerability information. By exploiting the vulnerabilities listed in Table 1, the attacker was able to launch three attacks: (i) compromise a workstation (CVE-2009-1918) to access the database server; (ii) leverage the product web application vulnerability (SWE89) to attack the database server; and (iii) exploit a cross-site scripting (XSS) vulnerability on a chat forum hosted by the portal web service to steal the administrator's session ID so that phishing

Table 1. Machine IP addresses and vulnerabilities.

Machine	IP Address/Port	Vulnerability
Attacker	129.174.124.122	
Workstations	129.174.124.184/185/186	HTML Objects Memory Corruption Vulnerability (CVE-2009-1918)
Webserver1 – Product Web Service	129.174.124.53:8080	SQL Injection (CWE89)
Webserver2 – Product Web Service	129.174.124.53:80	SQL Injection (CWE89)
Administrator	129.174.124.137	Cross-Site Scripting Flaw (XSS)
Database Server	129.174.124.35	

emails could be sent to clients, tricking them to update their confidential information.

In the experimental network, the installed intrusion detection system, configured web server and database server were able to detect some attacks and log malicious accesses. However, there were some false positives (e.g., when attack attempts were not successful). Also, because the Snort tool used for intrusion detection did not incorporate certain rules or the actual attack activities looked benign, some attacks were not detected and, therefore, no alerts were logged as evidence in these instances. Two examples are: (i) phishing URLs sent by the attacker to the clients requesting them to update their confidential information were not detected; and (ii) database server access by the attacker from the compromised workstation was deemed to be benign. In addition, the attacker compromised the workstation and obtained root privileges, which enabled him to use anti-forensic techniques to delete evidence left on the workstation. Under these conditions, when evidence is missing or destroyed, it is necessary to find a way to show how the attack might have occurred.

4. Attack Scenario Reconstruction

This section discusses the attack scenario reconstruction process.

4.1 Rules and Facts

As stated in Section 1, the vulnerability/forensics database constructed from MITRE's OVAL [10] was used to convert intrusion detection system alerts and the associated system logs to the corresponding vulnerability entries for attack scenario reconstruction (expert knowledge

Table 2. Evidence of alerts and logs from Figure 3.

Timestamp	Source IP Address	Destination IP Address	Content	Vulnerability
08\13-12:26:10	129.174.124. 122:4444	129.174.124. 184:4040	SHELLCODE x86 inc ebx NOOP	CVE-2009-1918
08\13-12:27:37	129.174.124. 122:4444	129.174.124. 184:4040	SHELLCODE x86 inc ebx NOOP	CVE-2009-1918
08\13-14:37:27	129.174.124. 122:1715	129.174.124. 53:80	SQL Injection Attempt	CWE89
08\13-16:19:56	129.174.124. 122:49381	129.174.124. 137:8080	Cross-Site Scripting	XSS
08\13-14:37:29	129.174.124. 53	129.174.124. 35	name='Alice' AND password='alice' OR '1'='1'	CWE89
...	...	...	...	...

is used only when an entry is not found in OVAL) [8]. Table 2 shows the converted evidence from the experimental network in Figure 3.

Figure 4 shows the concrete predicates for the items of evidence corresponding to the computer configuration and network topology, which instantiate the corresponding predicates in reasoning rules during a MulVAL run. In the figure, predicate "attackedHost" represents a destination victim computer; predicate "hacl" denotes a host access control list; predicate "advances" represents the access rights within the firewall that were used by the attacker to reach the next computer after the attacker had compromised a computer as a stepping-stone; predicate "timeOrder" ensures that the starting time and the ending time of an attack are within a reasonable interval; and predicates "vulExists," "vulProperty" and "networkServiceInfo" represent an attack step on the target computer (the first term in the predicate "networkServiceInfo" represents the target computer).

Figure 5 shows a reasoning rule that describes a generic attack. Each rule has Prolog tuples that derive the postconditions from the preconditions of an attack step. For example, the rule in Figure 5 stipulates that: if the attacker has compromised the victim's computer (Line 3) and the victim has the privilege "Perm" on his computer "Host" (Line 4) and the attacker can access the victim's computer (Line 5), then the evidence representing the three preconditions as the cause is correlated with the evidence that the attacker obtained the victim's privileges on the victim's computer (Line 2). Line 1 is a string that uniquely identifies a rule and Line 6 is the description of the rule.

```
/* Final attack victims */
attackedHost(execCode(admin,_)).
attackedHost(execCode(dbServer,_,_)).
attackedHost(execCode(admin,_)).

/* Network topology and access control policy */
attackerLocated(internet).
hacl(internet,webServer,tcp,80).
hacl(webServer,dbServer,tcp,3660).
hacl(workStation1,dbServer,tcp,3660).
hacl(workStation2,dbServer,tcp,3660).
hacl(internet,workStation1,_, _).
hacl(internet,workStation2,_, _).
hacl(internet,admin,_, _).
hacl(H,H,_, _).
advances(webServer,dbServer).
advances(workStation,dbServer).

/* Timestamps used to find the evidence dependency */
timeOrder(webServer,dbServer,14.3727,14.3729).
timeOrder(workStation1,dbServer,12.2610,14.3730).

/* Configuration and attack information of workStation1 */
vulExists(workStation1,'CVE-2009-1918',httpd).
vulProperty('CVE-2009-1918',remoteExploit,
privEscalation).
networkServiceInfo(workStation1,httpd,tcp,80,apache).
...
```

Figure 4. Input facts in the form of predicates representing evidence.

```
/* Interaction Rules */
1. interaction_rule(
2. (execCode(Host,Perm) :-
3.    principalCompromised(Victim),
4.    hasAccount(Victim,Host,Perm),
5.    canAccessHost(Host)),
6.    rule_desc('When a principal is compromised, any machine
      on which he has an account is also compromised',0.5)).
```

Figure 5. Example reasoning rule.

4.2   Evidence Graph Generation

Figure 6 shows the attack scenario that resulted from querying the logic-based system that was not integrated with an anti-forensic database and did not cover evidence acceptability standards. The table below the evidence graph provides a description of each node and the corre-

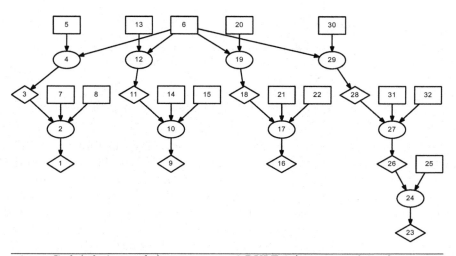

1:execCode(admin,apache)	2:RULE 2 (remote exploit of a server program)
3:netAccess(admin,tcp,80)	4:RULE 7 (direct network access)
5:hacl(internet,admin,tcp)	6:attackerLocated(internet)
7:networkServiceInfo(admin,httpd, tcp,80,apache)	8:vulExists(admin,'XSS',httpd, remoteExploit,privEscalation)
9:execCode(workStation1,apache)	10:RULE 2 (remote exploit of a server program)
11:netAccess(workStation1,tcp,80)	12:RULE 7 (direct network access)
13:hacl(internet,workStation1, tcp,80)	14:networkServiceInfo(workStation1, httpd,tcp,80,apache)
15:vulExists(workStation1, 'CVE-2009-1918',httpd, remoteExploit,privEscalation)	16:execCode(workStation2,apache)
17:RULE 2 (remote exploit of a server program)	18:netAccess(workStation2,tcp,80)
19:RULE 7 (direct network access)	20:hacl(internet,workStation2,tcp,80)
21:networkServiceInfo(workStation2, httpd,tcp,80,apache)	22:vulExists(workStation2, 'CVE-2009-1918',httpd, remoteExploit,privEscalation)
23:netAccess(dbServer,tcp,3660)	24: RULE 6 (multi-hop access)
25:hacl(webServer,dbServer,tcp,3660)	26:execCode(webServer,apache)
27:RULE 2 (remote exploit of a server program)	28:netAccess(webServer,tcp,80)
29:RULE 7 (direct network access)	30:hacl(internet,webServer,tcp,80)
31:networkServiceInfo(webServer, httpd,tcp,80,apache)	32:vulExists(webServer,'CWE89', httpd,remoteExploit,privEscalation)

Figure 6. Network attack scenario reconstructed from alerts and logs.

```
1. query:-
2.     tell('queryresult.P'),
3.     writeln('execCode(dbServer,user):'),
4.     listing(execCode(dbServer,user)),
5.     told.
```

Figure 7.   Querying the system for explanatory hypotheses.

sponding evidence in the logical form according to Definition 1. The facts, including primary facts (rectangles) and derived facts (diamonds) before a derivation node (ellipse), represent the preconditions before an attack step. All the facts after a derivation node represent postconditions after the attack step. Figure 6 shows the four attack paths constructed by this process: (i) the attacker used a cross-site scripting attack (XSS) to steal the administrator's session ID and obtain the administrator's privileges ($6 \rightarrow 4 \rightarrow 3 \rightarrow 2 \rightarrow 1$); (ii) the attacker used a web application that does not sanitize user input (CWE89) to launch a SQL injection attack on the database ($6 \rightarrow 29 \rightarrow 28 \rightarrow 27 \rightarrow 26 \rightarrow 24 \rightarrow 23$); (iii) the attacker used a buffer overflow vulnerability (CVE-2009-1918) to compromise workstations ($6 \rightarrow 12 \rightarrow 11 \rightarrow 10 \rightarrow 9$ and $6 \rightarrow 19 \rightarrow 18 \rightarrow 17 \rightarrow 16$).

Because some evidence is missing and destroyed, the phishing attack observed on the client computers and the attack on the database server launched from the compromised workstations could not be constructed or shown in Figure 6. Also, because the available evidence used for attack scenario reconstruction was not validated using standards of acceptability, Figure 6 might not reflect the real attack scenario and, hence, would have little weight in a court of law.

5.   Extending MulVAL

This section describes the extension of MulVAL to support attack scenario reconstruction.

5.1   Using an Anti-Forensic Database

Abductive reasoning and an anti-forensic database are engaged by the Prolog-based framework to explain how a host computer might have been attacked when evidence is missing or destroyed [6, 8].

By using abductive reasoning, the extended Prolog logic-based framework is able to provide all potential general explanations about how an attacker might have launched a particular attack. For example, in order to explain how the database server in Figure 3 might have been attacked, the file shown in Figure 7 was created to query the extended

Table 3. Anti-forensic database.

ID	A1	D1	
Category	attack tool	destroy data	...
Tool		BC-Wipe	...
Technique	obfuscate signature	delete content	...
Windows	all	98+	...
Linux	all	all	...
Privilege	user	user	...
Access	remote client	local client	...
Software	Snort		...
Effect	bypass detection	delete data permamently	...

logic-based system to show all the attack steps that would result in "execCode(dbServer,user)" (attack on the database server) as the explanatory hypothesis. In Figure 7, Lines 2 to 5 require the system to list all the attack steps of "execCode(dbServer,user)" and write the results to the file `queryresult.P` (Line 2 opens the output stream for writing to `queryresult.P` and Line 5 closes the output stream). The returned query results indicate that three possible hypotheses could result in "execCode(dbServer,user)." They are: (i) using a compromised computer as the stepping stone; (ii) exploiting the vulnerability of the database access software; and (iii) using a legitimate database server account to inject malicious input.

After all possible hypotheses have been generated, the extended Prolog logic-based framework uses an anti-forensic database to select the best explanation. Table 3 shows an example anti-forensic database from [6], which instantiates the predicate "anti_ Forensics(Category,Tool, Technique, Windows,Linux,Privilege,Access,Software,Consequence)" in Line 1 of Figure 8 so that it can work with the hypotheses obtained from the corresponding abductive rules to evaluate if a particular hypothesis could result in the postconditions collected from an attacked computer when evidence is missing or has been destroyed.

Figure 8 is a codification of an anti-forensic database for the purpose of providing explanations in the face of missing or destroyed evidence. Lines 2 through 11 specify two rules that use the predicate "anti_Forensics(Category,Tool,Technique,Windows,Linux,Privilege,Access,Software,Consequence)" to evaluate if the hypothesis that the attacker has used the vulnerability in the database access software to attack the database is the best explanation.

In the first rule (Lines 2–7), the head "vulHyp(H,_vulID,Software, Range,Consequence)" (the hypothetical vulnerability the attacker might

1. anti_Forensics(Category,Tool,Technique,Windows,Linux,Privilege,
Access,Program,Consequence).

2. vulHyp(H,_vulID,Software,Range,Consequence) :-
/* The following three predicates are from the abductive reasoning result */
3. vulExists(Host,_vulID,Software,Access,Consequence),
4. networkServiceInfo(Host,Software,Protocol,Port,Perm),
5. netAccess(Host,Protocol,Port).
/* Introduce a hypothetical vulnerability */
6. anti_Forensics(Category,Tool,Technique,OS,Privilege,Access,Software,Effect).
7. hostConfigure(Host,OS,Software).

8. with_hypothesis(vulHyp, Post-Condidtion) :-
9. cleanState,
10. assert(vulHyp(H,_vulID,Software,Range,Consequence)),
11. post-Condition.

Figure 8.   Codifying the anti-forensic database.

have used) is derived from three predicates: (i) hypothesis obtained from
one of the results of Figure 7 (Lines 3–5); (ii) "anti-Forensics" predicate
in Line 6 where the variable terms ("Category," "Tool," "Technique,"
"Windows," "Linux," "Privilege," "Access," "Program" and "Consequence") are instantiated by the corresponding concrete data from Table 3 during a system run; and (iii) configuration of the host (Line 7)
where the evidence has been destroyed by an anti-forensic technique used
by the attacker.

In the second rule (Lines 8–11), the derived fact "vulHyp(H,_vulID,
Software,Range,Consequence)" obtained from the first rule is asserted
to the logic runtime database (Line 10) and the asserted hypothetical condition is checked to see if it results in the postconditions (Line
11). The predicate "cleanState" (Line 9) is used to retract all previously asserted dynamic clauses that might affect the asserted predicate
"vulHyp(H,_vulID, Software,Range,Consequence)." After the asserted
"vulHyp" is proved to cause the postconditions, the hypothesis is evaluated as the potential cause of the attack. Note that an investigator
should perform an additional examination or even simulate the attack
for the purpose of validation, especially when multiple hypotheses can
explain the same attack.

5.2   Integrating Evidence Standards

Federal evidence admissibility criteria place additional constraints on
evidentiary data and data handling procedures, which include chain of
custody. Whenever the admissibility of digital evidence is called into

question, five federal rules are applied: (i) authenticity (Rules 901 and 902); (ii) hearsay or not (Rules 801–807); (iii) relevance (Rule 401); (iv) prejudice (Rule 403); and (v) original writing (Rules 1001–1008) [8], the most important being the relevance criterion. If these constraints are not considered, the evidence runs the risk of being ruled as insufficient.

The federal rules were codified in the Prolog logic-based framework [9] to determine the admissibility of evidence. The original MulVAL rules only use positive predicates in order to control complexity. The extended version incorporates negation to disqualify unacceptable evidence during an admissibility judgment.

Extended logic programs have two kinds of negations: (i) default negation that represents a procedural failure to find facts; and (ii) explicit negation (classic negation) that represents known negative facts [14]. Because a default negated predicate cannot be used as the head of a Prolog rule, default negated predicates (expressed using "\+" in XSB Prolog) are used in the body of a rule to exclude impossible facts, and an explicit negated predicate (expressed using "-" in XSB Prolog) is used in the head of a rule to judge if a derived fact that represents the corresponding evidence holds. If the logic program that includes negated predicates, including explicit negated predicates and the corresponding rules, generates execution cycles due to negated predicates, then it is necessary to ensure that the program is stratified [3]. Figure 9 shows a stratified Prolog program that uses positive and explicit negated predicates to determine if an attacker can gain access to a host computer (i.e., web server or workstation in the example) using the network protocol and ports (Lines 9–12). The conclusion (Lines 13–20) shows that the attacker can access the web server via TCP on Port 80, but not Port 8080. As such, only the evidence based on accessing the web server via TCP on Port 80 is acceptable when constructing an attack scenario.

In addition to using (explicit) negated predicates to exclude unacceptable evidence, in order to accommodate the federal rules of evidence, rules related to "timestamp," "relevance" and "not hearsay" were added to enhance the determination of evidence acceptability. Predicate "timeOrder" is used to verify if the attack steps are constructed in chronological order and the corresponding evidence falls in a reasonable timeframe. Predicate "vulRelevance" models expert knowledge, bug reports and vulnerability databases to determine if the given evidence is relevant to the observed attack. Predicate "notHearsay" is used to ensure that the evidence resource is not declared "hearsay" (a verbal report is generally not admissible). Interested readers are referred to [9] for a detailed discussion related to the federal rules of evidence in the context of the extended MulVAL framework.

1. nnetAccess(H,Protocol,Port):-
2. nattackerLocated(Zone),
3. nhacl(Zone,H,Protocol,Port).

4. -nnetAccess(H,Protocol,Port) :-
5. nattackerLocated(Zone),
6. -nhacl(Zone,H,Protocol,Port).

7. nattackerLocated(internet).
8. -nattackerLocated(webServer).
9. nhacl(internet,webServer,tcp,80).
10. nhacl(internet,workstation,tcp,4040).
11. nhacl(internet,workstation,udp,6060).
12. -nhacl(internet,webServer,tcp,8080).

13. | ?- -nnetAccess(webServer,tcp,8080).
14. yes
15. | ?- nnetAccess(webServer,tcp,8080).
16. no
17. | ?- nnetAccess(webServer,tcp,80).
18. yes
19. | ?- -nnetAccess(webServer,tcp,80).
20. no

Figure 9.   Rule using explicit negation.

6.   Experimental Results

The framework was supplied with the experimental evidentiary data and the new evidence graph shown in Figure 10 was obtained. The new evidence graph has several differences compared with the previous evidence graph in Figure 6. First, the attack path ($Node6 \rightarrow Node19 \rightarrow Node18 \rightarrow Node17 \rightarrow Node16$) on "Workstation 2" in Figure 6 is removed. This is because the evidence is not acceptable as false negatives are used (According to MITRE's OVAL database, "Workstation 2" is a Linux machine that uses Firefox as the web browser, which does not support a successful attack using "CVE-2009-1918" that only succeeds on Windows Internet Explorer). Second, a new attack path ($Node1 \rightarrow Node42 \rightarrow Node43$) corresponding to the phishing attack on the clients launched using the compromised administrator's session ID is added. This is obtained by using abductive reasoning on predicate "exec(client,_)" and a further investigation of the declared "hearsay" (the clients' phishing reports). Third, an attack path between the compromised workstation and the database server ($Node27 \rightarrow Node38 \rightarrow Node11$) is added; using the anti-forensic database, the reasoning system discovered that the attacker used the compromised workstation to gain

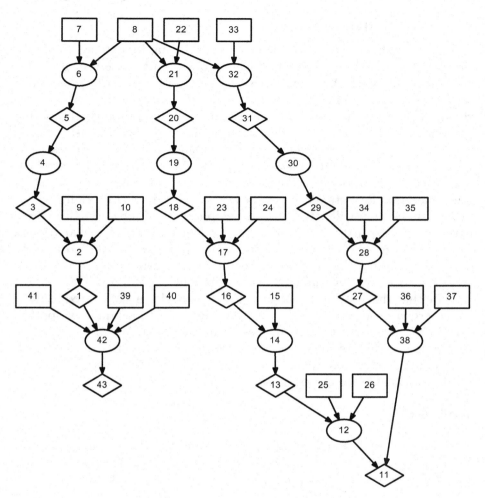

Figure 10. New reconstructed attack scenario.

access to the database server. Note that the reason why evidence could not be found is because the attacker was able to remove all the evidence using escalated root privileges that were obtained in a malicious manner.

Clearly, the reconstructed attack scenario obtained using the extended MulVAL framework (Figure 10) is considerably different from the reconstructed attack scenario obtained without the extension (Figure 6). This demonstrates that the extended framework can account for missing and/or destroyed evidence and can enhance the acceptability of a reconstructed attack scenario.

7. Conclusions

The network forensic model described in this chapter extends the MulVAL Prolog logic-based reasoning framework to automate the causality correlation of evidentiary data collected after a security event in an enterprise network. The extended model uses inductive and abductive reasoning, an anti-forensic database and legal acceptability standards for evidence to construct evidence graphs for network forensic analysis. The extension also excludes evidence such as false positives that are inadmissible and provides explanations for missing and destroyed evidence. In addition, it automates the process of using evidence that meets acceptability standards for attack scenario reconstruction.

Future research will attempt to develop a method for finding the best explanation of a network attack from among alternative explanations, validate the framework using realistic attack scenarios and work with attorneys to refine the evidence acceptability determination procedure. Also, attempts will be made to standardize the anti-forensic database.

Note that this chapter is not subject to copyright in the United States. Commercial products are only identified in order to adequately specify certain procedures. In no case does such identification imply a recommendation or endorsement by the National Institute of Standards and Technology, nor does it imply that the identified products are necessarily the best available for the purpose.

References

[1] O. Dain and R. Cunningham, Building scenarios from a heterogeneous alert stream, *Proceedings of the IEEE SMC Workshop on Information Assurance and Security*, pp. 231–235, 2001.

[2] H. Debar and A. Wespi, Aggregation and correlation of intrusion-detection alerts, *Proceedings of the Fourth International Symposium on Recent Advances in Intrusion Detection*, pp. 85–103, 2001.

[3] M. Fitting and M. Ben-Jacob, Stratified and three-valued logic programming semantics, *Proceedings of the Fifth International Conference and Symposium on Logic Programming*, pp. 1054–1069, 1988.

[4] J. Keppens and J. Zeleznikow, A model based reasoning approach for generating plausible crime scenarios from evidence, *Proceedings of the Ninth International Conference on Artificial Intelligence and Law*, pp. 51–59, 2003.

[5] C. Liu, A. Singhal and D. Wijesekera, Mapping evidence graphs to attack graphs, *Proceedings of the IEEE International Workshop on Information Forensics and Security*, pp. 121–126, 2012.

[6] C. Liu, A. Singhal and D. Wijesekera, Using attack graphs in forensic examinations, *Proceedings of the Seventh International Conference on Availability, Reliability and Security*, pp. 596–603, 2012.

[7] C. Liu, A. Singhal and D. Wijesekera, Creating integrated evidence graphs for network forensics, in *Advances in Digital Forensics IX*, G. Peterson and S. Shenoi (Eds.), Springer, Heidelberg, Germany, pp. 227–241, 2013.

[8] C. Liu, A. Singhal and D. Wijesekera, A model towards using evidence from security events for network attack analysis, *Proceedings of the Eleventh International Workshop on Security in Information Systems*, pp. 83–95, 2014.

[9] C. Liu, A. Singhal and D. Wijesekera, Relating admissibility standards for digital evidence to attack scenario reconstruction, *Journal of Digital Forensics, Security and Law*, vol. 9(2), pp. 181–196, 2014.

[10] MITRE, Open Vulnerability and Assessment Language: A Community-Developed Language for Determining Vulnerability and Configuration Issues in Computer Systems, Bedford, Massachusetts (oval.mitre.org), 2015.

[11] X. Ou, W. Boyer and M. McQueen, A scalable approach to attack graph generation, *Proceedings of the Thirteenth ACM Conference on Computer and Communications Security*, pp. 336–345, 2006.

[12] X. Ou, S. Govindavajhala and A. Appel, MulVAL: A logic-based network security analyzer, *Proceedings of the Fourteenth USENIX Security Symposium*, 2005.

[13] P. Sommer, Intrusion detection systems as evidence, *Computer Networks*, vol. 31(23-24), pp. 2477–2478, 1999.

[14] T. Swift, D. Warren, K. Sagonas, J. Friere, P. Rao, B. Cui, E. Johnson, L. de Castro, R. Marques, D. Saha, S. Dawson and M. Kifer, The XSB System Version 3.6.x, Volume 1: Programmer's Manual (xsb.sourceforge.net/manual1/manual1.pdf), 2015.

[15] W. Wang and T. Daniels, A graph based approach towards network forensics analysis, *ACM Transactions on Information and System Security*, vol. 12(1), article no. 4, 2008.

III

FORENSIC TECHNIQUES

Chapter 9

CHARACTERISTICS OF MALICIOUS DLLS IN WINDOWS MEMORY

Dae Glendowne, Cody Miller, Wesley McGrew and David Dampier

Abstract   Dynamic link library (DLL) injection is a method of forcing a running process to load a DLL into its address space. Malware authors use DLL injection to hide their code while it executes on a system. Due to the large number and variety of DLLs in modern Windows systems, distinguishing a malicious DLL from a legitimate DLL in an arbitrary process is non-trivial and often requires the use of previously-established indicators of compromise. Additionally, the DLLs loaded in a process naturally fluctuate over time, adding to the difficulty of identifying malicious DLLs. Machine learning has been shown to be a viable approach for classifying malicious software, but it has not as yet been applied to malware in memory images. In order to identify the behavior of malicious DLLs that were injected into processes, 33,160 Windows 7 x86 memory images were generated from a set of malware samples obtained from VirusShare. DLL artifacts were extracted from the memory images and analyzed to identify behavioral patterns of malicious and legitimate DLLs. These patterns highlight features of DLLs that can be applied as heuristics to help identify malicious injected DLLs in Windows 7 memory. They also establish that machine learning is a viable approach for classifying injected DLLs in Windows memory.

Keywords: Malware, DLL injection, memory analysis

1.   Introduction

Malware manifests itself in a variety of forms in Windows systems depending on the malware authors' needs and capabilities. For example, malware may run as its own process, as code injected into another process, as a service or as a driver. New techniques for executing malicious software in Windows systems arise occasionally, designed by malware authors in order to subvert detection and analysis. Each form of mal-

© IFIP International Federation for Information Processing 2015
G. Peterson, S. Shenoi (Eds.): Advances in Digital Forensics XI, IFIP AICT 462, pp. 149–161, 2015.
DOI: 10.1007/978-3-319-24123-4_9

ware has its own characteristics that distinguish it from others and each generates a different set of artifacts that may be used for detection.

Code injection describes any situation where malicious software might copy code to the memory space of an existing legitimate process, with the goal of executing the code either immediately or as part of a "hook" placed in the target process. Dynamic link library (DLL) injection is a form of code injection that inserts a malicious DLL into a separate legitimate process [7]. The DLL may be loaded directly at runtime or it could be loaded automatically the next time a process executes. This chapter focuses on malware that performs DLL injection to accomplish its goals.

Malware authors implement DLL injection for two primary reasons. First, injection provides a level of stealth to malware code as it executes; any actions taken by the DLL appear to originate from the process. Second, it grants malware the execution context of the "container" process. This allows malware to utilize system resources with the privileges of the host process such as the filesystem, registry and network access. If a botnet client needs to contact its command and control server, it may inject a DLL into a web browser to bypass host-level, process-specific firewalls that might otherwise block access.

This chapter explores the characteristics of malicious DLLs in Windows 7 x86 memory images. This is accomplished by executing malware samples in a sandboxed environment and acquiring memory. Volatility is used to extract features associated with a DLL sample, such as the host process, load path, base address and load count [16]. These features are analyzed to identify behavioral patterns in injected DLLs. Identifying these patterns serves two purposes. First, the patterns contribute to the general knowledge of malicious behavior in memory and can be used by forensic examiners as heuristics to aid in identifying malicious injected DLLs in Windows 7 memory images. Second, the patterns define characteristics of malicious injected DLLs that can help distinguish between malicious and legitimate DLLs. Distinctive behavioral patterns are necessary for machine learning to produce a robust model for reliably classifying new data. Machine learning has previously been used to classify malicious PE (portable executable) files using static and dynamic features [11]. Preliminary analysis reveals that it is also viable for classifying malware in Windows memory images.

This research makes two principal contributions. The first is a procedure for generating and processing large quantities of infected memory images to identify injected DLLs. The second contribution is the extraction of behavioral information drawn from the data as it relates to malicious and legitimate DLLs in a system.

2. Motivation

Several challenges are associated with identifying the use of malicious DLLs by a process. The use of legitimate DLLs by a process may make it more difficult to identify malicious DLL use. The variety of techniques used to inject malicious code, including DLLs, further increases the difficulty. This research address the complex and dynamic nature of DLL usage to identify DLLs in memory images that are considered to be malicious.

Runtime dynamic linking occurs when a DLL is loaded at runtime by a process or another DLL. A DLL loaded in this manner provides some required functionality and may be unloaded shortly after the requirement is met or it may persist within the process. Legitimate software that provides plug-in or add-on interfaces frequently uses this capability [12]. This leads to discrepancies in the DLLs loaded by a process based on the point in time at which its DLL list is examined.

Malware may be injected as a DLL into a running process by utilizing the same system code that is used to load legitimate runtime DLLs. The use of an identical loading mechanism enables malicious DLLs to better blend in with their legitimate counterparts. Many of the artifacts generated by this loading process are the same as, or at least not significantly different from, other legitimate DLL loading artifacts.

3. Related Work

While this work focuses on the effective identification of DLL injection events during dynamic analysis, a body of research covers the more general problem of detecting malware in memory. The Blacksheep rootkit detector [2], for example, compares memory images from multiple systems to perform a variety of analyses. Blacksheep compares the loaded kernel modules between memory images as well as the code in the kernel space itself. Kernel data structures and entry points to kernel code are also checked for differences. After the comparison procedure, memory images are clustered based on their combined distances from each other based on the comparison features.

Mandiant's Memoryze [8], when incorporated as a part of the Redline investigation tool, can be used to scan memory images and apply heuristics to assign scores to objects in memory that could be malicious. Other commercial products, such as Malwarebytes [1], scan memory in search of malicious software. However, the mechanisms and criteria used by these products are not always transparent and little information is published on the techniques that determine the features used to cluster and identify malicious code.

Gionta et al. [5] have designed an architecture for memory virus scanning as a service. The architecture allows for the efficient acquisition and scanning of memory in massive virtual environments. In this way, in-depth memory analysis techniques, such as those described in this chapter, can be efficiently used with minimal impact on virtual machine operations.

In the general case, determining if a piece of software would exhibit malicious behavior is undecidable [3]; extensive reverse engineering is typically required to understand the functionality of the underlying code and craft detection signatures. Signature-based scanners are grossly inadequate for detecting sophisticated modern malware [6]. This has led to the use of machine learning for classifying software as benign or malicious [11]. The research in this area is extensive, but the focus is normally on identifying features in a Windows PE file such as byte n-grams, API calls and opcodes, and using the features to train a classifier. The features listed in this work are based on in-memory structures and the way that observed malware uses the structures. However, there is some overlap with existing research because features are extracted from PE headers in memory.

4.   Test Data Generation

The test data was generated from a set of 33,160 malware samples obtained in 2012 from VirusShare [14]. The malware samples were subsequently processed by VirusTotal [15]: 97.29% of the samples were labeled as malicious by ten or more scanners. Additional verification was done using Metascan [10], which labeled 97.16% of the samples as malicious with a minimum detection rate of ten scanners.

The malware samples were then processed using the Cuckoo Sandbox [4]. The samples were submitted to a SQLite database where they were queued until they were processed. The Cuckoo host sent each queued sample to a Cuckoo analysis virtual machine running Windows 7 x86 with 512 MB of allocated memory. Since the sandbox does not provide external access to the Internet, INetSim was used to simulate various services; this caused some malware to exhibit additional functionality. The malware was executed in the Cuckoo analysis virtual machine for four minutes while being monitored by the Cuckoo agent, which runs as a Python script in the Cuckoo analysis virtual machine. The data collected about the malware included Windows API calls; network, registry and file interactions; and a memory capture of the system after malware execution. After this data was collected and compressed on disk, the Cuckoo analysis virtual machine was restored to the baseline

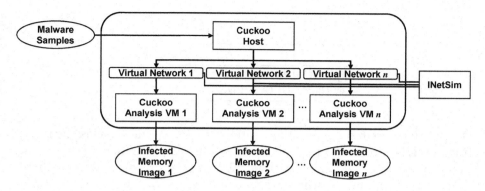

Figure 1. Data generation process.

snapshot and the next piece of malware from the queue was passed to the virtual machine. Figure 1 illustrates the process. Note that the data collected from Cuckoo by processing a piece of malware is referred to as a "cuckoo sample." A total of 33,160 cuckoo samples were generated.

While each cuckoo sample contains several types of information related to the execution of a piece of malware, this work focuses on data obtained solely from infected memory images. Volatility [16] was used to extract DLL artifacts from each memory image. The virtual address descriptor tree was traversed for each process to find nodes containing the mapped files. Artifacts were extracted from data structures associated with each node, including _LDR_DATA_TABLE_ENTRY, _MM-VAD and _EPROCESS. The artifacts were combined to create a data point describing a given DLL.

5. Data Classification

Each memory image in the dataset had between 615 and 1,645 loaded DLLs. Each of these DLL data points had to be classified before analysis could be performed. A DLL and its host process were classified into one of four categories:

- Legitimate processes containing legitimate DLLs.

- Legitimate processes containing malicious DLLs.

- Malicious processes containing legitimate DLLs.

- Malicious processes containing malicious DLLs.

A whitelist of all the files was created from the baseline snapshot of the analysis virtual machine. For a given data point, the process and

Table 1.   Dataset distribution.

	All	Unique
Injected DLLs	2,385	1,168
Legitimate DLLs	162,567	152,883

DLL were compared against the whitelist to determine the classification. Injected DLLs refers to DLLs categorized as "Legitimate processes containing malicious DLLs." Legitimate DLLs refers to either "Legitimate processes containing legitimate DLLs" or "Malicious processes containing legitimate DLLs." This work has opted to use the latter category because it provides a greater variety of legitimate DLLs than the former.

Each memory image contained the same legitimate processes. The processes tended to load the same DLLs across memory images, so using the set of "Legitimate processes containing legitimate DLLs" yielded large sets of repeated DLLs. When a malicious process is executed, it typically loads several system DLLs it requires for execution. These DLLs may not have been loaded by any of the other legitimate processes. Because the focus is on the DLLs and their behavior and appearance in memory, as long as they are legitimate, the nature of the loading process (whether malicious or legitimate) does not affect the analysis.

6.   Injected DLL Characteristics

This section discusses the various characteristics identified in the injected DLLs. The characteristics drawn from the set of injected DLLs were contrasted with those of legitimate DLLs where appropriate. As mentioned above, 33,160 cuckoo samples were generated for the study; 955 of the samples exhibited DLL injection behavior. It is plausible that more samples than the 955 identified performed DLL injection, but they did not in this instance due to the lack of a required resource (e.g., configuration file, Internet connection or installed software).

The analyzed data was split into two subsets. The first subset contained all the injected DLLs and all the legitimate DLLs, 2,385 and 162,567 DLLs, respectively. The second subset contained the unique injected and legitimate DLLs for a given memory image, 1,168 and 152,883 DLLs, respectively. Table 1 shows the dataset distribution.

Target Processes.   Malware that injects DLLs must specify a target process to host the malicious code. Figure 2 shows the target processes. In the dataset used in the study, some processes are more common than others. The most common processes targeted for injection

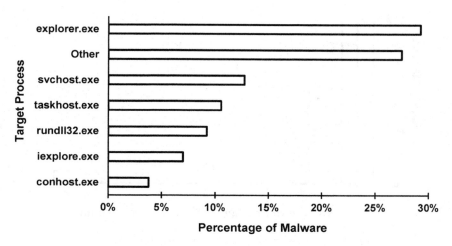

Figure 2. Target processes.

were `explorer.exe`, `svchost.exe` and `taskhost.exe`, accounting for more than 52% of injections. Each of these processes always runs on a Windows system and presents a large and/or varied set of DLLs at runtime. For example, `explorer.exe` had an average of 210 legitimate DLLs loaded at one time, and several instances of `svchost.exe` and `taskhost.exe` were typically in execution.

Number of Injections. A malware sample can choose to inject a DLL into any running process. Injecting DLLs into multiple processes can provide malware with greater survivability and versatility, but it also increases the chances of detection. In the dataset, 955 malware samples injected a DLL into a process. Figure 3 shows the number of injections per malware sample. Sixty percent (573) of the 955 samples targeted a single process while the remaining 40% (382) targeted two or more processes.

Simultaneous Loads. When malware injects a DLL into several processes, it often iterates through the active processes and injects the DLL as it finds its target(s). For malware that loaded into multiple processes, the load time extracted from _LDR_DATA_TABLE_ENTRY was examined to see how many DLLs had approximately the same load time. For a given DLL within a memory image, the DLL load time was compared against its load time in all the other processes containing the DLL. For every load time within one second, the simultaneous load value of the DLL was incremented by one (1). If the DLL appeared in multiple processes, but did not share a load time, then a value of zero (0) was

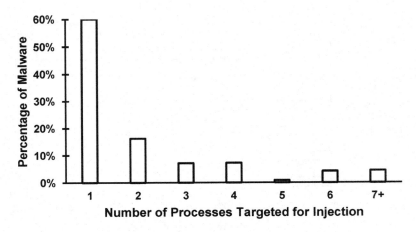

Figure 3.   Number of injections per malware sample.

assigned. If a DLL existed only once within an entire memory image, a value of minus one (-1) was assigned. Of the DLLs that existed in more than one process (those with a value of zero (0) or greater), the number of DLLs detected with at least one simultaneous load for injected DLLs was 73.3%. For legitimate DLLs, the corresponding percentage was 45.4%. This shows that malicious DLLs tend to have approximately the same load times whereas the load times of legitimate DLLs are more varied.

Load Position.   The *InLoadOrderModuleList* is a doubly linked list of _LDR_DATA_TABLE_ENTRY structures. The list is ordered based on when a DLL was loaded into a process, with the executable occupying the first position. The beginning entries are occupied by dynamically linked DLLs named in the import address table. DLLs loaded at runtime naturally appear at the end of the list. Some loaded DLLs are volatile in that they are loaded and unloaded repeatedly during the lifetime of a process while others are more stable, remaining loaded for longer periods of time.

The load position was calculated for each DLL that existed in the *InLoadOrderModuleList*. The average load position was calculated for injected and legitimate DLLs. The average load position for all the injected DLLs was 83.7. The average load position for legitimate DLLs was 52.6. Note that the system ran for a short period of time, which may have affected the reliability of the results. Depending on the number of DLLs unloaded by a process, an injected DLL may appear closer to the beginning of the list.

Init Position. Similar to the *InLoadOrderModuleList*, the *InInitializationOrderModuleList* represents the order in which the DLLMain function of a DLL was executed. The average init position for all the injected DLLs was 87.4. The average init position for legitimate DLLs was 51.3. This result may also be affected by the short execution time of the analysis system.

Base Address. The base address is the virtual address in a process where a DLL is loaded. The default base address for DLLs is 0x10000000. Since a process normally contains multiple DLLs and only one DLL can occupy a given virtual address within a process, many DLLs contain a .reloc section in the PE header that specifies how to translate its offsets. In all, 48% of the unique injected DLLs were loaded at the virtual address 0x10000000; this is in sharp contrast to legitimate system DLLs, for which 99.99% of the DLLs were loaded at an address other than 0x10000000.

Exported Function Count. The number of functions exported by each DLL were extracted and used to calculate the means and modes for the injected and legitimate DLLs. The injected DLLs exported considerably fewer functions on the average, with a mode of 2 and a mean of 13. Legitimate DLLs had a mode of 11 and a mean of 368.

Imported Function Count. The number of functions imported by each DLL were extracted and used to calculate the means and modes for the injected and legitimate DLLs. The mode of each type of DLL was similar with injected DLLs and legitimate DLLs having modes of 213 and 198, respectively. The means for injected DLLs and legitimate DLLs were 115 and 257, respectively.

Loaded from Temp. A common heuristic when looking for malware is searching binaries loaded from a temporary directory such as *%TEMP%* (*C:\Users\UserName\AppData\Local\Temp*). In all, 20% of the unique injected DLLs were loaded from a directory with *temp* in the path. Nearly all of these were from *%TEMP%*, but a small number were from the directories *C:\temp* or *C:\Windows\temp*.

Load Paths. Figure 4 shows the most common load paths for injected legitimate DLLs. In the case of legitimate DLLs, 97% were loaded from *C:\Windows\System32* or *C:\Windows\System32\en-us*.

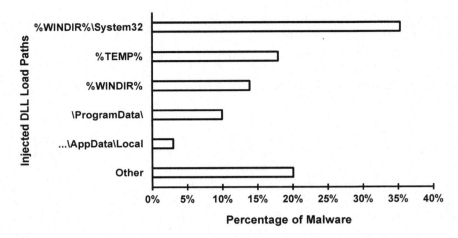

Figure 4. Malicious load paths.

COM Server. The Component Object Model (COM) is an interface standard used in the Windows operating system. It enables software to call code hosted by other software components without in-depth knowledge of its implementation. The calling component is the client and the hosting component is the server. Malware writers sometimes leverage the COM infrastructure to implement malicious code [13]. A COM server is required to export at least two Windows API functions: `DllGetClassObject` [9] and `DllCanUnloadNow` [9]. If these two API calls are seen in the exports of a DLL, then it is considered to be a COM server. Only 5.2% of the unique injected DLLs were implemented as COM servers.

COM Client. Windows binaries can call COM objects as clients. In order to use COM objects, the binary must call the `OleInitialize` [9] or `CoInitializeEx` [9] functions. DLLs importing either of these functions were considered to be COM clients. Only 2.1% of the unique injected DLLs in the dataset were capable of calling COM objects.

7.   Threats to Validity

Certain issues have to be accounted for in the generation process. The analysis described above was restricted to a specific Windows operating system version on a single architecture. While all versions of Windows share the same general linking and loading procedures, the details of the mechanism can change over time and across architectures. In the case of "user-land" malware, the details of the mechanism may not impact the results for newer versions of the operating system, but the behavior of malware that operates with elevated privileges may vary. This may be countered in future work by performing the data gathering and processing on multiple virtual machines with different operating system versions. The manner in which the resulting data is stored may have to be restructured to account for multiple DLL datasets for the different circumstances under which malware was executed.

Another issue is that the behavior of malicious software (and non-malicious software in the sandbox virtual machine) may vary based on the availability and status of the environmental resources and settings. Malware may choose not to act unless it determines that it can establish a "real" connection to a command and control server across the public Internet. It may choose not to inject DLLs into other processes unless it can detect the presence of email servers, active directory services or network shares. This would impact the ability to gather adequate DLL data, although it could be resolved by improving the fidelity and capability of virtual sandbox environments.

No additional software was installed on the system beyond the base installation. The legitimate DLLs referenced in this work are all Windows system DLLs. The behavior of third-party application DLLs may differ from that of the Windows system DLLs.

8.   Conclusions

The research described in this chapter generated Windows 7 x86 memory images for 33,160 malware samples obtained from VirusShare. The malware samples were executed in Cuckoo Sandbox, a sandboxed dynamic analysis environment. The memory images were processed using Volatility to extract several artifacts associated with DLLs. DLLs that had been injected into legitimate processes were identified. From among the 33,160 cuckoo samples that were generated, 955 samples injected a total of 2,385 (1,168 unique) DLLs into legitimate processes. There were also 162,567 (152,883 unique) legitimate DLLs in the dataset. Analysis of this data revealed several characteristics of malicious injected DLLs and legitimate Windows DLLs. The characteristics contribute to the understanding of malicious DLLs and can be applied as heuristics to assist in identifying malware in Windows memory images. Additionally, they demonstrate the applicability of machine learning to the identification of malicious DLLs in Windows memory images.

Future research will examine other forms of in-memory malware such as processes and drivers. The research will employ a similar methodology to identify characteristics that can assist in distinguishing malicious processes and drivers from their benign counterparts. The characteristics presented in this work will be used to build a feature set for training a machine learning classifier to identify malicious DLLs in memory. Feature selection algorithms will be applied to determine the most useful features and the resulting feature set will be evaluated using a variety of algorithms.

Acknowledgement

The authors wish to thank Puntitra Sawadpong for her assistance in formatting and proofreading this chapter.

References

[1] P. Arntz, Memory scan, Malwarebytes Unpacked, Official Security Blog, Malwarebytes, San Jose, California (`blog.malwarebytes.org/development/2014/03/memory-scan`), March 21, 2014.

[2] A. Bianchi, Y. Shoshitaishvili, C. Kruegel and G. Vigna, Blacksheep: Detecting compromised hosts in homogeneous crowds, *Proceedings of the ACM Conference on Computer and Communications Security*, 341–352, 2012.

[3] M. Christodorescu, S. Jha, S. Seshia, D. Song and R. Bryant, Semantics-aware malware detection, *Proceedings of the IEEE Symposium on Security and Privacy*, pp. 32–46, 2005.

[4] Cuckoo Foundation, Cuckoo Sandbox 1.2 (`www.cuckoosandbox.org`), 2014.

[5] J. Gionta, A. Azab, W. Enck, P. Ning and X. Zhang, SEER: Practical memory virus scanning as a service, *Proceedings of the Thirtieth Annual Computer Security Applications Conference*, pp. 186–195, 2014.

[6] D. Goodin, Antivirus pioneer Symantec declares AV "dead" and "doomed to failure," *Ars Technica*, May 5, 2014.

[7] M. Hale Ligh, A. Case, J. Levy and A. Walters, *The Art of Memory Forensics: Detecting Malware and Threats in Windows, Linux and Mac Memory*, John Wiley and Sons, Indianapolis, Indiana, 2014.

[8] Mandiant, Memoryze: Find evil in live memory, Alexandria, Virginia (`www.mandiant.com/resources/download/memoryze`), 2013.

[9] Microsoft, Windows API and Reference Catalog, Redmond, Washington (`msdn.microsoft.com/en-us/library/ms123401.aspx`).

[10] OPSWAT, Metascan Online, San Francisco, California (`www.metascan-online.com/en`).

[11] A. Shabtai, R. Moskovitch, Y. Elovici and C. Glezer, Detection of malicious code by applying machine learning classifiers on static features: A state-of-the-art survey, *Information Security Technical Report*, vol. 14(1), pp. 16–29, 2009.

[12] J. Shewmaker, Analyzing DLL injection, presented at the *GSM Conference*, 2006.

[13] M. Sikorski and A. Honig, *Practical Malware Analysis: The Hands-On Guide to Dissecting Malicious Software*, No Starch Press, San Francisco, California, 2012.

[14] VirusShare, VirusShare.com – Because sharing is caring (`www.virusshare.com`).

[15] VirusTotal, VirusTotal (`www.virustotal.com`).

[16] Volatility Foundation, Volatility (`github.com/volatilityfoundation`).

Chapter 10

DETERMINING TRIGGER INVOLVEMENT DURING FORENSIC ATTRIBUTION IN DATABASES

Werner Hauger and Martin Olivier

Abstract   Researchers have shown that database triggers can interfere with the attribution process in forensic investigations. Triggers can perform actions of commission and omission under the auspices of users without them being aware of the actions. This could lead to the actions being wrongly attributed to the users during forensic investigations. This chapter describes a technique for dealing with triggers during forensic investigations of databases. An algorithm is proposed that provides a simple test to determine if triggers played any part in the generation or manipulation of data in a specific database object. If the test result is positive, a forensic investigator must consider the actions performed by the implicated triggers. The algorithm is formulated generically to enable it to be applied to any relational SQL database that implements triggers. The algorithm provides forensic investigators with a quick and automated means for identifying the potentially relevant triggers for database objects, helping to increase the reliability of the forensic attribution process.

Keywords: Database forensics, database triggers, forensic attribution

1. Introduction

Database triggers are a feature of many relational databases. They were formally incorporated in the ISO/IEC 9075 SQL standard in 1999 and have since been updated [9]. However, the digital forensic community has not paid much attention to database triggers. While developing a new framework for database forensics, Khanuja and Adane [13] recognized that the actions performed by triggers are forensically important. Hauger and Olivier [8] have conducted research on the exact role that triggers play in database forensics. They studied trigger implementa-

© IFIP International Federation for Information Processing 2015
G. Peterson, S. Shenoi (Eds.): Advances in Digital Forensics XI, IFIP AICT 462, pp. 163–177, 2015.
DOI: 10.1007/978-3-319-24123-4_10

tions in a number of proprietary and open-source relational databases. Among other things, Hauger and Olivier discovered that the forensic attribution process is impacted by trigger actions.

Triggers can introduce side effects during the normal flow of operations. The side effects include performing additional actions or preventing the completion of the triggering operations. Certain types of triggers can also manipulate or completely replace the original operations. This means that what an original operation intended to do and what actually happened may not necessarily be the same.

As noted above, triggers can also lead to incorrect conclusions when the attribution of database operations is performed. This is because a trigger performs its actions with the same user credentials as the original operation that caused the trigger to fire. Some databases might log additional information with an operation to indicate that it was performed by a trigger. However, it cannot be assumed that such an extended log always will be available to a forensic investigator.

It is, therefore, important that a forensic professional be aware of triggers during an investigation. The first step is to determine if any triggers are present in the database under investigation. If triggers are indeed present, the next step is to establish if any of the triggers may have influenced the data being analyzed.

A database under investigation can potentially contain hundreds or even thousands of triggers. It is not feasible for a forensic investigator to analyze every single trigger to determine if it had an impact on the data being analyzed. A more efficient technique is required to identify the triggers that must be analyzed as part of an investigation.

This chapter proposes a test to quickly and easily establish if a trigger plays a role in the data of a database table being analyzed. A generic algorithm is presented that can be applied to any SQL database that supports triggers. The algorithm generates a list of triggers that potentially influence the data in a given database table, enabling a forensic investigator to focus only on the identified triggers.

2.   Background

This section briefly discusses forensic attribution and database triggers.

2.1   Forensic Attribution

Forensic attribution involves the use of technical means to establish the presence of a person or object at the scene of a crime after the fact [1]. In digital forensics, various techniques can be used to determine which actor, be it a person or a program, has performed specific actions in a digital system. However, determining the actual person responsible for actions in a digital system is problematic. This is because the physical person is located outside the boundaries of the digital system. Therefore, information from outside the digital system is required to positively link a specific person to the human-digital-system interface.

Attribution is performed during the digital evidence examination and analysis step. This step is part of the investigative processes as defined by the ISO/IEC 27043 draft standard [11]. The standard seeks to provide an overall framework for incident investigations and processing. It encompasses various other standards, each of which define the sub-processes in more detail.

Many digital systems create and maintain audit records and metadata [5]. These include dates, timestamps and file ownership, authentication and program execution logs, output files generated by program execution, network traffic logs and numerous other traces. The artifacts are created as part of normal system operation. They allow for the confirmation and review of activities as well as debugging errors.

A forensic investigator can employ authentication and authorization information to assist with the attribution process [5]. Authentication is implemented in many digital systems to identify users and grant appropriate system access. The access available to a user depends on the authorization afforded by the user's credentials. Unauthorized users are prevented from accessing and operating the system. Authentication information describes the actors in a digital system and authorization information describes the actions that the actors can perform.

Another attribution technique is to order and connect the various traces found in a digital system to create a chain of events [5]. The sequences of these events describe how the system reached a given state. By determining the actions that lead to the events and the actors that performed the actions, the person or program responsible for the actions can potentially be identified.

However, authentication information and the various traces are not infallible. Attackers can bypass authentication or steal the credentials of an innocent user. Traces can be modified or even removed to hide malicious activity. Furthermore, attribution techniques themselves can be abused by malicious actors. Stolen user credentials can be used to create traces that falsely implicate innocent users.

It is, therefore, important for a forensic investigator to attempt to obtain multiple independent traces that portray the same event. The independent traces can then be used to correlate the actions and identify possible manipulations. By excluding the manipulated information or reconstructing the original information, a forensic investigator can move closer to identifying the real actor or actors.

Olivier [15] has investigated attribution in forensic investigations involving databases. He noted that database forensics can use the same techniques as general digital forensics to perform attribution. The traces in a database are available in various log files and are also stored in system tables. The authentication of database users and the authorization of their operations is built into many databases. The same caveats that apply to general digital forensics also apply to database forensics.

2.2   Triggers

Database triggers originated in the mid 1970s in "active databases." It was not until the 1990s that this technology gained traction and was incorporated in commercial databases. The researchers at the time referred to triggers as event-condition-action rules [16]. The action portion of a rule was executed when the condition was true after being initiated by a triggering event. The condition was an optional part and a rule without a condition was called an event-action rule. The term database trigger was adopted when the technology was incorporated in the SQL standard in 1999.

Triggers are implemented for various reasons. Ceri et al. [2] distinguish between automatically-generated and manually-crafted triggers and suggest different uses for the two types of triggers. One use for manually-crafted triggers is the creation of internal audit trails. Developers now leverage this use case for auditing in their own external applications. When used for external auditing, the triggers normally take data from the original tables and store them in dedicated audit tables. Since the tables are part of the custom application, there is no particular layout or content. In general, the audit tables indicate which users performed operations, what operations were performed and when the operations were performed.

Independent of their usage, all the actions performed by triggers can be classified into two groups: (i) general actions; and (ii) condition-specific actions. A general action trigger performs its actions every time the triggering operation is performed. This makes the trigger suitable for general auditing. For example, a financial institution could use general action triggers to keep track of all the transactions performed on its system. A trigger would record relevant information such as the nature of a transaction, the time it was performed and the user who performed the transaction.

In contrast, condition-specific action triggers only perform their actions under specific circumstances. The circumstances are based either on the data that is manipulated by the triggering operation or on the user who performs the triggering operation. For example, a financial institution may have a legal requirement to report a certain type of monetary transaction that exceeds a specified amount. This requirement can be implemented using a condition-specific trigger that checks all transactions as they are executed. The trigger would only fire when a transaction type matches the type that has to be reported and the associated transaction amount exceeds the legislated amount.

Consider a situation where a financial institution might for security reasons only allow supervisors to execute certain transactions. However, due to the volumes of these transactions and the ratio of supervisors to normal operators, it may not possible to have only supervisors execute the transactions. To address this problem, the financial institution can implement an override that is invoked by a normal operator to enable him to execute a restricted transaction after a supervisor has authorized the transaction with his credentials.

Naturally, the financial institution would want to keep a very close eye on override transactions to identify any irregularities as soon as possible. A condition-specific action trigger can be used in this scenario to audit the restricted transactions. The trigger is created to fire only when a user who is not a supervisor executes a restricted transaction.

At first glance, it might appear that the two types of triggers would not interfere with a forensic investigation. However, one cannot assume that the triggers have not been modified by an attacker to perform malicious actions. For example, an attacker might wish to collect all the credit card numbers entered into a database. The attacker could set up his own general action trigger on the table that stores the credit card information or he could modify an existing audit trigger on the table. The trigger is created or the existing trigger is modified to place the credit card information in a separate location internal or external to the database. Another process is then scheduled to transmit the collected information to a location outside the financial institution from where the attacker can retrieve it at his convenience.

A malicious trigger can also be condition-specific. Consider a business that supports various forms of payment for its products and services. The attacker could add or modify a trigger so that it fires only when the payment method for a transaction is a credit card. This trigger then extracts the credit card information in the same manner as before. The attacker also may wish to perform malicious actions only when a specific user performs operations on the database. This could be because this particular user's actions are less likely to be scrutinized. Alternatively, the attacker may have a desire to implicate the user in the malicious actions.

3.   Trigger Identification

This section describes a systematic approach for identifying triggers that are potentially significant to an investigation of a database object. The approach is then formally specified as an algorithm that is database independent.

The simplest way to determine if a trigger has an effect on data contained in an object is to check if the name of the object is mentioned in the trigger. Having identified all such triggers, the next step is to manually check the kinds of SQL statements that refer to the object in question. Since SQL statements can be encapsulated in a user function or procedure, it is not enough to merely search the trigger content. The content of all called functions and procedures also have to be checked. Since additional functions and procedures can be invoked by a function or procedure, the contents of these additional functions and procedures also have to be checked. This process is repeated until the lowest level function or procedure has been reached that invokes no other function or procedure.

This top-down checking is formalized in Algorithm 1. To simplify the definition of the algorithm, procedures are assumed to be equivalent to functions. From a database perspective, there are differences between a function and a procedure. Some of the differences are general while some are database-specific.

Algorithm 1 (Top-Down): Identify all the triggers that directly or indirectly access an object of interest.

1. Assume that a trigger is an ordered pair (t, b_t) where t is the name of the trigger and b_t is the code (or body) of t. Assume that functions exist of the form (f, b_f) where f is the function name and b_f is the body of function f. The body b_x of a trigger or function x consists of primitive statements as well as calls to other functions. Let $f \in b_x$ indicate that f is used in the body of trigger or function x.

2. Let T be the set of all triggers and F be the set of all functions. Let ω be the name of the object that is the target of the search. Let $\omega \in b_x$ indicate that ω is used in the body of trigger or function x. Let R_1 the set of triggers that access ω directly. Then,

$$R_1 = \{t \in T \mid \omega \in b_t\}$$

3. Functions may be called by a trigger, where the function accesses ω, thereby providing the trigger with indirect access to ω. Therefore, the $\in$ notation is

extended to also indicate indirect access. The new relationship is denoted as $\in^*$. Then,

$$f \in^* b_x \Leftrightarrow \left\{ \begin{array}{ll} f \in b_x & \text{direct case} \\ \exists\, b_y \ni f \in b_y\ \&\ y \in^* b_x & \text{indirect case} \end{array} \right\}$$

Therefore, the complete set of functions used directly or indirectly by a trigger t is given by:

$$F^t = \{f \mid f \in^* b_t \ni t \in T\}$$

The subset of the functions that access ω is given by:

$$R_2 = \{t \in T \mid \exists\, f \in F^t \ni \omega \in b_f\}$$

The triggers that directly and indirectly access ω are then combined as:

$$R = R_1 \cup R_2$$

The algorithm produces a set of triggers R that refer directly or indirectly to the object (search target). At first glance, the algorithm seems simple and straightforward. However, a major problem arises when the steps are translated into SQL statements – How does one reliably identify other procedures in the content via string matching? The exact SQL syntax for invoking procedures is database-specific. It is possible to obtain the list of all the user function and procedure names and then search for each name in the content. However, this is not necessarily more reliable. Depending on the naming convention used by the database developers, the names of different object types could overlap (e.g., a table, a view and a procedure could all have the same name).

It is, therefore, necessary to design a new technique for finding the triggers that directly or indirectly refer to the object of interest. Alternatively, it is possible to start with all the triggers, functions and procedures and then narrow them down to only those that refer to the object of interest. Algorithm 2 formalizes this bottom-up technique.

Algorithm 2 (Bottom-Up): Identify all the triggers that directly or indirectly access an object of interest.

1. Assume that a trigger is an ordered pair (t, b_t) where t is the name of the trigger and b_t is the code (or body) of t. Assume that functions exist of the form (f, b_f) where f is the function name and b_f is the body of f. The body b_x of a trigger or function x consists of primitive statements as well as calls to other functions. Let $f \in b_x$ indicate that f is used in the body of trigger or function x.

2. Let T be the set of all triggers and F be the set of all functions. Let ω be the name of the object that is the target of the search. Let $\omega \in b_x$ indicate that ω is used in the body of trigger or function x. Let C be the combined set of all triggers T and functions F. Then,

$$C = T \cup F$$

3. Let U be the set of triggers and functions that access ω directly. Then,

$$U = \{c \in C \mid \omega \in b_c\}$$

Let U^t be the subset of triggers in set U. Then,

$$U^t = \{t \in U \mid t \in T\}$$

The subset U' of U without any triggers is given by:

$$U' = U - U^t$$

Let U_1 be the first iteration of a set of triggers and functions that access the functions in set U' directly. Then,

$$U_1 = \{d \in C \mid \exists\, e \in b_d \ni e \in U'\}$$

Let U_1^t be the first subset of all the triggers in the first set U_1. Then,

$$U_1^t = \{t \in U_1 \mid t \in T\}$$

The first subset of U_1 without any triggers is given by:

$$U_1' = U_1 - U_1^t$$

The sets U_2, U_2^t and U_2' can be constructed congruently. Specifically, the construction of the sets can be repeated i times ($i = 1, 2, \ldots$). Consequently, the ith iteration of set U_1 is given by:

$$U_i = \{x \in C \mid \exists\, y \in b_x \ni y \in U_{i-1}'\}$$

Furthermore, the ith subset of all the triggers in set U_i is given by:

$$U_i^t = \{t \in U_i \mid t \in T\}$$

Finally, the ith subset of set U_i without any triggers is given by:

$$U_i' = U_i - U_i^t$$

The combined set of all identified triggers $U^t, U_1^t ... U_i^t$ is given by:

$$R = U^t \cup U_1^t \cup ... \cup U_i^t$$

Since C is a finite set of triggers and functions, the algorithm reaches a point where set R no longer grows. Specifically, this is when the nth set U_n becomes empty, in other words $U_n = \phi$. At this point the algorithm terminates.

Algorithm 2 also produces a set of triggers R that refer directly or indirectly to the object of interest. However, it eliminates the need to search for calls to functions, which is difficult and database-specific. Instead, the algorithm repeatedly searches for known function and trigger names in the same way that it searches for the name of the object of interest.

4.   Algorithm Implementation

This section discusses the implementation of the proposed algorithm. Implementations are considered for the same databases discussed in [8].

The databases considered are all relational databases, so it can be assumed that data and metadata about triggers, functions and procedures are stored in relations. The most straightforward choice is to implement the algorithm using SQL. Each step of the algorithm is written as a simple SQL statement. SQL statements that are repeated are placed into functions. All the separate SQL steps and functions are then combined into a procedure.

An important point to keep in mind is that the database implementations available from vendors vary considerably. This includes the data dictionary that specifies what information is stored and how it is stored. Thus, in one implementation, retrieving all the triggers may involve just one select statement while in another it may require performing select statements on multiple differently-structured tables. Due to these differences, it is not possible to create template select statements that could be filled in with column and table names corresponding to a particular database. Instead, it is necessary to provide database-specific SQL statements for each database implementation.

A pure SQL implementation has two major drawbacks. The first drawback is that database vendors use different SQL dialects to extend the standard SQL statements. These extended features, such as variables, loops, functions and procedures, are required to implement the algorithm. Oracle uses an extension called PL/SQL that IBM DB2 version 9.7 and later support [3, 6]. Microsoft has a competing extension called Transact-SQL or T-SQL used by SQL Server and Sybase [12, 17]. Other databases such as MySQL more closely adhere to the official SQL/PSM extensions that are part of the SQL standard [10]. These differences would require a separate implementation for every database product. The second drawback is that the implementation has to be stored and executed within the database being investigated. However, this conflicts with the forensic goal of keeping the database uncontaminated.

Another approach is to implement the algorithm using a pure programming language. This provides the advantage of having to create only one application using a single syntax. The application is designed to read the database data from a file that conforms to a specific format. The drawback with this design is that the data first has to be extracted from the database in the correct format. This requires a separate extraction procedure for every database implementation. The extraction procedure also may have to be stored and executed on the database, which potentially contaminates the database.

The latter implementation choice involves a more involved two-step process. First, the required data is extracted from the database and transformed into the format expected by the application. Next, the standalone application is invoked with the created data file.

Thus, a hybrid approach that combines the advantages of the two choices is a better solution. A single application can be built using a conventional programming language that provides a database-independent framework for accessing and using databases. Next, database-specific formatted SQL statements in the application are used to select and retrieve data from the database under investigation. The database would remain unchanged because the algorithm logic as well as the SQL statements are external to the database.

The authors of this chapter are currently building a prototype that uses the hybrid approach to implement the bottom-up algorithm (Algorithm 2). The prototype comprises a standalone application written in Java that connects to the database being investigated via the JDBC programming interface. A JDBC database driver is required to handle database communications with each database.

The required data is selected and retrieved by executing database-specific SQL statements. These SQL statements, together with the database and JDBC driver configuration, are externalized to a definition file. This allows the pieces to be updated or changed without the need to modify the application. The architecture of the prototype enables it to be extended to support any SQL database with triggers by simply defining the new database, adding the required database and JDBC driver configuration and providing the SQL statements for each part of the algorithm.

5.   Implementation Challenges

This section discusses the challenges encountered when implementing the proposed algorithm. Some of the challenges are related to the general SQL syntax while others are related to database-specific implementation decisions.

5.1   Scope and Visibility

Most of the tested databases do not allow direct access to the data dictionary tables (these tables contain, among other things, lists of all the triggers, functions and procedures in a database). Instead, the databases provide access to the data in the tables via system views. The problem with the views is that they limit the results based on the permissions possessed by the user who accesses the view and on the scope of the database connection. Therefore, the user account employed to query the views must have access to all the database objects. However, even if the user account has the permissions to view all the objects, only the objects that fall within the scope of the connection would be listed. To work around this restriction, it is necessary to obtain a list of all the database scopes and iterate through them, changing the scope of the connection and repeating the query. The results obtained with each individual query are then combined.

5.2   Encryption

Some of the databases considered have the functionality to encrypt the contents of objects, including the triggers. This makes it impossible to search the content for the name of the object of interest. Due to flaws in current encryption implementations, it is possible to retrieve the decrypted content of an encrypted object [4, 14]. However, such workarounds are neither efficient nor practical. In any case, the flaws may be corrected in a future version, rendering the workaround worthless for the updated implementations.

5.3   Case Sensitivity

Since SQL is mostly case insensitive, the name of the object of interest may be spelled in many different ways. Therefore, searching the content for an exact match based on a particular spelling would be a hit and miss affair. The standard way to deal with this problem is to use lower case letters for the content and the object name being searched before executing the query [7]. This is usually done using a built-in function. The approach is feasible for a database with few objects that are to be searched. However, it would be very inefficient and impractical for a database with thousands of objects, each with thousands of lines of content. A better solution is to change the collation of the database to enable case-insensitive comparisons.

5.4   False Positive Errors

Since basic string matching is performed, any string in a trigger, function or procedure would match the object name. This includes comments, variable names and the names of other object types. Therefore, it would be necessary to manually check all the triggers listed by the algorithm and remove all the false positives. Since the SQL parser can identify comments based on the syntax, it is possible to pre-process the triggers, functions and procedures to remove the comments before initiating the search. However, other sources of matching strings could still produce false positives.

5.5   Data Types

Some of the considered databases do not store the contents of triggers, functions and procedures in table columns with the same data type. Many databases have moved from using the simple VARCHAR data type to one that can hold more data. Microsoft SQL Server, for example, uses the CLOB data type to store content while Oracle uses the older LONG data type. The problem is that all the data types that are used cannot be handled in the same way in the code. A more generic approach is needed to prevent the writing of various code exceptions. The approach would entail querying the database table metadata first to detect the data types that are used and invoke the relevant code to handle the specific data types.

5.6   Recursion

Database functions and procedures are allowed to call themselves either directly or indirectly. The recursion produces an endless loop in Algorithms 1 and 2. In Algorithm 2, R would stop growing at some point because no new elements are added. However, U_n would not become empty, which means that the termination criteria are never met. To address this problem, Algorithm 2 must keep track of all the elements seen in U_i' previously. U_n' should not contain any elements evaluated before and the following equality should hold:

$$U_n' \cap U' \cup U_1' \cup ... \cup U_{n-1}' = \phi$$

To achieve this, the second last line in Algorithm 2 is modified to:

$$U_i' = U_i - U_i^t - \bigcup_{j=1}^{i-1} U_j$$

This ensures that each function and procedure is only evaluated once.

5.7   Performance

The string matching component of the step $\omega \in b_x$ can be performed using the SQL LIKE command. The object name being searched can be located anywhere in the body of the trigger or function being searched. Thus, the SQL wildcard character "%" must be added around the object name as in "*%object_name%*." This makes the execution of the

SQL statement very slow because no index can be utilized. This does not pose much of a problem for a database with a small number of triggers, functions and procedures. However, the SQL statement can take a long time to complete if there are many such objects. This may occur in systems where auditing is performed with triggers or where the application utilizing the database performs a lot of transaction processing in functions and procedures. Depending on the time available to the forensic investigator, this could take a very long time to execute. It is also contrary to the goal of developing a quick test to establish trigger involvement.

6. Conclusions

A database trigger performs its actions under the credentials of the user who executed the database operation that initiated the trigger. Since the actions occur in the background without the user being aware of them, they can be abused by malicious actors. Malicious actions can be attached to legitimate operations and valid operations modified or even omitted. A forensic investigator who is tasked with analyzing these malicious actions could mistakenly attribute them to the wrong party.

Hence, it is important that a forensic investigator consider triggers very carefully when attributing actions. After suspicious data modifications have been identified, the forensic investigator must establish if a trigger interfered with the operations that lead to the data manipulation. Since a database under investigation might contain hundreds or even thousands of triggers, it is not feasible for the forensic investigator to analyze each trigger individually. An automated approach is needed to identify possibly significant triggers, which could then be analyzed in more detail.

The principal contribution of this chapter is an algorithm for identifying possible trigger involvement for a particular database object. The algorithm, which is simple and effective, is formulated in a generic manner so that it can be applied to any SQL database.

The prototype currently implements SQL statements for Microsoft SQL Server and Oracle. While the initial results are promising, more thorough tests are being conducted. Options such as moving the string comparison out of the database and into the prototype to enhance performance are being evaluated. The use of a local embedded database to temporarily store the content of all the triggers, functions and procedures is also being considered.

Future research will focus on optimizing the algorithm. Currently, only one object can be checked for trigger involvement at a time. Repeating the same check for every object is inefficient. Therefore, efforts will be made to search for multiple objects simultaneously in order to improve efficiency.

References

[1] M. Afanasyev, T. Kohno, J. Ma, N. Murphy, S. Savage, A. Snoeren and G. Voelker, Privacy-preserving network forensics, *Communications of the ACM*, vol. 54(5), pp. 78–87, 2011.

[2] S. Ceri, R. Cochrane and J. Widom, Practical applications of triggers and constraints: Success and lingering issues, *Proceedings of the Twenty-Sixth International Conference on Very Large Data Bases*, pp. 254–262, 2000.

[3] Y. Chan, N. Ivanov and O. Mueller, *Oracle to DB2 Conversion Guide: Compatibility Made Easy*, IBM Redbooks, Armonk, New York, 2013.

[4] D. Cherry, *Securing SQL Server*, Elsevier, Waltham, Massachusetts, 2012.

[5] F. Cohen, *Digital Forensic Evidence Examination*, Fred Cohen and Associates, Livermore, California, 2009.

[6] S. Feuerstein and B. Pribyl, *Oracle PL/SQL Programming*, O'Reilly Media, Sebastopol, California, 2014.

[7] P. Gulutzan and T. Pelzer, *SQL Performance Tuning*, Addison-Wesley, Boston, Massachusetts, 2003.

[8] W. Hauger and M. Olivier, The role of triggers in database forensics, *Proceedings of the Information Security for South Africa Conference*, 2014.

[9] International Standards Organization and International Electrotechnical Commission, ISO/IEC 9075-2:2011, Information Technology – Database Languages – SQL – Part 2: Foundation (SQL/Foundation), Geneva, Switzerland, 2011.

[10] International Standards Organization and International Electrotechnical Commission, ISO/IEC 9075-4:2011, Information Technology – Database Languages – SQL – Part 4: Persistent Stored Modules (SQL/PSM), Geneva, Switzerland, 2011.

[11] International Standards Organization and International Electrotechnical Commission, ISO/IEC 27043, Information Technology – Security Techniques – Incident Investigation Principles and Processes (Final Draft), Geneva, Switzerland, 2013.

[12] A. Jones, R. Stephens, R. Plew, R. Garrett and A. Kriegel, *SQL Functions Programmer's Reference*, Wiley Publishing, Indianapolis, Indiana, 2005.

[13] H. Khanuja and D. Adane, A framework for database forensic analysis, *Computer Science and Engineering*, vol. 2(3), pp. 27–41, 2012.

[14] D. Litchfield, *The Oracle Hacker's Handbook: Hacking and Defending Oracle*, Wiley Publishing, Indianapolis, Indiana, 2007.

[15] M. Olivier, On metadata context in database forensics, *Digital Investigation*, vol. 5(3-4), pp. 115–123, 2009.

[16] E. Simon and A. Kotz-Dittrich, Promises and realities of active database systems, *Proceedings of the Twenty-First International Conference on Very Large Data Bases*, pp. 642–653, 1995.

[17] P. Turley and D. Wood, *Beginning T-SQL with Microsoft SQL Server 2005 and 2008*, Wiley Publishing, Indianapolis, Indiana, 2009.

Chapter 11

USING INTERNAL MySQL/InnoDB B-TREE INDEX NAVIGATION FOR DATA HIDING

Peter Fruhwirt, Peter Kieseberg and Edgar Weippl

Abstract   Large databases provide interesting environments for hiding data. These databases store massive amounts of diverse data, they are riddled with internal mechanisms and data pools for enhancing performance, and they contain complex optimization routines that constantly change portions of the underlying file environments. The databases are valuable targets for attackers who wish to manipulate search results or hide traces of data access or modification. Despite its importance, research on data hiding in databases is relatively sparse. This chapter describes several data hiding techniques in MySQL and demonstrates the impact of data deletion on forensic analysis.

Keywords: Databases, data hiding, data deletion, index, InnoDB, MySQL

1.   Introduction

Strong interest in big data analytics has significantly increased the amount of data that is stored and accessed using high-performance techniques. Databases enhance the performance of operations, especially searching, and enable the reconciliation and linking of large data sets, while supporting the inclusion of many complex operations. Large corporations routinely use data warehouses with workflow engines that automatically enrich raw source data with operational information and data from other data streams. These databases are often massive and provide the foundation for many corporate activities (e.g., financial analysis and billing).

Large databases are perfect places to hide data, more so because they constitute a central and, usually, trusted part of an information technology environment. This trust is usually achieved by applying automated

© IFIP International Federation for Information Processing 2015
G. Peterson, S. Shenoi (Eds.): Advances in Digital Forensics XI, IFIP AICT 462, pp. 179–194, 2015.
DOI: 10.1007/978-3-319-24123-4_11

control systems, sanity checks and audits of the higher software layers, including the input data and results. The database itself usually functions as a black box due to its high level of complexity, massive data content, throughput and relatively opaque internal operations, often introduced to enhance performance. This also results in considerable background noise when examining the deeper layer of file operations; this effectively hinders classical forensic approaches. Furthermore, a database typically holds large amounts of sensitive data, making it easier to hide data inside the database instead of extracting the data and secreting it elsewhere.

Two types of techniques are used to hide data: (i) data removal; and (ii) data disguise. Data hiding seeks to make data inaccessible without leaving any traces while data disguise involves hiding data in other normal-looking data (e.g., using steganography). An important difference exists between data hiding and cryptography. According to Bender et al. [1], the goal of data hiding "is not to restrict or regulate access to the host signal, but rather to ensure that embedded data remain inviolate and recoverable."

The main requirements for data hiding techniques are [1]:

- Access to the hidden or embedded data must be regulated.

- The hidden data must be recoverable.

- The integrity of the hidden data must be ensured.

This chapter proposes several techniques for hiding data in database management systems using index manipulation. A novel approach is presented for evaluating the data hiding techniques. The practical applications of the techniques are showcased using MySQL/InnoDB index mechanisms.

2.   Background and Related Work

Databases not only store large amounts of information, but also substantial meta-information in order to facilitate fast searches and other operations on tables. Thus, considerable space is allocated that is invisible to database users, but that is, nevertheless, affected by operations and internal mechanisms. This section briefly discusses the use of database meta-information to hide data as well as the related topic of database forensics, especially forensic analyses of the index structure.

Traditional database forensics is mainly focused on analyzing the underlying filesystem layer to recover modified files [6, 13]. Internal mechanisms for guaranteeing database correctness and providing rollback functionality have been used for forensic purposes [4, 5].

Lahdenmaki and Leach [10] provide details of the internal workings of indices at a generic level, as well as related to database management systems and their underlying storage engines. They also discuss the efficient implementation of database indices, which is one of the basic requirements for creating slack space in real-world systems. Further analysis of the internal workings of index trees is provided in [11], where the possibility of using the structures for forensic purposes is also mentioned. Koruga and Baca [9] discuss how B-trees can be used for FAT32 filesystem forensics by searching for remnants of deleted data in the underlying navigation tree. Another approach utilizing the index tree for forensics is discussed in [12]: since the B^+-tree for a given set of elements is not unambiguous, the exact structure depends on the order in which the elements are inserted into the tree. Kieseberg et al. [8] have described several scenarios where manipulations of indexed data in a database can be detected by studying the structure of the underlying B^+-tree. Based on these observations, Kieseberg et al. [7] have proposed a new logging mechanism.

Pieterse and Olivier [14] have proposed some practical techniques for hiding data in PostgreSQL implementations. The techniques employ the SQL interface to hide structures, which makes them easy to implement, but also easy to detect in forensic investigations. In contrast, this research focuses on techniques that hide data deep inside the internal mechanisms, significantly hindering detection. Furthermore, several layers for manipulating query results are provided, allowing for targeted manipulations (e.g., of automated queries) without changing the results of manual investigations or audit routines.

3.   InnoDB Index

In InnoDB, data is stored in the form of an index tree based on the primary index, which is mandatory for every table. The data and the primary index are thus closely intertwined and directly affect each other; secondary indices are quite different because they solely exist for the purpose of speeding up specific searches. When creating a table, InnoDB generates an index for the primary key (an auto-incremented id-column is generated if no column is specifically selected). The actual data records are then stored directly inside the B^+-tree structure of the index. An additional index tree is generated for each secondary key, this index tree holds pointers to the respective pages in the primary key.

InnoDB uses a B^+-tree to locate pages. The first INDEX page in the tablespace is called the root node. All the data (keys and data records for the primary key and the corresponding links to the primary key pages in the case of secondary indices) are stored in the leaf nodes of the tree. All the other pages (i.e., inner nodes of the tree) are only used for navigation and do not contain any user records (note that, in very small tables, the root node may be the (only) leaf node). All the leaf nodes are sorted and are, therefore, implemented as a singly-linked list. For faster navigation within a page, InnoDB uses a page directory that directly links to every fourth to eighth element.

The index is physically stored in pages, which are containers of size of 16 KiB. The pages are stored in tablespace that resides in `ibdataX` files (global tablespace) or in `*.ibd` files if the `file-per-table` feature is active. Each `INDEX` page contains a `FIL` header, which incorporates meta-information about the page itself: an `INDEX` header with a lot of data related to the index, a `FSEG` header with certain pointers, infimum and supremum records and a `FIL` trailer containing checksums.

The user records are located right after the various headers in a page and are physically stored in order of their insertion. Next pointers are used for each record to create an ordered singly-linked list in which the infimum record points to the first record. The user records use the next pointer field to link to the next entry in ascending order. The next pointer of the last user record points to the supremum record that signals the index navigation algorithm that all the records of the page have been read.

4.   Data Removal

For performance reasons, InnoDB does not physically delete records. In fact, data records persist after deletion as a result of delete flags [2]. These garbage records are overwritten in the future if the space is needed.

As mentioned above, InnoDB uses a singly-linked list for navigation within a page. Specifically, InnoDB uses two `INDEX` header fields: (i) a pointer to the start of the free record list of a page; and (ii) a field that stores the number of bytes of deleted records. Figures 1 and 2 illustrate the deletion process of a data record (note that "@x" denotes an x-byte page offset, i.e., the physical data address in the filesystem). The garbage offset points to the first deleted record on the current page. As in the case of stored data records, InnoDB uses a singly-linked list for deleted records; the last deleted record points to itself, which signals the end of the list.

4.1   Physical Deletion of Data Records

When a record is deleted, InnoDB changes the deleted flag to one. Also, it updates the next pointer of the previous record in ascending

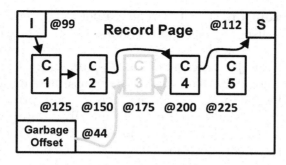

Figure 1. One deleted record.

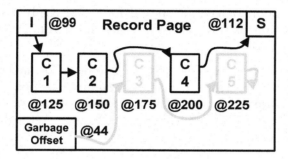

Figure 2. Pointer to deleted records in a page.

order and points to the next record or the supremum if the last record on the page is deleted. Additionally, the INDEX header is updated, i.e., the garbage size field is increased by the size of the deleted record and the pointer to the last inserted record is overwritten with 0x00000 (Offset: 0x0A). Internally, the last record of the deleted record list now points to the currently deleted record instead of to itself.

4.2 Forensic Impact

Previous research [2–4] has shown that physically-deleted records can be recovered by directly reading the filesystem. Several additional observations can be made based on the index and the actual algorithm that is used:

- **Timeline Analysis:** The design makes it possible to reconstruct the sequence of deletions using the next pointer of the singly-linked free record list of a page. A new deleted record is added to the end of the list.

■ **Data Retention:** InnoDB replaces deleted records in the page record free list only if certain conditions are met. First, a new record must be on the same page as the deleted record, which is determined by the structure of the B^+-tree. In the case of an auto-incrementing table, this is unlikely because new data records are only on the last page due to the incrementing primary key. If a new record is assigned to the page, InnoDB iterates over the page record free list to find a deleted record with the exact size. If the requirement is not met, InnoDB creates a new page and does not overwrite the deleted records. This method is very efficient, which is important for database management systems. However, it results in long retention times for deleted records, which is excellent from the point of view of digital forensics. Only a complete table recreation or table reorganization force InnoDB to overwrite deleted records.

■ **Slack Space:** InnoDB heavily uses pointers for navigation within pages. It is, therefore, possible to manipulate pointers to create areas that are not accessed by the storage engine, thereby creating slack space within stored files. This feature creates the basis for data hiding.

5.   Data Hiding

This section shows how the structure, and especially the removal mechanism, of the index can be used to create slack space for hiding data. The section also shows how to recover the hidden data. Several techniques for hiding data using the index are described along with their benefits and shortcomings.

5.1   Manipulating Search Results

In large-scale databases, data is usually retrieved with the help of secondary (search) indices to provide the desired performance. The dependency on the index can be used to hide data by making it invisible to common searches without actually removing the data from the table. This works by unlinking the index entries that point to the data hidden in the table from the rest of the index, but without modifying the underlying table. If this is done for all relevant searches and their indices, then the data is not retrievable via normal operations. However, the data can be accessed using SELECT statements that do not use modified indices or any index at all.

InnoDB uses two types of indices: (i) primary indices, where each table has exactly one primary index that is applied to the primary key

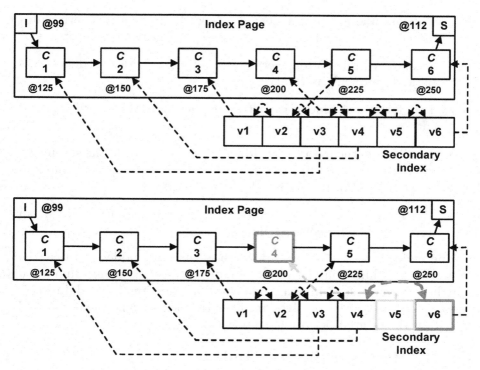

Figure 3. Manipulating search results.

of the table; and (ii) secondary indices that are used to enhance search performance. In this approach, the primary index is left unchanged and only the secondary indices are modified. This is reasonable because the primary index is usually an auto-incremented unique field that is not used for actual data retrieval in large databases.

Figure 3 shows how a secondary index can be manipulated to hide data. The index contains a copy of the indexed columns with pointers to the actual record pages where the records are stored. In order to hide a record, the links in the secondary index leading to and from the record and its neighbors are removed and replaced with a direct link between the two neighbors (e.g., v_5 in Figure 3 is unlinked from the tree structure and a new link is set to connect its former neighbors, v_4 and v_6). The record no longer exists in the search tree (secondary index) although it has not been removed from the primary index.

The following general approach is used to hide data:

- The table that will contain the hidden data is generated or selected. The primary index should be chosen in a way that makes it unsuitable for normal searches (e.g., by adding a generic auto-incrementing id-column that possesses the uniqueness property).

■ Secondary indices are generated for all SQL queries used to access table data during normal operations.

■ The data to be hidden is written to the table in the form of table entries.

■ The links to the data to be hidden are removed from the secondary indices using the approach described above. It is vital that the manipulation of the page index is not omitted.

■ The hidden data may be accessed using the primary index or an unmanipulated secondary index.

The main drawback of this approach is that the hidden data can be found by searching via the primary index or by employing unindexed searches. Nevertheless, in many real-world applications (e.g., data warehouses), all the queries involved in the extraction workflows are indexed to obtain the desired performance (e.g., for data cubes).

5.2   Reorganizing the Index

While the approach discussed in the previous section has merits, the actual pages holding the table data are still accessible by the database interface; only searching for them using secondary indices is thwarted. The countermeasures are to simply drop and recreate indices regularly or to use searches based on non-indexed columns or the primary index. Therefore, alternative techniques are proposed for hiding data inside the actual index pages. These techniques reorganize the next pointers to create slack space and force the database to skip the hidden records.

Figure 4 shows how a primary index can be manipulated to hide data. The index contains the actual data records, which are linked using the next pointers. In order to hide a record, the links in the primary index leading to/from the record and its neighbors are removed and replaced by a direct link. For example, C_8 in Figure 4 is unlinked from the tree structure and a new link is set to connect its former neighbors, C_7 and C_9. Also, the record must be removed from the page directory, which has a direct pointer to every fourth to eighth element to support faster searches within the page. Note that the directory has to be reorganized if the hidden record is referred to by the page directory.

The following general approach is used to hide data:

■ The table that will contain the hidden data is generated or selected.

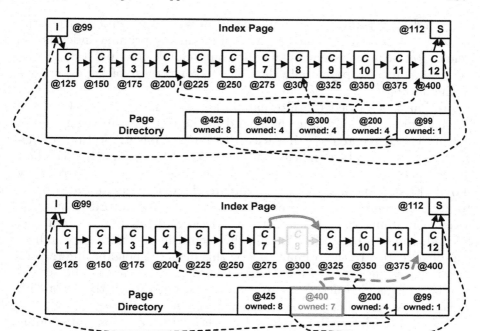

Figure 4. Reorganizing the index.

- The data to be hidden is written to the table in the form of table entries.

- The links to the data to be hidden are removed from the primary indices using the approach described in Section 5.1.

- The hidden data may be retrieved using classical forensic methods such as file carving on database records [2] or by reorganizing the pointers and using them to access the hidden data.

Note that the hidden records are still accessible via the secondary indices and have to be further hidden using the technique described in Section 5.1.

5.3 Hiding Data in Index Page Garbage Space

This section describes techniques for hiding data within the index pages, thus removing the data from the table altogether. These techniques can be seen as extending the original approach to the primary index. The main difference when removing a primary index compared with a secondary index is that the primary index constitutes the table content (i.e., all records belonging to a table are indexed by the primary index and any record removed from it is also removed from the table). The principal danger in manipulating the primary index is the generation of inconsistencies that not only enable manipulations to be detected, but also potentially destroy the correctness of large portions of the database.

Section 4 described the internal workings of data removal from the primary index by unlinking the record in the tree and linking it to the list of deleted records starting with the garbage offset. Section 5.1 described how secondary indices can be modified to manipulate searches. Thus, there are two starting points for hiding data from the primary index. First, it is possible to manipulate the delete operation in order to not link the deleted record to the list of deleted records; thus, the space containing the hidden data is not overwritten by the database. Second, the approach of unlinking the record in the secondary indices can be extended to the primary index; this links the neighboring records and removes the links to the hidden record. In the case of the second approach, it is also necessary to remove the links in all the secondary indices so as not to create inconsistencies in the database.

This approach can be extended to the primary index data hiding mechanisms (Section 5.2). Specifically, the hidden record stored in the table is unlinked as in the case of deletion, but it is not linked to the garbage collection. This also involves unlinking the record in every secondary index.

The following generic approach can be used to remove the data to be hidden from the primary index and, thus, from the table:

- The table that will contain the hidden data is generated or selected. No requirements are imposed on the primary index, especially related to its use in searches.

- The record holding the data to be hidden is removed from the table using a modified version of the delete operation (see the next step).

- When deleting the associated entry in the index tree, a modification of the delete operation is applied. While the record is unlinked from the tree as is done normally, it is not linked to the list of deleted records; thus, it is not marked as being available for future use. Since this is the only change with respect to the original deletion mechanism, all the secondary indices are updated normally.

- The hidden data may be retrieved using classical forensic methods such as file carving.

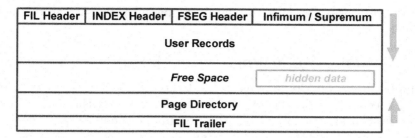

Figure 5. Physical structure of an index page.

The drawback of this method is that the insert and delete operations leave traces in the transaction log and other locations. This drawback is addressed by not hiding the data in the underlying table, but, instead, storing some arbitrary, unsuspicious data. Then, after unlinking the record from the index, the free space is filled with the data to be hidden using file carving. This has the additional benefit that the data can be changed later (i.e., the method is only used to create slack space that is not allocable by the database).

Unfortunately, navigation by file carving is rather tedious and inefficient if many reads need to be done. To enhance the usability of the slack space, a further enhancement is necessary. Analogous to the linked list of free space that starts with the garbage offset, the enhancement involves linking all the generated slack space in a page starting with a hidden page offset and a link to the first hidden record. The last record links to itself in order to signal the end of the list. This allows for easy navigation through the slack space in a page, because only the hidden page offset needs to be found by file carving.

Hidden page offsets can be linked together to further enhance searches in the slack space. This is done by generating a B^+-tree and creating a shadow index much like the primary index of a regular table.

5.4 Hiding Data in Index Page Free Space

Due to the physical structure of a page, some free space exists that is allocated by the storage engine but not used (see Section 3). Figure 5 shows the structure of an index page. New records are written to the user record space towards the FIL trailer in the order of their insertion. Simultaneously, the page directory grows towards the user records. If the two sections meet, the free space of the page is exhausted and the page is considered to be full. This free space is not used by the database management system and can be used to hide data. However, unlike the other data hiding techniques, this technique does not protect against overwriting because the database management system considers the space to be free.

5.5   Removing a Page from the Index

InnoDB uses pointers between pages to create a B$^+$-tree. These pointers are used to find the page where the requested data is stored. All the leaf nodes contain the actual record data, unlike the non-leaf nodes that only contain pointers to the next pages. All the pages at the same level are doubly-linked to their predecessors and successors. As in the case of index reorganization (Section 5.2), it is possible to change the pointers to unlink a page and use it to hide data. However, our experiments revealed that this approach is infeasible because, in general, a regular page contains considerable data that is also referred to by the secondary indices, which results in many additional updates. Furthermore, the B$^+$-tree has to be rearranged, which creates massive overhead.

According to the internal source documentation of InnoDB, the database storage engine accesses every data record exclusively via the primary index. If a record is not accessible via this index, the data record does not exist as far as the database management system is concerned. This architecture makes sense with regard to performance, but it can be misused for data hiding purposes as described above.

Since it would be imprudent to rely solely on the source code documentation, a new method was created in order to evaluate the data hiding techniques. The basic idea is to create a set of queries that are executed on a manipulated table space. A check is made if a test token that was hidden earlier can be retrieved and if the storage engine crashes as a result of the data hiding technique. It is impossible to cover all possible query combinations. However, it is feasible to use a fuzzy testing approach that generates a large test set that simulates a real-world environment and, because the navigation algorithms are limited, it is possible to guarantee with some certainty that all the query combinations are covered.

The `randgen` SQL generator (`launchpad.net/randgen`) was used in the evaluation. Originally designed for functional and stress testing, this tool implements a pseudorandom data and query generator. Test cases were generated using a context-sensitive grammar and input to `randgen`.

In the evaluations, only queries that actually rely on the existence of data (i.e., that reveal the existence of the hidden token) were considered. The following operations fulfill this requirement:

- `SELECT` operations
- `JOIN` operations

- INSERT operations with ON DUPLICATE UPDATE

Note that no functions, procedures, triggers, sub-queries or views were used. This is because they are handled by the same internal functions and mechanisms as the operations listed above.

The following (simplified) context-sensitive grammar specifying the SELECT syntax was used:

```
SELECT
  [ALL | DISTINCT | DISTINCTROW ] [SQL_CACHE | SQL_NO_CACHE]
  select_expr [, select_expr ...]
  [FROM table_references
  [WHERE where_condition]
  [GROUP BY {col_name | expr | position}
    [ASC | DESC], ... [WITH ROLLUP]]
  [HAVING where_condition]
  [ORDER BY {col_name | expr | position}
    [ASC | DESC], ...]
  [LIMIT {[offset,] row_count | row_count OFFSET offset}]
```

To generate a valid and adequate test set, the where_condition was used to force the database management system and the query optimizer to (preferably) use different types of index navigation (i.e., SQL caches, direct access and area searches).

The evaluation procedure executed concrete SQL statements derived using the grammar on a manipulated table containing the hidden token. A test case failed if the hidden token was not retrieved. When a failure occurred, MySQL internal tools such as EXPLAIN queries were used to determine the navigation algorithms that were used and the results were grouped into different categories: full-table scans (e.g., SELECT statements without an index or SELECT statements without WHERE conditions); direct access using a primary key (i.e., JOIN operations and WHERE conditions using primary key fields); and indirect access using secondary indices (i.e., WHERE conditions using a secondary index); and area scans using conditions (e.g., BETWEEN). Table 1 presents the evaluation results, including the availability of the hidden token using different queries and if the data hiding is persistent and resistant to accidental overwriting by the database management system.

Note that classical SQL uses full-table scans to create data backups. Due to its design, all the index information is lost; therefore, some modifications such as the manipulation of the search results would not be uncovered in digital forensic investigations. Such data tampering can only be detected by examining the live system. However, this is rarely done because of possible side effects to the production system.

Table 1. Hidden data accessible via an SQL interface.

	Full Table	Primary	Secondary	Persistent
Manipulating the search results	Yes	Yes	No	Yes
Reorganizing the index	No	No	Yes	Yes
Hiding data in index garbage space	No	No	No	Yes
Hiding data in index page free space	No	No	No	No
Removing a page from the index	Yes	Yes	No	Yes

6.   Conclusions

This research has demonstrated how indices in InnoDB can be manipulated in order to hide data. Five data hiding techniques were proposed, each with different characteristics and benefits. The techniques manipulate the underlying index structures, making it possible to hide data as well as create free slack space in InnoDB. Depending on the technique, the data may retrieved via an SQL interface by issuing suitable SELECT statements or by using advanced file carving methods.

An important practical application is the ability to adjust secondary indices so that hidden data still resides in database tables, making it available for sanity checks and forensic investigations. This is especially useful in the case of large data warehouses used for automated workflows. While the statements used in workflow routines are typically indexed to guarantee the desired performance, manual investigations usually target unindexed searches. Thus, it is possible to manipulate a database so that the hidden data is not accessible by indexed searches and, thus, also by the actual workflow, while making the manipulations invisible to sanity checks and forensic investigations. This also demonstrates that the results returned from a database using an SQL interface cannot be trusted.

The research also shows that an arbitrary amount of hidden slack space can be created in a database. The slack space cannot be searched or modified via an SQL interface and is, therefore, stable with respect to normal database operations. The slack space is especially valuable because it resides directly inside normal data files that are continually changed during normal operations, making additional changes practically impossible to detect via traditional digital forensic techniques (although file carving can be used to access the hidden data [2]). Additional structures are also implementable in this slack space in order to boost performance.

In conclusion, it is possible to manipulate and hide data inside databases with a potentially large impact on operations in data warehouses as well as on traditional filesystem-based forensics. Future research will extend the techniques to other prominent database management systems and will conduct large-scale case studies involving corporate databases.

Acknowledgement

This research was supported by the Austrian Research Promotion Agency (FFG) under the Austrian COMET Program and the Hochschuljubiläumsstiftung der Stadt Wien.

References

[1] W. Bender, D. Gruhl, N. Morimoto and A. Liu, Techniques for data hiding, *IBM Systems Journal*, vol. 35(3-4), pp. 313–336, 1996.

[2] P. Fruhwirt, M. Huber, M. Mulazzani and E. Weippl, InnoDB database forensics, *Proceedings of the Twenty-Fourth IEEE International Conference on Advanced Information Networking and Applications*, pp. 1028–1036, 2010.

[3] P. Fruhwirt, P. Kieseberg, K. Krombholz and E. Weippl, Towards a forensic-aware database solution: Using a secured database replication protocol and transaction management for digital investigations, *Digital Investigation*, vol. 11(4), pp. 336–348, 2014.

[4] P. Fruhwirt, P. Kieseberg, S. Schrittwieser, M. Huber and E. Weippl, InnoDB database forensics: Reconstructing data manipulation queries from redo logs, *Proceedings of the Seventh International Conference on Availability, Reliability and Security*, pp. 625–633, 2012.

[5] P. Fruhwirt, P. Kieseberg, S. Schrittwieser, M. Huber and E. Weippl, InnoDB database forensics: Enhanced reconstruction of data manipulation queries from redo logs, *Information Security Technical Report*, vol. 17(4), pp. 227–238, 2013.

[6] A. Grebhahn, M. Schaler and V. Koppen, Secure deletion: Towards tailor-made privacy in database systems, *Proceedings of the Fifteenth Conference on Database Systems for Business, Technology and Web*, pp. 99–113, 2013.

[7] P. Kieseberg, S. Schrittwieser, L. Morgan, M. Mulazzani, M. Huber and E. Weippl, Using the structure of B$^+$-trees for enhancing logging mechanisms of databases, *International Journal of Web Information Systems*, vol. 9(1), pp. 53–68, 2013.

[8] P. Kieseberg, S. Schrittwieser, M. Mulazzani, M. Huber and E. Weippl, Trees cannot lie: Using data structures for forensic purposes, *Proceedings of the European Intelligence and Security Informatics Conference*, pp. 282–285, 2011.

[9] P. Koruga and M. Baca, Analysis of B-tree data structure and its usage in computer forensics, *Proceedings of the Central European Conference on Information and Intelligent Systems*, 2010.

[10] T. Lahdenmaki and M. Leach, *Relational Database Index Design and the Optimizers*, John Wiley and Sons, Hoboken, New Jersey, 2005.

[11] H. Lu, Y. Ng and Z. Tian, T-tree or B-tree: Main memory database index structure revisited, *Proceedings of the Eleventh Australasian Database Conference*, pp. 65–73, 2000.

[12] G. Miklau, B. Levine and P. Stahlberg, Securing history: Privacy and accountability in database systems, *Proceedings of the Third Biennial Conference on Innovative Data Systems Research*, pp. 387–396, 2007.

[13] P. Stahlberg, G. Miklau and B. Levine, Threats to privacy in the forensic analysis of database systems, *Proceedings of the ACM SIGMOD International Conference on Management of Data*, pp. 91–102, 2007.

[14] H. Pieterse and M. Olivier, Data hiding techniques for database environments, in *Advances in Digital Forensics VIII*, G. Peterson and S. Shenoi (Eds.), Springer, Heidelberg, Germany, pp. 289–301, 2012.

Chapter 12

IDENTIFYING PASSWORDS STORED ON DISK

Shiva Houshmand, Sudhir Aggarwal and Umit Karabiyik

Abstract   This chapter presents a solution to the problem of identifying passwords on storage media. Because of the proliferation of websites for finance, commerce and entertainment, the typical user today often has to store passwords on a computer hard drive. The identification problem is to find strings on the disk that are likely to be passwords. Automated identification is very useful to digital forensic investigators who need to recover potential passwords when working on cases. The problem is nontrivial because a hard disk typically contains numerous strings. The chapter describes a novel approach that determines a good set of candidate strings in which stored passwords are very likely to be found. This is accomplished by first examining the disk for tokens (potential password strings) and applying filtering algorithms to winnow down the tokens to a more manageable set. Next, a probabilistic context-free grammar is used to assign probabilities to the remaining tokens. The context-free grammar is derived via training with a set of revealed passwords. Three algorithms are used to rank the tokens after filtering. Experiments reveal that one of the algorithms, the one-by-one algorithm, returns a password-rich set of 2,000 tokens culled from more than 49 million tokens on a large-capacity drive. Thus, a forensic investigator would only have to test a small set of tokens that would likely contain many of the stored passwords.

Keywords: Disk examination, stored passwords, password identification

1.   Introduction

Passwords continue to be the primary means for authenticating users. Because of the proliferation of websites related to banking, commerce and entertainment, the typical user necessarily maintains multiple accounts and passwords. Meanwhile, for security reasons, many websites have adopted password policies that force users to register passwords

© IFIP International Federation for Information Processing 2015

G. Peterson, S. Shenoi (Eds.): Advances in Digital Forensics XI, IFIP AICT 462, pp. 195–213, 2015.

DOI: 10.1007/978-3-319-24123-4_12

that conform to certain length, symbol and digit requirements. Since it is difficult to remember multiple, complex passwords, users increasingly save their passwords either on paper or on their computers. When storing passwords on disk, users typically use password management software or the password recall option provided by browsers or save passwords directly on their computers or cell phones. A 2012 survey by Kaspersky Lab [8] revealed that 29% of users do not remember passwords, but instead store them on media. The survey also reports that 13% of users create text documents with passwords that they store on their hard drives, 9% save passwords on their cell phones and only 7% use specialized password management software. As passwords become more complex, greater numbers of users will turn to storing their passwords on their computer hard drives. Indeed, an informal survey of 100 students conducted as part of this research revealed that 42% of the students store their passwords and 55% of these students save them on hard drives or cell phones without using encryption or specialized software.

Some researchers have developed techniques for extracting cryptographic keys and passwords stored in browsers [5, 10, 14]. However, a search of the literature does not reveal any research that attempts to distinguish passwords from other strings stored directly on disk by users. This problem, involving the identification of passwords in media, is the focus of this chapter.

An example scenario [4] is a disk containing encrypted files (of say illegal photographs) and there is a likelihood that the user has stored the passwords somewhere on the disk in order to easily access the encrypted files. A forensic investigator could review each saved file and attempt to determine, by context and structure, the strings that might correspond to passwords. This would, of course, be a very tedious task, especially if the disk has high capacity and holds numerous files.

Investigators sometimes use software tools to tokenize all the strings found on disks and incorporate them in dictionaries for offline cracking of encrypted files. However, it is often the case that the list of strings becomes too large to be used in dictionary-based password cracking. The identification problem is to distinguish the tokens that are likely to be passwords and winnow down the list to a manageable size. This problem is non-trivial because distinguishing the strings that may be passwords from a large set of strings has no obvious solution.

The solution described in this chapter first analyzes a disk image and attempts to retrieve all the strings that could possibly be passwords (these are called "tokens"). During the process of retrieval and subsequent processing, which is called "filtering," a potentially very large set of tokens is reduced to a manageable set that contains most of the passwords. This is accomplished by applying specialized filters to reduce the size of the token set. A previously-trained probabilistic context-free grammar [6, 16] is employed to decide which of the remaining tokens are likely to be passwords by assigning each token a probability. The probability values are used as input to ranking algorithms that produce ordered lists of tokens that represent possible passwords. The token lists can be used in dictionary-based password cracking.

This work is unique in its specification of the problem of identifying passwords on disk, its use of a probabilistic context-free grammar and its development of filters and ranking algorithms. Experiments demonstrate that the approach, on the average, identifies 60% of the passwords in the top 2,000 potential passwords returned to an investigator. Moreover, the approach is directly applicable to identifying passwords stored on cell phones and USB flash drives.

2. Related Work

Little, if any, research has focused on password identification in storage media. Garfinkel et al. [2] have studied the general problem of attempting to capture a storage profile of an individual computer to detect anomalous behavior. They propose the monitoring of the forensic content of the disk (or other media), such as email addresses and credit card numbers. The approach described in this chapter could, in fact, be used by their technique to capture potential password strings.

With respect to identifying passwords, many forensic tools exist for finding desired strings on disk; this means that the specific passwords being searched for are known. Forensic recovery tools such as EnCase and FTK can be used to find passwords on a hard disk, but these tools merely return a list of all the strings on the disk. As will be seen, the real problem is filtering the potentially large number of strings and determining the strings that are most likely to be passwords.

Sensitive Data Manager [7] is designed to search for data such as passwords, credit card numbers and social security numbers in several locations, including files, email, browsers, registry files, databases and websites. As far as searching for data on a hard disk is concerned, Sensitive Data Manager checks only the files that have metadata information available to the filesystem; it does not examine the unallocated space to search for passwords in deleted files. Sensitive Data Manager provides password search customization by enabling keyword and regular expression searches; this requires an investigator to conduct string searches as in the case of EnCase and FTK. Sensitive Data Manager, thus, does not tackle the password identification problem.

A related problem is to find a password that has been used to encrypt a file or to find the login password of a user. Hargreaves and Chivers [5] have attempted to recover encryption keys from memory; they demonstrated that if the memory is preserved when encrypted files are open, it is possible to find the encryption keys. Similarly, Lee et al. [10] have had success in finding login passwords by collecting and examining page files. Their work is interesting, but it is orthogonal to the password identification problem.

Attempts have also been made to find passwords that are stored by browsers. Chrome Password Recovery [14] is an open-source, command-line password recovery tool that retrieves login information (usernames, passwords and website links) from Google Chrome. However, it only focuses on recovering sensitive data such as encryption/decryption keys from encrypted Google Chrome password database files; it is not designed to identify passwords saved on hard disks.

3.   Background

This section discusses the principal concepts underlying the proposed solution to the password identification problem.

3.1   Probabilistic Context-Free Grammars

Probabilistic context-free grammars have been used to create better passwords as well as to crack passwords. This research uses a grammar to rank tokens recovered from a hard disk based on their likelihood of being user passwords. Specifically, the probabilistic password cracking approach described in [6, 16] is used to assign probability values to potential password tokens. In this approach, the base structure of a password is defined according to the component type (L for alpha string, D for digit string and S for special symbol string) and the length of the string is incorporated in the base structure. For example, the password string $alice123\#\%$ has the base structure $L_5D_3S_2$. A probabilistic grammar is then determined from a training corpus by calculating the frequencies of all the base structures and the component structures (of each length) found in the corpus. The resulting information is structured as a context-free grammar. For example, $alice123\#\%$ is derived as follows:

$$S \Rightarrow L_5D_3S_2 \Rightarrow aliceD_3S_2 \Rightarrow alice123S_2 \Rightarrow alice123\#\%$$

At each step, a probability is assigned to the rule transition. The product of the transition probabilities is the probability of the resulting string. As shown in [6], this approach can be used to compute the probability of any token given a context-free grammar derived from a realistic password corpus.

4. Examining a Disk

The goal is to identify passwords in files stored on disk by a user. Note that the assumption is that the user is not actively trying to hide passwords. In fact, the user simply stores the passwords in a file on disk that may or may not contain other text; this is done so that the user can easily access a forgotten password. The file may be in allocated space or unallocated space (i.e., the file has been deleted) or it may be hidden using the operating system.

A more sophisticated user might use specialized software to hide passwords in unallocated space in a partition, in file slack space or in some other non-filesystem space. Although this scenario is not the focus of this research, it should still be possible to find such data on the disk as long as encryption or steganography are not used. For example, if a user explicitly hides data or a file in the slack space of a file or partition, the slack space tool `bmap` or file carver `scalpel` could, respectively, be used to retrieve the data or file from slack space. The recovered data could be written to a text file for the tokenization process described in Section 4.2. The approach could fail under certain circumstances, such as when passwords are hidden in an arbitrary space on disk. Although the string stream could be viewed using a hex editor and the data echoed to a text file, it can be difficult to determine string boundaries when garbage data is intentionally or unintentionally added to the string stream. These circumstances greatly complicate the password identification problem.

4.1 Recovering Files from a Disk

The first step is to retrieve all the different types of files from the filesystem of a given disk image. This can be done using `tsk_recover`, a component of The Sleuth Kit, an open-source, digital forensics tool that provides several command-line tools for analyzing disk images. Note that `tsk_recover` can recover files from allocated space as well as unallocated space. This work specifically focuses on filesystems that are not corrupted. Files for which metadata information is lost or damaged are not considered. Data carving tools could also be used to retrieve files that might reside in other parts of the disk such as slack space, lost partitions and unallocated space in partitions. The tools could be used to create one or more files that could then be analyzed in the same way as the uncorrupted files.

4.2   Retrieving Tokens from Files

After recovering files from the disk, the next step is to extract the strings that are potential passwords. This is accomplished by extracting white-space separated strings from file types such as .doc, .docx, .xls, .xlsx, .rtf, .odt, .pdf and .txt.

Since some of the file types are not readable by text editors, these files must be converted to the text file format in order to be able to read their contents. The open-source tools, catdoc, docx2txt, xls2txt, unoconv and xls2txt, unrtf, odt2txt and pdftotext were, respectively, used to convert .doc, .docx, .xls, .xlsx, .rtf, .odt and .pdf files to the text file format.

Spaces, tabs and newlines were used as delimiters to tokenize string streams in a file; the associated text file was created by writing each token on a separate line. The resulting text files corresponding to all the files on disk were then searched to find potential passwords.

The accuracy of the tokens retrieved from the files is based entirely on the conversion performance of the tools. Two possible problems exist. First, some strings may be altered during the conversion process. Second, some new strings (i.e., not in the original file) may have been created by the tools. This latter situation only occurred when converting .xls and .xlsx files containing multiple spreadsheets for which the tool would add each sheet name. In the experiments conducted using the tools, a problem was rarely encountered during the conversion process. All the strings in the files were obtained, including from tables in .doc and .docx files and everything in the cells of .xls and .xlsx files. The only thing that was not obtained was text in the images residing in these files. Images sometimes create strings in the conversion process that are completely filtered out later.

4.3   Initial Filtering

Even an average-sized disk typically contains many different file types and files with text content; this results in a massive number of tokens. In order to reduce the number of tokens retrieved, rules were defined to filter some classes of tokens that are very unlikely to be passwords. Several revealed password sets (e.g., results of attacks on various websites such as Rockyou [15] and Yahoo [12]) were examined to obtain insights into the kinds of structures that are rarely seen in passwords. The following initial filters were defined and applied:

- **Non-Printable:** This filter eliminates ASCII characters that are almost always not valid password characters.

- **Length:** Passwords usually have certain lengths based on the password policy that is enforced. This filter applies a conservative bound and only tokens of length l, where $6 < l < 21$, are retained. In the Yahoo set, only 1.93% of the passwords have length less than seven and 0.047% of the passwords have length greater than 20.

- **Floating Point:** The files on disk (especially `.xls files`) often include many floating point numbers. It is a good idea to filter floating point numbers because studies of revealed password sets reveal that there is very little chance that such tokens correspond to passwords. Thus, this filter eliminates strings corresponding to the regular expression `[-+]?  [0-9]* .?  [0-9]+ ([eE][-+]?[0-9]+)?`.

- **Repeated Tokens:** This filter retains one copy of each repeated token in a file. One might assume that repeated tokens are unlikely to be passwords, but users often use the same password for multiple accounts, so there would be multiple instances of a given password string in a file.

- **Word Punctuation:** This filter eliminates punctuation patterns encountered in sentences. Specifically, tokens containing only alpha strings ending with one of the following characters ; : , . ? ! -) } were filtered. Also, tokens starting with (or { were filtered. An examination revealed that only 0.516% of such tokens were present in a sample of one million passwords in the Rockyou set.

4.4   Specialized Alpha String Filtering

It is obvious that English words constitute a very large part of every text file. Therefore, an extremely prevalent class of tokens found on a hard disk is the set of alpha strings (i.e., strings containing only alphabetic characters). This research considers various approaches for handling such strings. In particular, the following specialized alpha string filters are defined:

- **All-Alphas:** This filter eliminates tokens that only have alphabetic characters. The assumption is that the vast majority of passwords contain other symbols (e.g., digits and special characters). This assumption is validated by most password creation policies.

- **Sentences:** This filter eliminates all alpha strings that are only within sentences. The OpenNLP tool [1] was used to detect sentences after the file type conversion. This tool detects whether or not a punctuation character marks the end of a sentence. However, it cannot identify sentence boundaries based on sentence content. It only returns a set of indices for which each sentence (or non-sentence) is on a separate line. An additional problem encountered after the conversion process to a `.txt` file was that word wrapping was not preserved when line breaks were added; thus, sentences that ran over multiple lines were output as multiple indices by OpenNLP. Heuristics were used to detect indices that corresponded to sentences (and non-sentences). For example, an index that started with a capital letter and ended with a period [13] may be filtered.

- **Capitalization:** This filter eliminates all lower case alpha strings. This is because most password policies require passwords to have characters from one or more other classes (e.g., symbols, digits and capital letters).

- **Dictionary Words:** This filter eliminates alpha strings that appear in an English dictionary. This eliminates strings that are most likely words in sentences while retaining the remaining strings in the token set.

- **Multiwords:** This filter eliminates all alpha strings that are not multiwords. A multiword is a string that consists of two or more words in an English dictionary. Examples are passphrases (without whitespace) that are increasingly used as passwords.

5.   Identifying Passwords

This section focuses on the problem of distinguishing and finding a password from among a set of tokens. Specifically, after the hard disk has been examined and all the tokens separated by whitespace are obtained, a mechanism is required to distinguish passwords from other sequences of characters that appear in the text.

5.1   Calculating Token Probabilities

As discussed above, a probabilistic context-free grammar can be created from a large set of real user passwords. The probabilistic context-free grammar models a password distribution and the way users create passwords. Knowledge of the structure of passwords enables passwords to be differentiated from regular text.

Given a probabilistic context-free grammar, the probability of a string in the password distribution can be computed. This research employed the method described in [6] to calculate the probability. Each string was parsed into its components and the probability associated with each component of the probabilistic context-free grammar was computed.

As an example, consider the string *violin22*, which is represented as the base structure L_6D_2. The product of probabilities of the components (i.e., base structure L_6D_2, alpha string *violin*, all lower case capitalization M_6 and digit component *22*) is the estimated probability value of the string. Using this approach, the probabilities of all the retrieved tokens were computed. Note that in the remainder of the discussion, the retrieved tokens correspond to tokens that remain after the initial filtering.

5.2 Ranking Algorithms

After computing the probability of each token, the tokens must be ranked and a limited set of tokens (say the top N tokens called "potential passwords") must be provided to the investigator to examine as the most likely password candidates from the hard disk. Obviously, it is ideal to have high precision and high recall in the potential password set. Recall is generally more important in offline password cracking while precision is more important in online cracking. One might argue that, in the case of an offline attack, one could consider all the tokens found on the disk. However, it is very important to reduce the size of the potential password set – although password cracking is continually being sped up by GPUs, many hashing algorithms (e.g., the one used in TrueCrypt) can still take a very long time using the resources available to most law enforcement agencies.

In order to obtain the best precision and recall, several approaches were used to identify the top potential passwords from the retrieved tokens. This section describes three algorithms for ranking possible passwords. Note that the strings and the file they are associated with are maintained and this relationship is exploited by the algorithms. The algorithms incorporate a parameter N denoting the number of potential passwords to be returned to the investigator. The algorithms are:

- **Top Overall:** This algorithm selects the N highest probability tokens from among all the retrieved tokens. However, the results presented later in the chapter show that this is not the most effective approach.

- **Top Percent (per File):** This algorithm selects a fixed percentage of the highest probability tokens from each file such that the total number of tokens returned is N (thus, different numbers of tokens are selected from each file). The resulting tokens are then ordered according to their probabilities.

- **Top 1-by-1 (per File):** The first round of the algorithm chooses the highest probability token from each file and ranks them according to their probabilities. In the second round, the second highest probability token is selected from each file (if available) and they are ranked according to their probabilities. The rounds are continued until N tokens are obtained. Note that tokens in round j are ranked above tokens in round $j + 1$.

6. Experimental Evaluation

This section discusses the experimental results related to the utility of the filtering techniques as well as the effectiveness of the algorithms in identifying passwords. Since disk images containing real passwords were not available, test disk images were created by incorporating files containing a number of real passwords taken from revealed password sets.

6.1 Experimental Setup

The Govdocs1 digital corpus [3] was used as the source of files. This corpus contains about one million freely redistributable files in many formats. Five data disk images of different sizes (50 MB, 100 MB, 250 MB, 500 MB and 1 GB) were created with FAT filesystems. Each test disk image modeled a real disk and corresponded to a subset of a typical complete disk. A fairly large amount of space on a real disk is devoted to the operating system, media files (videos, music, images) and installed programs. The test disks only incorporated files that are likely to be created by users (.doc, .xls, .pdf, etc.). The sizes of the data disk images correspond to the total sizes of these files. For example, the 1 GB test data disk would likely have been derived from a 500 GB hard disk belonging to a typical user. The numbers of files analyzed in the five disks with sizes 50 MB, 100 MB, 250 MB, 500 MB and 1 GB were 108, 143, 426, 571 and 1,194, respectively.

Passwords were randomly selected from a revealed password set and files were randomly selected for storing the passwords. Since no data was available on how users store their passwords (either in one file or many files or at the end of large files, etc.), attempts were made to be as general as possible when adding the passwords. The experiments used passwords from three well-known revealed password sets: one million passwords from Rockyou [15], 300,000 from CSDN [9] and 300,000 from

Table 1. Percentage token reduction per filter.

Disk Filter	50 MB	100 MB	250 MB	500 MB	1 GB
Non-Printable	0	0	0	0.0015	0
Length	59.65	65.57	60.34	40.75	53.08
Floating Point	1.05	0.45	20.71	46.87	28.21
Repeated Token	85.04	82.79	73.78	75.63	70.10
Word Punctuation	68.96	11.90	8.27	6.28	20.42
All-Alpha	77.89	73.11	60.66	31.95	33.71

Yahoo [12]. Interested readers are referred to Ma et al. [11] for statistical information about these password sets.

6.2   Initial Filtering

Experiments were conducted to assess how the filters help reduce the number of tokens. The initial filtering techniques described previously were employed and the numbers of tokens obtained before and after applying each of the initial filters for each disk size were recorded. The most aggressive specialized filtering involving the removal of all alpha strings was also applied.

Table 1 presents the results. Note that all the filters, except non-printable, have a major impact on the results, reducing the large number of tokens obtained from the hard disk to a much smaller and manageable set. The non-printable filter turned out to be important in the next step involving the computation of probabilities, but it was rarely useful for token reduction. The order of application of the filters does not matter (except for the time requirements) because the same results are obtained regardless of the order in which filtering is performed.

Table 2. Token reduction by all filters.

	50 MB	100 MB	250 MB	500 MB	1 GB
# Before Filtering (mil.)	2.45	2.16	6.76	28.84	49.41
# After Filtering (mil.)	0.07	0.050	0.25	1.38	3.21
Total Reduction (%)	97.15	97.68	96.35	95.21	93.50

Table 2 shows the numbers of tokens (in millions) before and after filtering and the percentage reductions after all the filters were applied.

6.3   Ranking Algorithms

Experiments were conducted to evaluate the results of the three ranking algorithms. The Rockyou and CSDN revealed password sets were used to provide passwords that were stored on the test disks. The initial filters and the all-alpha filter were used in the experiments.

Some websites (e.g., Rockyou) did not enforce a password policy at the time they were attacked. Consequently, a good number of passwords in their lists have length less than seven or are alpha strings. Because this series of experiments only sought to evaluate the ranking algorithms, such passwords were not stored on the test disks. Specifically, five passwords were stored on each disk in one set of experiments and fifteen passwords were stored in the second set of experiments. The assumption was that users would typically store between five to fifteen passwords. The passwords were stored either in a file or in a deleted file. The Yahoo password set was used to train the probabilistic context-free grammar that was used to calculate the probabilities of potential passwords.

For each combination of disk size, revealed set and number of passwords stored, the number of passwords that could be found using the three algorithms (top overall, top percent and top 1-by-1) were determined. The results are presented in terms of N potential passwords provided to the investigator, where N is 1,000, 2,000, 4,000, 8,000 and 16,000.

Table 3 shows the results of storing five and fifteen passwords from CSDN. For example, the 1-by-1 algorithm, finds all five passwords in the 50 MB test data disk, three passwords in the 100 MB disk, two passwords in the 250 MB disk, etc., within the top $N = 1,000$ passwords returned by the algorithm.

The results obtained when storing five passwords are discussed first. When comparing the algorithms, given an N value and the number of stored passwords, higher recall implies higher precision and both values can be calculated from the number of passwords found. For example, the average recall value for the 1-by-1 algorithm across different disk sizes for $N = 8,000$ is 92%; for the top percent algorithm, the average recall value is 56%; and for the top overall algorithm, the average recall value is 40%. This shows that the 1-by-1 algorithm has higher precision and higher recall compared with the other algorithms.

The results obtained when storing fifteen passwords are similar. For $N = 8,000$, the average recall value of the 1-by-1 algorithm is 89.3% across the various disk sizes. Table 3 shows that the 1-by-1 algorithm has good performance and is better than the other algorithms.

Table 3. Number of CSDN passwords found.

N	Disk Size	50 MB	100 MB	250 MB	500 MB	1 GB	50 MB	100 MB	250 MB	500 MB	1 GB
		Out of 5 Passwords					Out of 15 Passwords				
1,000	Overall	1	2	0	0	2	1	7	0	2	2
	Percent	2	3	1	1	2	4	10	2	3	3
	1-by-1	5	3	2	3	3	11	12	7	8	9
2,000	Overall	1	2	0	0	2	1	9	0	2	2
	Percent	5	3	1	1	2	9	10	2	4	5
	1-by-1	5	4	2	3	4	12	14	9	9	11
4,000	Overall	5	2	0	0	2	11	10	0	2	2
	Percent	5	3	2	1	2	10	11	3	5	6
	1-by-1	5	5	3	4	4	15	15	12	10	12
8,000	Overall	5	3	0	0	2	13	11	0	2	2
	Percent	5	3	2	1	3	11	11	8	5	8
	1-by-1	5	5	4	4	5	15	15	13	10	14
16,000	Overall	5	4	0	0	2	15	14	0	2	2
	Percent	5	4	2	3	3	12	14	9	8	8
	1-by-1	5	5	4	5	5	15	15	13	11	14

Table 4 shows the results for stored passwords from the Rockyou password set. When five passwords from Rockyou were stored, the average recall value of the 1-by-1 algorithm for $N = 8,000$ is 84%, for the top percent algorithm the average recall value is 72% and for the top overall algorithm the average recall value is 60%. In the case of a smaller N value ($N = 1,000$), the average recall value for the 1-by-1 algorithm when fifteen passwords were stored is 81.3% and the average precision is 1.2%.

The amount of time taken by each algorithm was also measured. The total time taken for retrieving the tokens, filtering, ranking and returning the top potential passwords from the 1 GB data disk was less than three minutes. The total time for the smallest data disk (50 MB) was just thirteen seconds.

Examination of the results in Tables 3 and 4 reveals that the 1-by-1 algorithm has the most consistent performance.

6.4 Specialized Filtering

The filters used in the experiments described above eliminated all the alpha strings. This is reasonable because the vast majority of password policies would disallow such passwords. Nevertheless, the experiments

Table 4.   Number of Rockyou passwords found.

N	Disk Size	50 MB	100 MB	250 MB	500 MB	1 GB	50 MB	100 MB	250 MB	500 MB	1 GB
		Out of 5 Passwords					Out of 15 Passwords				
1,000	Overall	1	2	3	3	2	8	9	8	8	9
	Percent	3	2	1	2	0	8	10	4	3	2
	1-by-1	4	4	4	4	2	13	13	12	13	10
2,000	Overall	1	2	3	3	2	8	11	8	8	9
	Percent	4	2	2	3	1	10	10	7	4	5
	1-by-1	4	4	4	5	2	14	13	13	15	11
4,000	Overall	4	3	3	3	2	14	12	8	8	9
	Percent	4	4	3	5	2	13	13	9	10	6
	1-by-1	4	5	4	5	2	14	14	13	15	11
8,000	Overall	4	3	3	3	2	14	12	8	8	9
	Percent	4	4	3	5	2	13	13	12	13	7
	1-by-1	4	5	5	5	2	14	15	15	15	11
16,000	Overall	5	4	3	3	2	15	13	8	8	9
	Percent	4	4	4	5	2	14	13	13	14	7
	1-by-1	5	5	5	5	2	15	15	15	15	11

described in this section examine whether less restrictive filtering of alpha strings is useful.

In particular, the experiments used the specialized filters described previously to retain some of the alpha strings. The filters were applied in addition to the initial filters. The experiments used the 1 GB data disk with fifteen stored passwords from the Rockyou set. Alpha string passwords were permitted to be selected from the Rockyou set for storage. Note that these passwords could potentially be filtered before the identification process.

Table 5 shows the results for various specialized filters (N: no filter, C: capitalization, M: multiwords, D: dictionary, S: sentences and A: all-alphas). The numbers in parentheses correspond to how many of the fifteen passwords stored on the disk remained after the filtering process. For example, A (11) means that four of the fifteen passwords stored on the disk were filtered by the all-alphas filter.

The multiwords filter (M) eliminates all single words (whether they are dictionary words or not). The dictionary filter (D), however, only eliminates single words included in the dictionary and retains multi-words. Therefore, when applying the multiwords filter, a more limited set of alpha strings is retained. The dictionary filter used a moderate-sized English dictionary, which was designed for Scrabble-style computer

Table 5. Comparing specialized filters.

		N (15)	C (11)	M (14)	D (14)	S (15)	A (11)
	Overall	0	2	0	0	0	5
N=1,000	Percent	1	1	3	3	2	1
	1-by-1	2	2	4	4	0	8
	Overall	0	2	0	0	0	5
N=2,000	Percent	1	2	3	3	2	2
	1-by-1	2	2	4	5	0	10
	Overall	0	2	0	0	0	5
N=4,000	Percent	2	3	3	3	3	4
	1-by-1	2	2	5	5	1	10
	Overall	0	2	0	0	0	5
N=8,000	Percent	4	4	5	5	3	7
	1-by-1	2	2	7	7	1	10
	Overall	0	2	0	0	0	5
N=16,000	Percent	4	4	5	5	3	7
	1-by-1	4	5	8	8	7	10

word games; the dictionary was augmented with common names and common words from television and movie scripts. The results without any alpha string filtering (N) are also shown.

Table 5 shows that using less aggressive filters such as the multiwords and dictionary filters reduces password loss due to filtering. However, these filters are not as successful as the more aggressive approach of using the all-alphas filter and subsequently identifying the passwords because they retain too many alpha strings. Because of the large number of alpha strings that appear in the final token list and because of the way in which the probability of each token is calculated (words of the same length have equal probability), a large number of alpha strings with fairly high probabilities are obtained. Hence, when the top N potential passwords are selected by the algorithms, many of the passwords are not found as quickly as when all the alpha strings are filtered.

The sentences filter (S) is designed to reduce documents containing text but, as noted previously, the tool that was used was unable to distinguish between sentences and non-sentences. The results in Table 5 show that the sentences filter is not as useful as the other filters. Better tools for identifying sentences render the sentences filter more useful for password identification.

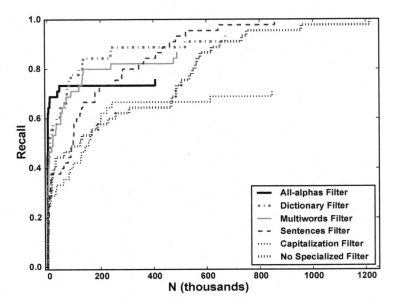

Figure 1.   Comparison of specialized filters for various N values.

The results in Table 5 also show that using all the filters is better than using no filters. Also, the all-alphas filter is much more effective than the other filters even though it may filter some passwords before the identification process. Furthermore, as before, the 1-by-1 algorithm has the best overall performance.

To assess how quickly passwords could be identified, the 1-by-1 algorithm was used along with the various specialized alpha string filters (in addition to the initial filters). Figure 1 shows plots of N versus the recall value until all the passwords that can be found by a given filter are obtained (the results are the averages of several runs). Note that some filters cannot achieve a recall value of one because some of the passwords were filtered before the identification process. For example, the aggressive all-alphas filter may not be able to find all of the passwords, but, on the average, it finds nine of the fifteen passwords with a recall of 0.6 and precision of 0.005 at $N = 1,659$. In comparison, when no specialized filters are applied, nine of the fifteen passwords are found only at the very much higher $N = 229,671$.

The results demonstrate that the filtering and identification approach enables an investigator to find most of the passwords at a very small value of N, eliminating the need to check a massive number of strings. Note that if the aggressive filter is not successful, an investigator could use a less aggressive filter. For example, using the dictionary filter, which

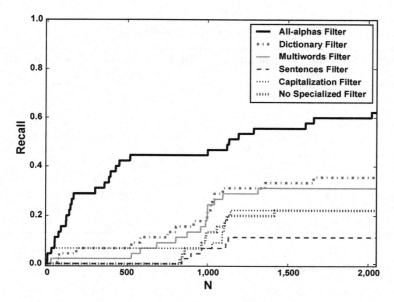

Figure 2. Comparison of specialized filters for small N values.

loses fewer passwords and finds an average of nine of the fifteen passwords at $N = 36,240$, is still much better than not using a specialized filter.

By choosing an appropriate value of N, an investigator can move between the online and offline password cracking modes. In order to better understand the implications of small values of N, Figure 2 presents the results for initial values of N up to 2,000. Note that the all-alphas filter identifies about half of the stored passwords within the first 500 tokens. Even finding just one password on a disk can be very helpful to an investigator because users often reuse a single password for multiple accounts. Note that, for the all-alphas filter in Figure 1, the first password was found on the average at $N = 11$.

Readers may be interested in seeing examples of the potential passwords returned by the 1-by-1 algorithm. Table 6 shows the top twenty potential passwords and their associated probabilities when using the all-alphas filter. Two of the fifteen passwords stored on the disk (i.e., *lyndsay1* and *blueberry1*) are among the top twenty potential passwords returned by the system. It is not clear how the filtering and ranking could be improved because all the other potential passwords appear to be possible passwords as well.

Table 6. Top twenty passwords.

Rank	Potential Passwords	Probability	Rank	Potential Passwords	Probability
1	*charles1*	6.384 E-6	11	*pdprog1*	5.370 E-8
2	*include3*	1.687 E-6	12	*report1*	5.370 E-8
3	*program4*	1.610 E-6	13	*cielo123*	5.080 E-8
4	*carolina23*	6.272 E-7	14	*soldiers1*	4.044 E-8
5	*light20*	1.112 E-7	15	*bluberry1*	4.044 E-8
6	*program97*	7.757 E-8	16	*listeria1*	4.044 E-8
7	*lyndsay1*	7.739 E-8	17	*compendia1*	3.110 E-8
8	*decagon1*	7.739 E-8	18	*framework1*	3.110 E-8
9	*dogbloo1*	7.739 E-8	19	*alpha1s*	2.972 E-8
10	*example1*	7.739 E-8	20	*address2*	2.538 E-8

7.   Conclusions

The proposed technique involving a probabilistic context-free grammar, specialized filters and ranking algorithms is very effective at identifying potential passwords stored on hard disks. Experiments demonstrate that the technique can provide a relatively small list of tokens that contain most of the stored passwords. For example, given approximately 49 million tokens from a large hard drive as input, the technique was able to output an ordered potential password set of 2,000 tokens, which contained nine of the fifteen stored passwords. Furthermore, the technique can very quickly find at least a few of the passwords – on the average, one password was found in the top eleven tokens and three passwords in the top fifty tokens.

Future research will apply the technique to other devices and media, including cell phones and USB drives. Also, the research will explore other approaches for identifying and filtering sentences. The filters and the ranking algorithms will also be adapted to leverage other information such as the password policy and the names and dates of birth of family members.

References

[1] Apache Software Foundation, OpenNLP, Forest Hill, Maryland (opennlp.apache.org), 2010.

[2] S. Garfinkel, N. Beebe, L. Liu and M. Maasberg, Detecting threatening insiders with lightweight media forensics, *Proceedings of the International Conference on Technologies for Homeland Security*, pp. 86–92, 2013.

[3] S. Garfinkel, P. Farrell, V. Roussev and G. Dinolt, Bringing science to digital forensics with standardized forensic corpora, *Digital Investigation*, vol. 6(S), pp. S2–S11, 2009.

[4] S. Grimm, Personal communication, Webster Groves Police Department, Webster Groves, Missouri, 2014.

[5] C. Hargreaves and H. Chivers, Recovery of encryption keys from memory using a linear scan, *Proceedings of the Third International Conference on Availability, Reliability and Security*, pp. 1369–1376, 2008.

[6] S. Houshmand and S. Aggarwal, Building better passwords using probabilistic techniques, *Proceedings of the Twenty-Eighth Annual Computer Security Applications Conference*, pp. 109–118, 2012.

[7] Identity Finder, Sensitive Data Manager, New York (`www.iden tityfinder.com/us/Business/IdentityFinder/SensitiveData Manager`).

[8] Kaspersky Lab, Perception and Knowledge of IT Threats: The Consumer's Point of View, Woburn, Massachusetts, 2012.

[9] M. Kumar, China Software Developer Network (CSDN) 6 million user data leaked, *The Hacker News*, December 21, 2011.

[10] S. Lee, A. Savoldi, S. Lee and J. Lim, Password recovery using an evidence collection tool and countermeasures, *Proceedings of the Third International Conference on Intelligent Information Hiding and Multimedia Signal Processing*, pp. 97–102, 2007.

[11] J. Ma, W. Yang, M. Luo and N. Li, A study of probabilistic password models, *Proceedings of the IEEE Symposium on Security and Privacy*, pp. 689–704, 2014.

[12] S. Musil, Hackers post 450K credentials pilfered from Yahoo, *CNET*, July 11, 2012.

[13] J. O'Neil, Doing Things with Words, Part Two: Sentence Boundary Detection, Attivio, Newton, Massachusetts, 2008.

[14] D. Riis, Google Chrome Password Recovery Tool (`www.bitbucket. org/Driis/chromepasswordrecovery`), 2012.

[15] A. Vance, If your password is 123456, just make it HackMe, *New York Times*, January 20, 2010.

[16] M. Weir, S. Aggarwal, B. De Medeiros and B. Glodek, Password cracking using probabilistic context free grammars, *Proceedings of the IEEE Symposium on Security and Privacy*, pp. 391–405, 2009.

Chapter 13

FRAGMENTED JPEG FILE RECOVERY USING PSEUDO HEADERS

Yanbin Tang, Zheng Tan, Kam-Pui Chow, Siu-Ming Yiu, Junbin Fang, Xiamu Niu, Qi Han and Xianyan Wu

Abstract   Many techniques have been proposed for file recovery, but recovering fragmented files is still a challenge in digital forensics, especially when the files are damaged. This chapter focuses on JPEG files, one of the most popular photograph formats, and proposes techniques for recovering partially-damaged standalone JPEG fragments by reconstructing pseudo headers. The techniques deal with missing Huffman tables and sub-sampling factors, estimate the resolution of fragments, assess the image quality of JPEG files with incorrect quantization tables, and create quantization tables that are very close to the correct quantization tables in a reasonable amount of time. Experiments with real camera pictures demonstrate that the techniques can recover standalone fragments accurately and efficiently.

Keywords: JPEG fragments, file recovery, pseudo headers

1.   Introduction

Operations such as creating, deleting, editing and appending files cause the fragmentation of user and system files, especially on hard drives that are filled to capacity and flash storage devices that employ wear-leveling mechanisms. Depending on the new file allocation rules of a filesystem [1], deleted files are overwritten by newly-created or edited files. JPEG is one of the most popular image file formats used in computers, digital cameras and smartphones and on the Internet. JPEG image files often constitute crucial evidence in criminal investigations. However, if the underlying filesystem is corrupted, it is difficult to recover files, especially when the files are fragmented, destroyed or incomplete.

© IFIP International Federation for Information Processing 2015
G. Peterson, S. Shenoi (Eds.): Advances in Digital Forensics XI, IFIP AICT 462, pp. 215–231, 2015.
DOI: 10.1007/978-3-319-24123-4_13

This chapter proposes techniques for recovering partially-damaged standalone JPEG fragments by reconstructing pseudo headers. The techniques deal with missing Huffman tables and sub-sampling factors, estimate the resolution of fragments, assess the image quality of JPEG files with incorrect quantization tables, and create quantization tables that are very close to the correct quantization tables in a reasonable amount of time. Experiments with real camera pictures demonstrate that the techniques can recover standalone fragments accurately and efficiently.

2.   Related Work

Many researchers have focused on file recovery and/or file carving. However, most of the techniques implemented in digital forensic tools (e.g., Encase, FTK and The Sleuth Kit) recover complete files by interpreting the filesystems in storage media. The vast majority of files are organized using specific structures or are encoded by specific algorithms. If a deleted file has been overwritten partially, it is difficult to recover the file fragments by exclusively analyzing filesystem data. The recovery of damaged encoded files and compressed files is also a major challenge. In such instances, it is necessary to analyze the file structures, obtain the necessary information and apply specific algorithms to read and display the damaged file content.

In the context of JPEG files, researchers have formulated the problem of reassembling JPEG fragments as a Hamiltonian path problem and have developed several greedy heuristic algorithms to identify the optimal path [8, 11, 13]. Garfinkel [3] has proposed a fast object validation technique to recover bi-fragmented files by exhaustively analyzing all possible combinations of data blocks between an identified file header and footer. Karresand and Shahmehri [6] have developed a method for reassembling a special type of JPEG file with "restart markers" that handles bit stream errors due to file corruption or unreliable transmission (however, not all JPEG files have such restart markers). Pal et al. [10] have proposed a sequential hypothesis testing algorithm that reassembles fragmented files by detecting JPEG file fragmentation points. However, if a file has been damaged or corrupted, the methods mentioned above reconstruct the file incorrectly or are simply unable to find the correct next fragmentation point.

Sencar and Memon [12] have proposed a technique for recovering JPEG files with missing fragments. The technique leverages the fact that image decoding information and content are stored separately in the JPEG header and the body. However, the technique is too general to construct pseudo headers. Inspired by Sencar and Memon's work, this research proposes an approach for constructing pseudo headers piece by piece.

Xu and Xu [18] have proposed an algorithm that estimates the width of JPEG pictures by measuring similarities between the differences of DC luminance coefficients in each row of an estimated picture width, which involves a brute force search from one up to the real width. When the estimated width is equal to the real width, the best (smoothest) features are obtained throughout the picture along with the closest similarity. However, the time consumption of this algorithm is as high as $(w \times h)^2$ where w is the width of the test image and h is the height.

Other researchers have attempted to predict the quantization tables of JPEG files [4, 17]. However, the technique only work for files with extended IJG standard quantization tables [5]. The technique estimates the similarity between coefficient differences by simulating the JPEG decoding and encoding processes with specific quality factors. However, the technique is very time consuming because it processes coefficients using discrete cosine transformation, quantization, dequantization and inverse discrete cosine transformation repeatedly for quality factors ranging from one to 100 to obtain the best result. The time requirements would be even more for test pictures with high image quality.

3. JPEG Background

A sound JPEG file has two parts, the header and the data (body). The header contains nearly all the configuration information used by the decoding process. The data part contains pure encoded binary data with an ending marker that indicates the end of the data section. The JPEG standard defines four encoding modes: lossless, sequential (or baseline), progressive and hierarchical. The sequential mode, which is the default and most commonly used JPEG mode, is the focus of this work.

The JPEG encoding algorithm transforms the color space (e.g., RGB) of an input image to the color components YCbCr. The three color components are divided into minimum coded units (MCUs), which are usually non-overlapping blocks of 8×8 pixels. The specific number of pixels per color component in a minimum coded unit is determined by the sub-sampling factor in the JPEG file header. The discrete cosine transform is used to transform the color pixels to frequency domain coefficients. The low-frequency coefficients are concentrated in the top-left portion of a minimum coded unit matrix while the high-frequency coefficients are in the bottom-right portion. Because humans are not sensitive to high-frequency information, after the quantization process, many of the high-frequency coefficients are rounded to zero or small numbers, thus achieving lossy compression.

The first element of a minimum coded unit is the direct component (DC) coefficient while the other elements are the alternating component (AC) coefficients. The DC coefficient is coded by differential pulse code modulation, which means that the differences between the DC coefficients of blocks are stored. AC coefficients are coded by run-length coding after zigzag scanning. The run-length coding can indicate the number of elements in a minimum coded unit matrix with an end of block (EOB) code. In the final step of the JPEG encoding process, all the coefficients are encoded by a variable bit length entropy coder that employs Huffman coding. The JPEG decoding process is performed by performing the steps in reverse order.

3.1 Essential Configurations in JPEG Headers

As described above, several processes and configurations are involved in JPEG encoding and decoding. To recover the content of a standalone JPEG fragment, it is necessary to construct a pseudo header to decode the fragment and then display it [12]. In the baseline JPEG encoding mode, four essential configurations are required to reconstruct a pseudo header: (i) Huffman code table; (ii) chrominance sub-sampling factor used in the minimum coded units; (iii) image resolution; and (iv) quantization table.

Figure 1 shows failed decodings of the `lena.jpg` file produced by incorrect components in the file header. Solutions for addressing the problems are discussed in Section 4.

3.2 Synchronization Point

The Huffman code as used in a JPEG file has the self synchronization property [7]. In other words, there is a synchronization point after which subsequent bits can be decoded correctly in any situation, even when starting from an unknown position.

In fact, the cost is only a few bits of error until the synchronization point is reached. An experiment was conducted with 700 pictures captured by several popular digital cameras and smartphones. The data part of each picture was truncated five times with a random size. Since DC coefficients are coded by differential pulse code modulation before the entropy encoding, there is only one DC coefficient in each color component of a minimum coded unit. Thus, a DC coefficient may occupy more minimum coded units before the synchronization point than an AC coefficient. The number of incorrect differential DC (dif_DC)

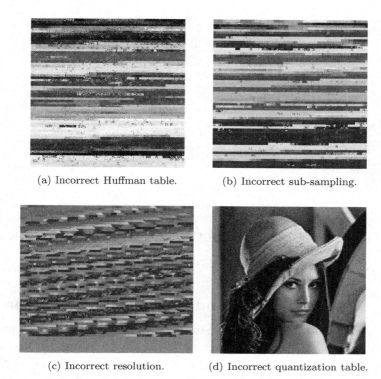

(a) Incorrect Huffman table.   (b) Incorrect sub-sampling.

(c) Incorrect resolution.   (d) Incorrect quantization table.

Figure 1. Versions of `lena.jpg` with incorrect components in the file header.

coefficients of luminance were counted to investigate the JPEG synchronization property. The results shown in Figure 2 demonstrate that more than 50% of the pictures reach the synchronization point after two minimum coded units and all the pictures become correct within 30 minimum coded units. Compared with the total number of minimum coded units in an image, the number of incorrect minimum coded units is negligible. Therefore, once the synchronization point is approached, all the entropy encoded data streams can be decoded successfully.

4.   JPEG File Recovery Methodology

This section describes the proposed methodology for reconstructing pseudo headers. First, the impact of the four essential configurations (Huffman code table, chrominance sub-sampling factor, image resolution and quantization table) are discussed. Following this, techniques for predicting these configurations are presented.

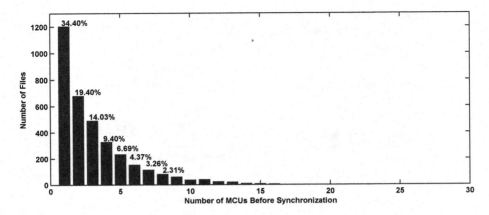

Figure 2.   Number of incorrect MCUs before the synchronization point.

4.1   Huffman Table and Sub-Sampling Factor

In a baseline JPEG file, a mismatched Huffman table or chrominance sub-sampling factor may result in failed decodings as shown in Figures 1(a) and 1(b). Estimating a Huffman table from an encoded data stream is a major challenge. Sencar and Memon [12] have analyzed if Huffman tables from two fragments are identical considering a unique n-bit pattern. The probability of finding the bit pattern from an m-bit fragment is as low as $m/(2^n)$; when $n = 15$, the probability is around 3×10^{-05}. In order to reduce implementation costs, however, most digital camera manufacturers prefer to use the standard Huffman table [5], which was developed based on the average statistics of a large set of images. In fact, Karresand and Shahmehri [6] found that 69 of 76 popular digital cameras use the standard Huffman table. Consequently, the JPEG files considered in this work are assumed to use the standard Huffman table.

As specified in the JPEG standard, AC coefficients are encoded by run-length coding in interleaved order, which is defined by the sub-sampling factor. Also, an end of block (EOB) code exists at the end of each encoded minimum coded unit to identify the end of the current block. Thus, for each minimum coded unit, if a decoding is performed using an incorrect sub-sampling factor, the total size of the AC coefficients might go below or above the stipulated value (e.g., 63 for an 8×8 minimum coded unit block). Moreover, the number of sub-sampling factors used are very limited; the most popular settings in digital cameras are 4:1:1, 2:1:1 and 1:1:1. Therefore, by enumerating the limited sub-

Table 1. DC and dif_DC coefficients in MCU units from (0,0) to (7,5).

DC	0	1	2	3	4	5	dif_DC	0	1	2	3	4	5
0	46	46	46	46	47	47	0	46	0	0	0	1	0
1	61	60	59	59	59	60	1	1	-1	-1	0	0	1
2	60	59	60	61	**5**	-13	2	0	-1	1	1	**-56**	-18
3	59	59	59	61	**9**	-8	3	-1	0	0	2	**-52**	-17
4	59	59	59	61	**5**	-4	4	-1	0	0	2	**-56**	-9
5	59	59	59	61	**-3**	-7	5	23	0	0	2	**-64**	-4
6	59	59	59	55	-14	-5	6	79	0	0	-4	-69	9
7	59	59	53	-37	-9	-4	7	53	0	-6	-90	28	5

sampling factors and determining the total size of the run-length coded AC coefficients, it is possible to discover the correct configuration.

4.2   Image Resolution

If the width or height are mismatched, the decoded picture might appear to be filled with random data as shown in Figure 1(c). This chapter proposes a new technique to estimate the image resolution by analyzing the distances between similar dif_DC chains of luminance.

After the discrete cosine transformation, the first top-left DC coefficient holds the average intensity of the minimum coded unit block; it contains high energy because it is the most important coefficient. As specified in Property 1 below, real-world images have smooth transitions in object intensity and color; in other words, a specific profile or significant change always extends to adjacent areas. Thus, the DC coefficients can represent the luminance profile of a picture and the values are distributed sparsely to reflect the exact image pattern. Since the dif_DC coefficients are computed as the differences between the DC coefficients of adjacent encoding blocks from left to right, the dif_DC coefficients hold the change patterns in a compact form and concentrate on small values.

Property 1. Smoothness Phenomenon: *Generally, the luminance intensity and chrominance of a captured picture changes gradually over a localized area.*

Table 1 shows the DC and dif_DC coefficients in the minimum coded units (0,0) to (7,5) of Figure 3. The object intensity and color change significantly in the chimney region in Figure 3. Accordingly, the DC coefficient values drop significantly in column 4 from row 2 to 6 (shown in boldface). The dif_DC coefficients exactly represent this profile as shown in boldface on the right-hand side of Table 1. Comparing the DC

Figure 3.   JPEG image of a house with the minimum coded units shown.

and dif_DC coefficients reveals that the dif_DC coefficients have smaller values for adjacent similar blocks.

The problem of estimating the image resolution can be transformed to finding the distance between two vertically adjacent minimum coded unit blocks. As demonstrated above, when there is a significant change, the pattern has a high probability of being extended to an adjacent area. As a result of improvements in image quality, the pattern would be covered by more than one minimum coded unit block in a high-resolution picture. In order to find the significant patterns of the dif_DC coefficients, a unique dif_DC chain is chosen as a sample chain. This sample chain begins with a high contrast dif_DC coefficient. Upon comparing nearby data areas, the most similar chains are found using cosine similarity:

$$cos(A, B) = \frac{A \cdot B}{\|A\|\|B\|} = \frac{\sum_{i=1}^{n} A_i \times B_i}{\sqrt{\sum_{i=1}^{n} (A_i)^2} \times \sqrt{\sum_{i=1}^{n} (B_i)^2}} \tag{1}$$

Accordingly, the distance between the most similar dif_DCs chains would be the width of the image.

In order to reduce noise and improve performance, m sample chains are chosen in each fragment and then the top k most similar chains are found. After evaluating the distances between the top $m \times k$ dif_DC chains, the distance value with highest frequency is chosen as the candidate width. Experiments revealed that the size l is less than 20, k

Figure 4. Image of `lena.jpg`.

is as small as five and m is smaller than ten, depending on the size of examined JPEG fragments.

In fact, human-vision-detectable vertical luminance changes are not necessarily required for fragments. As a result of improvements in image quality, even a small (significant) spot might contain several minimum coded unit blocks. In the case of the `lena.jpg` file with 512×512 resolution in Figure 4, the starting minimum coded units of the chosen sample dif_DC chains are indicated as circles and the evaluated similar chains as boxes. In this case, some of the sample chains also evaluated as the most similar chains. The distance values for points in the top-left portion and on the hat of `lena.jpg` have the highest frequencies. In other words, the highest frequency distance value is exactly equal to the width of the picture.

4.3 Quantization Table

This work focuses on original (unmodified) pictures. Unlike the situation involving image forgery detection in double quantized files[2], histogram patterns are inadequate for original photos. Also, when testing different quantization tables for files, distorted images do not have an impact on features such as Gaussian noise or Gaussian blurring. This section presents an image quality assessment (IQA) algorithm called Blocking_IQA for measuring the quality of JPEG files with incorrect quantization tables. Also, a quantization table prediction algorithm called QT_Blocking is described.

Image Quality Assessment (Blocking_IQA). Image quality assessment attempts to measure the quality of distorted pictures caused by restoration, transmission, compression and so on. Depending on the availability of a reference image, objective image quality assessment metrics can be classified into three types: (i) full reference (FR); (ii) no-reference (NR); and (iii) reduced-reference (RR). The full reference metrics, such as peak signal-to-noise ratio (PSNR) and SSIM [15], evaluate picture quality using the original picture as the reference. In contrast, no-reference metrics, such as jpeg_quality_score [16] and BRISQUE [9], predict the quality of a test picture only using information from the test picture. In fact, as elaborated by Wang et al. [16], it is still a major challenge to find a no-reference metric that can handle every distorted picture.

As defined by the JPEG standard decoding process, if a quantization table mismatch exists, color coefficients are increased or decreased after the dequantization process during decoding. Thus, the smooth features of a decoded picture with regard to luminance and color are seriously degraded, especially with blocking at the boundaries of JPEG minimum coded units as stated in Property 2:

Property 2. Blocking Phenomenon: *For a non-artifact picture, if a mismatch exists in the quantization table, there is visual degradation of luminance and chrominance and an impact on blocking at the boundaries of minimum coded units.*

Figure 5(a) shows a zoomed image of an eye in `lena.jpg` while Figure 5(b) shows a version of the same picture with an incorrect quantization table. Note that Figure 5(b) has darker luminance and worse chrominance than the original picture (Figure 5(a)). Most importantly, there is serious blocking around the eye, which is located at the boundaries of minimum coded units.

In order to analyze the image quality of pictures with incorrect quantization tables, the blocking property is evaluated by comparing the color differences between the internal and boundary blocks of minimum coded units. First, CIE76 (or Euclidean distance)[14] is used to measure the

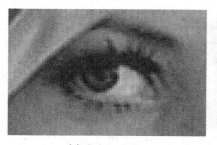 

(a) Original file.   (b) Incorrect quantization table.

Figure 5.   Blocking phenomenon when zooming into an eye in `lena.jpg`.

color difference between two adjacent pixels:

$$CIE_i = \frac{1}{n}\sqrt{\sum_{i=1}^{n}(x_i - x_{i+1})^2} \qquad (2)$$

where $i \bmod 8 = \{6, 7\}$.

In the vertical direction, two CIE color differences are evaluated, one for the last two columns of each minimum coded unit and the other for two columns of two nearby minimum coded units. The blocking phenomenon ΔCIE is measured by comparing two adjacent CIEs as follows:

$$\Delta CIE = |CIE_i - CIE_{i+1}| \qquad (3)$$

The estimated image quality score in the vertical direction $BlockingIQA_v$ is the average value of all the corresponding ΔCIE values:

$$BlockingIQA_v = \overline{\Delta CIE} \qquad (4)$$

The image quality score in the horizontal direction $BlockingIQA_h$ is evaluated similarly. The final image quality score $BlockingIQA$ is the average of $BlockingIQA_v$ and $BlockingIQA_h$:

$$BlockingIQA = \frac{1}{2}(BlockingIQA_v + BlockingIQA_h) \qquad (5)$$

A smaller $BlockingIQA$ score corresponds to better image quality and greater smoothness at the boundaries of decoded minimum coded units.

Quantization Table Estimation (QT_Blocking). The standard quantization table is used as a reference to find the closest quantization table for a JPEG fragment. The standard basis table $T_b[i]$ is scaled by

Table 2.   Average values of coefficients.

519.39	17.37	9.27	5.79	2.59	0.82	0.32	0.12
22.59	11.36	7.35	4.84	1.62	0.44	0.20	0.12
12.61	8.32	5.91	2.66	0.86	0.32	0.16	0.10
8.04	5.91	2.91	1.56	0.46	0.13	0.07	0.05
5.39	2.70	1.18	0.49	0.23	0.05	0.02	0.02
2.23	0.99	0.47	0.22	0.08	0.03	0.01	0.01
0.55	0.26	0.15	0.09	0.03	0.01	0.01	0.01
0.15	0.09	0.07	0.04	0.02	0.01	0.01	0.01

a quality factor Q to obtain the new table $T_s[i]$. The scaling function is given by:

$$T_s[i] = \left\lfloor \frac{S \times T_b[i] + 50}{100} \right\rfloor \qquad (6)$$

where $T_b[i]$ is the standard quantization table, Q is the quality factor that ranges from 1 to 100, $S = (Q < 50)? \frac{5000}{Q} : 200 - 2Q$, and if $T_s[i] \leq 0$, then $T_s[i] = 1$.

The advantage of the discrete cosine transform is its tendency to aggregate most of the signal in one corner of the result. In other words, most of the energy is concentrated in the low-frequency area located at the top-left corner. Due to the fact that the human eye is not sensitive enough to distinguish high-frequency brightness variations, when designing a quantization table, the quantization steps in the high-frequency area are usually larger than those in the low frequency area. Thus, the information of many zero-valued high-frequency components can be greatly reduced without much visual impact. Depending on the compression ratio, most AC coefficients have zero values after dividing the quantization steps – especially those at the high frequencies – in a zigzag pattern [5]. As a result, most of the energy in the original image is concentrated in the non-zero low frequency coefficients, whereas the DC coefficient is the most important coefficient.

Property 3. Quantized Zeros: *After discrete cosine transformation and quantization, the low-frequency coefficients are usually coded as a few non-zero coefficients in the top-left of image blocks and the high-frequency coefficients are coded as many zero-valued coefficients in the bottom-right.*

Experiments were conducted on 500 pictures taken by several popular digital cameras and smartphones. Table 2 shows the absolute mean values within a decoding block while Table 3 shows the probabilities of

Table 3. Probabilities of quantized zero coefficients (%).

0.04	6.46	11.11	16.78	33.11	58.86	77.92	91.60
5.38	9.38	13.20	18.50	41.61	69.29	85.69	91.25
10.38	13.16	17.48	37.46	61.56	76.74	88.89	92.37
15.56	18.58	37.01	44.06	74.53	88.70	94.88	95.73
24.82	38.92	57.31	73.52	83.75	95.37	98.15	97.96
46.08	61.50	74.06	85.32	94.18	97.97	99.24	99.06
70.94	82.00	87.45	93.70	97.83	99.27	99.56	99.38
89.11	91.95	93.55	96.15	98.43	99.09	99.36	99.18

the quantized zero coefficients. The results satisfy Property 3. The coefficients in the high-frequency area not only have smaller values, but also have higher probabilities of being zero. Therefore, when reconstructing a quantization table, the most important task is to correctly predict the quantization steps in the low-frequency areas.

In a JPEG image, the pixels of the original color YCbCr components in the spatial domain are coded using eight bits (corresponding to the range $[0, 255]$). After the discrete cosine transformation, the DC and AC coefficients take up eleven bits (corresponding to the range $[-1,024, 1,023]$). Conversely, in the decoding process, the coefficients must be dropped from the range $[-1,024, 1,023]$ after dequantization. Although the DC coefficients may be decoded incorrectly, the amplitudes of the DC coefficients are fixed. The amplitudes of the DC and AC coefficients can be found from the maximum and minimum coefficients in a decoding block. Therefore, the upper bound for the first quantization step can be restricted by dividing 2,048 by the amplitude of a DC coefficient as follows:

$$DC : Q_{ij} \leq \left\lfloor \frac{2,048}{abs(max(S_{ij})) + abs(min(S_{ij}))} \right\rfloor \tag{7}$$

where $(i, j) \in X$, $X = \{(i,j)| i \bmod 8 = 0 \wedge j \bmod 8 = 0\}$.

Equivalently, the upper bound of the quantization step of an AC coefficient is given by:

$$AC : Q_{ij} \leq \left\lfloor \frac{1,024}{max(abs(S_{ij}))} \right\rfloor \tag{8}$$

where $(i, j) \in \overline{X}$, S_{ij} is the decoded entropy coefficient at horizontal frequency i and vertical frequency j, and Q_{ij} is the estimated upper-bound quantization step for coefficient S_{ij}.

As shown in Table 2, the DC coefficient holds the most energy in each minimum coding unit, so the rough range of the estimated quantization

Table 4.   Width estimations of two fragment groups.

| Dataset | Large Fragments (242) | | Small Fragments (28) | |
Metric	Accuracy(%)	Time(s)	Accuracy(%)	Time(s)
Brute Force	98.35	183.6	75.00	1.094
Similarity Search	95.46	0.282	64.29	0.093

table can be improved by only finding the step at Q_{00}. Generally, Q_{00} can be restricted to a very small range such as less than two when the quality factor is larger than 92.2 and one when the quality factor is greater than 95.4. The Blocking_IQA algorithm is used in a brute force manner to evaluate pictures with all possible quality factors. The picture with the best quality score is the best estimated result.

5.   Experimental Results

The performance of the proposed methodology was evaluated using an SD card containing approximately 1 GB of JPEG files – 207 high-resolution JPEG files and 120 unique quantization tables. All the pictures were captured by a BenQ DC E1050 digital camera. In the experiment, all the file headers were removed to simulate fragments without file headers. A total of 270 fragments were obtained, including sequential and fragmented files. Fragments that are too small have insufficient information for decoding. Therefore, the fragments were divided into two sets: 28 small fragments containing than 50 KB of data and 242 large fragments.

The computer used in the experiments had a 3.40 GHz CPU and 4 GB memory. Matlab (version 2013b) was used for all the computations, `libjpeg` (version 8b) was used as the default JPEG decoder/encoder and JPEG Toolbox (version 2.0) was used for coefficient extraction.

The proposed width estimation algorithm, called the similarity search algorithm, was applied to the small and large fragment sets. Table 4 shows the results along with those obtained using the brute force JPEG width estimation technique of Xu and Xu [18]. The similarity search algorithm yields an average accuracy of 95.46% for large fragments with an average time requirement of 0.282 seconds. Although the brute force algorithm has a better accuracy of 98.35%, the average time requirement per fragment is extremely high (183.6 seconds). Due to the limited information provided by small fragments, both the algorithms do not perform well. It is also pertinent to note that eight of the 28 small fragments had sizes less than 32 KB, meaning that the decoded pixel data was much less than the width of the image.

Since both the width estimation algorithms did not perform well on small fragments, additional quantization table prediction experiments were only conducted on the large fragment dataset. The quantization estimation experiments used the original picture and the saturated overflow algorithm of Huang et al. [4] for purposes of comparison.

The deviation of each element in the estimated quantization table was evaluated as:

$$\Delta Q = \frac{|Q_O - Q_E|}{|Q_O|} \tag{9}$$

where Q_O is the original quantization table and Q_E is the estimated quantization table.

The results show that the QT_Blocking algorithm performs better that the saturated overflow algorithm. The mean value of the deviation for the QT_Blocking algorithm was 0.1631 whereas the saturated overflow algorithm had a mean value of 0.6556.

Image quality was also evaluated using SSIM [15]. SSIM generates a score between zero and one, with a higher score indicating greater similarity between a test picture and original picture. A total of 157 beginning fragments were used for testing since the original fragments could be recovered easily from the image dump. The QT_Blocking algorithm had an average quality score of 0.9939 and required only 18.13 seconds; on the other hand, the saturated overflow algorithm had an average quality score of 0.9587 and required 142.5 seconds. Both algorithms had some quality scores lower than 0.85 due to failures in width prediction.

The performance of Blocking_IQA was also compared against that of JPEG_IQA, a popular no-reference image quality assessment algorithm [16]. After evaluating the rough quality factor range, the Blocking_IQA and JPEG_IQA algorithms were applied to find the picture with best quality score from among all the conditional quantization tables. The dataset comprised 207 complete pictures (the quantization tables were removed). Also, SSIM [15] was chosen as the reference algorithm to evaluate the image quality between the original picture and the estimated quantized files. The experiments revealed that the quality scores of pictures estimated by Blocking_IQA were higher than those of JPEG_IQA. Also, the Blocking_IQA required 0.7509 seconds for one file per round while JPEG_IQA required 1.3102 seconds. In other words, when assessing the quality of JPEG image files with incorrect quantization tables, the Blocking_IQA yielded better results than the well-known JPEG_IQA algorithm.

6. Conclusions

This methodology proposed in this chapter is specifically designed to recover partially-damaged standalone JPEG fragments by reconstructing pseudo headers. Extensive experiments with real camera pictures demonstrate that it can recover fragments with missing headers accurately and efficiently. However, the no-reference nature of the methodology renders it effective only on original pictures; this is because blocking features may be changed in edited or doubly-compressed pictures. Future research will examine blocking features in pictures in the context of image quality assessment as well as image forgery detection. Also, it will focus on extending the approach to other multimedia files such as videos.

Acknowledgement

This research was partially supported by International Cooperation and Exchange Project No. 61361166006, National Nature Science Foundation of China Project No. 61401176 and Natural Science Foundation of Guangdong Province (China) Project No. 2014A030310205.

References

[1] B. Carrier, *File System Forensic Analysis*, Pearson Education, Upper Saddle River, New Jersey, 2005.

[2] H. Farid, Digital image forensics, *Scientific American*, vol. 298(6), pp. 66–71, 2008.

[3] S. Garfinkel, Carving contiguous and fragmented files with fast object validation, *Digital Investigation*, vol. 4(S), pp S2–S12, 2007.

[4] L. Huang, M. Xu, H. Zhang, J. Xu and N. Zheng, A method of approximately reconstructing JPEG quantization table via saturated overflow, *Proceedings of the SPIE International Conference on Graphic and Image Processing*, vol. 8768, 2013.

[5] International Telecommunication Union, Information Technology – Digital Compression and Coding of Continuous-Tone Still Images – Requirements and Guidelines, Recommendation T.81, Geneva, Switzerland, 1993.

[6] M. Karresand and N. Shahmehri, Reassembly of fragmented JPEG images containing restart markers, *Proceedings of the European Conference on Computer Network Defense*, pp. 25–32, 2008.

[7] S. Klein and Y. Wiseman, Parallel Huffman decoding with applications to JPEG files, *The Computer Journal*, vol. 46(5), pp. 487–497, 2003.

[8] N. Memon and A. Pal, Automated reassembly of file fragmented images using greedy algorithms, *IEEE Transactions on Image Processing*, vol. 15(2), pp. 385–393, 2006.

[9] A. Mittal, A. Moorthy and A. Bovik, No-reference image quality assessment in the spatial domain, *IEEE Transactions on Image Processing*, vol. 21(12), pp. 4695–4708, 2012.

[10] A. Pal, H. Sencar and N. Memon, Detecting file fragmentation points using sequential hypothesis testing, *Digital Investigation*, vol. 5(S), pp. S2–S13, 2008.

[11] A. Pal, K. Shanmugasundaram and N. Memon, Automated reassembly of fragmented images, *Proceedings of the IEEE International Conference on Acoustics, Speech and Signal Processing*, vol. 4, pp. 732-735, 2003.

[12] H. Sencar and N. Memon, Identification and recovery of JPEG files with missing fragments, *Digital Investigation*, vol. 6(S), pp. S88–S98, 2009.

[13] K. Shanmugasundaram and N. Memon, Automatic reassembly of document fragments via context based statistical models, *Proceedings of the Nineteenth Annual Computer Security Applications Conference*, pp. 152–159, 2003.

[14] G. Sharma and R. Bala (Eds.), *Digital Color Imaging Handbook*, CRC Press, Boca Raton, Florida, 2002.

[15] Z. Wang, A. Bovik, H. Sheikh and E. Simoncelli, Image quality assessment: From error visibility to structural similarity, *IEEE Transactions on Image Processing*, vol. 13(4), pp. 600–612, 2004.

[16] Z. Wang, H. Sheikh and A. Bovik, No-reference perceptual quality assessment of JPEG compressed images, *Proceedings of the International Conference on Image Processing*, vol. 1, pp. I-477–I-480, 2002.

[17] M. Xu, L. Huang, H. Zhang, J. Xu and N. Zheng, Recovery method for JPEG file fragments with missing headers, *Journal of Image and Graphics*, vol. 18(1), pp. 24–35, 2013.

[18] Y. Xu and M. Xu, Width extraction of JPEG fragment via frequency coefficients scale similarity measuring, *Proceedings of the Second International Conference on Future Computer and Communication*, vol. 2, pp. 513–517, 2010.

IV

MOBILE DEVICE FORENSICS

Chapter 14

FORENSIC-READY SECURE iOS APPS FOR JAILBROKEN iPHONES

Jayaprakash Govindaraj, Rashmi Mata, Robin Verma and Gaurav Gupta

Abstract   Apple iOS is one of the most popular smartphone operating systems, but it restricts the installation of apps that are not from the Apple App Store. As a result, users often jailbreak their iPhones to defeat this restriction. Jailbroken iPhones are making their way into enterprises that have a Bring Your Own Device (BYOD) policy, but these devices are often barred or restricted by mobile device management software because they pose security risks. This chapter describes the iSecureRing solution that secures mobile apps and preserves the dates and timestamps of events in order to support forensic examinations of jailbroken iPhones. An analysis of the literature reveals that iSecureRing is the first forensic-ready mobile app security solution for iOS applications that execute in unsecured enterprise environments.

Keywords: Jailbroken iPhones, enterprise environments, forensic examinations

1.   Introduction

According to a 2013 Pew report [19], 40.98 % of the smartphones used by adult Americans are Apple iPhones. Apple's iOS operating system does not allow the installation of applications, extensions and themes that are not obtained from the Apple App Store. As a result, users frequently jailbreak their devices to obtain root access and defeat the installation restrictions [4]. A jailbroken iPhone allows the retrieval of applications and their associated data, potentially compromising the security of the applications and the confidentiality of the data [4, 16].

Since jailbreaking is a reality [8, 11], it is increasingly important to design mobile applications that can run securely on jailbroken iPhones. The requirement of having an application execute securely in an unsecure environment is critical to scenarios where a proprietary applica-

© IFIP International Federation for Information Processing 2015
G. Peterson, S. Shenoi (Eds.): Advances in Digital Forensics XI, IFIP AICT 462, pp. 235–249, 2015.
DOI: 10.1007/978-3-319-24123-4_14

tion should work without impacting enterprise security. At this time, enterprises that have a Bring Your Own Device (BYOD) policy generally detect and restrict jailbroken iPhones using mobile device management software such as Citrix's XenMobile and IBM's Endpoint Manager. Thus, employees have to un-jailbreak their iPhones or install enterprise applications on other approved devices. The solution proposed in this chapter enables enterprises to install their applications securely on jailbroken iPhones. New apps and existing apps can be secured and be made forensic-ready. The forensic readiness of the apps enables enterprises to check if the apps run securely and also ensures that forensic artifacts are available in the event of security incidents.

2.   Related Work

D'Orazio et al. [2] have proposed a concealment technique that enhances the security of unprotected (class D) data that is at rest in iOS devices, along with a deletion technique to reinforce data deletion in iOS devices. Hackers and malicious users resort to techniques such as jailbreaking, running an app in the debug mode, reverse engineering, dynamic hooking or tampering in order to access or compromise sensitive data stored by iOS apps:

- **Jailbreaking:** Attackers use jailbreaking to obtain system-level (root) access to iOS devices, potentially compromising the security of applications and their associated data [15].

- **Debugger Mode:** Attackers run targeted applications in the debug mode, obtain memory dumps and overwrite the memory with malicious code [9, 13].

- **Reverse Engineering:** Apps from the Apple Store are encrypted using Apple's Fairplay DRM, which complicates the task of reverse engineering binaries. However, an attacker can overwrite the encryption information of an application in a jailbroken device to obtain the memory dump and analyze it to create new attacks [3, 16].

- **Dynamic Code Hooking:** After a device is jailbroken, an attacker can hook malicious code to an app at runtime in order to bypass security checks, potentially compromising the security of the application and its data [20].

- **Tampering:** Attackers can modify the dates and timestamps of artifacts in order to cover their tracks. Verma et al. [21] have recently proposed a mechanism for preserving dates and timestamps in support of forensic examinations of Android smartphones.

This chapter presents a technique for protecting applications and data in jailbroken iOS devices. In the event of a security incident, the technique can be used to support a forensic examination of a jailbroken device.

3. Implementation Methodology

The solution has two modules: (i) a static library that wraps apps running on jailbroken devices with an extra layer of protection, making them difficult to crack and preventing access to their data; and (ii) a module that preserves authentic dates and timestamps of events related to the secured apps to support forensic examinations. The captured dates and timestamps are stored outside the device on a secure server or in the cloud. The modules are discussed in following subsections.

3.1 Securing Apps

The static library, which is designed to secure apps, incorporates APIs that may be used to identify and mitigate security vulnerabilities in jailbroken iPhones [6]. Functions in the library include: isCheck1(), which checks if an iPhone is jailbroken; isCheck2(), which checks if an application is running in the debug mode; enableDB(), which disables the gdb (debugger) for a particular application (process); isAppC(), which checks if an application binary is encrypted and also checks the integrity of application bundle files (Info.Plist); initialize(), which checks if static library functions are hooked; CheckA(), which checks if critical methods (functions) passed as arguments are hooked; CheckS(), which checks if methods (functions) related to SSL certificate validation are hooked; createCheck() and createCheckTest(), which check if an application has been tampered with; and resetZeroAll(), which wipes sensitive data from memory.

3.2 Preserving Dates and Timestamps

The dynamic library has been created using the MobileSubstrate framework. This framework provides APIs for adding runtime patches or hooks to system functions in jailbroken iOS devices [18]. The solution architecture shown in Figure 1 incorporates three components:

- **Dynamic Library (dylib):** This component hooks system open calls and captures kernel-level dates and timestamps of selected files and writes them to the log file. It is loaded into running applications. Filters are applied so that it is only loaded into specified applications.

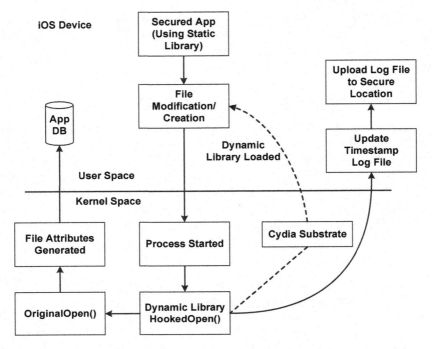

Figure 1. Solution architecture for preserving date and timestamps.

- **Timestamp Log File:** This component is stored in the internal memory of an iPhone. It is not directly accessible to applications, which secures it from unauthorized deletion.

- **Log File:** This component is generated by the DLL. It is uploaded at regular user-defined intervals to an external server or cloud storage based on network connectivity.

3.3   Static Library

The static library is designed to secure applications and their associated data. The library wraps apps in an additional layer of protection, which makes them more difficult to crack in a jailbroken iOS device. The static library contains several APIs (Table 1) that can be used to identify security vulnerabilities in jailbroken devices. The library implements the detection of jailbroken devices, the disabling of application debuggers, the checking of application encryption (for App Store binaries) and the detection of dynamic code hooking. Note that the function names are intentionally not very descriptive in order to enhance code obfuscation and hinder malicious reverse engineering efforts.

Table 1. Static library APIs.

API	Description
isCheck1()	Checks if a device has been jailbroken
isAppC()	Checks if the application encryption provided by the App Store is intact
enableDB()	Disables the application debugger
isCheck2()	Checks if an app is running in the debug mode
Initialize()	Checks if library APIs are hooked by method swizzling techniques
checkA()	Checks if a function is hooked by a method swizzling technique
checkS()	Checks if the SSL validation methods provided by the iOS SDK are hooked
makeZero()	Finds the data portion of object memory and zeroes it out
encPwd()	Encrypts object data in memory using a secret
decPwd()	Decrypts object data in memory using a secret
listed()	Adds an object to the pointer list used by the APIs
unlisted()	Removes an object from the pointer list
resetAllZero()	Wipes all tracked objects
createCheck()	Provides and statically stores a string of all the tracked memory addresses and object checksums
createCheckTest()	Checks if the current memory states of all the tracked objects match their states when checksumMem() was called

3.4 Dynamic Library

The dynamic library was created using the MobileSubstrate framework, now known as the Cydia Substrate [18]. The framework provides a platform and APIs for adding runtime patches or hooks to system functions as well as other applications on jailbroken iOS and rooted Android devices. The MobileSubstrate framework incorporates three components: (i) Mobilehooker; (ii) Mobileloader; and (iii) Safemode.

- **Mobilehooker:** This component replaces the original function with the hooked function. Two APIs may be used for iOS devices: (i) MSHookMessage(), which is mainly used to replace Objective-C methods at runtime; and (ii) MSHookFunction(), which is used to replace system functions, mainly native code written in C, C++ or assembly.

- **Mobileloader:** Cydia Substrate code is compiled to create the dynamic library, which is placed in the directory */Library/Mobile Substrate/DynamicLibraries/* in jailbroken iOS devices. The main task of Mobileloader is to load the dynamic library into running applications. The Mobileloader initially loads itself and then invokes `dlopen` on all the dynamic libraries in the directory and loads them at runtime.

The dynamic libraries are configured using Property List (PList) files, which act as filters, controlling if a library should be loaded or not. The PList file should have the same name as that of `dylib` and should be stored in the same directory as `dylib`. The PList should contain a set of arrays in a dictionary with the key Filter. The other keys used are: (i) Bundles (array) – the Bundle ID of a running application is matched against the list, if a match occurs, then `dylib` is loaded; (ii) Classes (array) – the `dylib` is loaded if one of the specified Objective-C classes in the list is implemented in the running application; and (iii) Executables (array) – `dylib` is loaded if an executable name in the list matches the executable name of the running application.

An example is:

```
Filter = Executables = ("mediaserverd"); Bundles =
     ("com.apple.MobileSlideShow"); Mode = "Any";;
```

In the example, the filter ensures that `dylib` is loaded only for the iOS built-in application Photos, whose executable name matches `mediaserverd` or Bundle ID is `com.apple.MobileSlideShow`. The Mode key is used when there are more than one filters. By specifying Mode = Any, `dylib` is loaded if one of the filters has a match.

- **Safemode:** In this mode, all third-party tweaks and extensions are disabled, preventing the iOS device from entering the crash mode. Following this, the broken `dylib` can be uninstalled from the device.

Compilation Procedure. The Theos [10] development suite was used to edit, compile and install the dynamic library on a device. It provides a component named Logos, which is a built-in pre-processor-based library designed to simplify the development of MobileSubstrate extensions. In order to compile the dynamic library, Theos must be installed on a Mac machine. A Mac OS X has most of the tools required by Theos; however, Xcode command line tools must be installed if they are not present. Additionally, it is necessary to install the `ldid` tool, which is used to sign apps or tweaks so that they can be installed on jailbroken iOS devices.

To start the project, it is necessary to obtain all the iOS private headers of the functions intended to be hooked. The headers can be dumped using the Class-Dump-Z command line tool [5]. This reverse engineering tool provides complete header information of the Objective-C code of an iOS application. Dumping the headers can take some time because headers from all the frameworks, including private frameworks, are also collected. The dumped headers are saved in a folder with the corresponding framework name. Instead of dumping the headers, headers collected by other researchers can be used (e.g., headers from GitHub). All the headers are saved at /opt/theos/include.

The next step is to create the Theos project. This involves executing the file /opt/theos/bin/nic.pl from the command line and choosing the project template, name, etc. The project type should be library because the goal is to hook a system function. After the project has been created, a new file named tweak.xm is found in the project directory; this file is used to store the hooking code.

The following pseudocode for hooking an open() system call is added in the tweak.xm file:

```
extern "C"
{ int orig\_open(const char *path, int oflags);}
int hijacked\_open(const char *path, int oflags)
{    // do something, then
    return orig\_open(path, oflags);
}
\%ctor{ NSAutoreleasePool *pool=[[NSAutoreleasePool alloc] init];
MSHookFunction(open(), \&hijacked\_open, \& orig\_open);
[pool drain];}
```

The MSHookFunction() API is used to hook the open() system call. The replacement function is hijacked_open(). The makefile is then modified to add the required frameworks. Note that the Foundation framework is used to create the hooking code. The target SDK version and the architecture needed to support it are also added:

```
TARGET := iPhone:7.0
ARCHS := armv7 arm64
ProjectName\_FRAMEWORKS = Foundation

Once done, call make from command line as below.
xyz:test xyz make
Making all for application test...
Copying resource directories into the application wrapper...

Signing test...
```

The project is then compiled and a DLL is created in the obj folder.

DLL Loading. After the DLL is created, it can be installed on a device by the Theos suite using the command `make package install`. This command creates a Debian package of the DLL and installs it in the proper location on the device. Before this is done, the environment variable must be set to `export THEOS_DEVICE_IP=iPhone Device IP`. Next, the package is transferred to the device for installation via SFTP. The iOS device should be on the same network as the computer used for development [20].

4.   Preventing Attacks and Anti-Forensics

The section discusses how attacks and anti-forensic approaches can be mitigated using the static and dynamic libraries.

4.1   Using the Static Library

- **BOOL isCheck1():** This function is used to check if an iOS device is jailbroken. It returns yes if the iOS device is jailbroken; otherwise no. This function can be called before application launch.

- **API for Checking Debug Mode:** The application exits when launched in the debug mode using the `enableDB()` function. This function can be called from `main()` and from elsewhere in the project to disable debugging at any stage. By calling `enabledDB()` in `main()` or before app launch, the application can be prevented from running in the debug mode. Therefore, the function should be called in the release mode.

- **isCheck2():** This function gives information about how the application is running. If the application was started in the debug mode, then a value of one is returned; otherwise zero is returned.

- **BOOL isAppC(char* inBundlePath):** This function checks if the application has been hacked. The parameter `inBundlePath` can be any character pointer; it is only added for obfuscation and is not used inside the function. It includes an app encryption check (if the App Store encryption is broken), signer identity checks, etc. If the app is cracked, the function returns yes; otherwise no. The function is primarily used to check if App Store binaries are cracked.

- **int Initialize():** This function checks if the APIs in the static library are themselves hooked. The function has to be called initially, preferably during app launch, to check if the library APIs are hooked by method swizzling, after which the appropriate actions must be taken. If the functions are hooked, then it makes no sense to use the APIs to protect applications.

- **int checkA(const char* MCl, const char* MFr, const char* MFn, void *funcPTR):** This function checks if any hooking is done for a critical method within an application passed as an argument to the function. The function returns one if no hooking is discovered and zero if a function is hooked. It requires the method name, method class and the path of the framework (for a framework method) or app bundle path (for an application method).

- **int checkS():** This function checks if SSL certificate validation methods provided by the iOS SDK are hooked. This function is invoked within an application before calling SSL validation methods so that the proper actions can be taken. The function returns one if there is no hooking and zero if a function is hooked.

- **makeZero(obj):** This function is used to zero the value of a sensitive variable after its use.

- **encPwd() and decPwd():** These APIs are used for encrypting sensitive data immediately after the data is created and decrypting the data only during its use. After the sensitive data has been used, it should be cleared from memory permanently.

- **listed() and unlisted():** These functions track several objects in order to clear them from memory simultaneously. Sensitive objects are added to the list to keep track of them; they are all cleared at one time using an API. For example, when a device is locked and/or an app is closed (hidden or terminated), it may be necessary to wipe all the sensitive data. In this case, it is necessary to add `resetZeroAll()` to the state-change notify functions in `AppDelegate`. Several tools are available for attackers to modify the values of critical data and change the behavior of an application at runtime. Such modifications can be tracked using the `createCheck()` and `createCheckTest()` APIs to create a checksum of the critical data and check it periodically to ensure that the data is not modified by an attacker.

4.2   Using the Dynamic Library

Whenever files are modified, accessed or created, the hijacked `open()` call is invoked and the modified, accessed, created dates and timestamps (MAC DTS) are captured and stored in the log file. The log file is stored

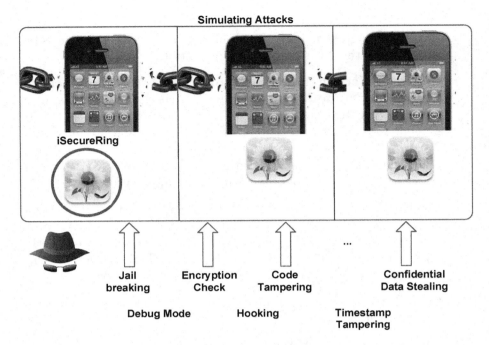

Figure 2. Simulating attacks on devices.

outside the iPhone at a secure location such as a server or in the cloud. The information in the log file can be used in a forensic investigation of the smartphone in the event of a security incident.

5. Experimental Results

The experiments involved the creation of two apps, one without any protection and the other protected by iSecureRing. The apps were then deployed on a jailbroken iPhone 4 (iOS 7.0.6).

A series of attacks were simulated on the apps and their data to validate the proposed solution (Figure 2). At the application level, the apps were subjected to various attacks to exploit the lack of binary protection [2]. The results in Table 2 demonstrate that an app with iSecureRing running on a jailbroken iPhone (Row 3) is just as secure as a normal app running on a non-jailbroken iPhone (Row 1).

Performance benchmarking was conducted for the three cases considered in the experiments. Figure 3 summarizes the results of the initial tests (five runs). The results show no significant differences in device performance.

Table 2. Attacks and results.

iPhone 4 (iOS 7.0.6)	Jail-broken	Debug Mode	Encryption Check	Hooking	Code Tampering
Not Jailbroken (App without protection)	Yes	No	No	No	No
Jailbroken (App without protection)	N/A	Yes	Yes	Yes	Yes
Jailbroken (App with iSecureRing)	N/A	No	No	No	No

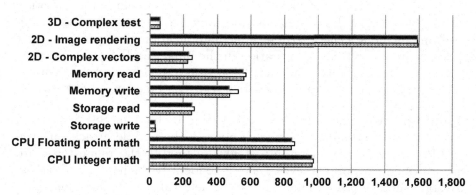

■ **Jailbroken with iSecureRing** □ **Jailbroken without iSecureRing** ▥ **Not Jailbroken**

Figure 3. Performance benchmark results.

```
file=/System/Library/PrivateFrameworks/TextInput.framework/Info.plist
Mtime=Wed Feb 19 11:10:02 2014
 Atime=Wed Feb 19 11:10:02 2014
 Ctime=Wed Feb 19 11:10:02 2014
 Flag=0

file=/var/mobile/Media/PhotoData/Thumbnails/V2/DCIM/100APPLE/IMG_0002.PNG/5003.JPG
Mtime=Sun Mar  2 23:27:24 2014
 Atime=Sun Mar  2 23:27:24 2014
 Ctime=Sun Mar  2 23:27:24 2014
 Flag=0
```

Figure 4. MAC DTS logs for an image file.

iSecureRing also helps detect attempts to exploit known or unknown vulnerabilities by capturing the timestamps of activities associated with a secured app. One experiment involved timestamp tampering attempts on images from Apple's Photo app. iSecureRing successfully captured all the events in the log. An analysis of the log clearly revealed the tampering attempts. Figure 4 shows the MAC DTS logs for one of the images.

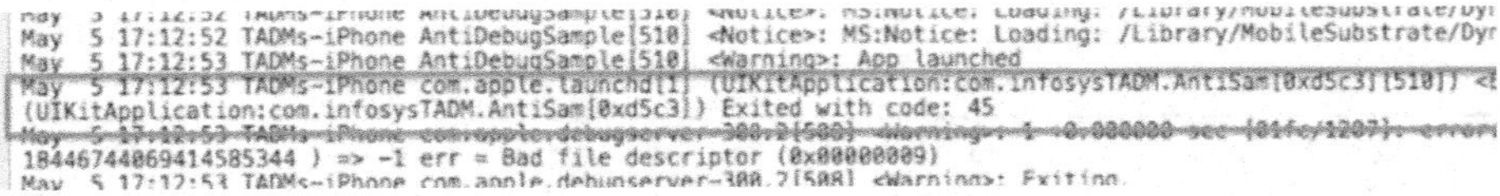

May 5 17:12:52 TADMs-iPhone AntiDebugSample[510] <Notice>: MS:Notice: Loading: /Library/MobileSubstrate/Dy
May 5 17:12:53 TADMs-iPhone AntiDebugSample[510] <Notice>: MS:Notice: Loading: /Library/MobileSubstrate/Dyr
May 5 17:12:53 TADMs-iPhone AntiDebugSample[510] <Warning>: App launched
May 5 17:12:53 TADMs-iPhone com.apple.launchd[1] (UIKitApplication:com.infosysTADM.AntiSam[0xd5c3][510]) <
(UIKitApplication:com.infosysTADM.AntiSam[0xd5c3]) Exited with code: 45
May 5 17:12:53 TADMs-iPhone com.apple.debugserver-300.2[580] <Warning>: -1 -0.000000 sec [01fc/1207]: error
18446744069414585344) => -1 err = Bad file descriptor (0x00000009)
May 5 17:12:53 TADMs-iPhone com.apple.debugserver-300.2[580] <Warning>: Exiting.

Figure 5.   Preventing a debug mode attack.

Debug Mode Attack.   Figure 5 shows a screenshot of an Xcode application running in the debug mode [17] while it was being protected by iSecureRing.

Encryption Attack.   Clutch [17] was used to simulate an encryption attack (Clutch may be downloaded from `cydia.iphonecake.com`). iSecureRing includes a check to determine if application encryption is intact by analyzing encryption information in the binary and also the `cryptid` flag value. If the application encryption is found to be broken, then the user is alerted and the application behavior can be changed at runtime.

Hooking.   A hooking attack was simulated by hooking SSL validation methods. It is possible to launch a man-in-the-middle attack on even HTTPS requests to understand, steal and modify the requested data. iSecureRing incorporates several checks to identify the hooking of critical methods such as SSL validation and authentication. Applications that use iSecureRing are protected against the attacks because the user is alerted and the app behavior can be changed.

Code Tampering.   A code tampering attack was simulated using Cycript [7], a JavaScript interpreter. The tool was used to modify iOS application behavior at runtime (e.g., bypassing some authentication checks and accessing critical information from memory). An application compiled with iSecureRing provides APIs for identifying code tampering of critical instance variables and class objects using CRC checksums. Also, APIs are provided for wiping sensitive data from memory.

6.   Case Study

The iSecureRing implementation was successfully used to secure an iPhone mobile app for a leading bank in India.

Problem Statement.   The bank had a security incident in which the application running on a jailbroken device revealed sensitive data.

Jailbreaking Attack.   The attacker had used the latest jailbreaking tool for iOS 7.1.2 Pangu [1]. The attacker also used certain tweaks to defeat jailbreak detection. Some tweaks within Cydia bypass the jailbreak detection check of an application and make the application run normally even on jailbroken devices. One such tweak is xCon [12], which hooks low-level APIs used for jailbreak detection such as file-related APIs and other system calls, thus bypassing the jailbreak detection functions used in the application. No configuration is required for xCon, a MobileSubstrate dynamic library that can be installed from Cydia.

iSecureRing Results. The bank app was secured using iSecureRing. The jailbreak detection function was robust enough to check if the device was jailbroken and if any jailbreak detection bypassing functions were present. The solution was tested with xCon 39 beta 7 on iPhone 4 devices with iOS version 7.1.2. xCon was unable to bypass the jailbreak detection techniques used by iSecureRing. The iSecureRing solution checks for the existence of file-related system function hooking, rendering xCon-like tweaks useless. The solution also mitigates the jailbreak detection bypassing mechanism provided by the xCon dynamic library.

7.   Conclusions

The iSecureRing solution secures apps on jailbroken iOS devices. The static library helps detect security vulnerabilities and alerts users to take appropriate actions. The dynamic library helps detect malicious tampering of data by storing authentic copies of MAC DTS values on a local server or in the cloud; this also supports offline digital forensic investigations after security incidents. Thus, iSecureRing enables existing and new apps to be secured and made forensic-ready even if the iOS device has been jailbroken. With enterprises implementing BYOD policies and jailbroken devices making their way into enterprises, the iSecureRing solution helps enterprises mitigate the security risks while enabling employees to use one device for official and personal activities.

Future research will focus on analyzing anomalous interactions with secured apps, blocking attacks and raising alerts. Efforts will also be made to create similar solutions for Android and Windows smartphones.

References

[1] J. Benjamin, How to jailbreak iOS 7.1.x with Pangu 1.1 on Windows, *iDownloadBlog*, June 29, 2014.

[2] C. D'Orazio, A. Ariffin and K. Choo, iOS anti-forensics: How can we securely conceal, delete and insert data? *Proceedings of the Forty-Seventh Hawaii International Conference on System Sciences*, pp. 4838–4847, 2014.

[3] D. Ertel, Decrypting iOS apps (www.infointox.net/?p=114), 2013.

[4] S. Esser, Exploiting the iOS kernel, presented at *Black Hat USA*, 2011.

[5] P. Gianchandani, iOS Application Security Part 2 – Getting Class Information of iOS Apps, Infosec Institute, Elmwood Park, Illinois, 2014.

[6] GitHub, Tools for securely clearing and validating iOS application memory, San Francisco, California (github.com/project-imas/memory-security), 2014.

[7] S. Guerrero Selma, Hacking iOS on the run: Using Cycript, presented at the *RSA Conference*, 2014.

[8] A. Hoog and K. Strzempka, *iPhone and iOS Forensics: Investigation, Analysis and Mobile Security for Apple iPhone, iPad and iOS Devices*, Syngress, Waltham, Massachusetts, 2011.

[9] iPhoneDevWiki, debugserver (iphonedevwiki.net/index.php/Debugserver), 2015.

[10] iPhoneDevWiki, Theos (iphonedevwiki.net/index.php/Theos), 2015.

[11] iPhoneHacks, Jailbreaking your iPhone remains legal in US, but it is illegal to jailbreak your iPad and unlock your iPhone under DMCA, October 26, 2012.

[12] iPhone Wiki, xCon (theiphonewiki.com/wiki/XCon), 2014.

[13] C. Miller, Owning the fanboys: Hacking Mac OS X, presented at *Black Hat Japan*, 2008.

[14] C. Miller, Mobile attacks and defense, *IEEE Security and Privacy*, vol. 9(4), pp. 68–70, 2011.

[15] S. Morrissey, *iOS Forensic Analysis for iPhone, iPad and iPod Touch*, Apress, New York, 2010.

[16] M. Renard, Practical iOS apps hacking, *Proceedings of the First International Symposium on Grey-Hat Hacking*, pp. 14–26, 2012.

[17] B. Satish, Penetration Testing for iPhone Applications – Part 5, Infosec Institute, Elmwood Park, Illinois, 2013.

[18] SaurikIT, Cydia Substrate, Isla Vista, California (www.cydiasubstrate.com), 2014.

[19] A. Smith, Smartphone Ownership 2013, Pew Research Center, Washington, DC, June 5, 2013.

[20] B. Trebitowski, Beginning Jailbroken iOS Development – Building and Deployment, Pixegon, Albuquerque, New Mexico (`brandon treb.com/beginning-jailbroken-ios-development-building-and-deployment`), 2011.

[21] R. Verma, J. Govindaraj and G. Gupta, Preserving date and time-stamps for incident handling in Android smartphones, in *Advances in Digital Forensics X*, G. Peterson and S. Shenoi (Eds.), Springer, Heidelberg, Germany, pp. 209–225, 2014.

Chapter 15

A FRAMEWORK FOR DESCRIBING MULTIMEDIA CIRCULATION IN A SMARTPHONE ECOSYSTEM

Panagiotis Andriotis, Theo Tryfonas, George Oikonomou and Irwin King

Abstract   Contemporary mobile devices allow almost unrestricted sharing of multimedia and other types of files. However, because smartphones and tablets can easily access the Internet and exchange files wirelessly, they have also become useful tools for criminals who perform illegal activities such as sharing contraband and distributing illegal images. Thus, the need to investigate the source and destination of a multimedia file that resides in the internal memory of a smartphone is apparent. This chapter presents a framework for illustrating and visualizing the flow of digital images extracted from Android smartphones during a forensic investigation. The approach uses "big data" concepts to facilitate the processing of diverse (semi-structured) evidence from mobile devices and extends the idea of digital evidence bags. The data used for evaluation was obtained by running experiments that involved image exchange through channels such as Bluetooth, Internet and cloud services. The study presents information about the locations where evidence resides and uses graph databases to store metadata and to visualize the relationships that connect images with apps and events.

Keywords: Android forensics, graph database, content, analysis, NoSQL

1.   Introduction

The proliferation of smartphones and fast mobile telephony networks offer countless opportunities for users to exchange text messages, photographic images, videos and multimedia content. Unfortunately these smart applications, which are equipped with convenient interfaces that facilitate the smooth and rapid flow of information, have become tools

© IFIP International Federation for Information Processing 2015
G. Peterson, S. Shenoi (Eds.): Advances in Digital Forensics XI, IFIP AICT 462, pp. 251–267, 2015.
DOI: 10.1007/978-3-319-24123-4_15

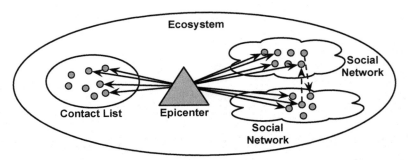

Figure 1. Smartphone ecosystem.

in the hands of criminals who commit crimes such as sharing contraband and distributing illegal images.

Smartphones are often seized in investigations and the evidence extracted from them is used in courts to establish the guilt or innocence of defendants. They are valuable evidence containers because they hold large amounts of personal information and are fully integrated with their owners' lifestyles. Smartphones are equipped with a variety of sensors that enable developers to create powerful applications (apps). They have also become very efficient with regard to their processing power and the accuracy of their sensors. Users are able to connect to the Internet, upload and download material through cloud services, capture images, sound recordings and videos, monitor their health and well-being, create and edit documents and spreadsheets, and obtain personalized information from various sources based on their locations and interests. All these actions leave artifacts that can be used as evidence.

A smartphone can be viewed as defining a unique "ecosystem" where the owner of the device is a central entity: the epicenter. The ecosystem consists of smaller groups that include entities linked with each other via various types of relationships. For example, the contact list of a smartphone corresponds to an entity group in which an analyst can find people who are connected with the epicenter. Another entity group might include the accounts of friends in a social network or the contacts in a professional network like LinkedIn. One of the problems that a forensic analyst has to solve is whether an entity is a real person or whether it represents a fake, secondary or parody account. The forensic analysis of a smartphone can also reveal entities from different groups that are linked together (especially, if the smartphone owner has used the contact syncing utility provided by many social network apps).

Figure 1 shows a smartphone ecosystem. The epicenter is linked with the contact list group (neighborhood) and with two other social networks. Some entities in the ecosystem are also linked together (dashed lines) via the automated contact linking process. During a forensic analysis, the different neighborhoods can be linked via the artifacts found in various databases in the internal memory of the smartphone. In Android smartphones, applications store data in specific folders in the data partition [8]. Most of the application folders contain the folders *databases*, *cache*, *lib* and *files*. The *databases* folder is usually where information about the user is maintained in SQLite databases. The stored information can help reconstruct the profile and activities of the epicenter. Furthermore, a forensic analysis can be enhanced using reporting tools that provide visual metaphors of the underlying data [18].

This approach involves separating diverse data existing in the smartphone internal memory into distinct categories such as entities, groups and multimedia. It also focuses on the relationships with the epicenter. However, despite the practicality of the representations of social connections, certain disadvantages exist. The approach does not provide additional information about the events linked to entities. For example, if a forensic analyst wishes to visualize the entity in the ecosystem who is responsible for capturing and distributing an illegal image, Figure 1 would not provide any useful hints because the entities are not linked with actions they performed using the various apps. Consequently, it is necessary to incorporate functionality that links actions with entities.

This chapter focuses on cases involving the circulation of digital images (photographs) in a smartphone ecosystem. The goal is to construct a network that depicts the distribution of multimedia in the ecosystem defined by an Android mobile device. The main contribution is a framework that solves the problem of linking entities with events and digital artifacts during forensic analyses of smartphones while highlighting the relationships between apps and multimedia. The approach uses big data concepts and extends the concept of digital evidence bags, utilizing modern storage methods and focusing on the ecosystem epicenter and its actions. Information stored about an individual under investigation is augmented with visualizations of the interactions in his ecosystem using graph databases. The conceptual design is readily extended to cover other types and aspects of evidence found in smartphones. In addition, the framework can represent multiple smartphone ecosystems that are linked in a case.

2. Related Work

Several researchers have highlighted the importance of identifying traces that reveal access to illegal content. For example, Howard [9] has presented a technical analysis of the cache and the methods that a forensic analyst may use in a child pornography case to find data stored in the *Temporary Internet Files* folder of a browser.

More recently, the seamless information flow provided by peer-to-peer (P2P) networks has transformed digital neighborhoods to blooming areas of illegal image and video trafficking. Hurley et al. [11] have analyzed multimedia trafficking in two popular P2P networks (eMule and Gnutella) and have studied various subgroups such as peers that use Tor, peers that bridge multiple P2P networks and peers that contribute to file availability. They conclude that these groups are more active than others with regard to child pornography trafficking. Wolak et al. [20] have examined data from Gnutella using the RoundUp investigative tool [13] and propose that data should be systematically gathered and analyzed to prioritize investigations in P2P networks. However, these tools cannot be applied to smartphones and used to reconstruct and present the exchange of information between different apps.

Traditional digital image forensics [5] can be employed to perform tasks such as device identification and linking, and digital forgery detection. Despite the plethora of anti-forensic software [17], certain information sources exist that can provide indications (e.g., sensor data) that can be used during forensic analyses of smartphones [16]. However, this data is usually volatile and is not available during a post-mortem analysis.

Several novel approaches have been proposed to automatically collect and analyze non-volatile data from Android devices, especially devices used in sensitive enterprise environments [7]. Marturana and Tacconi [15] have proposed a machine-learning-based triage scheme to automate digital media categorization, essentially blending digital forensics and machine learning. Liu et al. [14] have used support vector machines to identify the smartphone camera sources of digital images and to reveal operations that may have been applied to the digital images. Turner [19] has presented an approach for unifying digital evidence from disparate sources using digital evidence bags (i.e., universal containers for capturing and processing digital evidence from different sources). Flaglien et al. [4] have highlighted the obstacles posed by diverse file formats with regard to digital evidence processing; several solutions have been proposed to overcome these obstacles. For example, Garfinkel [6] developed the DFXML scheme to facilitate the exchange of structured forensic data from multiple sources.

Digital forensic researchers have studied the diverse data that can be drawn from the disparate sources existing in a smartphone ecosystem. Chung et al. [3] have analyzed artifacts from various sources (desktop machines and mobile devices) connected to cloud storage services, revealing traces of activity in file paths, XML files and databases. Huber et al. [10] have collected and categorized information from social media networks, including user data, posts, private messages, photograph images and associated metadata; Kontaxis et al. [12] have used this information to detect if cloned profiles exist in social networks. Anglano [2] has analyzed the traces that remain from the use of the popular chatting app, WhatsApp Messenger, on Android devices. However, no work has focused on the circulation of images (or multimedia) in smartphone ecosystems. The framework presented in this chapter integrates all the valuable data existing in a smartphone ecosystem, facilitating flexible and extensible evidence visualization and analysis.

3.   Using Graph Databases

Forensic investigations of smartphones involve four basic steps: (i) smartphone seizure; (ii) logical and/or physical data acquisition; (iii) data analysis; and (iv) data presentation and preservation. This study focuses on the data presentation step and proposes a methodology for automating forensic investigations of illegal image trafficking in smartphone ecosystems. Of particular interest are images that have entered or exited an ecosystem via five paths: (i) wireless technologies such as Bluetooth, Wi-Fi Direct and near field communications (NFC); (ii) email; (iii) Internet downloads; (iv) cloud storage services; and (v) smartphone applications such as Facebook Messenger and Twitter.

The mapping approach highlights the relationships between photographic images and their sources or destinations. For example, the most obvious relationship between a JPEG image and a Camera application is if the photographic image was captured using the app or if it was downloaded or distributed using another app. This information is critical to determining if an individual under investigation was involved in producing illegal content or merely distributing the content.

The storage capacity of modern mobile devices is constantly increasing and forensic analyses of mobile devices involve the processing of very large amounts of information. As a result, a medium such as a database is required to safely migrate and store all the acquired data and its relationships for further analysis. Traditional databases (e.g., relational databases) require very complicated design strategies to depict relations, foreign keys, joins and tables as reference points to link different entities. However, new types of databases have been introduced for social media and big data. These include NoSQL and graph databases such as Cassandra, MongoDB and Neo4j. The principal advantage of a graph database over a relational database is its ability to easily handle and depict relationships between linked entities.

This chapter investigates relations that occur between linked entities. For example, to locate images that were downloaded from the Internet, connections and/or relationships with the attribute DOWNLOADED must be targeted. Thus, a graph database is the most appropriate storage medium because it supports searches for patterns within paths created by nodes that are linked together. In a graph database, nodes can be stored and connected together using different attributes based on the types of relationships existing between the nodes. The result is an expandable graph that can store different kinds of information. Indeed, photographic images, videos, music and sound clips, and documents can all be stored in a graph database without the need for database refactoring.

4.   Use Case Experiments

A scenario involving numerous user activities was designed in order to capture the traces left in smartphone internal memory after the use of several common applications. The smartphone used was a Samsung Galaxy Fame GT-6810P running Android Operating System (version 4.1) and equipped with an external secure digital (SD) card and superuser privileges (su).

The following actions were performed to simulate illegal image exchange and trafficking in the smartphone ecosystem:

- Images were emailed to the user's account. The user viewed and downloaded them to the smartphone. The standard Android Email and Gmail apps were used.

- Images were captured using the smartphone camera and stored on the smartphone.

- Images were exchanged using wireless interfaces (Bluetooth and NFC).

- Applications such as Snapchat (chatting while exchanging images) were used. Other apps included the popular Facebook Messenger, WhatsApp and Google Hangouts.

- Images were uploaded and downloaded from the smartphone via cloud services (Dropbox and Google Drive apps).

- Images were downloaded to the smartphone using applications such as Twitter and Instagram.

- Images were downloaded from the Internet using the standard Android Internet browser and Google Chrome, which is shipped with most recent versions of the Android operating system.

After the actions were performed, the data was collected via a physical acquisition of the smartphone data partition. During this process, the USB Debugging option on the smartphone was enabled and the Android Debug Bridge (`adb`) tool was utilized. As described in [1], this is a common way to extract physical images of smartphone partitions. Physical data acquisition also includes the extraction of deleted images using open source tools such as `scalpel`. Deleted images can be incorporated in the graph database as nodes connected to the epicenter with relationships marked DELETED.

5. Results

Table 1 presents the locations (in the form of lists of folders) where information related to the circulation of images in the ecosystem is stored. It also describes the traces found in the internal memory of a smartphone. Of special interest is the data folder (`data/data/`) of a smartphone where most applications store significant amounts of information. Note also that the databases listed in this section are not encrypted and an individual with superuser privileges can access and view them in an open source SQLite browser such as `sqliteman`. Note that [SQLite] in Table 1 denotes a SQLite3 database. Anglano [2] provides information about decoding `.nomedia` image files.

The Android operating system is installed on a variety of devices with different characteristics. A smartphone, for example, may be equipped with external disk storage (an SD or microSD card), internal emulated storage or both. The test smartphone had two storage folders: emulated and external SD. When an SD card is inserted in a smartphone, images captured by the Camera app are usually stored on the SD card. Logical copies of the folders in the external and emulated media reveal only the images that can be seen by the operating system. However, these images may contain important information in their Exif metadata headers, such as user location if the GPS was enabled when the image was captured. A logical copy of the storage media may be obtained by connecting the smartphone to a computer via a USB cable and issuing a pull command to the `adb` tool. Collecting this data augments a visualization with information about the types of connections that link nodes in the graph. Table 2 lists the possible locations of digital images in the test smartphone.

Table 1. Resources that provide information about image sharing.

Path	Type	Details
com.android.bluetooth/ /databases/btopp.db [SQLite]	Sent, received, deleted	In table btopp, see uri and direction
com.android.email/ /cache/[folder_e.g._1.db_att]	Received, attached (via Email app)	May not be visible via Gallery app
com.android.email/databases/ /EmailProvider.db [SQLite]	Sent, received, downloaded	In attachment and message tables
com.android.providers.downloads/ /databases/downloads.db [SQLite]	Downloaded	Downloaded (Internet) chat apps (e.g., Hangouts)
com.dropbox.android/ databases/db.db [SQLite]	Deleted, uploaded	Tables dropbox and photos
com.facebook.orca/cache/fb-temp/	Uploaded	Uploaded content
com.facebook.orca/cache/image/ /v2.ols100.1/[folders]/	Sent, received, seen (via Gallery app)	Thumbnails from Gallery (if accessed by Messenger)
com.google.android.apps.docs/cache/ /diskCache/fetching/account_cache_1/	Uploaded, downloaded	Images residing in Google Docs app
com.google.android.apps.docs/ /databases/DocList.db [SQLite]	Deleted, data owners	Tables like entry111
com.google.android.apps.docs/ /files/fileinternal/[folders]/	Downloaded, pinned	Pinned images to be viewed offline
com.google.android.gm/ /cache/[user's_gmail_address]	Unknown, sent, received	Images and other attachments
com.google.android.talk/ /cache/scratch/	Sent	Sent images via Hangouts app.
com.google.android.talk/ /databases/babel1.db [SQLite]	Sent, received	In messages, see attribute local_uri
com.instagram.android/cache/	Pending, captured, sent, received	Names flagged with timestamps
com.sec.android.gallery3d /databases/picasa.db [SQLite]	Various	Table photos (if auto-uploading is on)
com.sec.android.providers.downloads/ /databases/sisodownloads.db [SQLite]	Downloaded	Downloaded via Internet browser
com.snapchat.android/cache/ /received_image_snaps/	Received (.nomedia files)	May be encrypted (version dependent)
com.snapchat.android/cache/ /stories/received/thumbnail/	Received (.nomedia files)	May be encrypted (version dependent)
com.snapchat.android/ /databases/tcspahn.db	Various	Entries about sent, received images

Table 2. Locations of images in external and emulated storage.

Path	Type
mnt/extSdCard/DCIM/Camera/	Photos captured via the Camera app
mnt/sdcard0/Download/	Downloaded via the Chrome browser
mnt/extSdCard/Download/	Downloaded via the Internet browser
mnt/sdcard0/Pictures/Twitter/	Uploaded and downloaded via Twitter
mnt/sdcard0/Pictures/Facebook/	Captured and uploaded via Facebook
mnt/sdcard0/Pictures/Messenger/	Downloaded via Messenger
mnt/sdcard0/Beam/ or /sdcard0/Bluetooth/	Exchanged via wireless
mnt/sdcard0/Snapchat/	Downloaded photos via Snapchat
mnt/sdcard0/WhatsApp/Media/ /WhatsApp Images/	Received and sent images via WhatsApp
mnt/sdcard0/Android/data/	Folders containing photos from distinct apps

6. System Design

A graph database is a graph and a database at the same time. Entities, photographic images and applications are represented as nodes in the graph. This feature makes the entire system expandable and able to hold diverse types of information (e.g., videos, sound recordings and documents). In the proposed framework, each case is represented as a node in the graph (because, in the future, different cases with unique ecosystems may have to be linked). For example, a person under investigation might be involved in multiple cases. In the graph database, nodes are connected with relationships such as DOWNLOADED, UPLOADED and DELETED, and contain information from the original SQLite databases. Nodes and relationships both contain attributes/properties that can be used by a forensic analyst to find patterns and paths inside the graph by issuing SQL-like queries.

The work described in this chapter used the Neo4j graph database (available from www.neo4j.org) and its Cypher query language. Cypher is a graph database language that uses ASCII art expressions and a limited number of commands to issue graph queries. An example of the ASCII art writing style used by Cypher is:

(a)->[:UPLOADED]-(b)-[:DELETED]->(c)

where (a), (b) and (c) are nodes and [:UPLOADED] and [:DELETED] are relationships. Thus, (a) is linked with (b) via the [:UPLOADED]

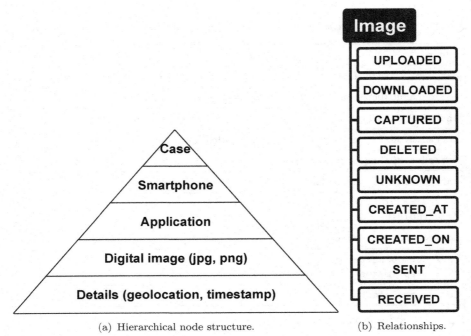

(a) Hierarchical node structure.   (b) Relationships.

Figure 2.   Graph database conceptual design.

relationship that points from (a) to (b), and so on. In a large graph, the query output can be presented graphically, viewed using a browser or outputted as a table. Graph databases are very useful in forensic analysis because they provide the opportunity to visualize data and simultaneously support searches for patterns and paths in the ecosystem using a common infrastructure (which is the graph database itself).

Figure 2(a) presents the hierarchical design of a system that incorporates the findings of the case study discussed in Section 5. The graph has nodes that represent: (i) the case; (ii) the seized smartphone (linked with the case); (iii) the applications existing in the smartphone ecosystem; (iv) the images found in the cache and other storage media; and (v) important details such as geolocations and timestamps. It was decided to depict geolocations and timestamps as distinct nodes and not as node attributes due to the importance of this information and also because it may be necessary to link more actions in the future with specific geolocations and timestamps. Figure 2(b) shows the main relationships that link images with other graph entities. CAPTURED is related to the Exif metadata, which identifies the camera type (or smartphone) used

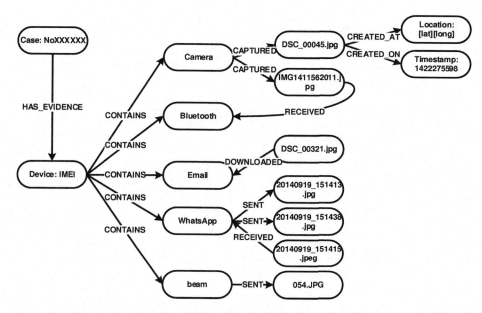

Figure 3. Nodes and their relationships in the graph database.

to capture the image. CREATED_AT is a relationship that links images and locations and CREATED_ON links images with timestamps. Figure 3 shows an example of the principal entities and their relationships in the graph database.

One of the advantages of this system is that it is easily extended to incorporate new nodes corresponding to videos, sound recordings and documents. In addition, it allows for the integration with other ecosystems that might exist in a case. It is also possible to add nodes that represent entities such as social media accounts and individuals in a contact list. Thus, data and evidence found in different devices involved in a case can be linked.

Another advantage of the proposed framework is its graph representation, which makes it possible to apply graph-theoretic approaches and metrics to extract information. Example metrics are the degree, indegree and outdegree of a node corresponding to an application (e.g., Facebook Messenger) that describe the usage frequency of the app and the incoming and outgoing digital evidence, respectively. At a larger scale, these metrics provide information about the most preferred application for image exchange.

The timestamp nodes help focus on different periods of time and highlight potential changes in user behavior. Additionally, data from Neo4j graph databases are easily stored as GraphML files. GraphML files can

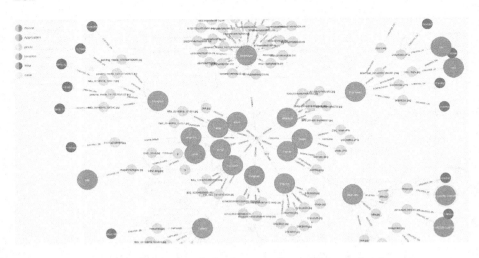

Figure 4.   Screenshot from the experimental graph database.

be fed to sophisticated graph visualization tools to significantly enhance data analysis.

Figure 4 shows a screenshot of the graph database after data collection. To view the graph, it is necessary to establish a connection with `http://localhost:7474/browser` when the database server is running and type the command MATCH (n) RETURN n.

Figure 5 shows an example of further analysis of the graph using the Gephi open source visualization tool (available from `gephi.github.io`). The "busy" nodes (i.e., the apps most used for image sharing) were identified by extracting the graph as a GraphML file and plotting the nodes according to their degrees.

The graph database also provides information about data sharing in a more concise way, projecting results (degree, indegree, outdegree) onto tables in order to observe the data circulation in an ecosystem. Let $\mathcal{R}$ be the set of relationships that link apps with images, i.e., $\mathcal{R}$ = {RECEIVED, SENT, DOWNLOADED, CAPTURED, UNKNOWN, DELETED, UPLOADED}. Let $\mathcal{I}$ be the set of incoming relationships and $\mathcal{O}$ be the set of outgoing relationships, i.e., $\mathcal{I}$ = {RECEIVED, DOWNLOADED, CAPTURED} and $\mathcal{O}$ = {SENT, UNKNOWN, DELETED, UPLOADED}. Additionally, let $\mathcal{A}$ be the set of app sources in an ecosystem, i.e., $\mathcal{A}$ = {Bluetooth, Beam, Email, Downloads, Messenger, Drive, Gmail, Hangouts, Instagram, Dropbox, Snapchat, Camera, Facebook, Twitter, WhatsApp}. In general, $\mathcal{A} = \{A_i, i = 1, \ldots, n\}$, where n is the number of different apps in the ecosystem. If m is the number of different relationships that link app A_i, then the relationships

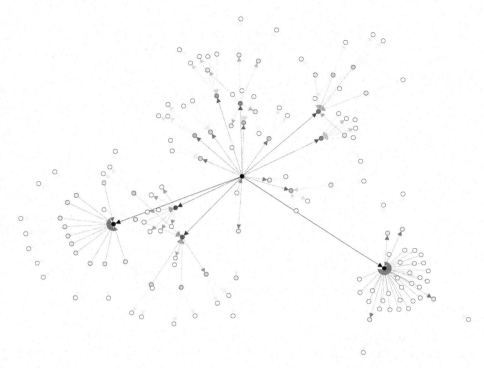

Figure 5. Graph with "busy" nodes highlighted.

may be expressed as $r^{(i)}{}_j$, $j = 1, \ldots, m$ and $r^{(i)}{}_j \in \mathcal{A}$. For simplicity, $r^{(i)}{}_j$ is expressed as:

$$r^{(i)}{}_j = \begin{cases} \kappa & \text{if } r^{(i)}{}_j \in \mathcal{I} \\ \lambda & \text{if } r^{(i)}{}_j \in \mathcal{O} \end{cases} \tag{1}$$

Thus,

$$indegree = \sum_{i=1} \kappa \tag{2}$$

$$outdegree = \sum_{j=1} \lambda \tag{3}$$

$$degree = indegree + outdegree \tag{4}$$

Table 3 shows the results of applying Equation (4) on the graph database. The results indicate that Messenger stores more information compared with the other apps. Also, the user of the smartphone exchanged images using Bluetooth and NFC (Beam) (indegree $\neq 0$). Other information can be gleaned about the use of chatting apps for image exchange

Table 3.   Numbers of relationships between images and apps.

App	Indegree	Outdegree	Degree
Bluetooth	5	2	7
Beam	1	0	1
Email	2	0	2
Downloads	6	0	6
Messenger	28	4	32
Drive	2	1	3
Gmail	0	3	3
Hangouts	2	2	4
Instagram	0	5	5
Dropbox	2	6	8
Snapchat	1	0	1
Camera	11	0	11
Facebook	3	0	3
Twitter	0	2	2
WhatsApp	3	2	5

(WhatsApp and Hangouts). For example, the person under investigation cannot claim that no image left the device via WhatsApp because the outdegree for WhatsApp equals two. This means that at least two images were sent via WhatsApp to another ecosystem. Additionally, if the image nodes were to be connected to time nodes, it would be possible to see when these transactions occurred.

7.   Conclusions

The framework presented in this chapter provides a novel approach for capturing and analyzing the flow of images in smartphone ecosystems. The relevant information is collected from SQLite databases in the caches and data partitions of Android smartphones (and tablets) and stored in a Neo4j graph database for forensic analyses. The graph database supports rapid and accurate searches based on pattern matching. The framework is extensible and can be adapted to provide big data functionality by adding diverse, semi-structured data from a variety of sources. An unexpected discovery during the study was that applications such as Facebook can access the smartphone Gallery app and copies of images in the particular folders are retained by the applications. This means that even if a user has deleted the original images from Gallery, the cached files corresponding to the app can reveal the deleted content.

Future research will leverage the advantages of graph databases to accommodate multiple entities in a single graph. These entities, which could be fake or secondary social media accounts or friends, colleagues or family members in the contact list of a seized smartphone, will be linked with actions and events to produce additional evidence. For example, if an individual under investigation has exchanged via Bluetooth an image with embedded geolocation data that was taken at a specific time, then the recipient's location could also be derived from the information that is collected and organized in a graph database. Thus, the framework presented in this chapter can be extended to hold diverse data that produces additional information related to entities who interact with an individual under investigation.

Acknowledgement

This research was supported by the EU DG Home Affairs – ISEC (Prevention of and Fight Against Crime)/INT (Illegal Use of Internet) Programme (HOME/2012/ISEC/AG/INT/4000003892) and by the Systems Centre of the University of Bristol.

References

[1] P. Andriotis, G. Oikonomou and T. Tryfonas, Forensic analysis of wireless networking evidence of Android smartphones, *Proceedings of the IEEE International Workshop on Information Forensics and Security*, pp. 109–114, 2012.

[2] C. Anglano, Forensic analysis of WhatsApp Messenger on Android smartphones, *Digital Investigation*, vol. 11(3), pp. 201–213, 2014.

[3] H. Chung, J. Park, S. Lee and C. Kang, Digital forensic investigation of cloud storage services, *Digital Investigation*, vol. 9(2), pp. 81–95, 2012.

[4] A. Flaglien, A. Mallasvik, M. Mustorp and A. Arnes, Storage and exchange formats for digital evidence, *Digital Investigation*, vol. 8(2), pp. 122–128, 2011.

[5] J. Fridrich, Digital image forensics, *IEEE Signal Processing*, vol. 26(2), pp. 26–37, 2009.

[6] S. Garfinkel, Digital forensics XML and the DFXML toolset, *Digital Investigation*, vol. 8(3-4), pp. 161–174, 2012.

[7] J. Grover, Android forensics: Automated data collection and reporting from a mobile device, *Digital Investigation*, vol. 10(S), pp. S12–S20, 2013.

[8] A. Hoog, *Android Forensics: Investigation, Analysis and Mobile Security for Google Android*, Syngress, Waltham, Massachusetts, 2011.

[9] T. Howard, Don't cache out your case: Prosecuting child pornography possession laws based on images located in temporary Internet files, *Berkeley Technical Law Journal*, vol. 19, pp. 1227–1273, 2004.

[10] M. Huber, M. Mulazzani, M. Leithner, S. Schrittwieser, G. Wondracek and E. Weippl, Social snapshots: Digital forensics for online social networks, *Proceedings of the Twenty-Seventh Annual Computer Security Applications Conference*, pp. 113–122, 2011.

[11] R. Hurley, S. Prusty, H. Soroush, R. Walls, J. Albrecht, E. Cecchet, B. Levine, M. Liberatore, B. Lynn and J. Wolak, Measurement and analysis of child pornography trafficking on P2P networks, *Proceedings of the Twenty-Second International Conference on World Wide Web*, pp. 631–642, 2013.

[12] G. Kontaxis, I. Polakis, S. Ioannidis and E. Markatos, Detecting social network profile cloning, *Proceedings of the IEEE International Conference on Pervasive Computing and Communications Workshops*, pp. 295–300, 2011.

[13] M. Liberatore, R. Erdely, T. Kerle, B. Levine and C. Shields, Forensic investigation of peer-to-peer file sharing networks, *Digital Investigation*, vol. 7(S), pp. S95–S103, 2010.

[14] Q. Liu, X. Li, L. Chen, H. Cho, P. Cooper, Z. Chen, M. Qiao and A. Sung, Identification of smartphone-image source and manipulation, in *Advanced Research in Applied Artificial Intelligence*, H. Jiang, W. Ding, M. Ali and X. Wu (Eds), Springer, Berlin-Heidelberg, Germany, pp. 262–271, 2012.

[15] F. Marturana and S. Tacconi, A machine-learning-based triage methodology for automated categorization of digital media, *Digital Investigation*, vol. 10(2), pp. 193–204, 2013.

[16] A. Mylonas, V. Meletiadis, L. Mitrou and D. Gritzalis, Smartphone sensor data as digital evidence, *Computers and Security*, vol. 38, pp. 51–75, 2013.

[17] M. Stamm and K. Liu, Anti-forensics of digital image compression, *IEEE Transactions on Information Forensics and Security*, vol. 6(3), pp. 1050–1065, 2011.

[18] S. Teelink and R. Erbacher, Improving the computer forensic analysis process through visualization, *Communications of the ACM*, vol. 49(2), pp. 71–75, 2006.

[19] P. Turner, Unification of digital evidence from disparate sources (digital evidence bags), *Digital Investigation*, vol. 2(3), pp. 223–228, 2005.

[20] J. Wolak, M. Liberatore and B. Levine, Measuring a year of child pornography trafficking by U.S. computers on a peer-to-peer network, *Child Abuse and Neglect*, vol. 38(2), pp. 347–356, 2014.

V

CLOUD FORENSICS

Chapter 16

A TRUSTWORTHY CLOUD
FORENSICS ENVIRONMENT

Shams Zawoad and Ragib Hasan

Abstract   The rapid migration from traditional computing and storage models to cloud computing environments has made it necessary to support reliable forensic investigations in the cloud. However, current cloud computing environments often lack support for forensic investigations and the trustworthiness of evidence is often questionable because of the possibility of collusion between dishonest cloud providers, users and forensic investigators. This chapter presents a forensics-enabled cloud environment that supports trustworthy forensics in cloud environments. The forensic environment is designed on top of the OpenStack open-source cloud operating system. The environment enables cloud service providers to provide trusted digital forensics support to customers and forensic investigators, and enables customers to establish their own forensics-friendly infrastructures without making significant financial investments.

Keywords: Cloud computing, cloud forensics, trustworthy environment

1.   Introduction

Consumers around the world avail of cloud computing services when they access Gmail, Google Calendar, Dropbox, Microsoft Office Live, or run Amazon Elastic Compute Cloud (EC2) instances. According to Gartner [8], consumers will store more than one third of their digital content in the cloud by 2016. A recent Market Research Media study [16] states that the global cloud computing market is expected to grow at a 30% compounded annual growth rate, reaching $270 billion in 2020.

However, the highly-scalable computing and storage resources offered by the cloud can be targeted by machines within the cloud [9, 13] or abused to store and distribute illegal images [22]. As a result, investigators are increasingly called upon to conduct digital forensic examina-

© IFIP International Federation for Information Processing 2015
G. Peterson, S. Shenoi (Eds.): Advances in Digital Forensics XI, IFIP AICT 462, pp. 271–285, 2015.
DOI: 10.1007/978-3-319-24123-4_16

tions of cloud environments. This particular branch of digital forensics is known as cloud forensics.

Many of the traditional digital forensic assumptions do not transfer to cloud forensics. One of the major hurdles is that neither users nor investigators have physical access to the cloud. Moreover, each cloud server contains files belonging to multiple users, raising issues of privacy and cross-contamination. Even with a subpoena, it is not feasible to seize servers from a cloud service provider without violating the privacy of many other users. The trustworthiness of the collected evidence is also questionable because, aside from the cloud service provider's word, no consistent approach is available to determine the integrity of the evidence.

To control costs, cloud providers do not generally support persistent storage of terminated virtual machines (VMs). Hence, data residing in a cloud virtual machine is unavailable after it has terminated. This significantly hinders forensic investigations of illegal activities involving a virtual machine that has already terminated. Additionally, cloud providers or forensic investigators can collude with malicious users to hide traces of illegal activities or frame innocent users. For these reasons, it is imperative to provide reliable digital forensics support in cloud computing environments.

Several researchers have proposed solutions to address the challenges of cloud forensics [3, 7, 20, 23]. However, the solutions do not provide a complete cloud computing architecture that supports the extraction and preservation of trustworthy evidence. Moreover, the solutions do not consider the possibility of malicious cloud stakeholders and collusions between cloud stakeholders.

To support trustworthy forensics in cloud environments, it is necessary to collect and securely preserve logs, data attribution and provenance information, and timestamps. The required evidence should be made available to users, forensic investigators and legal authorities.

This chapter proposes a forensics-friendly cloud architecture – FECloud, which is designed on top of the OpenStack architecture and meets the major cloud forensics requirements discussed above. FECloud introduces five new components into the OpenStack architecture: (i) Logger (Themis); (ii) Data Possession Manager (Metis); (iii) Timestamp Manager (Chronos); (iv) Provenance Manager (Clio); and (v) Proof Publisher (Brizo). New functions are added to the OpenStack block storage (Cinder) and compute node (Nova) to communicate with the new components. The OpenStack dashboard (Horizon) and identity manager (Keystone) are augmented to provide user interfaces and authenticate the new OpenStack components. Finally, a forensics-enabled image for virtual machines is available to provide digital forensic features. The FECloud environment enables cloud service providers to provide trusted digital forensics support to customers and forensic investigators. Also, it enables customers to establish their own forensics-friendly cloud infrastructures without making significant financial investments.

2. Related Work

McCormick et al. [17] have emphasized that digital evidence is not the counterpart of statements provided by humans, which should ideally be tested by cross-examination. Instead, the admissibility of digital evidence should be determined based on the reliability of the system and the processes that generated the evidence. Thus, the collection and preservation of trustworthy evidence are priorities in digital forensic investigations as well as in cloud forensic investigations.

Recognizing that isolation helps protect evidence from contamination, Delport et al. [6] have focused on isolating virtual machine instances to mitigate the multi-tenancy issue. Hay and Nance [12] have shown that if a virtual machine instance is compromised by installing a rootkit to hide the traces of malicious activity, it is still possible to identify the malicious activity by performing virtual machine introspection. To make the activity logs available to customers and forensic investigators, Birk and Wegener [3] have proposed that cloud providers only expose read-only APIs. Zawoad et al. [23] have proposed the concept of secure logging-as-a-service as a means to store virtual machine activities, which ensures the integrity and confidentiality of logs despite the possibility of malicious cloud providers and forensic investigators. Thorpe and Ray [20] have developed a log auditor for cloud environments that detects temporal inconsistencies in virtual machine timelines.

Dykstra and Sherman [7] have recently implemented FROST, a forensic data collection tool for OpenStack. Cloud users and forensic investigators can use FROST to acquire images of the virtual disks associated with user virtual machines and validate the integrity of the images using cryptographic checksums. It is also possible to collect logs of all API requests made to a cloud provider as well as OpenStack firewall logs for virtual machines. Data provenance in cloud computing is a relatively new research area that was first proposed by Muniswamy-Reddy et al. [18]; the researchers also developed a solution for gathering provenance data from Xen hypervisors [15]. More recently, Lu et al. [14] have introduced the concept of secure provenance in cloud environments; they proposed a trusted third party based scheme for secure cloud provenance that ensures data confidentiality, unforgeability and full anonymity of signatures, and full traceability from a signature. Schmidt [19] has proposed a legal hold framework in cloud environments; however, the approach does not consider the trustworthy management of litigation holds to protect evidence from dishonest cloud providers, users or forensic investigators.

3.   Desired Properties

Five properties are required for a trustworthy forensics environment to meet the unique characteristics of cloud systems:

- **Trustworthy Log Management:** It is often the case that experienced attackers tamper with system logs to hide their traces [1]. An adversary who hosts a botnet server, spam email server or phishing website in a cloud virtual machine can remove the traces of malicious activity by modifying the logs. Hence, a forensics-enabled cloud should acquire all activity logs from the virtual machines and store them in persistent storage while ensuring their integrity and confidentiality.

- **Proof of Data Possession:** Preserving proof of data possession is important to prove the presence of a specific file in a storage system at a certain time and to ensure the preservation of a litigation hold. In order to capture evidence that a suspect accessed a file in cloud storage at a certain time, a forensics-enabled cloud should preserve the proof of data possession. This also meets the requirements of a litigation hold, which is a notice to an organization to preserve all the electronically stored information (ESI) relevant to a lawsuit for a stipulated time period [21, 22].

- **Secure Timestamps:** Timestamps associated with digital evidence can be crucial to convict or acquit a suspect [5]. An attacker could change the system clock on a virtual machine before launching an attack and later reset it to the correct time as an anti-forensic measure. Tampering with the system clocks of a cloud host and virtual machine produces a set of events that are temporally coherent but different from the actual event times. Any event timeline generated from the system clocks of a host and guest virtual machines can, therefore, have an integrity problem. In order to guarantee trustworthy timelines in forensic investigations, it is necessary to ensure that all cloud system clocks have not been tampered with.

- **Secure Provenance:** Provenance is the history of an object, which includes its origins and use. Secure provenance helps a digital forensic investigator maintain proper chain of custody. However, because files and their access histories are under the control of cloud service providers, it is possible that the provenance records could be modified intentionally or unintentionally. An attacker who can access provenance records may obtain valuable and sensitive information about data stored in the cloud. A secure provenance scheme [10] must be implemented to protect provenance records from attacks on integrity and confidentiality.

- **Evidence Availability:** The physical inaccessibility of evidence residing in the cloud is always a challenge. A cloud service provider can support evidence acquisition by offering a secure software interface to authorized entities. Using the interface, customers and forensic investigators can collect network, process and database logs, as well as other digital evidence and the provenance records of the evidence.

4. Challenges

Achieving trustworthy forensic properties in current cloud infrastructures is challenging for several reasons:

- **Collusion:** Cloud customers and forensic investigators have limited control over evidence stored in the cloud. Despite the availability of state-of-the-art frameworks for collecting evidence from cloud systems, customers and investigators have no other option than to trust cloud service providers because they cannot verify the completeness and integrity of the evidence recovered from cloud systems.

  For example, an employee of a cloud provider could collude with a malicious user to hide important evidence or fabricate evidence that points to the innocence of the malicious user. A malicious cloud provider employee could also provide incomplete or modified logs, remove documents and their traces, maintain false timestamps and tamper with provenance information. A forensic investigator could also intentionally alter the evidence before presenting it in court. In a traditional computer system, only the user and investigator can collude. The three-way collusion in a cloud environment increases the attack surface and makes cloud forensics more challenging.

- **Volatile Data:** Data residing in a virtual machine is volatile, meaning that no data is preserved after the virtual machine is terminated. The volatile data includes documents, network logs, operating system logs and registry logs. An entity who terminates a virtual machine after conducting malicious activities can cause vital evidence to be lost.

Cloud service providers can constantly monitor running virtual machines and store the volatile data in persistent storage in order to provide logs or proofs of data possession when needed. However, the routine preservation of the data of terminated virtual machines would overwhelm the storage resources of cloud providers. Therefore, it is necessary to find effective ways to preserve logs, data possession histories and provenance records.

■ **Multi-Tenancy:** In cloud environments, multiple virtual machines share the same physical infrastructure (e.g., data belonging to multiple customers is co-located). A suspect could claim that the evidence collected from a cloud environment is associated with other cloud tenants, not the suspect. In this case, the forensic investigator has to prove that the evidence is actually associated with the suspect. In contrast, the owner of a traditional computing system is solely responsible for the electronically stored information in the computing system. Additionally, when conducting a forensic investigation of a cloud environment, it is imperative to protect the privacy of other cloud tenants.

5.   FECloud Architecture

The FECloud forensics-enabled cloud architecture provides forensic investigators with the means to obtain and preserve cloud-based evidence in a secure manner. FECloud enhances the OpenStack cloud operating system by incorporating five components:

■ **Logger (Themis):** This component collects logs from virtual machines, Cinder and Nova compute nodes and preserves them in a secure manner.

■ **Data Possession (DP) Manager (Metis):** This component collects trace evidence about data possession from Cinder and stores the records in a secure manner.

■ **Timestamp Manager (Chronos):** This component handles the timestamp verification cycles between the virtual machines, Nova compute node and itself, and preserves the verification information in a secure manner.

■ **Provenance Manager (Clio):** This component collects various provenance records (data, application and state) from the virtual

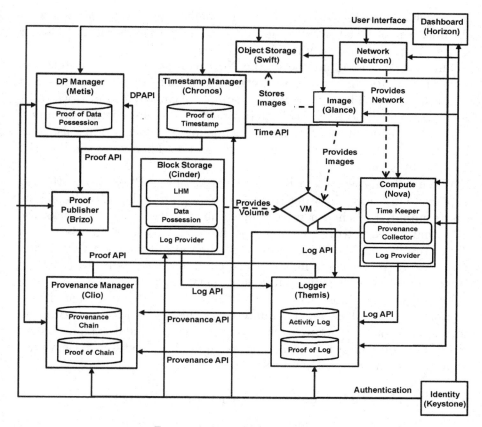

Figure 1. FECloud architecture.

machines, Nova compute node and Themis and securely creates and preserves the provenance chain.

- **Proof Publisher (Brizo):** This component distributes evidence traces so that any evidence alteration by cloud service providers, users or investigators can be detected.

Figure 1 presents the FECloud architecture. FECloud incorporates augmentations to the OpenStack dashboard (Horizon) and identity manager (Keystone) to support a user interface and the authentication of the new components. A forensics-enabled image for virtual machines that provides various forensic features is also available.

5.1 Logger (Themis)

The Logger (Themis) communicates with the OpenStack compute node (Nova), block storage (Cinder) and the running virtual machines to collect all possible activity logs. To facilitate communications with Themis, a new Log Provider module is added to the Nova and Cinder nodes of OpenStack and virtual machine images.

The Log Provider module of the Nova compute node monitors the network activity and processor usage of running virtual machines and sends the logs to Themis. Logs that cannot be gathered from Nova (e.g., operating system logs) are collected directly from the virtual machines. The Log Provider module of Cinder sends logs of block storage usage to Themis. Logs from different entities are sent to Themis by the log API exposed by Themis.

When Themis receives a log entry via the log API, it stores the log in persistent storage in order to retain the log after the virtual machine has terminated. When a virtual machine is active, Themis tracks the data that belongs to the virtual machine and associates the data with the virtual machine user, ensuring that the data of multiple virtual machine users are not co-mingled. Data confidentiality is protected from unauthorized entities using public key encryption.

To prevent collusion between cloud service providers, forensic investigators and cloud users, Themis creates hashes of the logs using an accumulator data structure such as a one-way accumulator [2] or Bloom filter [4]. The computed hashes are compared with stored hash values to verify the integrity of the logs.

5.2 Data Possession Manager (Metis)

The Data Possession Manager (Metis) collects information about data possession from Cinder and stores the data possession records in a data possession database. Cinder is augmented with a Data Possession module to communicate with this new component.

A naive way to preserve data possession records is to store them in persistent storage. However, this increases the storage cost significantly. A more efficient way to preserve the records is to use an accumulator data structure [2, 4]. The accumulator also enables Metis to preserve data possession records without revealing the original data. Specifically, the membership checking method of the accumulator checks the data possession record of a suspect to verify if a document of interest belongs to the suspect without having to examine the document content.

Data possession records can also be used to identify violations of litigation holds. In such a scenario, a litigant presents all the documents that are under a litigation hold to the court. The verification method creates data possession information of the documents provided by the litigant. It then compares the generated data possession information with the data possession records collected from the cloud. Document deletions are detected when the generated data possession information does not match the stored data possession records.

5.3   Timestamp Manager (Chronos)

Since it is not possible to prevent a virtual machine owner from changing the system time of a guest virtual machine or prevent a malicious system administrator from changing the system time of the host, a verification protocol is implemented using the Timestamp Manager (Chronos) to reveal clock changes. This secure timestamp verification protocol involves three entities, the Nova compute node, a running virtual machine and Chronos, in which each entity verifies the timestamp of the other two entities to detect timestamp alterations. Traces pertaining to the verification phase are stored securely using a hash-chain scheme in a timestamp database. Before beginning the verification cycle, the virtual machine and Chronos determine the round trip times with the Nova compute node. The validity of a requestor's timestamp depends on the current timestamp of the verifier and the round trip time values. The timestamp of one requestor is attested by the other two entities and each attestation is subsequently certified by an entity other than the verifier and requestor. A new Time Keeper module is incorporated in the Nova compute node to handle timestamp verification. Public key encryption and signature generation are used in all communications to preserve confidentiality and integrity.

This new feature enables a forensic investigator to present timestamp verification information along with the evidence collected from the cloud. Because the timestamp verification information is preserved using a hash-chain scheme, malicious entities cannot change the system time without breaking the verification chain.

5.4   Provenance Manager (Clio)

The Provenance Manager (Clio) extracts provenance records related to data, application and virtual machine state from the log database as well as from the provenance layer of the Nova compute node and the running virtual machines. Since the Logger (Themis) collects logs of data modifications from block storage, Clio collects the necessary log records to build the data provenance from Themis via the provenance API. Provenance records for the Virtual File System and applications running within virtual machines are directly collected from the virtual machines using the same API. Finally, provenance records for establishing the system level provenance of the Nova compute node are collected from the provenance layer of Nova.

After collecting the various provenance records, Clio applies secure provenance chaining [11] to preserve the integrity of the provenance records. The secure provenance information is stored in the provenance chain database. To ensure that a malicious cloud service provider cannot modify the chain, the head of the provenance chain is stored in the proof of chain database after certain time periods.

5.5   Proof Publisher (Brizo)

The Proof Publisher (Brizo) periodically publishes the records of logs, data possession, timestamp verification and provenance chain on the web. Making these records publicly available prevents cloud service providers and investigators from altering or fabricating evidence because any manipulated evidence would not exist in the published record.

Information published by Brizo can be made available by an RSS feed to protect it from manipulation by cloud service providers. A trust model can also be established by engaging multiple cloud service providers in the publication process. Whenever one cloud service provider publishes a record, it is shared with the other cloud service providers. Therefore, a record can be considered to be valid as long as more than 50% of the cloud service providers are honest.

5.6   Evidence Access Interface (Horizon)

The OpenStack dashboard (Horizon) has been augmented to provide computerized access to cloud-based electronically stored information. Thus, physical access to cloud infrastructures is not necessary to acquire logs and data possession and provenance information. Four new modules are incorporated in Horizon to provide user interfaces for Metis, Chronos, Clio and Themis, with one module dedicated to each component. These modules enable users and investigators to collect activity logs, provenance, proof of data possession and proof of timestamp information in a secure and reliable manner.

5.7   Forensics-Enabled Image

The Nova compute node and Cinder do not provide all the evidence relevant to incidents in cloud environments. Indeed, without introducing new capabilities for virtual machines, it would not be possible to develop a complete forensics-enabled cloud environment.

Figure 2 shows a proposed forensics-enabled virtual machine image. A virtual machine launched using this image would be able to support

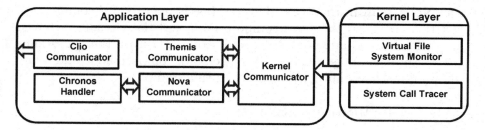

Figure 2. Forensics-enabled virtual machine image.

all the required forensic features. Some of the modules would be inside the kernel while others would be in the application layer. The following are the names and functionalities of the seven modules:

- **Virtual File System (VFS) Monitor:** This module is placed inside the kernel to trace virtual file system operations, which are important for constructing data provenance records for virtual machines.

- **System Call Tracer:** This module is placed inside the kernel to track all system calls. System call information can reveal the activities of cloud users and is important for establishing application and state provenance.

- **Kernel Communicator:** This module resides inside the application layer and acts as a bridge between the kernel and application layer. The module collects information from the Virtual File System Monitor and the System Call Tracer module in the kernel and feeds the information to other modules in the application layer.

- **Chronos Handler:** This application layer module participates in the timestamp verification step to verify the timestamps of the Nova compute node and Chronos, and also to have its own timestamp verified by the other two entities.

- **Themis Communicator:** This module collects the system call information and virtual file system activities from the Kernel Communicator and sends the logs to Themis using the log API.

- **Clio Communicator:** This module sends provenance records of applications, virtual file system and virtual machine state to Clio using the provenance API. The provenance records are collected from the Virtual File System Monitor and System Call Tracer via the Kernel Communicator module.

■ **Nova Communicator:** This module is required for communications between the Nova compute node and the virtual machines. The Nova Communicator is also required during the timestamp verification phase during which the Nova compute node and a virtual machine mutually verify their timestamps.

5.8   Preliminary Results

The proof-of-concept FECloud implementation incorporates cryptographic frameworks for Metis [24] and Themis [23]. A Bloom-filter-based data possession scheme is available for storage-as-a-service cloud environments [24]. Experiments revealed that a FECloud user has 0.13% to 3.73% overhead in terms of time to upload files based on the file size and security properties. This overhead decreases as the file size increases and becomes almost constant when the file size is greater than 6 MB. The storage overhead on the cloud service provider side is also low. Regardless of the file size, approximately 1,262 bytes are required to preserve the data possession records for 1,000 files.

Themis uses the secure logging scheme from [23], which incorporates a Bloom filter and RSA accumulator to achieve the desired security properties. The design has $O(n)$ time and space complexity for log insertion and storage. The verification algorithm requires a constant amount of time to verify logs using both the accumulator schemes.

Current work related to FECloud involves securing the system time of the Nova compute node and the virtual machines with the assistance of Chronos. Initial experiments indicate that the timestamp verification cycle between the three entities can be executed every 60 seconds while introducing less than 1% system overhead on each entity. Another experiment, which involved running the verification protocol between 20 virtual machines, a Nova compute node and Chronos for 24 hours with a verification frequency of 60 seconds, recorded that the system was 99.98% stable.

6.   Conclusions

At this time, forensic investigators are dependent on cloud service providers to identify and extract evidence from cloud computing environments. Unfortunately, under these circumstances, there is no way to verify if a cloud service provider has transmitted all the evidence that is relevant to a case and that the integrity of the evidence has been maintained. As a result, a forensic investigator has no way of knowing if the evidence is complete and valid. The FECloud architecture described in this chapter supports trustworthy forensics in cloud computing environments. Designed on top of the OpenStack open-source cloud operating system, FECloud enables cloud service providers to provide trusted forensics support to customers and investigators, and enables customers to establish their own forensics-friendly infrastructures without making significant financial investments.

Future research will focus on the design of an efficient and secure cloud provenance scheme for Clio and the complete integration of all the proposed components within OpenStack. Following this, the overhead and stability of individual components and the integrated system will be evaluated using OpenStack benchmarking tools to establish the feasibility of using FECloud in real-world cloud environments.

Acknowledgement

This research was supported by National Science Foundation CA-REER Award CNS 1351038, a Google Faculty Research Award and Department of Homeland Security Grant FA8750-12-2-0254.

References

[1] M. Bellare and B. Yee, Forward Integrity for Secure Audit Logs, Technical Report CS98-580, Department of Computer Science and Engineering, University of California at San Diego, San Diego, California, 1997.

[2] J. Benaloh and M. de Mare, One-way accumulators: A decentralized alternative to digital signatures, *Proceedings of the Workshop on the Theory and Application of Cryptographic Techniques*, pp. 274–285, 1994.

[3] D. Birk and C. Wegener, Technical issues of forensic investigations in cloud computing environments, *Proceedings of the Sixth IEEE International Workshop on Systematic Approaches to Digital Forensic Engineering*, 2011.

[4] B. Bloom, Space/time trade-offs in hash coding with allowable errors, *Communications of the ACM*, vol. 13(7), pp. 422–426, 1970.

[5] E. Casey, Error, uncertainty and loss in digital evidence, *International Journal of Digital Evidence*, vol. 1(2), 2002.

[6] W. Delport, M. Kohn and M. Olivier, Isolating a cloud instance for a digital forensic investigation, *Proceedings of the Information Security for South Africa Conference*, 2011.

[7] J. Dykstra and A. Sherman, Design and implementation of FROST: Digital forensic tools for the OpenStack cloud computing platform, *Digital Investigation*, vol. 10(S), pp. S87–S95, 2013.

[8] Gartner, Gartner says that consumers will store more than a third of their digital content in the cloud by 2016, Stamford, Connecticut (www.gartner.com/newsroom/id/2060215), June 25, 2012.

[9] D. Goodwin, Amazon cloud hosts nasty banking Trojan, *The Register*, July 29, 2011.

[10] R. Hasan, R. Sion and M. Winslett, Preventing history forgery with secure provenance, *ACM Transactions on Storage*, vol. 5(4), article no. 12, 2009.

[11] R. Hasan, R. Sion and M. Winslett, The case of the fake Picasso: Preventing history forgery with secure provenance, *Proceedings of the Seventh USENIX Conference on File and Storage Technologies*, pp. 1–14, 2009.

[12] B. Hay and K. Nance, Forensics examination of volatile system data using virtual introspection, *ACM SIGOPS Operating Systems Review*, vol. 42(3), pp. 74–82, 2008.

[13] Infosecurity Magazine, DDoS-ers launch attacks from Amazon EC2, July 30, 2014.

[14] R. Lu, X. Lin, X. Liang and X. Shen, Secure provenance: The essential of bread and butter of data forensics in cloud computing, *Proceedings of the Fifth ACM Symposium on Information, Computer and Communications Security*, pp. 282–292, 2010.

[15] P. Macko and M. Chiarini, Collecting provenance via the Xen hypervisor, *Proceedings of the Third Workshop on the Theory and Practice of Provenance*, article no. 23, 2011.

[16] Market Research Media, Global cloud computing market forecast 2015-2020, San Francisco, California (www.marketresearchmedia.com/?p=839), January 8, 2014.

[17] C. McCormick, C. Tilford and J. Strong (Eds.), *McCormick on Evidence*, West, St. Paul, Minnesota, 1992.

[18] K. Muniswamy-Reddy, P. Macko and M. Seltzer, Making a cloud provenance-aware, *Proceedings of the First Workshop on the Theory and Practice of Provenance*, article no. 12, 2009.

[19] O. Schmidt, Managing a Legal Hold on Cloud Documents, U.S. Patent Application 20140012767, 2014.

[20] S. Thorpe and I. Ray, Detecting temporal inconsistency in virtual machine activity timelines, *Journal of Information Assurance and Security*, vol. 7(1), pp. 24–31, 2012.

[21] United States District Court (Southern District of Ohio, Eastern Division), Robert A, Brown et al. v. Tellermate Holdings Ltd. et al., Case No. 2: 11-cv-1122, 2014.

[22] United States District Court (Southern District of Texas, Houston Division), Quantlab Technologies Ltd. and Quantlab Financial LLC v. Godlevsky et al., Civil Action No. 4:09-CV-4039, 2014.

[23] S. Zawoad, A. Dutta and R. Hasan, SecLaaS: Secure logging-as-a-service for cloud forensics, *Proceedings of the Eighth ACM SIGSAC Symposium on Information, Computer and Communications Security*, pp. 219–230, 2013.

[24] S. Zawoad and R. Hasan, Towards building proofs of past data possession in cloud forensics, *ASE Science Journal*, vol. 1(4), pp. 195–207, 2012.

Chapter 17

LOCATING AND TRACKING DIGITAL OBJECTS IN THE CLOUD

Philip Trenwith and Hein Venter

Abstract   One of the biggest stumbling blocks in a cloud forensic investigation is the inability to determine the physical location of a digital object in the cloud. In order to provide better accessibility to users, data in the cloud is not stored at a single location, but is spread over multiple data centers. This chapter proposes a model for providing data provenance and reporting on the provenance of a digital object in the cloud. It also examines how data provenance can be used to track where a digital object has been in the cloud and where the object can be found at any point in time. A special file type (wrapper) that encapsulates a digital object and its provenance data is proposed. The design helps preserve the integrity of provenance data and meets many of the requirements set for data provenance, including the support of cloud forensic investigations. The implementation requires each cloud service provider to maintain a central logging server that reports on the locations of wrapped objects in its domain.

Keywords: Cloud computing, cloud forensics, data provenance, central logging

1.   Introduction

This chapter explores how data provenance can be stored in a forensically-ready manner and how provenance data can be used in cloud forensic investigations to trace where an object is located in the cloud and where the object has been. In a traditional digital forensic investigation, it is customary to seize a device suspected to be involved in illegal activities in order to examine it. However, this approach does not scale to the cloud for several reasons, the most important being that the physical locations of "devices" are often unknown due to the virtual nature of cloud environments. Data in the cloud is also spread across a range of hosts and data centers, which renders the task of identifying the physical

© IFIP International Federation for Information Processing 2015

G. Peterson, S. Shenoi (Eds.): Advances in Digital Forensics XI, IFIP AICT 462, pp. 287–301, 2015.

DOI: 10.1007/978-3-319-24123-4_17

location of an object even more challenging. It is, therefore, necessary to investigate how digital forensic readiness and data provenance can provide a technique for acquiring potential evidence that is better suited to the architecture and operation of cloud computing environments.

The primary challenge in cloud forensic investigations is determining the locations of relevant data [15]. The ability to trace a digital object in the cloud is made possible by Locard's principle of exchange (as stated in [7]): "Whenever two objects come into contact with each other, each object is left with a trace of the other object."

An example of such a trace is seen in the registry of a machine running the Windows 7 operating system. When a flash drive is connected to the Windows 7 machine, a record is written to the registry. This record contains the hardware ID of the flash drive and the time it was inserted [1]. The record remains in the registry even after the flash drive has been removed.

The principle of exchange provides a means, in theory, of tracing an object in the cloud. However, collecting potential evidence from the cloud is a challenge because the approach is reactive. The challenge can potentially be addressed by establishing a proactive approach based on digital forensic readiness, in which an organization prepares in advance for the possibility that an event might occur that requires an investigation to be conducted.

The primary research question discussed in the chapter is: How can a digital object be tracked in the cloud and its history be recorded in order to obtain accurate location information during a cloud forensic investigation?

2.   Background

This section discusses cloud computing, digital forensics and data provenance.

2.1   Cloud Computing

Cloud computing is a scaled-up, virtual environment for distributed computing that has become immensely popular in recent years. The U.S. National Institute of Standards and Technology (NIST) defines cloud computing as "a model for enabling convenient, on-demand network access to a shared pool of configurable computing resources that can be rapidly provisioned and released with minimal management effort or service provider interaction" [11]. The cloud provides three common service models. Infrastructure as a service (IaaS) offers computing and storage services to cloud users. Platform as a service (PaaS) offers platform support for software development. Software as a service (SaaS) offers fully functional applications to cloud users. These service models can be deployed in one of four modes: (i) private cloud; (ii) public cloud; (iii) hybrid cloud; and (iv) community cloud [11]. The primary difference between cloud computing and traditional computing is that storage is distributed throughout the cloud and the stored data is not necessarily in the same location as the device being used to access the data. The picture seen by an end user is much the same as in traditional computing, but the picture for a digital forensic investigator is very different.

Virtualization makes it difficult to tell the physical location of a data object in the cloud. The locations of objects in the cloud are important because the objects have to be found and retrieved in order to present them (and their constituent data) as evidence. Therefore, it is very important to maintain the locations and histories of cloud objects.

Consider, for example, the European Union's Data Protection Directive [6], which stipulates that no sensitive data may leave the European Union. Implementing this directive makes it necessary to always know the locations of cloud objects containing sensitive data. Cloud service providers also duplicate and distribute data between multiple data centers to enhance availability, but this makes it difficult to assure that the data is (or is not) stored in a specific jurisdiction and that all copies of the data are removed if a deletion request is made. Pearson and Benameur [14] discuss many of the challenges associated with cloud services and securing the data that is generated and used by the services. Some of these challenges are considered later in this chapter in developing a solution for locating and tracking digital objects in the cloud.

2.2   Digital Forensics

Digital forensics is a formal process involving several steps that are executed on computing devices to answer questions related to investigations of computer crime and other incidents. Traditionally, if it is found that a device is needed for an investigation, the device is seized in order to examine it for evidence. This approach does not scale to cloud computing environments primarily because of their virtual nature. Indeed, seizing and examining a single device would almost certainly be insufficient to produce all the evidence related to an incident in a cloud computing environment. Reilly et al. [15] emphasize that obtaining access to physical devices in the cloud is one of the main stumbling blocks in cloud investigations. Gaining physical access to devices in the cloud may not always be possible but, if adequate logs are maintained and if the information is made available to investigators when required, then the stumbling block could be overcome.

Traditional digital forensic investigations follow a reactive approach. An investigation is only initiated after an incident has occurred and the incident has been identified as one that requires further investigation. The reactive approach must be adapted to a proactive approach in order to perform successful cloud investigations. The proactive approach is better known as digital forensic readiness, which is defined by Rowlingson [16] as "the ability of an organization to maximize its potential to use digital evidence whilst minimizing the costs of an investigation." Digital forensic readiness requires an organization to take proactive measures to continuously collect and store data for a period of time to ensure that it is adequately prepared to conduct future investigations.

The intersection of digital forensics and cloud computing has created the new discipline of cloud forensics, which is defined by Ruan et al. [17] as "a cross discipline of cloud computing and digital forensics." Cloud forensics offers many challenges to investigators, including the inability to perform independent investigations because cloud service providers maintain full control of their computing environments and, thus, the sources of evidence. Barbara [3] states that the biggest challenges in cloud forensics are to determine the who, what, when, where, how and why of cloud-based activity. These challenges can potentially be addressed by the provision of data provenance – as Birk and Wegener [4] state, the history of a digital object, combined with a suitable authentication scheme, are crucial to cloud forensic investigations.

2.3   Data Provenance

Muniswamy-Reddy and Seltzer [13] define data provenance as the history of a digital object. Data provenance is valuable data in a digital forensic investigation because it reveals information such as when a digital object was modified and who accessed it. Some researchers [10, 13, 23] have investigated the use of data provenance in the cloud as a tool for supporting digital forensic investigations.

Lu et al. [10] discuss one of the challenges of cloud forensics known as anonymous authentication. Cloud computing offers anonymous authentication, which enables a user to log into a service using group authentication. In other words, a group of users may be granted access to specific objects and services in the cloud with the same access rights. While each user has unique credentials to access the service, there is no way to identify a specific user. This is because the credentials of the users in the group are related through mathematical inverses. Therefore, the credentials are not stored by the system, only the inverse function is stored. The authentication scheme calculates the mathematical inverse of the provided credentials and compares it with the function value. Therefore, the credentials cannot be used to uniquely identify one individual from the other members of the group. This is advantageous to users but a challenge to forensic investigators. Lu et al. [10] argue that this is the reason why provenance is required in the cloud. They further state that the addition of provenance data that can be used to report on the history of a digital object would contribute to the wider acceptance of cloud computing by the general public. However, when implementing data provenance in a cloud computing environment, care must be taken not to infringe on the confidentiality and privacy of data owners.

3.   Related Work

Muniswamy-Reddy et al. [12] have proposed a system that creates and maintains provenance-aware network storage. However, this system does not scale well to the cloud because it requires the network to be set up in a specific way to provide provenance data. The system is, thus, not compatible with all cloud environments.

Trenwith and Venter [23] have proposed a system that obtains provenance data from cloud service provider logs in network infrastructures (e.g., TCP/IP networks) to identify the physical locations of objects in the cloud. The underlying approach is leveraged in this work to provide data provenance for cloud objects while also addressing the challenges related to cloud forensics. One of the challenges, involving the provision of cryptographic proofs to verifying cloud data integrity, has been listed as a requirement for cloud forensics in [9, 18].

Trenwith and Venter [22] have developed a technique for proving the integrity of log files stored at a central log server. This is accomplished by computing a hash value when the logs are captured, encrypting the hash value with a secret key and storing the encrypted hash value along with the log. The integrity of the log file may be verified at any time by recomputing the hash value and then encrypting the hash value with a validation application that holds the secret key. The application then compares the newly encrypted value with the original encrypted value that was saved with the log file.

3.1   Storing Provenance Data

The provenance of a digital object can be stored in one of two ways. One is to embed provenance data in the digital object. The other is to store the provenance data separately in a second digital object [19].

- **Embedded Provenance Storage:** This technique modifies a digital object to incorporate provenance data within the object. The provenance data is typically stored in the file header. The main advantage of this technique is that it helps maintain the integrity of the provenance data because the data is stored with the object and can easily be verified. A disadvantage is that it is difficult to search the provenance data [19]. This technique is used by NASA's Flexible Image Transport System [8] and by the Spatial Data Transfer Standard [2] used by GIS systems to reference spatial data.

- **Separate Provenance Storage:** This technique stores provenance data separately from the object. The need to maintain a separate data object can be viewed as a disadvantage. However, Tan [21] suggests that centralized logging is vital to an efficient digital forensic strategy. Thus, with proper maintenance, the disadvantage of separate provenance storage can be turned into an advantage. Trenwith and Venter [23] have suggested the use of this technique with a central log server to store provenance data. The implementation is discussed later in this chapter.

3.2   Data Provenance Requirements

Lu et al. [10] identify three requirements for a provenance record:

R1: A provenance record must be unforgeable.

R2: A provenance record must be kept confidential.

R3: The integrity of a provenance record must be maintained by the system.

Trenwith and Venter [23] suggest an additional requirement that addresses the cloud forensics challenges faced by investigators. In particular, a provenance data should produce sufficient information to answer most of the questions asked by investigators during cloud forensic investigations. The new requirement is:

R4: A provenance record must answer the who, what, when, where and how of an event. These terms are defined as [23]:

  R4.1: Who: The identity of the process or user account associated with the modification.

  R4.2: What: The object that was modified.

  R4.3: When: The time of the modification.

R4.4: Where: The location of the object at the time of the modification.

R4.5: How: The hash values of the object before and after the modification.

4. Cloud-Based Provenance Model

The primary research question discussed in the chapter is: How can a digital object be tracked in the cloud and its history be recorded in order to obtain accurate location information during a cloud forensic investigation? Trenwith and Venter [23] have proposed the use of a central log server for storing the provenance data of digital objects. Although central logging provides advantages with regard to digital forensics, this approach is not without challenges. The principal challenge is the bandwidth required to ensure that the central server can continuously receive the provenance data of every object maintained by a cloud service provider. Therefore, this work investigates if a technique can be developed that provides the advantages of central storage while reducing the bandwidth requirements. This is accomplished by revisiting the embedding techniques used to store provenance data.

Trenwith and Venter [23] have made good arguments for storing provenance data separately from digital objects. Their goal was to use provenance data to identify and track object locations in the cloud. An examination of the requirements set for provenance data reveals that some of the requirements are easily met if provenance data is embedded within digital objects.

- **R1: A provenance record must be unforgeable:** Lu et al. [10] stipulate that it should not be possible to forge a provenance record. Because provenance records are produced by the system, it may be possible for a malicious attacker to forge a record that looks like a valid record. Therefore, instead of addressing the procedure that creates provenance records, it is necessary to see how provenance data is validated to prove its integrity. The approach is similar to that proposed in [22] and discussed above with regard to validating log files. If provenance data is embedded in a data object, the most recent provenance record can easily be validated against the data object. Taking this one step further, the system should store a second hash value to validate historical provenance data. Having the system encrypt the provenance data ensures that the non-forgeability requirement is met.

- **R2: A provenance record must be kept confidential:** This requirement can also be met using encryption. Encrypting provenance records and user data prevents cloud service provider employees as well as other parties from accessing the data, thus maintaining confidentiality. This concept is leveraged by Venters et al. [24] in their implementation of a secure provenance service.

- **R3: The integrity of a provenance record must be maintained by the system:** The integrity of a provenance record is more easily maintained if the record is embedded within the object. The integrity can easily be verified by checking the record against the data object. The integrity of historical provenance data can also be maintained by including historical data when computing the hash value of an object.

- **R4.1: Who (Identity of the process or user account associated with the modification):** This requirement can be met by recording the user account that was used to edit the object. If this is not possible, the identity of the process that modified the object should be recorded.

- **R4.2: What (Object that was modified):** When data provenance is embedded with the object, the issue of what was modified is irrelevant because provenance data is stored in the object that was modified.

- **R4.3: When (Time of the modification):** The time of the modification should be saved with the provenance data. To avoid confusion regarding timestamps, a cloud service provider should synchronize the time on all its servers [22].

- **R4.4: Where (Location of the object at the time of the modification):** A process running on a machine can easily record the machine name and the IP address assigned to the machine. However, this information is not enough to identify the location of a machine in the cloud. If the IP address is recorded along with the modification time, a cloud service provider can identify the location of an object by examining a log that stores the identity of the machine that was associated with the IP address at the time of interest. This approach assumes the worst case scenario where IP addresses are assigned dynamically. This is often not the case in the cloud, but adopting this approach ensures that dynamic IP address allocation is not a concern at a later stage.

This work leverages digital forensic readiness principles to help locate objects in the cloud. However, the difficulty is to identify the location of an object of interest when the data that identifies the object is stored within the object. One way to solve this problem is to maintain a central logging service for all objects being monitored.

Embedding provenance data within an object has the advantage that it is not necessary to transmit all the provenance data to a central server. This addresses the bandwidth issue identified in [23]. The approach only requires an identification tag to be transmitted to the central server along with the current location of the object. Hence, if additional provenance data has to be retrieved from the object, the current location of the object can be looked up at the central server after which the object can be retrieved from the cloud for further investigation. This is only possible if the user has not deleted the object from the cloud. If the object has been deleted, its provenance data is no longer available.

The problem posed by a deleted object can be addressed by a data deletion policy implemented by a cloud provider. For example, the provider could mark an object as deleted, but retain the object for a certain period of time, in case the object or its provenance data may constitute evidence in a future investigation.

- **R4.5: How (Hash values of the object before and after the modification):** Hash values are used to verify object integrity and to indicate when the object was modified. This work uses the SHA-256 hash algorithm. According to NIST [5], any hash algorithm stronger than 112-bits should be adequate until the year 2030.

5.   Using a Central Logging Server

As discussed in the previous section, embedding provenance data in objects overcomes some of the disadvantages of current systems and helps meet most of the data provenance requirements. However, one problem that remains to be addressed is that only a few file types allow user-defined metadata to be appended to the file header. Therefore, the successful implementation of an embedded provenance system requires the creation of a file type that can be used to wrap a digital object and its provenance data in a single object. The next section discusses the design of a file wrapper that can embed provenance data with any digital object.

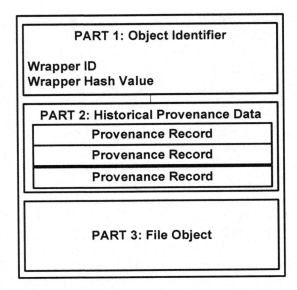

Figure 1. Wrapper design.

5.1   File Wrapper

This section describes the design of the wrapper used to embed a file and its provenance data in a single digital object. Figure 1 presents a schematic diagram of the file wrapper. The file wrapper has three components:

- **Object Identifier:** This component consists of the wrapper ID and a hash value. The wrapper ID is a unique key that is assigned to the object when it is constructed. The key, which is stored at the central server, is used to uniquely identify the object. This is necessary because there may be thousands of file objects wrapped with provenance data and it is necessary to know which wrapper contains a specific object. The hash value stored in the object identifier is computed by taking the hash value of the file object concatenated with its historical provenance data.

- **Historical Provenance Data:** This component is the provenance data of the object, which is covered by the requirements R4.1 through R4.5. The historical provenance data identifies when the object was constructed and includes information about subsequent modifications along with the time of each modification and the process or user account responsible for the modification. It also contains the hash value of the file object. Note that the historical provenance data includes not only the most recent modification,

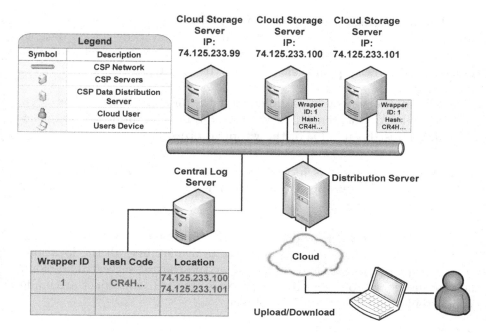

Figure 2. Wrapper implementation.

but also the provenance data associated with each modification and the file object hash value after each modification.

- **File Object:** This component is the user file; by design, it can be any type of file. A cloud service provider can decide what data is to be wrapped and how it is used. A cloud service provider may maintain provenance data for all the objects associated with its client accounts or it may maintain provenance data for a subset of objects associated with critical user data.

5.2   Tracking Wrapper Locations

Figure 2 shows a wrapper implementation by a cloud service provider such as Google Drive that could be used to track files uploaded by users. The cloud service provider implements the model by wrapping a file uploaded by a user before it is stored in the cloud. Before the wrapped file is stored in the cloud, the system registers the file and calculates a unique ID to identify and keep track of the wrapper. The hash value of the object is also computed and stored at the central server along with its location. The distribution server in Figure 2 distributes the object among its storage servers.

When a user logs in to access and modify the file, the object is un-wrapped. When the user saves the file, the new provenance data is created and stored, and the file is wrapped. The wrapped object is required to connect to the central server to update its record:

- When the object is modified and the new hash value has been calculated, the central server records must be updated to reflect the latest hash value of the wrapped object.

- When the object is moved from one location to another, the location of the wrapped object that is stored at the central server must be updated.

If the cloud service provider maintains multiple copies of its data for backup purposes or to provide better data availability, all the locations of a wrapped object should be stored at the central server. The cloud service provider should ensure that changes made to an object are made concurrently to all copies of the object.

6.   Discussion

Reilly et al. [15] note that the lack of knowledge of the physical locations of objects in the cloud is one of the main stumbling blocks in cloud forensics. The primary goal of this research has been to identify the physical locations of data in the cloud and, thereby, enhance cloud forensic investigations. The design helps preserve the integrity of provenance data and meets many of the requirements set for data provenance. In particular, the embedded data provenance system and the use of a central server enables digital forensic investigators to track the histories of digital objects and to easily identify their locations in the cloud if and when this becomes necessary.

Takabi et al. [20] emphasize that the owner of a data object should have full control over who accesses the data and what is done with the data. Encryption is the obvious solution to maintain data confidentiality, but this may introduce a performance penalty. However, the encryption technique is not intended to be employed by end users to encrypt their data. For this reason, it is suggested that user data be encrypted when it is uploaded to the cloud.

The technique also benefits the cloud service provider that controls the data. Since the data remains encrypted and is only decrypted when it is actually in use by the end user, there is no way for a malicious cloud provider employee to view, let alone compromise, the data. Thus, the user maintains full control over who can view or modify the data because only individuals who are granted access to the data by the user may view or modify the data.

A potential problem is that provenance data can grow to become larger than the digital object it describes [19]. Data compression can be used to reduce the storage requirements. However, since there is no maximum limit on the size of the provenance data or the wrapper, the cloud service provider may wish to consider time and storage limits on the provenance data maintained with digital objects.

7. Conclusions

The proposed approach for locating and tracking digital objects in the cloud uses wrappers to encapsulate digital objects and their provenance data. The design helps preserve the integrity of provenance data and meets many of the requirements set for data provenance, including the support of cloud forensic investigations Also, it combines the advantages of embedded provenance storage with the strategic advantage of central logging.

Future research will address issues related to keeping user data inside specific jurisdictions and preventing data from crossing jurisdictional boundaries. Also, efforts will focus on developing a prototype and evaluating its performance.

8. Acknowledgement

This work was partially supported by the National Research Foundation of South Africa under Grant Nos. 88211, 89143 and TP13081227420.

References

[1] K. Alghafli, A. Jones and T. Martin, Forensic analysis of the Windows 7 registry, *Proceedings of the Eighth Australian Digital Forensics Conference*, 2010.

[2] P. Altheide, Spatial Data Transfer Standard, in *Encyclopedia of GIS*, S. Shekhar and H. Xiong (Eds.), Springer, New York, pp. 1087–1095, 2008.

[3] J. Barbara, Cloud computing: Another digital forensic challenge, *Digital Forensic Investigator News*, October 1, 2009.

[4] D. Birk and C. Wegener, Technical issues of forensic investigations in cloud computing environments, *Proceedings of the Sixth IEEE International Workshop on Systematic Approaches to Digital Forensic Engineering*, 2011.

[5] B. Burr, NIST Hash Function Standards: Status and Plans, National Institute of Standards and Technology, Gaithersburg, Maryland (`csrc.nist.gov/groups/SMA/ispab/documents/minutes/2005-12/B_Burr-Dec2005-ISPAB.pdf`), 2005.

[6] F. Cate, The EU data protection directive, information privacy and the public interest, *Iowa Law Review*, vol. 80, pp. 431–443, 1995.

[7] Y. Guan, Digital forensics: Research challenges and open problems, tutorial presented at the *Thirteenth ACM Conference on Computer and Communications Security*, 2007.

[8] R. Hanisch, A. Farris, E. Greisen, W. Pence, B. Schlesinger, P. Teuben, R. Thompson and A. Warnock, Definition of the flexible image transport system, *Astronomy and Astrophysics*, vol. 376, pp. 359–380, 2001.

[9] A. Juels and B. Kaliski, PORs: Proofs of retrievability for large files, *Proceedings of the Fourteenth ACM Conference on Computer and Communications Security*, pp. 584–597, 2007.

[10] R. Lu, X. Lin, X. Liang and X. Shen, Secure provenance: The essential of bread and butter of data forensics in cloud computing, *Proceedings of the Fifth ACM Symposium on Information, Computer and Communications Security*, pp. 282–292, 2010.

[11] P. Mell and T. Grance, The NIST Definition of Cloud Computing, Special Publication 800-145, National Institute of Standards and Technology, Gaithersburg, Maryland, 2011.

[12] K. Muniswamy-Reddy, U. Braun, D. Holland, P. Macko, D. MacLean, D. Margo, M. Seltzer and R. Smogor, Layering in provenance systems, *Proceedings of the Annual USENIX Technical Conference*, 2009.

[13] K. Muniswamy-Reddy and M. Seltzer, Provenance as first class cloud data, *ACM SIGOPS Operating Systems Review*, vol. 43(4), pp. 11–16, 2010.

[14] S. Pearson and A. Benameur, Privacy, security and trust issues arising from cloud computing, *Proceedings of the Second IEEE International Conference on Cloud Computing Technology and Science*, pp. 693–702, 2010.

[15] D. Reilly, C. Wren and T. Berry, Cloud computing: Forensic challenges for law enforcement, *Proceedings of the International Conference on Internet Technology and Secured Transactions*, 2010.

[16] R. Rowlingson, A ten step process for forensic readiness, *International Journal of Digital Evidence*, vol. 2(3), 2004.

[17] K. Ruan, J. Carthy, T. Kechadi and M. Crosbie, Cloud forensics, in *Advances in Digital Forensics VII*, G. Peterson and S. Shenoi (Eds.), Springer, Heidelberg, Germany, pp. 35–46, 2011.

[18] Y. Shi, K. Zhang and Q. Li, A new data integrity verification mechanism for SaaS, *Proceedings of the International Conference on Web Information Systems and Mining*, pp. 236–243, 2010.

[19] Y. Simmhan, B. Plale and D. Gannon, A Survey of Data Provenance Techniques, Technical Report IUB-CS-TR618, Computer Science Department, Indiana University, Bloomington, Indiana, 2005.

[20] H. Takabi, J. Joshi and G. Ahn, Security and privacy challenges in cloud computing environments, *IEEE Security and Privacy*, vol. 8(6), pp. 24–31, 2010.

[21] J. Tan, Forensic readiness: Strategic thinking on incident response, presented at the *Second Annual CanSecWest Conference*, 2001.

[22] P. Trenwith and H. Venter, Digital forensic readiness in the cloud, *Proceedings of the Information Security for South Africa Conference*, 2013.

[23] P. Trenwith and H. Venter, A digital forensic model for providing better data provenance in the cloud, *Proceedings of the Information Security for South Africa Conference*, 2014.

[24] C. Venters, P. Townend, L. Lau, K. Djemame, V. Dimitrova, A. Marshall, J. Xu, C. Dibsdale, N. Taylor and J. Austin, J. McAvoy, M. Fletcher and S. Hobson, Provenance: Current directions and future challenges for service oriented computing, *Proceedings of the Sixth IEEE International Symposium on Service Oriented System Engineering*, pp. 262–267, 2011.

VI

FORENSIC TOOLS

Chapter 18

A TOOL FOR EXTRACTING STATIC AND VOLATILE FORENSIC ARTIFACTS OF WINDOWS 8.x APPS

Shariq Murtuza, Robin Verma, Jayaprakash Govindaraj and Gaurav Gupta

Abstract   Microsoft Windows 8 introduced lightweight sandboxed applications called "apps" that provide a full range of functionality on top of touch-enabled displays. Apps offer a wide range of functionality, including media editing, file sharing, Internet surfing, cloud service usage, online social media activities and audio/video streaming for the Windows 8 and 8.1 operating systems. The use of these apps produces much more forensically-relevant information compared with conventional application programs. This chapter describes MetroExtractor, a tool that gathers static and volatile forensic artifacts produced by Windows apps. The volatile artifacts are extracted from the hibernation and swap files available on storage media. MetroExtractor creates a timeline of user activities and the associated data based on the collected artifacts. The tool appears to be the first implementation for extracting forensically-sound static and volatile Windows 8 app artifacts from a system hard disk.

Keywords: Windows forensics, Windows Metro apps, forensic timelines

1.   Introduction

Microsoft Windows dominates the world's desktop operating system market with a 91% share as of 2014 [15]. Windows 8 (launched in October 2012) and Windows 8.1 (launched in October 2013) have market shares of 6.29% and 6.35% respectively. During the initial period after the launch of Windows 8, there was not much migration to the operating system. However, sales of Windows 8 received a push when touch-screen laptops and monitors became available. Windows 8.1 brought enhanced

© IFIP International Federation for Information Processing 2015
G. Peterson, S. Shenoi (Eds.): Advances in Digital Forensics XI, IFIP AICT 462, pp. 305–320, 2015.
DOI: 10.1007/978-3-319-24123-4_18

user interaction and better software integration, which further increased
sales. Although, Windows 7 still has about 50% market share, the situation is expected to change in 2015 when Microsoft terminates its main-
stream support [10], encouraging users to upgrade to Windows 8 or 8.1
(Windows 8.x).

Windows 8 introduced lightweight application programs called "apps"
that work across a variety of computing devices, including desktops, laptops, tablets and smartphones; Microsoft chose touch screens to be the
default user interaction medium for all the devices. The apps are more
task-oriented compared with full-fledged application programs. For example, there are dedicated apps for checking news and weather, making
restaurant reservations, managing finances, accessing online social networks, shopping online and logging health and fitness information. The
use of these apps produces much more forensically-relevant information
than full-fledged application programs. From the digital forensics perspective, Windows 8.x is similar to Windows 7 in that most forensic
artifact extraction methods for application program data that work on
Windows 7 can also be used on Windows 8.x. However, the apps, which
are exclusive to Windows 8.x, are responsible for the primary difference
between Windows 8.x and Windows 7 forensics.

The apps that come bundled with the operating system are called
native apps; the remaining apps are downloaded from the Windows app
store by the user. The static artifacts of an app mainly include its data
and associated metadata stored on the relatively static hard disk drive.
These artifacts are available in the local folders and related registry
entries of the app. The volatile artifacts of an app include the RAM space
allocated to it in physical memory. The hibernation file contains volatile
artifacts of apps, desktop applications and other processes in the form of
a compressed and encoded dump of the physical memory that contains
their most recent running states. The RAM space of an app that is
written to the hibernation file contains valuable volatile forensic artifacts
that are not present in the app's local folders or registry entries. For
example, a Facebook app's RAM space contains news feeds, comments,
notifications and likes that cannot be extracted via static analysis. The
RAM slack space in the hibernation file can also have archival artifacts
pertaining to apps. Similarly, the swap file in Windows 8.x may also
contain volatile artifacts related to apps; however, this is limited by the
physical memory size and the frequency of the RAM freeing up process.
The private data of running apps is flushed to the swap file during a
memory crunch [9], which transfers the volatile contents of the apps
to the hard disk. Small physical memory size tends to increase the

frequency of RAM freeing up and, consequently, the chances of finding forensic artifacts related to apps.

This chapter describes the design and implementation of the MetroExtractor tool that collects static and volatile artifacts of Windows 8.x apps. The static artifacts are extracted from the hard disk drive and volatile artifacts from the hibernation and swap files present on a Windows 8.x installation disk. The MetroExtractor tool also creates a combined timeline for the static and volatile artifacts collected for a particular app. The tool was tested on the Facebook and Twitter social network apps and the Dropbox and OneDrive cloud data storage apps. The integrity of the results was verified by comparing the findings with a live RAM capture made at the same time. A survey of the literature indicates that MetroExtractor is the first tool capable of extracting forensically-sound static and volatile Windows 8.x app artifacts from a system hard disk.

2. Related Work

This section briefly discusses Windows 8 forensics and the forensic analysis of apps.

2.1 Windows 8 Forensics

This work focuses on the collection of forensically-relevant static and volatile Windows 8.x app artifacts from a hard disk. Johnson [8] has investigated the feature of Windows 8.0 and subsequent versions that helps the users to easily refresh or reset their workstations. He has shown that a user can use these options to restore the original system settings by keeping the user files, removing everything else and reinstalling Windows. However, he did not consider the extraction of volatile data from the hard disk drive.

Thompson [19] has performed similar work, primarily analyzing the app folder structure and the operation of basic apps. His research also investigated the artifacts generated by apps. This work takes a step further by incorporating Thompson's findings in the analysis of app artifacts found in the hibernation and swap files. Thompson also examined Windows 8 registry files in order to collect artifacts. However, the work was done using Windows 8 Consumer Preview and, thus, the results may not be directly applicable to Windows 8.1

Dija et al. [3] have investigated the extraction of volatile artifacts from the hibernation file. Their work concentrates on application programs that can be searched for in the hibernation file; however, it does not consider Windows 8.x apps and the associated page and swap files. Mrdovic and Huseinovic [13] have recovered encryption keys from a physical memory dump with a hibernation file as the source. Gupta and Mehte [5] have conducted similar work on the Sandboxie application in a non-encrypted system.

2.2   Forensic Analysis of Apps

This work analyzes some of the common Windows 8.x apps so that correlation techniques can be used to obtain data about online social network activities related to a particular user and/or account. The analysis focuses on the cache of the targeted app and its local information from the corresponding SQLite 3 database. The hibernation, page and swap files are also examined to gather physical memory remnants of the app in the event that the local artifacts of the app were tampered with or deleted.

Iqbal et al. [7] have investigated the Surface tablet with a standard Windows 8 RT installation. However, their work is limited to Windows 8 RT and covers only the Surface tablet, which, compared with Windows 8.x, is restricted in terms of its hardware and operating system functionality. Iqbal et al. have also discussed techniques for obtaining RAM dumps from Windows 7 phones.

Carvey [2] has described the procedures that should be followed during an incident response involving a Windows 8.0 device. He has also identified Windows 8 artifacts that can be extracted. Additionally, he stresses the importance of the hibernation file and the fact that malware and other data can remain resident in the file even after anti-virus software and other temporary space cleaners have been employed.

Quick and Choo [16–18] discuss methods for extracting artifacts related to the use of SkyDrive, Dropbox and Google Drive. The remnants gathered include user-related information and files. Quick and Choo [17] have also analyzed RAM captures and local sources for the Dropbox application, but they did not consider the fact that the hibernation file may contain sensitive data related to the application. Similarly, Wong et al. [20] have focused on finding Facebook artifacts from web browsers and RAM dumps. Beverly et al. [1] have proposed a methodology for extracting network packet data from a hibernation file and using the data in network forensic investigations.

3.   Background

This section discusses the hibernation and swap files, and static and volatile artifacts in Windows 8.x systems.

3.1   Hibernation File

Windows 8.x apps are lightweight programs that run on limited resources while providing well-defined functionality to users. User activity information and other data collected by an app is lucrative from a forensic perspective. For example, a map app typically retains all the user queries, including the places searched, routes explored and user location (if a laptop was used). The apps store their data and activity information in their respective local folders and registry entries on the hard disk. However, some of the information is not written back to the hard disk and remains in the app's RAM space when it executes. For example, the Facebook app's RAM space contains news feeds, comments and likes that are not written back to the app's local folders on disk. However, the availability of this extra information in RAM space depends on the type of app and its design.

Experiments were conducted on the hibernation file (`hiberfil.sys`), a large file about the size of the physical memory of the system. The file is overwritten by the RAM contents. At the time of writing the RAM contents to the file, the operating system compresses and encodes the data. Windows 8.x uses the Xpress algorithm for compression and the Huffman and LZ algorithms for encoding [6]. This speeds up the process of writing to and reading from the hibernation file during the shutdown and restart operations. The encoded content of the hibernation file can be converted back to a RAM dump (i.e., in a data format exactly similar to the RAM) using the MoonSols tool [11]. Although Volatility can be used to convert an encoded hibernation file to a RAM dump, MoonSols was found to produce an error-free output at a faster rate. A hibernation file also contains archival data in slack space that is the result of previous writes. The amount of archival data present in a hibernation file depends on the size of the file and the frequency of writes. A general rule of thumb is that the larger the hibernation file, the greater the chances of finding app artifacts related to earlier sessions.

3.2   Swap File

According to the official MSDN blog [9], the runtime design of Windows 8 enables it to suspend an app when it is minimized by a user. The suspended apps do not use the processor as soon they are not in active use. When Windows 8 Metro apps are suspended, the RAM space allocated to them remains untouched. When there is a memory crunch, the operating system flushes all the memory of the suspended apps to a swap file. The memory dump stored in the swap file can be brought back to the RAM later without terminating the apps [9]. Morrison [12] states that the mechanism of writing the private RAM space of a suspended app to the swap file on disk until it resumes is analogous to the hibernation of an app. Note that the swap file contains the flushed-out private memory dump of an app during a memory crunch, so it does not necessarily hold the last used instance of the app. Hence, the swap file generally provides a random memory snapshot of an app.

3.3   Static vs. Volatile Artifacts

Although the static artifacts of an app on disk give useful insights into user activity and data, the volatile artifacts from the hibernation and swap files are also required to completely reconstruct the sequence of events in a digital forensic case. The importance of collecting static and volatile artifacts of Windows 8.x apps is clarified using two example scenarios. The two scenarios assume that the hibernation file on the system disk cannot be touched by the user because it is inaccessible to all user level apps, applications and processes on a running Windows 8.x system.

- **Unintentional Deletion of Forensic Artifacts:** Assume that a user installs a Windows 8.x app that clears the cache of apps that are already installed on the system. The user has no intention of modifying any evidence related to the pre-installed apps; instead, the user merely wishes to free up some storage space. In this case, the static artifacts are deleted from the system, but can be recovered using forensic tools. However, there is a good chance they are overwritten over time and are unrecoverable. Volatile artifacts in the hibernation and swap files may retain the same archival data that was deleted from the static collection. Additionally, certain forensic artifacts are only present in the volatile space. Therefore, collecting volatile artifacts from the hibernation and swap files is as just important as collecting static artifacts from the disk.

- **Intentional Deletion and Anti-Forensics:** In the second scenario, the user employs anti-forensics to securely delete or tamper with the static artifacts of an app. If the user securely deletes the static artifacts of the app, the artifacts cannot be recovered using conventional forensic tools. If the user tampers with the static artifacts, then there is the possibility that a forensic tool could find traces of the tampering, but there is a good chance that the traces would have been overwritten over time. However, the volatile artifacts in the hibernation and swap files may still have the same archival data that was in the static space.

The two scenarios demonstrate that collecting volatile artifacts from the hibernation and swap files is as worthwhile as collecting artifacts from static space.

4. Experimental Methodology

Windows Metro app static data is present on disk in the form of databases and app registry files. It is important to emphasize that not all the data displayed by the Metro app is stored on disk as database files. Some artifacts are present only in volatile memory. These include, in the case of the Facebook app, the user's news feed, posts made or viewed by the user and the comments made about posts. This data, which is fetched via the Facebook API, is stored in volatile memory and is not reflected on the disk. For example, a user may post a status update on his wall and may decide to delete the post some time later. If such posts were to be reflected on the disk, then errors would exist. Some chat applications require that the recipient should get a message even if it was deleted by the sender. Such activities are, therefore, reflected on the disk. For these reasons, a complete forensic picture may only be available if an investigator considers both static and volatile artifacts. Tools such as Privacy Eraser and other Windows 8 cache cleaners such as Modern UI Apps Cleaner enable users to clean the cache, cookies, Internet history files and other temporary app files from Windows 8 apps folders. This cleaning results in the loss of potential static evidence from the disk.

The MetroExtractor tool described in this chapter gathers static and volatile forensic artifacts of Windows apps. It incorporates a graphical user interface front-end written in Java; its back-end activities are implemented by a collection of shell scripts. MetroExtractor collects static artifacts, arranges them according to their timestamps and presents a timeline of activities. The tool then extracts the hibernation file from the hard disk/dd image/user-provided image or E01 file, and converts it to the corresponding RAM dump using the MoonSols memory toolkit. Volatility is then used to extract app-specific memory chunks from the RAM dump. The next step is to extract timestamped data from the chunks. The data is usually present in the form of a JSON file that is received by the (Facebook) app as a response to the API request that it sent. The JSON file is received and parsed by the Facebook app and displayed. The file contains user data such as chats, notifications, image links, textual content and, most importantly, timestamps (Unix epoch timestamps). The JSON data is extracted using regular expressions and is then classified as chats, notifications, posts, etc. on the basis of variable names. The timestamps are then extracted and plotted on a timeline. Finally, the artifacts obtained via the static and volatile analyses are incorporated in the timeline and displayed to the investigator.

The experiments involved the following steps:

1. An app was launched and allowed to load completely and display the data.

2. A RAM dump was created using the MoonSols DumpIt program.

3. The system was made to hibernate.

4. The hibernation file was extracted using a Linux Live CD.

Figure 1 presents the experimental methodology. A RAM dump was obtained just before the system was made to hibernate. This was done to ensure that the RAM content and the content stored in the hibernation file would be as similar as possible to the RAM dump. Two different dumps (one from RAM and the other from the hibernation file) were obtained to verify the findings and if the hibernation file could be used for forensic analysis with the same credibility as the RAM dump. The time difference between taking the RAM dump and hibernating the system was minimized. The app specific memory chunks that were extracted from RAM memory were found to have comparable sizes. The difference in sizes (if present) was never more than 100 MB. The size difference was most likely due to the hibernation file containing some RAM slack.

The MoonSols memory toolkit was then used to convert the hibernation file to a RAM dump. The Volatility Framework could also have been used for this task, but experimentation revealed that MoonSols performs faster conversions. Next, Volatility was used to inspect the RAM dump created from the hibernation file. After obtaining the extracted memory, Foremost was used to perform string searches on the memory dump.

As mentioned above, the back-end functionality of the MetroExtractor tool is implemented by a collection of shell scripts. MoonSols is only used to convert the hibernation file to a RAM dump. MetroExtractor runs on a Linux system or a Windows platform with Cygwin installed. It takes as input a dd image, ewf file or a hard disk. The tool first converts the hibernation file to an equivalent RAM dump using MoonSols. The RAM dump is then processed by MetroExtractor using the Volatility API to extract the process memory space for the required app. The memory chunk of the app is then processed and classified by MetroExtractor as a chat, comment, notification, etc. Note that the Facebook API responses are in a form specific to JSON with variable names (used for activity

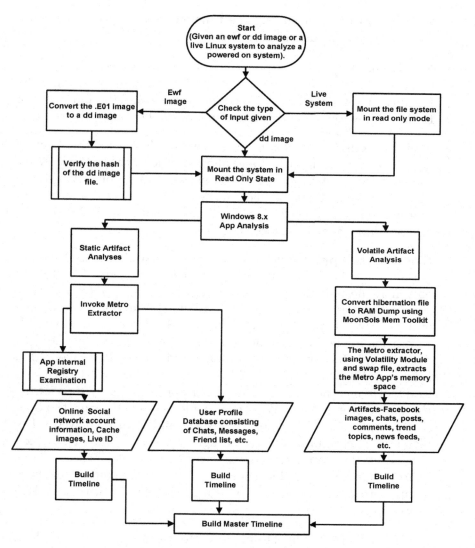

Figure 1. Experimental methodology.

classification) and timestamps. The timestamps are exported into a CSV file along with the corresponding activity.

The MetroExtractor tool also collects static app artifacts from disk. The data is stored in databases from which timestamps are extracted and a timeline plotted. The static and volatile timelines are then merged. Merging the two timelines gives insights about activities that were performed simultaneously, such as commenting and chatting while receiving a notification. The unified timeline representation provides a comprehensive picture of user activities. The timeline is displayed by opening the CSV file using spreadsheet software.

- **Facebook App:** The experiment began by launching the Facebook app and allowing it to load all the content. After this, the RAM dump was made and the system was put in hibernation. The RAM dumps were then processed using the Foremost tool.

- **Twitter App:** A similar procedure was followed for the Twitter app. The app was launched and allowed to load the content. After the content was loaded and the app was stable, the RAM dump was made using DumpIt. Following this, the system was put in hibernation, the hibernation file was extracted and the process described above was performed.

- **One Drive App:** By default, documents saved to OneDrive are not downloaded from the cloud; instead, they are downloaded only if requested by users or if users explicitly specify that they should be made available offline. While conducting experiments on OneDrive, it was discovered that the `Skydrive.exe` service always runs in the background in order to synchronize all the data files. Sample files were created and stored in the OneDrive folder. Like the Windows 8 Dropbox app, the Windows 8 Modern app for OneDrive is not designed for synchronization, only for viewing the online stored files. Whenever a file is opened using the app, it is downloaded to temporary storage and then displayed. The files are synchronized by the background service `Skydrive.exe`. Whenever the app was used, it started with the process name `FileManagerexe`. In due course, this process spawned itself as a child process. A similar procedure was followed with the child process.

- **Dropbox App:** The Dropbox Windows 8 app was launched. Dumps were made of the RAM and the hibernation file.

- **OneNote App:** The OneNote Windows 8 app was launched. Dumps were made of the RAM and the hibernation file.

5.   Experimental Results

During the experiments, app-specific memory chunks were extracted from the RAM dumps. A similar procedure was followed with the hibernation files after converting them to RAM dumps using the MoonSols memory toolkit. This section presents the experimental results and com-

Table 1. Hibernation file artifacts with live RAM capture (social network apps).

Apps	Hibernation File Data	Live RAM Data	Result
Facebook	Username, profile ID, profile info JSON, profile pic URL, other images, chat messages, Facebook feed status, login email id and trending items.	Username, profile ID, profile info JSON, profile pic URL, other images, chat messages, Facebook feed status, login email id, trending items, news feed, comments, notifications and likes.	The findings were verified to a large extent, the only exceptions were the news feed, comments, notifications and likes.
Twitter	Twitter handle, profile JSON, profile pic URL, tweets at the current instant, embedded pictures, direct messages and email id. The data was present in the form of JSON.	Twitter handle, profile JSON, profile pic URL, tweets at the current instant, embedded pictures, direct messages and email id. The data was present in the form of JSON.	The hibernation file is as good as the live RAM capture.

pares the results obtained from the RAM dumps and the hibernation files.

5.1 Facebook

Table 1 presents the results for the Facebook app. It was possible to extract the images displayed in the user's Facebook feed. Chat messages were found along with user activity and user profile data such as the Facebook profile ID, JSON data pertaining to conversations, timestamps, etc. All the results were verified except for Facebook notifications because the notifications were displayed for a very short time during the live RAM capture. In addition to these artifacts, it was possible to find previous chat messages in the dumps, because the Facebook app was loading them to show the user his chat history. Static artifacts were extracted from the on-disk app databases. These databases contained many details, including the friends list, notifications and chat content.

A timeline was created from the static artifacts, mainly the notification and chat timestamps. The static timeline was merged with the volatile timeline (Figure 2), yielding vital activity clues such as notifications that arrived during chats, when they occurred and the individuals with whom the user was chatting during specific time windows.

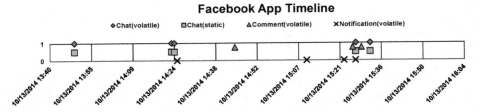

Figure 2. Combined timeline for the Facebook app.

Creating the combined timeline is important because the static and volatile artifacts complement each other. User activities can be verified from the combined timeline. Activities such as chats and friend requests were easily verified from the static artifacts. Many new insights were gained when the static timeline was combined with the volatile timeline. These included the images that were viewed (carved from the dump using Foremost), the verification of the chat history and the comments posted by the user, and the correlation of posts from other users in the user's home page feed.

Table 2. Hibernation file artifacts with live RAM capture (cloud storage apps).

Apps	Hibernation File Data	Live RAM Data	Result
Dropbox	Name list of all files stored in the cloud account, Dropbox user ids with whom files were shared, user login email id, multiple location-based data such as locale and DTS.	All this data was also found in the RAM with no other artifacts being present.	The hibernation file is as good as the live RAM capture.
OneDrive	File list, user name and id (profile and email), SHA1 hash, DTS, sharing level, UID and file sizes.	All this data was also found in the RAM with no other artifacts being present.	The hibernation file is as good as the live RAM capture.

5.2   Other Apps

Other apps, including Twitter, Dropbox and OneDrive, have common artifacts in their static and volatile spaces. Tables 1 and 2 present the results.

In the case of Windows 8 OneNote, the app was started and allowed to synchronize. Following this, the hibernation file and live RAM dump

Table 3. Average time taken by MetroExtractor to process data.

Processor	System Configuration	Operating System	Time
Intel Core2Duo (2.2 GHz)	HDD: 320 GB; RAM: 4 GB	Ubuntu 12.04 LTS (32 bit)	32 min.
Intel Core i5 (2.8 GHz)	HDD: 320 GB; RAM: 4 GB	Ubuntu 12.04 LTS (64 bit)	21 min.

were collected. Microsoft OneNote organizes and stores data in the form of pages called Notebooks. Foremost was able to recover all the images that were pasted in the Notebooks along with the text content. A hex editor revealed an XML structure similar to Office documents. The creator's Live ID and the creation time of the notes were found in the XML structure.

5.3 Performance

The primary time consuming activities of MetroExtractor are the conversion of a hibernation file to the corresponding RAM dump and the extraction of the individual process memory chunks from the RAM dump. Table 3 shows the average time (over ten replications) taken by the tool to process artifacts for a particular app.

Finally, it is useful to compare the performance of bulk_extractor [4] and MetroExtractor. The bulk_extractor tool works by scanning a disk without parsing the file system structure. MetroExtractor, on the other hand, uses the file system structure to locate active files and extract the corresponding artifacts. Both the tools attempt to find the maximum amount of evidence in the input disk or image. The bulk_extractor tool extracts all possible artifacts, including information from other applications. However, the current version of MetroExtractor finds artifacts only for Windows 8 Metro apps. MetroExtractor generates timelines using the timestamps of the collected artifacts whereas bulk_extractor simply lists all the evidence present without correlating it or arranging it in chronological order.

6. Conclusions

The MetroExtractor tool described in this chapter gathers forensic artifacts related to Windows 8 and 8.1 Metro apps. Static artifacts from the local app folders and registry entries along with volatile artifacts extracted from the hibernation and swap files are mapped to a single timeline to provide comprehensive reconstructions of events. The tool was tested on the Facebook and Twitter apps and the OneDrive and Dropbox cloud data storage apps. The integrity of the methodology was verified experimentally by comparing the results from a live RAM capture with those from a hibernation file written to disk at the same time. A survey of the literature indicates that MetroExtractor is the first tool capable of extracting forensically-sound static and volatile Windows 8.x app artifacts from a system disk.

MetroExtractor considers only active hibernation files. Because the Windows 8.x disk optimization options are enabled by default, some portions of a hibernation file may be defragmented. Since the Windows operating system corrupts the beginning of the hibernation file every time the system reboots, a defragmentation operation can cause portions of the corrupted file to be found in the slack space [1].

Future research will focus on developing similar tools for Microsoft Windows phones and tablet devices. Also, research will attempt to analyze synced data that moves between devices.

References

[1] R. Beverly, S. Garfinkel and G. Cardwell, Forensic carving of network packets and associated data structures, *Digital Investigation*, vol. 8(S), pp. S78–S89, 2011.

[2] H. Carvey, *Windows Forensic Analysis Toolkit: Advanced Analysis Techniques for Windows 8*, Syngress, Waltham, Massachusetts, 2014.

[3] S. Dija, T. Deepthi, C. Balan and K. Thomas, Towards retrieving live forensic artifacts in offline forensics, in *Recent Trends in Computer Networks and Distributed Systems Security*, S. Thampi, A. Zomaya, T. Strufe, J. Alcaraz Calero and T. Thomas (Eds.), Springer-Verlag, Berlin Heidelberg, Germany, pp. 225–233, 2012.

[4] S. Garfinkel, Digital media triage with bulk data analysis and bulk_extractor, *Computers and Security*, vol. 32, pp. 56–72, 2013.

[5] D. Gupta and B. Mehte, Forensic analysis of Sandboxie artifacts, in *Security in Computing and Communications*, S. Thampi, P. Atrey, C. Fan and G. Martinez Perez (Eds.), Springer-Verlag, Berlin Heidelberg, Germany, pp. 341–352, 2013.

[6] M. Hale Ligh, A. Case, J. Levy and A. Walters, *The Art of Memory Forensics: Detecting Malware and Threats in Windows, Linux and Mac Memory*, John Wiley and Sons, Indianapolis, Indiana, 2014.

[7] A. Iqbal, H. Al Obaidli, A. Marrington and A. Jones, Windows Surface RT tablet forensics, *Digital Investigation*, vol. 11(S1), pp. S87–S93, 2014.

[8] W. Johnson, Journey into Windows 8 recovery artifacts, *Proceedings of the Conference on Digital Forensics, Security and Law*, pp. 87–100, 2013.

[9] B. Karagounis, Reclaiming Memory from Metro Style Apps, Microsoft Developer Network, Microsoft, Redmond, Washington (`blogs.msdn.com/b/b8/arxchive/2012/04/17/reclaiming-memory-from-metro-style-apps.aspx`), 2012.

[10] Microsoft, Windows Lifecycle Fact Sheet, Redmond, Washington (`windows.microsoft.com/en-us/windows/lifecycle`), 2014.

[11] MoonSols, MoonSols Windows Memory Toolkit, Hong Kong, China (`www.moonsols.com/windows-memory-toolkit`), 2015.

[12] B. Morrison, Windows 8/Windows Server 2012: The New Swap File, Technet, Microsoft, Redmond, Washington (`blogs.technet.com/b/askperf/archive/2012/10/28/windows-8-windows-server-2012-the-new-swap-file.aspx`), 2012.

[13] S. Mrdovic and A. Huseinovic, Forensic analysis of encrypted volumes using hibernation files, *Proceedings of the Nineteenth Telecommunications Forum*, pp. 1277–1280, 2011.

[14] S. Mrdovic, A. Huseinovic and E. Zajko, Combining static and live digital forensic analysis in virtual environments, *Proceedings of the Twenty-Second International Symposium on Information, Communication and Automation Technologies*, 2009.

[15] NetMarketShare, Desktop operating system market share, Irvine, California (`www.netmarketshare.com/operating-system-market-share.aspx?qprid=8\&qpcustomd=0`), 2014.

[16] D. Quick and K. Choo, Digital droplets: Microsoft SkyDrive forensic data remnants, *Future Generation Computer Systems*, vol. 29(6), pp. 1378–1394, 2013.

[17] D. Quick and K. Choo, Dropbox analysis: Data remnants on user machines, *Digital Investigation*, vol. 10(1), pp. 3–18, 2013.

[18] D. Quick and K. Choo, Google Drive: Forensic analysis of data remnants, *Journal of Network and Computer Applications*, vol. 40, pp. 179–193, 2014.

[19] A. Thomson, Windows 8 Forensic Guide, George Washington University, Washington, DC (`propellerheadforensics.files.wordpress.com/2012/05/thomson\_windows-8-forensic-guide2.pdf`), 2012.

[20] K. Wong, A. Lai, J. Yeung, W. Lee and P. Chan, Facebook Forensics, Valkyrie-X Security Research Group (`www.fbiic.gov/public/2011/jul/facebook_forensics-finalized.pdf`), 2011.

Chapter 19

CRITERIA FOR VALIDATING SECURE WIPING TOOLS

Muhammad Sharjeel Zareen, Baber Aslam and Monis Akhlaq

Abstract   The validation of forensic tools is an important requirement in digital forensics. The National Institute of Standards and Technology has defined standards for many digital forensic tools. However, a standard has not yet been specified for secure wiping tools. This chapter defines secure wiping functionality criteria for NTFS specific to Windows 7 and magnetic hard drives. The criteria were created based on the remnants of user actions – file creation, modification and deletion – in $MFT records, the $LogFile and the hard disk. Of particular relevance is the fact that the $LogFile, which holds considerable forensic artifacts of user actions, is not wiped properly by many tools. The use of the proposed functionality criteria is demonstrated in an evaluation of the Eraser secure wiping tool.

Keywords: Tool validation, secure wiping functionality, NTFS, $LogFile forensics

1.   Introduction

To ensure the integrity of digital evidence and the results of forensic investigations, digital forensic professionals must use validated tools based on state-of-the-art technology and tried and tested procedures [1, 8]. In addition to ensuring the integrity of evidence, this protects the credibility of digital forensic professionals [5].

The U.S. National Institute of Standards and Technology (NIST) conducts extensive digital forensic tool validation under its Computer Forensics Tool Testing (CFTT) Program [4]. Prior to validating the functionality of a forensic tool, it is necessary to define standards (i.e., validation criteria) for tool functionality. NIST standardization procedures involve defining tool specifications, test assertions, test cases and a test methodology [4].

G. Peterson, S. Shenoi (Eds.): Advances in Digital Forensics XI, IFIP AICT 462, pp. 321–339, 2015.
DOI: 10.1007/978-3-319-24123-4_19

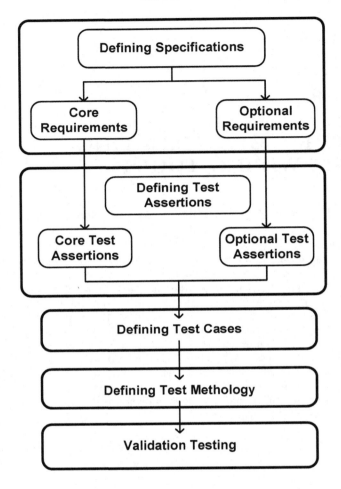

Figure 1. NIST validation cycle.

Each specification includes the required functions and technical features. These provide a basis for defining test assertions and test cases. Test assertions are defined to help ascertain that a tool meets each specification. Based on the test assertions, test cases and a methodology for testing tool functionality are defined. Figure 1 shows the NIST tool validation cycle.

Unfortunately, a standard has not as yet been specified for secure wiping tools. This chapter defines secure wiping criteria for the New Technology File System (NTFS) specific to Windows 7 and magnetic hard drives.

Data deletion is the process of removing digital data from digital storage. The goal of deletion is to remove all the data and its related information from digital storage in order to ensure data confidentiality. When data is deleted from NTFS using standard deletion functions, the operating system only marks the master file table ($MFT) records as deleted and makes minor changes such as removing links in cluster maps and directories [3].

Since no data overwriting is done, the data is recoverable using digital forensic tools, provided that the original data has not been overwritten by new data. Secure wiping tools delete files in order to prevent data retrieval. A general perception is that once files have been deleted using secure wiping tools, no information about the files can be extracted. However, this chapter shows that, even after secure wiping, critical information is left behind, especially in the $LogFile, including the names, contents and temporal information of files and information about the wiping operation. Moreover, each wiping tool leaves behind a signature pertaining to how the data was overwritten; this signature can be used to identify the tool. This chapter evaluates the functionality of Eraser, a popular secure wiping tool, and identifies the artifacts left behind after a secure wiping operation.

Validation criteria for secure wiping functionality are defined in this chapter to ensure that all the data and related information are wiped from $MFT records, the $LogFile and the hard disk (clusters containing non-resident data, index entries and other non-resident payloads of attributes). The criteria also ensure that no signature remains that could reveal information about the wiping operation and the tool that was used.

Digital forensic examinations of deleted data involve collecting evidence that includes: (i) what was deleted; (ii) when it was deleted; (iii) when the deleted files were created; (iv) what the deleted files contained; and (v) what were the sizes of the deleted files. In the light of these objectives, the forensic artifacts of a deleted file are divided into three main categories: (i) name; (ii) time; and (iii) contents. Information about the name of a file and its parent folder falls in the name category. Information about the file creation, modification and deletion times fall in the time category. Information about file content and size comes under the contents category.

User actions have effects on different areas of an NTFS. When a file is created or modified, changes are made to:

- $MFT records of the file and folder and related records ($BitMap, $MFT, etc.) that store resident data and metadata under various attributes.

- $LogFile logs that record transactions related to user actions.

- The hard disk that contains non-resident data and non-resident payloads of various attributes.

When a file has been dormant for an extended period of time, its operational records in the $LogFile are overwritten; the exact duration depends on the volume of the activities performed on the hard drive. However, related information remains in $MFT records and on the hard disk. When a file is deleted, it leaves artifacts in $MFT records, the $LogFile and hard disk. Moreover, after deletion, all previous artifacts of file creation and modification are available in the $LogFile and on the hard disk, and partially in $MFT records (new user actions generate new attributes that overwrite previous attributes). This chapter only discusses the deletion process in detail because artifacts that remain after file deletion must be considered when characterizing the secure wiping process.

The primary contribution of this work is the identification of the effects of user actions performed on a file in various segments of an NTFS, including the $MFT records, $LogFile and hard disk, and the identification of the remnants in these entities after a deletion process. These remnants are used to define the validation criteria for secure wiping functionality; specifically, to ensure that all file data and information about the wiped file and the wiping tool are removed from the filesystem (NTFS in a Windows 7 environment).

2.   Deletion Effects and Deletion Types

This section briefly discusses the effects of user actions on $MFT records, the $LogFile and the hard disk. Note that only the remnants of deletion processes are discussed because these remnants must be removed by secure wiping tools. Also, the section describes two types of deletion.

2.1   Deletion Effects

A user action on a file in an NTFS has the following effects:

- **$MFT Record:** The end state of a user action is recorded in the $MFT record of the file and associated $MFT records such as the parent folder, $BitMap and $MFT. The $MFT record carries the $LogFile sequence number (LSN) in its header, which links the $MFT record to the corresponding chain of operational records in the $LogFile.

- **$LogFile:** A user action generates a chain of operational records in the $LogFile. Each record represents an NTFS transaction that is performed to complete the user action. When a new action is performed, the records in the $LogFile are not replaced with new records corresponding to the file. Instead, new records are stored in the next available space in the $LogFile [7]. The writing of records in the $LogFile is circular in nature. After the $LogFile is filled, new records are written starting from the beginning of the $LogFile [6]. The $LogFile thus contains artifacts of user actions that constitute valuable digital evidence. Interested readers are referred to [10] for details about the $LogFile structure and how it is read. Details about chains of operational records in the $LogFile for user actions and the linking of the chains with corresponding $MFT records are discussed in [9].

- **Hard Disk:** The hard disk, as well as the $MFT and $LogFile, which carry non-resident data and non-resident index entries, are updated.

2.2 Deletion Types

NTFS provides two types of file deletion: (i) deletion via the recycle bin; and (ii) permanent deletion.

Deletion via the Recycle Bin. This deletion process has two stages. In the first stage, the file is deleted and sent to the recycle bin. In the second stage, the file is removed from the recycle bin.

During the first stage, the following actions are performed by NTFS on $MFT records:

- **Deleted File:** The name of the deleted file is changed to a random name of seven characters starting with $ and followed by the letter "R" (R is for the renamed file in the recycle bin; this file is referred to as $Rxxx in this chapter). The renamed file is moved to the recycle bin and its temporal information in attribute 0x10 $Standard_ Information and attribute 0x30 $File_Name of the $MFT record are updated.

- **New File Generation:** At the same time, a new file with the same random name $Rxxx is also generated in the current user folder of the recycle bin, but it starts with $I (I is for information). The new file is referred to as $Ixxx in this chapter. A corresponding entry is made in the $MFT for the newly-generated $MFT record of $Ixxx. The file contains the file name, location and temporal information about the original file and the file deletion process. The $Ixxx file facilitates the NTFS recovery process when the file is to be recovered from the recycle bin.

- **Deleted File Index Entry:** The index entry of the deleted file is moved from the parent folder to the current user folder of the recycle bin. Temporal information in attribute 0x10 of the $MFT record of the current user folder and the parent folder are updated to show the deletion time. The parent file index entry in its own parent folder is also updated with the time and size. In addition, if the name was indexed at the end of attribute 0x90 $Index_Root or attribute 0xA0 $Index_Allocation, then the deletion leaves the index entry (name + time + size) in the slack space.

A chain of operational records is generated in the $LogFile in which all the above transactions are logged. If a deleted file is non-resident, no changes occur to the non-resident data contents of attribute 0x80 $Data (i.e., data residing on the hard disk outside the $MFT record). Details of the changes are discussed in [9].

Clearing the file from the recycle bin during the second stage results in the following changes:

- **$Rxxx and $Ixxx:** The $MFT record headers of the $Rxxx and corresponding $Ixxx files are updated to show the new $LogFile sequence number, record sequence number, flag with the $MFT record status as deleted and update sequence number. In addition, the update sequence numbers of the sector boundaries of the $MFT record (0x1FE–0x1FF and 0x3FE–0x3FF) are updated accordingly. The remaining attributes of the $MFT record are not altered or wiped. This makes information contained in the attributes available to digital forensic professionals.

- **Parent Folder:** The $MFT record of the current user folder of the recycle bin is updated to show its modified size (after the removal of two files) and temporal information in attribute 0x10 of the $MFT record. The index entries of the deleted files are removed and the next file records in line are shifted up to these locations.

A chain of operational records is accordingly generated in the $Log-File in which all the above transactions are logged. If the deleted file is non-resident, no changes occur to the non-resident data contents of attribute 0x80 $Data (i.e., data residing on the hard disk outside the $MFT record). This data is recoverable using digital forensic tools.

Permanent File Deletion. When a file is deleted via a command prompt or using `shift + delete`, the file does not go to the recycle bin, but is deleted permanently. This type of deletion leaves more forensic information than a recycle bin deletion. Almost all the attributes of the $MFT records of the deleted file are unaltered, except for the $MFT record header. The deletion remnants include:

- **Deleted File:** The $MFT record header of the deleted file is updated showing the updated $LogFile sequence number, record sequence number, flag with the $MFT record status as deleted and update sequence number. In addition, the update sequence numbers of the sector boundaries of the $MFT record (`0x1FE-0x1FF` and `0x3FE-0x3FF`) are updated accordingly. The remaining attributes of the $MFT record are not altered or wiped. This makes all the information contained in the attributes available to digital forensic professionals.

- **Index Entry of Deleted File:** The index entry of the deleted file in the $MFT record of the parent folder is removed and its attribute `0x10` is updated. This reveals the time of file deletion. In addition, if the name was indexed at the end of attribute `0x90` or the index of attribute `0xA0`, then the deletion leaves the index entry (name + time + size) in slack space. The parent file index entry in its own parent folder is also updated with the new time and size.

A chain of operational records is accordingly generated in the $LogFile in which all the above transactions are logged. If the deleted file is non-resident, no changes occur to the non-resident data contents of attribute `0x80` $Data (i.e., data residing on the hard disk outside the $MFT record). This data is recoverable using digital forensic tools.

3.   File Deletion Artifacts

Forensic artifacts are divided into three categories based on their locations: (i) $MFT records; (ii) $LogFile; and (iii) hard disk. The following sections discuss each category of artifacts for the two deletion methods.

3.1 $MFT Records (Recycle Bin Deletion)

The following artifacts are present in $MFT records.

- **Name Information:** The name of the $Rxxx deleted file is present in attribute `0x30` of the $MFT record of the deleted file. The actual name and location of the parent folder under which the original file was indexed are available in the $MFT record of $Ixxx. This file also reveals the name of the original file and its original path. The altered file name is also indexed in the current user folder of the recycle bin. If the original/renamed file is indexed at the end of attribute 0x90 or index of attribute 0xA0, then the deletion process leaves the index entry (name + time + size) in the slack space of the original parent folder/current user folder; this information is recoverable using digital forensic tools.

- **Temporal Information:** Temporal information about file creation and deletion (file modification time when the file was renamed to $Rxxx and the $MFT record update time) is available in attribute 0x10 $Standard_Information. Temporal information about the renaming of the file to $Rxxx is also available in attribute 0x30 $File_Name. The renamed index entry (name + time + size) of the file in the current user folder of the recycle bin also reveals the deletion time (i.e., file deletion to the recycle bin). Temporal information about the original/renamed file is also available in the slack space if the original/renamed file is indexed at the end as mentioned above.

- **Content Information:** Information about file contents is available in attribute 0x80 $Data of the $MFT record of $Rxxx. In the case of resident data, the content is also available in the same attribute. In the case of non-resident data, information about the size of the data and clusters is available in attribute 0x80. The original file size is also available in the $MFT record of $Ixxx.

3.2 $LogFile (Recycle Bin Deletion)

The $LogFile is a gold mine when it comes to forensic artifacts. All the transactions related to file creation, modification and deletion are logged here. As mentioned above, the $LogFile records produced during file creation are unchanged during file modification and deletion. These records are only overwritten from the start in a circular manner after the $LogFile is filled.

The following artifacts are present in the $LogFile:

- **Name Information:** The file name is present in previous records related to file creation, file renaming and file deletion. The records related to adding and deleting the index entry of a deleted file to/from parent folder also hold file name information.

- **Temporal Information:** Temporal information is logged about the creation, renaming and access times of the file along with the

$MFT record update time. These logs are related to changes in the $MFT records of the associated files (original file, $Rxxx and $Ixxx) and their parent folders and the parents of their parent folders. Indirect information, such as the bit representing $MFT record allocation in the non-resident location of attribute 0xB0 $BitMap of the $MFT, also provides temporal information.

- **Content Information:** File size information is logged to show the data payload in various logs related to $MFT changes in the file and its parent folder, and the parents of the parent folder all the way up to the $Root filename index. Data contents are not logged in the $LogFile except when a resident file is converted to a non-resident file, in which case the old resident content is logged in the $LogFile and is retrievable as discussed in [9]. However, if the data content is modified, it is logged in the $LogFile and the sizes of the old and new data are both available. All these records are not altered during the deletion process and are, therefore, available to digital forensic professionals.

3.3   Hard Disk (Recycle Bin Deletion)

Non-resident data of attributes stored outside $MFT records on the hard disk are included in this category. All this data is available to digital forensic professionals because it not overwritten during the deletion process. Even when the $MFT record of non-resident data is overwritten, the non-resident data may exist if the new overwritten $MFT record is resident or, in the case of a non-resident record, some other clusters are allocated if the size of new non-resident data is different from the previously-deleted data (if the number of clusters required is the same, then NTFS reuses the clusters and overwrites the data).

3.4 $MFT Records (Permanent File Deletion)

Almost all the attributes of the $MFT record of a deleted file are left unaltered, except for the header of the $MFT record. The following artifacts remain after the deletion process:

- **Name Information:** All the information in attribute 0x30 of the $MFT record of the deleted file is left unaltered, thus giving away the name of the deleted file and name of the parent folder under which the file was indexed. If the deleted file is indexed at the end of attribute 0x90 or index of attribute 0xA0 of the parent folder, the deletion process leaves the index entry (name + time + size) in the slack space of the parent folder, thus revealing the file name.

Information in attribute 0x40 $Object_ID in the $MFT record of
the deleted file reveals the file GUID.

- **Temporal Information:** All the information in attribute 0x10
  in the $MFT record of the deleted file is unaltered, thus giving
  away temporal information of the $MFT record update, owner ID
  and security ID. In the $MFT record of the parent folder, the
  index entry of the deleted file is removed and its attribute 0x10 is
  updated; this reveals the file deletion time. If the original deleted
  file is indexed at the end of attribute 0x90 or index of attribute
  0xA0 of the parent folder, the deletion process leaves the index
  entry (name + time + size) in the slack space of the parent folder,
  thus revealing temporal information about the deleted file.

- **Content Information:** All the information in attribute 0x80 in
  the $MFT record of the deleted file is left behind, thus giving away
  information about the content size and contents (for resident data)
  and the location (for non-resident data).

3.5 $LogFile (Permanent File Deletion)

The $LogFile chain of operational records generated as a result of
permanent deletion is smaller than the chain generated by recycle bin
deletion. However, the artifacts related to name, temporal and content
information are similar. The missing items are the changes related to
the creation of the $Rxxx and $Ixxx files and the moving of the deleted
file to the recycle bin.

3.6   Hard Disk (Permanent File Deletion)

The artifacts of this deletion process are the same as those of the
recycle bin deletion process.

4.   Validation Criteria

Under its Computer Forensics Tool Testing Program, the U.S. National Institute of Standards and Technology has defined validation criteria and standards (i.e., specifications, test assertions, test cases, test plans and test images) for a number of forensic functions [4]. However, no standards or criteria are available for secure wiping functionality. As a result, the claims made by vendors about the accuracy and efficacy of their secure wiping tools cannot be validated.

Three validation criteria for secure wiping tools that meet the standards of digital forensic investigations are:

- Specifications of the capabilities of secure wiping tools. These are further divided into core requirements (i.e., mandatory features of secure wiping tools) and optional requirements (i.e., requirements that are applicable only if a vendor claims that its tool has the features).

- Test assertions that ascertain the secure wiping tool capabilities based on the defined specifications. These are divided into core test assertions and optional test assertions.

- Test cases defined for particular environments in order to test the claimed secure wiping tool functionality based on the test assertions.

4.1 Specifications

The specifications fall into two categories: (i) core requirements; and (ii) optional features.

Secure Wiping Core Requirements (SW-CR). The following secure wiping core requirements must be met by a tool claiming to have secure wiping functionality:

- **SW-CR-01:** The tool shall overwrite the entire $MFT record of the file being wiped and accordingly make the record available in $MFT.

- **SW-CR-02:** The tool shall overwrite the entire allocated cluster(s) of non-resident data of the file being wiped and accordingly make the cluster(s) available in $BitMap.

- **SW-CR-03:** The tool shall overwrite the index entry of the file in the parent folder.

- **SW-CR-04:** The tool shall overwrite the entire chain of operational records in the $LogFile of the file being wiped.

- **SW-CR-05:** The secure wiping of a file and its parent folder shall not generate a chain of operational logs in the $LogFile of the file being wiped.

- **SW-CR-06:** The tool shall overwrite all the previous chains of operational logs in the $LogFile of the file being wiped.

- **SW-CR-07:** The tool shall overwrite the entire $MFT record of the folder being wiped along with the $MFT records of all its files and make their corresponding records available in $MFT.

0	1	2	3	4	5	6	7		8	9	A	B	C	D	E	F			
46	49	4C	45	30	00	03	00		38	10	40	00	00	00	00	00		FILE0	8 @
01	00	00	00	38	00	00	00		40	00	00	00	00	04	00	00		8	@
00	00	00	00	00	00	00	00		00	00	00	00	5B	00	00	00			[
02	00	00	00	00	00	00	00		FF	FF	FF	FF	00	00	00	00			ÿÿÿÿ

Figure 2. Empty unallocated $MFT record.

Secure Wiping Optional Features (SW-OF). The following secure wiping optional features may be met by a tool claiming to have secure wiping features:

- **SW-OF-01:** If the tool supports the overwriting of index entries of the parents of the parent folder (until $Root filename index), then it shall change the file sizes and temporal information in the index entries accordingly.

- **SW-OF-02:** If the tool supports the overwriting of deleted files, then it shall follow the SW-CR-01 and SW-CR-02 requirements for the wiped files.

4.2   Test Assertions

Assertions are used to ascertain tool functionality vis-a-vis specifications. The assertions fall into two categories: (i) core test assertions; and optional test assertions.

Secure Wiping Core Test Assertions (SW-CA). The following core test assertions are specified for testing and validating secure wiping functionality:

- **SW-CA-01:** When a tool overwrites an entire $MFT record, the first 0x3C bytes shall be written with the standard information of an empty $MFT record as shown in Figure 2. The remaining bytes shall be written with all zeros with the update sequence number at the sector boundaries at offsets 1xFE and 3xFE as entered in offset 0x30.
  Justification: Some wiping tools leave signatures based on the manner in which they overwrite $MFT records. The complete wiping of the record with zeros removes the signature.

- **SW-CA-02:** The tool shall set the record allocation bit in the $MFT for the file being wiped.
  Justification: This removes any mismatch between the $MFT

and status flag in the $MFT record after it has been wiped and marked as available.

- **SW-CA-03:** The tool shall delete the corresponding index entry and, if the deleted entry is not the last entry, shift the remaining index entries to occupy the space.
  Justification: This removes traces of the wiped file from the folder under which it is indexed. Shifting the remaining index entries upwards to occupy the space vacated by the wiped file removes all traces of the wiping operation.

- **SW-CA-04:** The tool shall overwrite the $MFT records of $Rxxx and $Ixxx and their corresponding record allocation bits in $MFT as mentioned in SW-CA-01 and SW-CA-02. Where applicable, SW-CA-05 shall also be followed.
  Justification: This removes traces of the wiped file from the recycle bin. Also, it removes any mismatch between the $MFT and the status flag in the $MFT records of the $Rxxx and $Ixxx files after the file has been wiped and its space is marked as available.

- **SW-CA-05:** For non-resident files, the tool shall overwrite the entire cluster containing non-resident data with all zeros and set the corresponding cluster allocation bit in $BitMap to zero.
  Justification: This ensures the wiping of non-resident data; data that is left in slack space is recoverable. Moreover, if the data is not wiped with all zeros, traces of the wiping operation remain. Some tools may also leave signatures based on the way they overwrite non-resident data; overwriting with all zeros removes the signatures. This also removes any mismatch between the cluster allocation status of $BitMap and the wiped cluster.

- **SW-CA-06:** The tool shall locate the entire chain in the $LogFile associated with the file being wiped and copy randomly-selected contents from the $LogFile so that the entire chain is overwritten. Also, record page headers that specify the last $LogFile sequence number or file offset and last end $LogFile sequence number and update sequence numbers at sector boundaries shall be placed carefully.
  Justification: This ensures that the chain of operational records that log the latest actions performed on the file before secure wiping are overwritten; this removes all traces of the actions. The adjustments to the various fields eliminate mismatches and ensure secure wiping.

- **SW-CA-07:** The tool shall search and identify the previous chains of operational records associated with the file being wiped and overwrite them according to SW-CA-06.
  Justification: This ensures that no information related to the name, time and contents of the wiped file is present in $LogFile.

- **SW-CA-08:** The secure wiping operation shall not generate a chain of operational records in $LogFile.
  Justification: This ensures that no traces of wiping functionality are present in $LogFile. Otherwise, it is possible to obtain information about the wiping operation and the file that was wiped.

- **SW-CA-09:** The tool shall overwrite all $MFT records of a folder and its files and their corresponding record allocation bits in $MFT as mentioned in SW-CA-01 and SW-CA-02. Where applicable, SW-CA-05 shall also be followed.
  Justification: This ensures that, when a folder is being wiped, all the files and folders contained in the folder are also wiped. This removes all traces of the folder and the wiping operation.

Secure Wiping Optional Test Assertions (SW-OA). The following optional test assertions are specified for testing and validating secure wiping functionality:

- **SW-OA-02:** If the tool supports the removal of artifacts from the parents of the parent folder, then it shall adjust their index entries according to the reduced sizes of the parent folders (i.e., without the wiped file index) and accordingly adjust their temporal information.

- **SW-OA-02:** If the tool supports the secure wiping of deleted files, then it shall perform SW-CA-04, SW-CA-06 and SW-CA-07.

4.3   Test Cases (SW-TC)

The following test cases are defined to test the functionality of secure wiping tools:

- **SW-TC-01:** Overwriting the $MFT record of the resident file when it is not in the recycle bin.

- **SW-TC-02:** Overwriting the $MFT record of non-resident data and overwriting the non-resident data when the file is not in the recycle bin and setting the corresponding record allocation bit in the $MFT of the wiped file to zero.

Table 1. Relational summary table.

No.	Requirements	Test Assertion	Test Cases
1	SW-CR-01	SW-CA-01, SW-CA-02, SW-CA-04	SW-TC-01 or SW-TC-02 or SW-TC-03 or SW-TC-04 or SW-TC-05 or SW-TC-06
2	SW-CR-02	SW-CA-05	SW-TC-02 or SW-TC-04
3	SW-CR-03	SW-CA-03	SW-TC-01 or SW-TC-02 or SW-TC-03 or SW-TC-04 or SW-TC-05 or SW-TC-06
4	SW-CR-04	SW-CA-06	-do-
5	SW-CR-05	SW-CA-08	-do-
6	SW-CR-06	SW-CA-07	-do-
7	SW-CR-07	SW-CA-09	SW-TC-07
8	SW-OF-01	SW-OA-01	SW-TC-01 or SW-TC-02 or SW-TC-03 or SW-TC-04 or SW-TC-05 or SW-TC-06
9	SW-OF-02	SW-OA-02	SW-TC-05, SW-TC-06

- **SW-TC-03:** Overwriting the $MFT record of the resident file when the file is in the recycle bin.

- **SW-TC-04:** Overwriting the $MFT record of the non-resident data and overwriting the non-resident data when it is in the recycle bin.

- **SW-TC-05:** Overwriting the $MFT record of the resident file after it has been deleted.

- **SW-TC-06:** Overwriting the $MFT record of the non-resident data after it has been deleted.

- **SW-TC-07:** Overwriting the $MFT records of a folder and all its files.

4.4 Relational Summary Table

Table 1 shows the relational table of specifications, assertions and test cases.

5.   Validation Testing of Eraser

Eraser is an open source software tool that is often used to securely wipe files and folders [2]. The tool was selected for validation testing because it is one of the top secure wiping tools. Experiments were conducted on Eraser 6.0.10.2620 to check its secure wiping functionality on NTFS (Windows 7 Professional, Service Pack 1) against the verification standard for secure wiping functionality presented in this chapter.

Eraser was configured with the following settings:

- Default file erasure method of German VSIRT (seven passes).

- Default unused space erasure method using pseudorandom data (one pass).

- Random data source of RNGCryptoServiceProvider. A higher number of passes was not required because hardware data extraction is out of scope.

A non-resident file (converted from a resident file) was used as a test case. The target file, which was stored in a folder in the root directory of a physical drive, was securely wiped using Eraser. WinHex 16.9 x86 was used to view and analyze the information in the $MFT records, non-resident locations (including index entries) and $LogFile records. The following observations were made:

- Eraser marked the $MFT record of the target file as deleted and the corresponding record allocation bit in $MFT was set to zero.

- Eraser overwrote all the attributes of the $MFT record of the target file.

- The target file name in attribute 0x30 was overwritten with a random name.

- Eraser overwrote the entire cluster containing non-resident data with random entries. The corresponding cluster allocation bit in $BitMap was set to zero.

- Eraser replaced the corresponding index entries in the parent folder with random entries.

- Eraser did not wipe any entries from the $LogFile. Instead, it generated its own chain of operational records in the $LogFile.

The performance of Eraser with regard to overwriting data in $MFT records and non-resident data locations was satisfactory. However, it

Table 2. Eraser compliance matrix.

No.	Requirements	Test Cases	Results of Test Assertions
1	SW-CR-01	SW-TC-02	– SW-CA-01 non-compliant as the $MFT record was not overwritten as required – SW-CA-02 compliant – SW-CA-04 non-applicable
2	SW-CR-02	SW-TC-02	SW-CA-05 compliant
3	SW-CR-03	SW-TC-02	SW-CA-03 non-compliant as the corresponding entry was not deleted and the remaining entries moved up; instead, the entries were replaced with with random entries
4	SW-CR-04	-do-	SW-CA-06 non-compliant as the latest chain of operational records in the $LogFile related to the target file was not wiped
5	SW-CR-05	-do-	SW-CA-08 non-compliant as chains of operational records were generated in the $LogFile
6	SW-CR-06	-do-	SW-CA-07 non-compliant as previous chains were not wiped
7	SW-CR-07	SW-TC-07	SW-CA-09 non-applicable
8	SW-OF-01	SW-TC-07	SW-OA-01 non-applicable
9	SW-OF-02	SW-TC-05 SW-TC-06	SW-OA-02 non-applicable

failed to wipe critical forensic artifacts residing in the $LogFile. Table 2 shows the compliance matrix for Eraser based on the secure wiping criteria presented in this chapter. Researchers can replicate this validation test by creating a resident file in Notepad. The resident file must then be converted to a non-resident file by adding data to the file.

6. Conclusions

The $LogFile is a valuable source of information about deleted files and the tools used to delete the files. However, a standard has not as yet been specified for secure wiping tools. The validation criteria for secure wiping functionality defined in this chapter ensure that all the data and related information are wiped from the $MFT records, $LogFile and hard disk. The criteria also help ensure that no signature remains that could reveal information about the wiping operation and the wiping tool that were used.

The popular Eraser secure wiping tool was evaluated against the validation criteria. Eraser's performance with regard to overwriting data in $MFT records and non-resident data locations was satisfactory. However, it failed to wipe critical forensic artifacts residing in the $LogFile.

Future research will attempt to specify similar criteria for the Resilient File System (ReFS) of Windows 8. This research will advance digital forensic efforts as well as efforts focused on protecting sensitive personal and proprietary information.

References

[1] J. Beckett and J. Slay, Digital forensics: Validation and verification in a dynamic work environment, *Proceedings of the Fortieth Annual Hawaii International Conference on System Sciences*, 2007.

[2] T. Fisher, 36 free file shredder software programs, About Tech (www.pcsupport.about.com/od/data-destruction/tp/free-file-shredder-software.htm), 2015.

[3] M. Miroshnichenko, Why deleted files can be recovered? Hetman Software, Walnut, California (www.hetmanrecovery.com/recovery_news/why-deleted-files-can-be-recovered.htm), 2012.

[4] National Institute of Standards and Technology, Computer Forensics Tool Testing Program, Gaithersburg, Maryland (www.cftt.nist.gov/documents.htm), 2015.

[5] B. Nelson, A. Phillips and C. Steuart, *Guide to Computer Forensics and Investigations*, Course Technology, Boston, Massachusetts, 2009.

[6] J. Oh, NTFS Log Tracker (www.forensicinsight.org/wp-content/uploads/2013/06/F-INSIGHT-NTFS-Log-TrackerEnglish.pdf), 2013.

[7] R. Russon and Y. Fledel, NTFS Documentation (www.dubeyko.com/development/FileSystems/NTFS/ntfsdoc.pdf), 2005.

[8] J. Vacca, *Computer Forensics: Computer Crime Scene Investigation*, Charles River Media, Hingham, Massachusetts, 2005.

[9] M. Zareen, Provision of Validated Toolset of Freeware Computer Forensic Tools, M.S. Thesis, Department of Information Security, Military College of Signals, National University of Sciences and Technology, Islamabad, Pakistan, 2014.

[10] M. Zareen and B. Aslam, $LogFile of NTFS: A blueprint of activities, presented at the *Seventeenth IEEE International Multi-Topic Conference*, 2014.

Chapter 20

DO DATA LOSS PREVENTION SYSTEMS REALLY WORK?

Sara Ghorbanian, Glenn Fryklund and Stefan Axelsson

Abstract   The threat of insiders stealing valuable corporate data continues to escalate. The inadvertent exposure of internal data has also become a major problem. Data loss prevention systems are designed to monitor and block attempts at exposing sensitive data to the outside world. They have become very popular, to the point where forensic investigators have to take these systems into account. This chapter describes the first experimental analysis of data loss prevention systems that attempts to ascertain their effectiveness at stopping the unauthorized exposure of sensitive data and the ease with which the systems could be circumvented. Four systems are evaluated (three of them in detail). The results point to considerable weaknesses in terms of general effectiveness and the ease with which the systems could be disabled.

Keywords: Data leakage prevention systems, evaluation, forensic implications

1.   Introduction

The theft of sensitive corporate information has always been, and continues to be, a serious problem. While the insider threat (malicious and accidental) should not be exaggerated, fully half of all security incidents reported by businesses are attributed to insiders [4]. The potential loss from insider crime is very high because malicious insiders are difficult to detect, they often have access to sensitive information and they have intimate knowledge of what to take.

Systems specifically designed to identify and protect sensitive data leakage were first introduced in 2006 [6]. They have come to be known as data leakage prevention systems or data loss prevention systems. The purpose of these systems is to detect and stop unauthorized attempts to

© IFIP International Federation for Information Processing 2015
G. Peterson, S. Shenoi (Eds.): Advances in Digital Forensics XI, IFIP AICT 462, pp. 341–357, 2015.
DOI: 10.1007/978-3-319-24123-4_20

leak or export sensitive data. Several data loss prevention systems are available for various operating systems and mobile platforms.

Data loss prevention systems are commonly used in corporate environments and are, therefore, beginning to be encountered in forensic investigations of suspected data leaks. However, very little research has focused on how these systems operate and their ability to prevent data loss. This chapter examines the effectiveness of four well-known data loss prevention systems in a range of leakage scenarios. The results point to considerable weaknesses in terms of general effectiveness and the ease with which the systems could be disabled.

2.   Related Work

Considerable enterprise-related research has been conducted in the data loss prevention area, but the academic research is relatively sparse. Most of the research has focused on identifying the best data loss prevention system based on user needs. One example is the report by Ouellet [10], which compares systems from Trustwave, McAfee, Symantec and eleven other vendors, and lists their strengths and weaknesses.

Blasco et al. [2] have examined methods for bypassing data loss prevention systems using trusted applications. A trusted application is a piece of software that has been approved to be used in an otherwise restricted environment. Blasco et al. demonstrate that, by encrypting secret data and using only trusted applications (in this case, an ordinary spreadsheet), a user is able to leak information. The data loss prevention system did not identify the data as sensitive and, because the application was classified as trusted, the data leakage was not detected.

Carvalho and Cohen [3] have proposed a technique for preventing email leakage in scenarios where emails with sensitive information are sent (intentionally or unintentionally) to unauthorized recipients. The technique, which relies on machine learning, was able to detect leakage in 82% of the test cases.

Kim and Kim [7] have proposed a data loss prevention architecture that takes user privacy into consideration. Their research examines the trade-off between information leakage prevention and privacy protection. A scoring module is suggested for computing the levels of security and privacy. The scores are used to discern the number of times private information has been reviewed by a data loss prevention system.

Luft [8] investigated if data loss prevention systems can actually stop data leakage. Evaluations of two data loss prevention systems indicated that the systems had problems preventing data from leaking. Luft also discovered that the systems did not properly secure communications between the data loss prevention server and agents, making it possible to intercept and eavesdrop on information such as incident reports about secret or sensitive data that had been being blocked. Since 2009, when the evaluation was conducted, data loss prevention systems have made rapid advancements; nevertheless, continued evaluations of the systems are required. Although Luft examined the security of data loss prevention systems, no research has specifically focused on how data loss prevention systems can be manipulated to cause data leakage. This is one of the important issues discussed in this work.

Balinsky et al. [1] and Wuchner and Pretschner [11] have studied agent-based implementations of data loss prevention systems. Balinsky et al. propose the interception of operating system calls to manage read and write access to data. Wuchner and Pretschner continued the work of Balinsky et al. by applying an adapted policy model. Both solutions require restrictions to be imposed on user permissions and access to critical files. The two groups of researchers also identify vulnerabilities in their data loss prevention solutions. One is the possibility of bypassing their solutions because all possible function calls that could be used to access data are not intercepted. Other weaknesses exist in policy management, which make it possible to execute man-in-the-middle attacks.

3.   Evaluated Systems

Data loss prevention systems constantly monitor data to prevent the unauthorized movement of data from secured sites. In general, data exists in three states [2]:

- **Data in Motion:** This corresponds to data that is being transferred from one location to another. It could involve a file being moved from one hard drive or an email moving across the Internet.

- **Data in Use:** This corresponds to data that is actively being used by software. It could involve a Word document that has not recently been saved to the hard drive.

- **Data at Rest:** This corresponds to data that is stored on some media and is not actively being used or transferred.

A data loss prevention system operates under a set of policies that guide decisions and help achieve rational outcomes. The policies are set by administrators and incorporate rules governing the network and endpoints (i.e., what usage is allowed and what is not). The policies can be set on specific applications or web pages, and on anything that makes file transfer possible, such as email, instant messaging and transfers to an external hard drive. Different policies may be set according to the levels of access granted to users. The more specific the policies, the lower the number of false positive and false negative alerts, which results in a more accurate data loss prevention system.

Data loss prevention systems can be categorized into three types: agent-based, agentless and hybrid systems. An agent-based system incorporates an agent at each endpoint, which communicates with a data loss prevention server that delegates policies [9]. An agentless system incorporates one or more servers that monitor and analyze network traffic; every endpoint is forced to have its traffic routed through a server and nothing is installed at the endpoints. A hybrid system is a combination of agent-based and agentless systems; it incorporates an agent at each endpoint as well as one or more monitoring servers.

To gain an understanding of how data loss prevention systems operate and their ability to prevent data loss, the following four systems were evaluated:

- **My Endpoint Protector:** `www.endpointprotector.com`

- **Trustwave:** `www.trustwave.com`

- **MyDL:** `www.mydlp.com`.

- **OpenDLP:** `code.google.com/p/opendlp`

My Endpoint Protector was chosen because it is a data loss prevention system that is deployed in the cloud; it engages the software as a service (SaaS) paradigm. A ten-day trial version of My Endpoint Protector with complete access to all the data loss prevention functionality was used in the study. Trustwave was chosen as a representative commercial data loss prevention system; access to its virtual test environment for the study was set up by Trustwave via a third party, Hatsize (`hatsize.com`). MyDLP and OpenDLP were chosen as representative open-source data loss prevention systems. Unfortunately, after closer examination, it turned out that OpenDLP was only able to operate on data at rest. Since the study focused on data in motion, extensive evaluations could not be performed for OpenDLP.

3.1   Agent-Based Solution

My Endpoint Protector is an agent-based, 100% cloud-managed data loss prevention solution. Everything is managed via a web user interface, from policy creation to downloading and deploying the agent at an endpoint. The trial version Endpoint Protector was used in the tests. It runs on a variety of platforms, including Windows 7 and 8, Mac OS

X, and Apple and Android tablets and phones. Tests were conducted on Windows 7 and Mac OS X Maverick to see if they differed in their protection services.

Upon using the Windows version of My Endpoint Protector, the following problems and suggestions for improvements were discerned:

Problems:

- An image was sent via Windows Live Mail, even if the action was to block images, because Live Mail uploads the image to Microsoft SkyDrive, which is not included in the list of checked applications for Windows.

- The data loss prevention agent disabled the print screen button, but was unable to disable the snipping tool for taking screenshots, which is pre-installed on Windows.

- The agent was unable to decompress files and analyze their contents, even if they contained sensitive data.

- Printing with a network printer was not detected by the agent.

- The agent could not detect if sensitive text was being written to a document or chat, only if the user was attempting to copy the text.

- When the connection between the agent and server was lost, and an incident occurred, the logs were not sent to the server after reconnection.

Suggested Improvements:

- Make it possible to add applications that should be monitored.

- Since the agent analyzes MIME-type files, the administrator should have the ability to add more file types as necessary.

- Save logs locally but encrypt them and send them to the server as soon as a connection is reestablished.

- Decompress compressed archived files and analyze their contents.

3.2   Agentless Solution

Trustwave is a commercial, agentless data loss prevention solution that performs content filtering and monitoring on dedicated servers in a network. In order for this to work, it is necessary to configure each endpoint to route its traffic through the servers. To ensure that the traffic does not bypass the servers, it is recommended to prevent all outgoing SSL/HTTPS traffic (encrypted traffic) from leaving the network, with the exception of traffic from the data loss prevention servers. Ordinary non-encrypted traffic is covered by a monitoring server that receives copies of the outgoing traffic and logs instances of sensitive data leaving the network.

Access was provided to Trustwave's pre-installed virtual environment, which is used to demonstrate the product to new customers. The experimental setup comprised six servers and one Windows 7 desktop.

The virtual environment froze whenever the connection between data loss prevention components at the endpoint and at the server was cut by adding and activating rules in a Windows Firewall (as was done with the other data loss prevention systems). Unfortunately, this situation prevented further testing of Trustwave.

The following problems and suggestions for improvements were discerned for the Windows platform (because the pre-installed environment was used):

Problems:

- The uploading of `.zip` and `.rar` files was blocked, but not `.7z` files.

- Encrypted files containing sensitive data were not discovered.

- When attaching a document with sensitive data to an email, the only notification received was: "Something went wrong, could not attach document. Please try again."

Suggested Improvements:

- The Trustwave vendor was informed about the problem with `.7z` files; the problem will be fixed in a future version.

- Simplify the addition of file types from a scripting language to adding MIME types. The method for doing this should be clarified in the documentation.

- Present users with more information about the files that were blocked and why they were blocked.

3.3   Hybrid Solution

MyDLP is a combination of the two data loss prevention solutions discussed above. As in the case of Trustwave, content filtering is done within the network using dedicated servers. However, MyDLP also enables data loss prevention agents to be installed at endpoints (these agents only run on Windows systems). Each endpoint must be configured to route its traffic through a data loss prevention server.

MyDLP is a open-source data loss prevention system with two licenses, Community Edition and Enterprise Edition. No support is available for the Community Edition.

MyDLP extracts compressed files before determining if they are sensitive or not; this is not done by My Endpoint Protector. MyDLP even extracts .docx files to check if anything is hidden in .docx folders. As in the case of Trustwave, it was not possible to force Skype and Teamviewer to go through the proxy.

Unlike the situation with My Endpoint Protector, when the agent-server is disabled and a file that is blocked is attempted to be transmitted, a log entry is sent to the server as soon as the connection is reestablished. MyDLP has built-in filesystem scan functionality called Discovery, but this has a very high impact on performance.

One advantage of MyDLP is that, even if the data loss prevention agent is disabled on a machine, the rules enforced via the proxy are still operational; however, the use of USB storage and local printers is no longer prevented. If the connection to the data loss prevention server is blocked, the last active operational policies are still enforced.

Problems:

- Attachments in web mail clients were blocked, but not attachments in local mail clients. Blocking was not implemented even after the proxy settings were set up.

- An email containing a .docx file with an image added in the extracted folder was detected, but not when the file was sent via Facebook.

- Only printing to a locally-connected printer can be blocked. Printing to a wirelessly-networked printer is not blocked.

- Notifications are not presented to users when something has been blocked. This could lead to frustration if the user is not aware of the information or the file type that was blocked.

- When applying a rule for blocking applications/octet-streams and MIME types for *inter alia* encrypted files, the entire web pages contained octet-streams, which made it impossible to test encrypted files as attachments.

- The screenshot rule was able to block the snipping tool in Windows, but not the print screen button. Other screenshot tools were not blocked.

Suggested Improvements:

- Extract .docx files for all types of file transfers.

- Present information about the reasons for blocking to users.

- Differentiate between file transfers and web browsing when it comes to octet-streams.

- Block all types of screenshot attempts.

3.4   File System Scanning Tool

OpenDLP is marketed as "a free and open source, agent- and agentless-based, centrally-managed, massively distributable data loss prevention tool" [5]. However, while this data loss prevention tool analyzes locally-stored data, it does not monitor network traffic or prevent data from being leaked. As such, OpenDLP is an example of what happens when the notion of a "proper data loss prevention solution" is not well-defined. By the time the scanner reaches a file containing sensitive information in order to quarantine it or block its dissemination, the file could be attached to an email or printed without being detected. The scanning tool does not affect performance as much as in the case of MyDLP, but because every scanning log entry is saved in a database, the performance could become noticeable if the database is overwhelmed with log entries.

This research focuses on data loss prevention systems that monitor data in motion. Since OpenDLP only analyzes data at rest, no tests were performed on the data loss prevention tool.

4.   Experimental Setup

The virtual test environments incorporated the following operating systems:

- Windows 7 running Service Pack 1

- Linux running Ubuntu 13.10

- Mac OS X Maverick

The advantage of using a virtual environment is that it is fairly easy to create clones of entire experimental setups, which significantly reduces the time required for experimentation.

The four data loss prevention systems were installed and thoroughly tested one at a time on the different platforms. The experiments involved leaking sensitive data using webmail clients (Gmail), local mail clients (Windows Live Mail), cloud syncing software (Google Drive), social media (Facebook), instant messaging software (Skype), remote control software (Teamviewer), printers (network and local) and USB devices. The experiments also considered a situation where a user has different privileges on a local machine. The data that was attempted to be leaked included:

- A text file containing the secret words: "Hemlig," "Stopp," "Credit card information" and "Confidential." These were added to a custom content dictionary to see if the system could detect files containing the words. The credit card number: "4485630591171087" was also added to the text file to test the built-in credit card number finders.

- Compressed versions of the text file in the .zip, .7z and .rar formats.

- Encrypted version of the text file (stored in a Truecrypt file container).

- A 5,370 KB .mp3 audio file.

- A 15 KB .png image file.

- Compressed version of the encrypted text file in the .zip format.

- A Microsoft Office Word .docx file; this file type is an archive that can be decompressed and files added to it without anyone being the wiser.

In every experiment, one file type at a time was set to be blocked with the remaining files being allowed; this was done to see if there was any way to fool the system. The experiments with the compressed files were done twice: the first experiment was set to block compressed file types while the second experiment allowed them, but blocked their contents (i.e., the text file). A similar set of experiments was done with the encrypted files. Experiments with the Microsoft Office file were also performed twice: the first was set to block the .docx file type and the second was set to allow it while blocking image files. The .docx file was also extracted and an image was added in the archive.

The experiments were performed in three phases for each data loss prevention system. During the first phase, a data loss prevention system was set up as recommended to prevent data leakage. Attempts to move/leak the data were made using the applications and software mentioned above and the results were graded as Passed, Passed with Comments or Failed, depending on whether or not data leakage was prevented. Experiments that could not be conducted were graded as Comments while experiments for which a system did not cover the functionality were graded as N/A. The first phase also involved a study of how well each data loss prevention solution reported a blocked attempt to administrators and users.

The second phase involved attempts to disable or bypass a data loss prevention solution and then investigate how well it performed in a "crippled" state. The experiments were run again and graded using the same scores as before. The following attacks were implemented on the data loss prevention solutions:

- Booting the computer from another media (i.e., CD) and accessing the hard drive (i.e., a live CD attack).

- Corrupting or manipulating important binaries or configuration files used by a data loss prevention solution.

- Stopping or killing a data loss prevention solution to prevent it from executing.

The third phase involved disabling communications between the central server and the endpoint. To accomplish this, rules were configured in the local firewall at the endpoint to prevent communications between the central server and the endpoint. The same experiments as in the two previous phases were then conducted to evaluate the effects with respect to data loss prevention.

Table 1 presents the test cases and configurations used in the experiments.

5. Experimental Results

This section summarizes the experimental results obtained for the three phases. The data loss prevention systems tested were: (i) My Endpoint Protector (MEP); (ii) Trustwave (TW); and (iii) MyDLP (MD). As mentioned above, the following grades were used to assess data loss prevention performance:

- **Passed (P):** The system successfully blocked the leakage attempt.

- **Passed with Comments (PC):** The system was partially successful at blocking or identifying the leakage attempt, but this did not qualify as a pass and comments are provided.

Table 1. Test cases.

Test Case	Configuration
Transfer a text file	Policy to block text files is active
Transfer a text file with sensitive data	Policy to block text files is inactive; policy to block sensitive data is active
Transfer a compressed file	Policy to block compressed files is active
Transfer a compressed file with sensitive data	Policy to block compressed files is inactive; policy to block sensitive data is active
Transfer an encrypted file	Policy to block encrypted files is active
Transfer an encrypted file with sensitive data	Policy to block encrypted files is inactive; policy to block sensitive data is active
Transfer an encrypted file	Policy to block encrypted files is active
Transfer an encrypted file with sensitive data	Policy to block encrypted files is inactive; policy to block sensitive data is active
Transfer a media file	Policy to block media files is active
Transfer an image	Policy to block image files is active
Write sensitive data	Type blocked words from content dictionary
Transfer a compressed file containing an encrypted file	Compress an encrypted file while the policy to block encrypted files is active; policy to block compressed files is inactive
Transfer a Microsoft Office file	Policy to block Microsoft Office files is inactive; policy to block image files is active

- **Failed (F):** The system did not block the leakage attempt.

- **Comments (C):** The test case was not conducted for some reason.

- **Not Applicable (N/A):** The system functionality did not cover the test case.

Phase 1: Clean Install. The experiments involved installing the data loss prevention software at the endpoints, setting up policies according to the documents and manuals, and transferring the test files. The data loss prevention software was not tampered with during the first phase. Figure 1 shows the detailed results of the Phase 1 experiments. Note that the systems tested were: My Endpoint Protector (MEP); (ii) Trustwave (TW); and (iii) MyDLP (MD). Table 2 summarizes the main results.

Description	Mail MEP	Mail TW	Mail MD	Printer MEP	Printer TW	Printer MD	Google Drive MEP	Google Drive TW	Google Drive MD	Facebook MEP	Facebook TW	Facebook MD	Skype MEP	Skype TW	Skype MD	Teamviewer MEP	Teamviewer TW	Teamviewer MD	USB MEP	USB TW	USB MD
Attach/send text file	P	P	PC	P	N/A	F	N/A	F	F	P	F	P	P	C	C	P	N/A	C	P	N/A	P
Attach/send text file with sensitive data	P	P	PC	PC	N/A	N/A	P	C	F	P	C	P	F	C	C	F	N/A	C	P	N/A	F
Attach/send compressed file	PC	PC	PC	N/A	N/A	N/A	PC	C	F	F	C	F	F	C	C	F	N/A	F	N/A	N/A	P
Attach/send compressed file with sensitive data	F	PC	PC	N/A	N/A	N/A	C	C	F	F	C	P	F	C	C	F	N/A	F	N/A	N/A	P
Attach/send encrypted file	P	F	PC	N/A	N/A	N/A	PC	C	F	P	C	F	F	C	C	F	N/A	F	N/A	N/A	F
Attach/send encrypted file with sensitive data	F	F	N/A	N/A	N/A	N/A	C	C	F	P	C	P	F	C	C	F	N/A	F	N/A	N/A	F
Attach/send media file	P	N/A	PC	PC	N/A	PC	PC	N/A	F	N/A	N/A	P	N/A	N/A	C	N/A	N/A	F	N/A	N/A	F
Attach/send image	PC	N/A	PC	PC	N/A	F	PC	F	F	P	F	P	P	C	C	P	N/A	C	P	N/A	F
Write sensitive data	N/A	N/A	N/A	N/A	N/A	N/A	N/A	F	F	N/A	C	N/A	N/A	C	C	N/A	C	C	P	N/A	N/A
Attach/send compressed file with encrypted file within.	F	F	PC	N/A	N/A	N/A	C	F	F	P	C	P	F	C	C	F	N/A	F	N/A	N/A	F
Attach/send Microsoft Office files	P	N/A	PC	N/A	N/A	F	PC	F	F	PC	C	PC	P	C	C	P	N/A	F	P	N/A	P

Figure 1.   Test results for a clean install.

Description	Mail MEP	Mail TW	Mail MD	Printer MEP	Printer TW	Printer MD	Google Drive MEP	Google Drive TW	Google Drive MD	Facebook MEP	Facebook TW	Facebook MD	Skype MEP	Skype TW	Skype MD	Teamviewer MEP	Teamviewer TW	Teamviewer MD	USB MEP	USB TW	USB MD
Attach/send text file	F	PC	PC	F	N/A	F	F	F	F	F	F	F	F	C	C	F	N/A	C	F	N/A	F
Attach/send text file with sensitive data	F	PC	PC	P	N/A	N/A	F	F	F	F	F	F	F	C	C	F	N/A	C	F	N/A	F
Attach/send compressed file	PC	PC	PC	N/A	N/A	N/A	PC	F	F	F	F	F	F	C	C	C	N/A	C	F	N/A	F
Attach/send compressed file with sensitive data	F	N/A	PC	N/A	N/A	N/A	C	F	F	F	F	F	F	C	C	C	N/A	C	F	N/A	F
Attach/send encrypted file	F	N/A	N/A	N/A	N/A	N/A	C	F	F	F	F	F	F	C	C	C	N/A	C	F	N/A	F
Attach/send encrypted file with sensitive data	F	F	N/A	N/A	N/A	N/A	C	F	F	F	F	F	F	C	C	C	N/A	F	F	N/A	F
Attach/send media file	F	N/A	PC	PC	N/A	N/A	C	N/A	F	F	N/A	P	F	N/A	C	C	N/A	F	N/A	N/A	F
Attach/send image	F	PC	PC	F	N/A	F	F	F	F	F	F	F	F	C	C	N/A	N/A	F	N/A	N/A	F
Write sensitive data	P	F	PC	N/A	N/A	N/A	F	F	F	F	C	P	F	C	C	N/A	C	F	N/A	N/A	F
Attach/send compressed file with encrypted file within.	F	F	PC	N/A	N/A	N/A	C	F	F	F	C	F	F	C	C	C	C	F	N/A	N/A	F
Attach/send Microsoft Office files	F	N/A	PC	F	N/A	F	N/A	C	F	F	F	PC	P	C	C	F	N/A	N/A	N/A	N/A	P

Figure 2.   Test results for a disabled data loss prevention agent.

Table 2. Summary of results from Figure 1.

	My Endpoint Protector	Trustwave	MyDLP
Passed	37	2	14
Passed with Comments	8	1	10
Failed	22	2	23
Comments	0	19	21
N/A	9	53	9
Total	77	77	77

Table 3. Summary of results from Figure 2.

	My Endpoint Protector	Trustwave	MyDLP
Passed	0	2	14
Passed with Comments	0	1	10
Failed	68	2	23
Comments	0	19	21
N/A	9	53	9
Total	77	77	77

Comments:

- **Trustwave:** SSL/HTTPS could not be tested because of configuration problems. Also, Trustwave does not cover endpoints, so the printer and USB received N/A scores.

- **MyDLP:** Skype and Teamviewer could not be forced to go through the proxy.

Phase 2: Disabled Agent. The experiments involved attempts to disable data loss prevention software at the endpoints (described previously). Figure 2 shows the detailed results of the Phase 2 experiments. Table 3 summarizes the main results.

Comments:

- **Trustwave:** Trustwave is an agentless data loss prevention system, so there is no agent to disable. Also, the comments are the same as in Phase 1.

- **MyDLP:** The comments are the same as in Phase 1.

Table 4. Summary of results from Figure 3.

	My Endpoint Protector	Trustwave	MyDLP
Passed	34	0	7
Pass with Comments	8	0	1
Failed	26	0	39
Comments	0	24	21
N/A	9	53	9
Total	77	77	77

Phase 3: Disconnected Server. The experiments involved disabling communications between the central server and the endpoint. Figure 3 shows the detailed results of the Phase 3 experiments. Table 4 summarizes the main results.

Comments:

- **Trustwave:** The virtual environment halted when a firewall rule was added and activated. Also, the comments are the same as in Phase 1.

- **MyDLP:** The comments are the same as in Phase 1.

6. Discussion

The experimental results demonstrate that the data loss prevention systems have severe "blind spots" in some test cases. This is understandable given that they implement different strategies based on host operation or network operation. Even so, some of the systems draw complete blanks for certain test cases, which means that they can hardly be relied on in operational environments. Also, it is not unreasonable to assume that some users could inadvertently identify these flaws and leverage them to transfer and store sensitive files. This, of course, makes the situation trickier for a forensic investigator because any evidence of leakage could be argued to be the result of an accident instead of malicious behavior.

The evaluation results with regard to disabling the data loss prevention systems are even more disheartening. The systems were relatively easy to disable or fool (even by non-expert users), which renders their effectiveness more questionable, especially as standalone solutions. It also appears that attempts at disabling the systems could go unnoticed. For example, stopping a data loss prevention agent from contacting a server by activating firewall rules would leave few traces on the server.

Description	Mail			Printer			Google Drive			Facebook			Skype			Teamviewer			USB		
	MEP	TW	MD	MEP	TW	MD	MEP	TW	MD	MEP	TW	MD	MEP	TW	MD	MEP	TW	MD	MEP	TW	MD
Attach/send text file	P	N/A	F	F	N/A	F	PC	N/A	F	P	N/A	F	P	N/A	C	P	N/A	C	P	N/A	P
Attach/send text file with sensitive data	P	C	F	F	N/A	PC	P	C	F	P	C	F	P	C	C	P	C	C	P	N/A	P
Attach/send compressed file	PC	N/A	F	N/A	N/A	N/A	PC	N/A	F	P	N/A	F	P	N/A	C	P	N/A	C	P	N/A	P
Attach/send compressed file with sensitive data	F	C	F	N/A	N/A	N/A	F	C	F	F	C	F	F	C	C	F	C	C	F	N/A	P
Attach/send encrypted file	P	N/A	F	N/A	N/A	N/A	PC	N/A	F	P	N/A	F	P	N/A	C	P	N/A	C	P	N/A	P
Attach/send encrypted file with sensitive data	F	C	F	N/A	N/A	N/A	F	C	F	F	C	F	F	C	C	F	C	C	F	N/A	F
Attach/send media file	P	N/A	F	N/A	N/A	N/A	PC	N/A	F	P	N/A	F	P	N/A	C	P	N/A	C	P	N/A	F
Attach/send image	PC	N/A	F	F	N/A	F	PC	N/A	F	P	N/A	F	P	N/A	C	P	N/A	C	P	N/A	P
Write sensitive data	F	C	F	N/A	N/A	N/A	F	C	F	F	C	F	F	C	C	N/A	N/A	N/A	N/A	N/A	N/A
Attach/send compressed file with encrypted file within.	F	C	F	N/A	N/A	N/A	F	C	F	F	C	F	F	C	C	F	C	C	F	N/A	F
Attach/send Microsoft Office files	P	N/A	F	F	N/A	F	PC	N/A	F	P	N/A	F	P	N/A	C	P	N/A	C	P	N/A	P

Figure 3. Test results for a disconnected data loss prevention server.

As a result, checking for information that is not in the logs becomes as important as checking what is actually in the logs.

In summary, the data loss prevention field is currently immature. Consequently, it is imprudent to place too much trust on data loss prevention solutions when attempting to prevent data leakage as well as when conducting forensic investigations.

7.   Conclusions

This chapter describes the evaluation of four data loss prevention systems in order to ascertain their effectiveness at stopping the unauthorized exposure of sensitive data and the ease with which the systems could be circumvented. Although the focus was on agent-based systems that do not have connections to data loss prevention servers, agentless systems were considered as well. The experimental results reveal that none of the data loss prevention systems is 100% secure and all have potential weaknesses and lack complete coverage when identifying and protecting data. In general, the evaluated systems perform rather poorly and several improvements have been suggested to address the problems.

The research has identified various threats to the data loss prevention agents themselves; the measures to protect agents include restricting user privileges, using full disk encryption and monitoring process status. Another key issue is to create policies that cover the proper identification and categorization of data, especially when the data is hidden or obfuscated.

Future research will investigate the forensic aspects of data loss prevention systems, especially the traces of data leakage that remain and those that are not retained. Also, additional applications will be used to reveal more information about data loss prevention systems and their weaknesses. Finally, improved agent-based and agentless solutions will be developed to prevent data leakage from devices such as network printers.

References

[1] H. Balinsky, D. Perez and S. Simske, System call interception framework for data leak prevention, *Proceedings of the Fifteenth IEEE International Conference on Enterprise Distributed Object Computing*, pp. 139–148, 2011.

[2] J. Blasco, J. Hernandez-Castro, J. Tapiador and A. Ribagorda, Bypassing information leakage protection with trusted applications, *Computers and Security*, vol. 31(4), pp. 557–568, 2012.

[3] V. Carvalho and W. Cohen, Preventing information leaks in email, *Proceedings of the SIAM International Conference on Data Mining,* pp. 68–77, 2007.

[4] Computer Security Institute, 2010/2011 Computer Crime and Security Survey, New York, 2011.

[5] A. Gavin, OpenDLP – Data Loss Prevention Suite, version 0.5.1 (code.google.com/p/opendlp), 2012.

[6] P. Kanagasingham, Data Loss Prevention, InfoSec Reading Room, SANS Institute, Bethesda, Maryland, 2008.

[7] J. Kim and H. Kim, Design of internal information leakage detection system considering the privacy violation, *Proceedings of the International Conference on Information and Communication Technology Convergence,* pp. 480–481, 2010.

[8] M. Luft, Can Data Leakage Prevention Prevent Data Leakage? Bachelor's Thesis, Laboratory for Dependable Distributed Systems, University of Mannheim, Mannheim, Germany, 2009.

[9] R. Mogull, Understanding and Selecting a Data Loss Prevention Solution, Technical Report, Securosis, Phoenix, Arizona, 2010.

[10] E. Ouellet, Magic Quadrant for Content-Aware Data Loss Prevention, Technical Report G00224160, Gartner, Stamford, Connecticut, 2013.

[11] T. Wuchner and A. Pretschner, Data loss prevention based on data-driven usage control, *Proceedings of the Twenty-Third IEEE International Symposium on Software Reliability Engineering,* pp. 151–160, 2012.

Printed in the United States
By Bookmasters